The Raymond Tallis Reader

Also by Raymond Tallis

BETWEEN THE ZONES (*poetry*)

CLINICAL NEUROLOGY OF OLD AGE (*editor*)

ENEMIES OF HOPE: A Critique of Contemporary Pessimism

EPILEPSY IN ELDERLY PEOPLE

THE EXPLICIT ANIMAL: A Defence of Human Consciousness

FATHERS AND SONS (*poetry*)

INCREASING LONGEVITY: Medical, Social and Political Implications (*editor*)

IN DEFENCE OF REALISM

NEWTON'S SLEEP: Two Cultures and Two Kingdoms

NOT SAUSSURE: A Critique of Post-Saussurean Literary Theory

ON THE EDGE OF CERTAINTY

PSYCHO-ELECTRONICS

THE PURSUIT OF MIND (*co-editor with Howard Robinson*)

TEXTBOOK OF GERIATRIC MEDICINE AND GERONTOLOGY (*co-editor with John Brocklehurst and Howard Fillett*)

THEORRHOEA AND AFTER

The Raymond Tallis Reader

Edited by

Michael Grant
Senior Lecturer
Rutherford College
The University of Kent
Canterbury

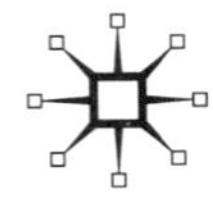

First published 2000 by
PALGRAVE
Houndmills, Basingstoke, Hampshire RG21 6XS and
175 Fifth Avenue, New York, N. Y. 10010
Companies and representatives throughout the world

PALGRAVE is the new global academic imprint of
St. Martin's Press LLC Scholarly and Reference Division and
Palgrave Publishers Ltd (formerly Macmillan Press Ltd).

ISBN 0–333–77271–7 hardback
ISBN 0–333–77272–5 paperback

This book is printed on paper suitable for recycling and made from fully managed and sustained forest sources.

A catalogue record for this book is available from the British Library.

Library of Congress Cataloging-in-Publication Data
Tallis, Raymond.
The Raymond Tallis reader / edited by Michael Grant.
p. cm
Includes bibliographical references (p.) and index.
ISBN 0–333–77271–7
1. Philosophy of mind. 2. Criticism (Philosophy) I. Grant, Michael, 1940– II. Title.
BD418.3 .T357 2000
192—dc21

00–033264

10 9 8 7 6 5 4 3 2 1
09 08 07 06 05 04 03 02 01 00

Printed and bound in Great Britain by
Antony Rowe Ltd, Chippenham, Wiltshire

Dedicated to Tim Farmiloe and Charmian Hearne, without whom Raymond Tallis would have had neither a Reader *nor readers*

I am enormously grateful to Michael Grant for his energy, enthusiasm and painstaking care in putting together this Reader, *I could not have been better read.*

Raymond Tallis
May 2000

Contents

Acknowledgements

Grateful acknowledgement is made to Macmillan for permission to reprint selections from the work of Raymond Tallis; to *The Times Higher Education Supplement* for permission to reprint 'The Shrink from Hell' (Reading 10); and to Oxford University Press for permission to reprint 'Evidence-based and Evidence-free Generalisations' (Reading 12).

I would like to acknowledge the unfailing support and encouragement of Raymond Tallis himself during the sometimes difficult but always pleasurable task of putting this Reader together. I would also like to acknowledge the help and kindness of Eleanor Birne of Macmillan, and to offer my thanks to Ruth Willats for her indispensable work on the text.

Michael Grant

Introduction: Raymond Tallis and the Bewitchment of Theory

Michael Grant

> What has to be overcome is a difficulty having to do with the will, rather than with the intellect.
>
> Wittgenstein

Raymond Tallis is a man of the Enlightenment. His work represents a reaffirmation of the values of the Enlightenment, even, one might say, of 'the Enlightenment project'. And yet, while he would undoubtedly see the promotion of health, freedom, justice, tolerance and peace as a good in itself, the reaffirmation in question is one that has been profoundly chastened by reflection on the experience of the last two hundred years. The values to which Tallis has committed himself are indeed those of a certain enlightenment, but an enlightenment stripped of the scientism and the scientistic utopianism that have helped to give birth to the dystopian nightmares of totalitarian regimes and succoured those who would engineer the human soul. At the same time, the reaffirmation of what are for him values fundamental to the purpose and meaning of human life has put him on a collision course with the progenitors and contemporary exponents of poststructuralism and postmodernism. He has castigated what he sees as the hypocritical complacency of their nihilism and excoriated the low standards of their scholarship, while making no bones about his loathing for what he describes as the carelessness, methodological shoddiness and out-and-out fraud that all too often characterise their investigative procedures. The result, he insists, disfigures a great deal of what passes for academic activity within the humanities departments of modern universities. This connects with another of his major preoccupations, the clarification of what kinds of general assertion are admissible and what kinds are not, an issue vigorously pursued in relation to Lacan and Derrida. There is frequently, then, a polemical edge to his writing, and against this background of controversy the force and importance of the themes and ideas that engage him are seen to advantage. Tallis places human consciousness at the very centre of human affairs, having the gravest reservations about contemporary notions of the unconscious. He is emphatic about the complexity of that consciousness and has insisted on its inexplicability in terms of physical science. He is eager to reassert the role of the human agent in individual action and the shaping of human culture and destiny. And in his far-reaching criticisms of modern theorists of pessimism – 'the enemies of hope' – he seeks to instigate, through the reaffirmation of the irreducible significance of the consciously intending human agent, an act of cultural transformation. His aim is to challenge the facile attractions of negativity and to secure grounds for hope. There is, for Tallis, nothing chimerical about the idea of progress, and it is one of the more urgently pressed parts of his undertaking to make the case for its principled rehabilitation.

I

In his writings critical of contemporary literary theory Tallis has given accounts of the ideas in question and emphasised their genesis in the work of Saussure. In so doing, he has been at pains to exonerate Saussure himself from what he sees as the excesses and confusions inflecting the writings of those such as Derrida and Lacan who claim him as their exemplar. Tallis considers that 'many eminent interpreters' of Saussure have been misled into using 'sign', 'linguistic sign' and 'word' as though they were synonyms of either the signifier or the signified, or both. It is characteristic of literary theorists, he argues, to write as if the negative and differential properties of signifier and signified could be ascribed to other elements of language as well. This is the essential step in many post-Saussurean misreadings of Saussure, and it is 'unforgivable', particularly since Saussure himself distinguishes between them very exactly. For Tallis, the error of theory – Theorrhoea, as he later calls it – is the ascription to speech of properties that belong to the language system alone.[1]

As Tallis presents it, Saussure's work embodies and exemplifies a model of what a theory of language is, one which later writers did not so much develop or build upon as distort. The model in question is inseparable from the idea of what Saussure calls value, and he reaches it by way of a conceptualisation of language that has as its primary requirement the founding of linguistics as an authentic and rigorous science. Tallis has succinctly characterised Saussure's vision of what lies at the heart of language:

> Verbal meaning is ... carried not by a relationship between a particular physical sound and a thing but by the relationship between one word and all the others. It is the *differences* between the linguistic units that carry meanings; and the units, defined by such differences, can be grasped only through the network of other such units. At the heart of language is not an external relationship between a particular physical sound and a material thing but an internal relationship between oppositions at the phonetic level and oppositions at the semantic level.[2]

Saussure believed that to found linguistics on the basis of difference so understood was to define language in such a way that it became possible to say for the first time what the nature of linguistic theory essentially is. The opening move in this direction is to recognise that the founding act of a theory of language is to constitute out of the diverse phenomena of language in general an integral and unique object.[3] It was the failure of his predecessors, the comparative philologists, to seek out the nature of their proper object of study that, in Saussure's view, had resulted in their failure to develop a scientific method. However, the search for the object of linguistics poses a crucial problem: 'Other sciences work with objects that are given in advance and that can then be considered from different viewpoints; but not linguistics' (8). The problem arises from the fact that linguistic phenomena present themselves as dualities. For example, the consonant *n* is a duality involving movements of the vocal organs and an auditory impression; similarly, the French word *nu* (naked) is an audible sound and an inaudible meaning. Furthermore, language has an individual and a social aspect, the one being inconceivable without the other. Language is also 'both an established system and an evolution; at every moment it is an existing institution and a product of the past' (8). As Samuel Weber has noted:

> The phenomena of language do not present a unified aspect to the observer. The object of language is not accessible to empirical observation.[4]

Saussure concludes that these dualities can be put to one side only in so far as linguistics takes as its object of study the language system.

However, the distinctions that Saussure makes between language as a whole (*langage*), speech (*parole*) and the language system (*langue*) are not simply observable distinctions within the fact of language: 'they are products of a point-of-view seeking to construct its object in a manner which will enable linguistics to establish itself as an autonomous science; that is, as a self-contained and autonomous object of analysis and classification.'[5] The language system is therefore to be the primary concern of linguistics, and all other linguistic manifestations are to be related to it (9). The system itself is defined in terms not of what it is but of what it is not. Both language in its entirety and speech are disparate phenomena that lack the essential unity of the system, a unity crucial to the object of science. Language as a whole is 'many-sided and heterogeneous'. Because it straddles several areas simultaneously – physical, physiological and psychological – it belongs 'both to the individual and to society'; it is not possible to find a place for it in a system of classification since it has no evident unity (9). So far as speech is concerned, speaking and the language system are interdependent, the system being both the instrument and the product of speech, and yet they are two 'absolutely distinct things' (19). On the other hand, language as a system is a self-contained whole and 'a principle of classification' (9), the study of which will be synchronic, not diachronic.

Such a system can be compared to a set of chessmen, in which the identity of a given piece depends on its function in the game. This function within the whole Saussure calls 'value':

> We see then that in semiological systems like language, where elements hold each other in equilibrium in accordance with fixed rules, the notion of identity blends with that of value and *vice versa*. (110)

Language emerges as 'a system of pure value', which is as distinct from meaning as it is from sound:

> Psychologically, our thought – apart from its expression in words – is only a shapeless and indistinct mass. Philosophers and linguists have always agreed in recognizing that without the help of signs we would be unable to make a clear, consistent distinction between two ideas. Without language, thought is like a vague, uncharted nebula. There are no pre-existing ideas, and nothing is distinct before the appearance of language. (111–12)

As Weber has argued, this is a crux in Saussure's thought: the argument 'is not simply that language is indispensable for the articulation of ideas, but for their very constitution'.[6] Tallis is emphatic on this point also, since, as he sees it, it is the failure to distinguish between system and speech that underpins the confusions endemic in post-Saussurean theory:

> The signifier and the signified are not *things* but *values*; and they are valorised only within the *system* where they coexist with other opposing or different values.[7]

It is the idea of value that allows Saussure to envisage the language system as the 'domain of articulations'. He sees each linguistic sign or unit as a member, 'an *articulus* in which an idea is fixed in a sound and a sound becomes the sign of an idea' (112). The characteristic role of the language system with respect to thought is not to create a phonic and material means of expressing ideas, but to serve as an intermediary between thought and sound (112). It is not that thought is given material form, or that sounds become transformed into mental entities: it is rather the 'mysterious' fact that 'thought-sound' implies division, 'and that language works out its units while taking shape between two shapeless masses' (112). Saussure visualises the air in contact with a sheet of water: if the air pressure changes, the water will break up into waves. The waves resemble the 'union or coupling' of thought with phonic substance.[8] The notion of value thus defines, for Saussure, not only the essence of language, but also the means by which that essence is to be isolated, perceived and understood:

> The idea of value ... shows that to consider a term as simply the union of a certain sound with a certain concept is grossly misleading. To define it in this way would isolate the term from its system; it would mean assuming that one can start from the terms and construct the system by adding them together when, on the contrary, it is from the interdependent whole that one must start and through analysis obtain its elements. (113)

Value is 'interior' to language, inasmuch as it comes between thought and sound, and 'exterior' to it, inasmuch as it is the whole that constitutes the relations between elements that comprise language as a system. This point is further exemplified in the distinction between value and signification – another distinction hopelessly confused in the writings of theorists. Signification is that area of language involved in representation, reference and semantics, and is achieved through value, without reference being identical to value. The essence of language does not lie in reference, naming or meaning: 'it is not signification ... that produces value, but value that produces signification'.[9] For example, the French *mouton* has the same signification as English *mutton*, but their values are distinct, *mutton* being limited in its usage by *sheep*, a distinction lacking in French. For Saussure, this can be taken to show that, since words do not have 'exact equivalents in meaning from one language to the next', they do not stand for pre-existing concepts. Signs do not signify pre-existing ideas: the concepts expressed by language are values 'emanating from the system' (117).

> When they are said to correspond to concepts, it is understood that the concepts are purely differential and defined not by their positive content but negatively by their relations with the other terms of the system. Their most precise characteristic is in being what the others are not. (117)

The idea that the language system is a system of pure values is glossed in terms of difference: 'in language there are only differences *without positive terms*' (120). This means that value cannot be given specific embodiment: since words cannot be identified as the units of the system, it is not possible to regard spoken or written discourse as an aspect of value:

> If I state simply that a word signifies something when I have in mind the association of a sound-image with a concept, I am making a statement that may suggest what actually happens, but by no means am I expressing the linguistic fact in its essence and fullness. (117)

It is this urge to express the linguistic fact in its essence and fullness that justifies the primacy Saussure gives to difference: in order to establish the units of the system, it is essential to assume that 'the characteristics of the unit blend with the unit itself' (121). In language, as in any semiological system, 'whatever distinguishes one sign from the others constitutes it' (121). Difference constitutes that which it differentiates, and in so doing constitutes value and the units of value. The nature of the object studied is in this way deduced from the nature of the methods used to study it: the method of analysis is to 'predicate of the thing what lies in the method of representing it'.[10] The failure to observe these distinctions, between the methodological constraints on the study of language and the properties of the object studied, has as its consequence the multiple confusions of structuralist and poststructuralist thought, the fundamental flaw of which is, according to Tallis, 'the incorrect assumption that the "system" can be defined in isolation from its actual use in specific situations and without reference to extra-linguistic reality'.[11] The assimilation of all forms of human utterance and linguistic endeavour – particularly those of literature and the novel – to a model of structure based on a misunderstanding of Saussure's ideas on value and system has had dire consequences for literary study as such, and the humanities in general. Tallis has made the nature of this confusion unequivocally clear: structure alone cannot found meaning, for where there is no meaning in language there can be no such thing as structure in language.

II

What this amounts to is the view that post-Saussurean thinkers such as Barthes, Lacan and Derrida have identified a differential understanding of the structure of language with the experience of the world itself. In other words, they have each in their own way distorted Saussure's theory so as to define language in terms of a certain experience of what leading one's life with language is like, and to define what it is like to live with language in terms of a certain structure of difference, whether of the 'signifier' or *différance*. The assimilation of self to language understood differentially is what engenders and apparently justifies the notion of the split subject and the unconscious. It is an ordering of experience that the contemporary philosopher, Richard Eldridge, has characterised in the following terms:

> These lives – our words, thinkings, speakings, intendings, and actings – are familiar, everyday, and yet strange. In leading them we live with and within an unsatisfiable desire for mastery, wholeness, completion, transparency (with oneself and others), and for perfect expressiveness. We want to get beneath everything that seems exterior, derivative, secondary, and

> imperfect to what is essential: what makes anyone able at all to think speak, intend, and will, thence to perfect our own performances by giving them a perfect derivation. ... But what we wish for does not come.[12]

It is a sense of ordinary language similar to this, of its exteriority, of its having derivative and partial character, that in Derrida combines with a Hegelian understanding of language as the murderer of the thing and with an atheistic desire to undermine the Christian doctrine of the Word. The result is the heady intellectual brew from which deconstruction and poststructuralism more generally have emerged, and to which they owe their undeniably potent appeal.

It is against this background that Tallis places Derrida, in an account that is both sympathetic and moving. This last point may seem surprising, given the general rigour and unyielding nature of his attack on the foundations of deconstruction (and of literary theory in general). None the less, for Tallis, Derrida appears as 'a tragic case', a man who, despite his immense talent and erudition, has been unable to say the things he most wished to say. He has been compelled to make interminable approaches to, and circlings around, the issues that have most powerfully coerced his thought, and as such he seems trapped, without hope of escape, inside the fly-bottle of his own confusions.[13] He is the victim of 'a disappointed longing for the union of absolute lucidity and undeniable substantiality, of thing-like thereness with thought-like transparency, for an absolute coincidence of knowing and being'.[14] This is a desire for the impossible, inasmuch as it is composed of a double movement: as being approaches the transparency of thought it is deprived of substance, and where it gains in substance it also gains in opacity. It is an impossibility based on a choice between mutually exclusive elements, between being and meaning, a choice that in Lacan's notorious expositions of subjectivity is called alienation, a self-differing that he sees as the founding condition of what it is to be a human subject. As Tallis presents the matter, it is a similar idea of the riven nature of subjectivity that is also crucial to Derrida's thought on human subjectivity. Contradiction, for Derrida, is the condition of experience itself. Since absolute presence is impossible – the possibility of its realisation having been undermined by contradiction – ordinary presence, as we have it in daily experience, must also be a mirage. The contradictions that strike absolute presence down must also strike at our ordinary notions of presence. Our thoughts, our feelings, our sensations, our perceptions, must all be subject to difference and contradiction at all times and at every level. Our sense of what is present, for example, must be divided or split across the no longer of the past and the not yet of the future, and what we remember and what we intend must likewise be alienated from themselves. If one takes this view, one is compelled to say that experience is nothing other than the experience of difference and deferral, the self-differing that for Derrida is *différance*. In other words, *différance* is what constitutes experience as such, creating it and structuring it much as the language system creates and structures the utterances of the individual speaker. This vision is explicitly that of Lacan, whose graphs, algorithms and formulae are attempts to make manifest the double experience of self-difference and deferral across a wide range of psychic experience (neurosis, psychosis, perversion, and so on). When one looks at a Lacanian formula, it is as though one were being required to participate in the structuring principle of the formula itself, in order to participate in what gave rise to that formula in the first place. Something similar holds for his prose style, which, like his mathematical entities, is also intended to articulate what one might call an impossible position, both inside and outside representation (or language) at one and the same time. Lacan would say that what he intends to represent is the lack – that is, the unconscious psychic function or operation – that underlies and engenders language as such. His claim is that he can dig down below meaning and representation, and by so doing allow us a direct experience of the unconscious as that which subverts determinate meaning in the very act of constructing it.

Tallis comments on the significance of this kind of approach for the understanding of how we use language:

> Self-presence *chez* Derrida requires total self-possession. If the signs I use do not originate with me and if I do not explicitly intend all the conventions and, indeed, all the utterance-conditions, that make meaning possible, then I am not present in my act.[15]

Clearly, since the signs I use do not originate with me, and since I do not, indeed could not, make all the conditions surrounding my utterance, the context, the ramifications of what I say, and so on, fully explicit, Derrida's position must lead to the view that meaning is always already elsewhere, lost to us, and that we ourselves are divided from ourselves, the speech act itself annihilating us in the very act of speaking.

These kinds of argument confront us with the kinds of problem that arise when we lose our bearings in language, and words leave us at a loss. We no longer know our way around. The arguments of scepticism, for example, are couched in a speech that denies the importance of our shared forms of life, inasmuch as the sceptic seeks to establish an inhuman and unconditioned certainty concerning the existence of other minds and the world. To repudiate in this way our common life in language is to deprive oneself of meaning and the power of coherent speech, and it is a repudiation that follows from what Stanley Cavell has called a 'chronic distrust of the ordinary'. It is the cardinal sin of philosophy, and Cavell comes across it not only in scepticism but throughout modern thought. He finds on it especially in certain kinds of radical modern sensibility, most obviously that of deconstruction, but widespread beyond it, and he thinks of it 'as a horror of the common, expressed as a flight from the banal, typically from banal pleasures. It stretches from a horror of the human, to a disgust with bourgeois life, to a certain condescension toward the popular'.[16] It amounts to 'a modern inflection of the prideful human craving to be God, of the perennial human desire to deny one's own humanity'.[17]

One of the most extraordinary examples of this refusal or repudiation of our shared forms of life is to be found in an account given in 1954 by Lacan of what the human subject is. Lacan asks the auditors of his seminar to imagine the world when all human beings have disappeared from it:

> This is enough to ask oneself the question – *What is left in the mirror?* But let us take it to the point of supposing that all living beings have disappeared. There are only waterfalls and springs left – lightning and thunder too. The image in the mirror, the image in the lake – do they still exist?[18]

He goes on to assert that, despite the disappearance of human life, indeed of all life, a complex machine, such as a Polaroid camera, complicated enough to store the images it takes, can replace what we think of as consciousness. Though the camera lacks an ego (*moi*), it does have an I (*je*). Lacan's thought here would seem to be as follows: the ego is the self as it (mis)recognises itself in its own image. The I is the self as decentred, as other than itself, the real condition of subjectivity, of which the ego is oblivious. The camera, obviously, lacks an ego, since it neither recognises nor misrecognises anything. However, the relation between image and what is imaged is such that Lacan can see in it that which structures the decentring of the subject: it is decentring similar to that which is effected in language, or, as he would have it, in the Symbolic. An object in a photograph is both itself and only an image of itself. So in language I am revealed as other than myself: I am myself and at the same time lost to myself in what represents me – my name, for example, or the word 'I'.

> The machine is the structure detached from the activity of the subject. The symbolic world is the world of the machine.[19]

As Manfred Frank has pointed out, Lacan is here taking the view that 'consciousness arises as an effect of the differential relations between elements of an order'.[20] For Frank, Lacan seems to be implying that the camera can substitute for the eye in all essential respects: 'The surface of a lake can also be replaced by the *area striata* of the occipital lobe, for the *area striata* with its fibrillary layers is exactly like a mirror.'[21] It would seem that the *area striata* of the occipital lobe of the brain operates just as a camera does, with its film inside it. The confusions here are multiple, but, as Frank indicates, a fundamental objection was indicated during the course of Lacan's seminar by J.B. Lefèbvre-Pontalis, who put his finger on 'the sore point' of Lacan's position. As Frank has it, Lefèbvre-Pontalis's argument amounts to saying that 'there is nothing intrinsic to the play of visual reflections that would indicate that the mirror images that are sent back and forth are for themselves what they are'.[22] In other words, the basic problem is that all attempts to derive consciousness from relations between elements, of whatever kind – whether images, words or objects – are doomed to failure, since any such attempt must already presuppose consciousness. The same objection holds for Derrida's attempt to derive consciousness, or subjectivity, from the differential play of elements that make up *différance*.

III

Tallis responds to theories that attempt to derive subjectivity and consciousness from ahistorical and transcendent linguistic structures by returning us to the actualities of our ways of life. He asks us to consider a non-linguistic act, such as walking:

> Walking, analysed as a set of physical events, may not have discernible formal properties. The individual movements comprising my journey to the pub cannot easily be related to 'movement-types' whose successive realisations amount to a 'sentence' whose resultant meaning is 'arrival at a pub'.[23]

I may, for example, pause on the way, chatting to the people I meet, looking at the varieties of flowers beside the road, avoiding an unpredictable dog, and so on. None the less, if I am asked what I am doing, I can say what my purpose is and where I am going, though in order to do this there is no necessary or sufficient condition that I am obliged to meet or cite. However, an action will imply choice, inasmuch as I might have decided to do something else. And, given that there are alternative courses of action, which I have rejected, the meaning of my action can therefore be said to depend on the opposition of the elements that compose it to other actions that have different meanings. Since choice would seem to involve differentiation and exclusion, differing and deferral appear as intrinsic to meaning conveyed non-verbally – the meaning of gestures, actions, and so on – as to meaning that is given strictly verbal expression. Tallis's point has a direct bearing on the notion that language is to be explained in terms of a system. The idea of a language system, whether as we have it in Saussure, or in the more extreme forms of linguistic fetishism to be found in Lacan, Derrida and their disciples, assumes that a language consists only of verbal symbols or signs. Tallis's account of walking suggests why this won't do: the gestures, rhythms and movements of the body, are, like differing tones of voice, inseparable from how in practice we say what we mean. If theories of meaning have no place for gesture and movement, this is because the language system has no place for them. But gesture and deixis utilise the fact that one is physically located in space and time, and to exclude them from our ideas of what it is to have mastered a natural language, such as French or English, is a distortion of those ideas. As Tallis indicates, the meaning of a walk to the pub may plausibly be said to involve not only everything that I have been and done up until that moment but also a complex, and uncertain, relation to the future. Other writers have come to similar conclusions. G.P. Baker and P.M.S. Hacker, for example, have drawn attention to how the many aspects of language use – the carrying on of conversations, the answering and putting of questions, the giving and obeying of orders and requests, and much more – are interwoven with a wide range of other activities, involving many kinds of skill and knowledge. As they put it: 'The ability to speak English merges into other abilities, such as social skills, memory and motor skills, and the ability to express knowledge clearly and precisely. This means that the ability to speak a language is not sharply circumscribed and properly described independently of other abilities.'[24] Rush Rees has also remarked on what is at issue here, in a discussion of Wittgenstein's builders:

> [It] is important to emphasize, as Wittgenstein was doing, that to understand what is said in the language you must understand more than the vocabulary and rules of grammar. But the differences between one form of life and another are not like the differences between one form of some institution (say marriage customs or financial institutions) and another. And the activity of the builders does not give you an idea of a people with a definite sort of life. Do they have songs and dances and festivals, and do they have stories and legends? And are they horrified by certain sorts of crimes, and do they expose people to public ridicule? ... Language is something that can have a literature. This is where it is so different from chess.[25]

These remarks make it clear that the understanding of a language is not to be isolated from gesture and bodily expression. As Baker and Hacker note, the way people look, their grimaces, facial expressions and smiles, for example, all indicate whether or not an utterance has been understood. The expression in the eyes, the set of the mouth, are often excellent guides to as to whether someone is lying or joking, while misunderstandings of an utterance are often manifest in wrong or inappropriate behaviour.

These reflections serve to reinforce the implausibility of post-structuralist theories of meaning, and so of the notions of subjectivity based on them. The same point emerges from the account Tallis gives of the human person:

> The other day, on a hot bus, I sat behind a girl with her hair drawn up into a pony tail. This left her neck, emphatically denuded by the sunshine, exposed to my gaze. As I looked at the shadow cast by her sternomastoid muscle over the anterior triangle of her neck and observed the soft pulsing of the carotid artery, I had an overwhelming sense, beyond that of the girl's bodily presence to me, of her presence to herself, mediated by this, her body. She *was*, in some sense I found difficult to characterise, this body. And I was reminded of the extent to which *I* was, more or less, *my* body. I was reminded, that is to say, of the material tautology of my own existence.[26]

Tallis here seems to be giving himself over to the temptation to say 'I *am* my body', a temptation that he is, however, quick to repudiate. His novelistic (and medical) evocation of the girl on the bus emphasises the way he imagines the girl's presence to herself being mediated by her body. He remarks that from time to time he has been prone, like Sartre's Antoine Roquentin and Rilke's Malte Laurids Brigge, to have a sudden awareness of his own right hand. It is an uncanny experience, in which the hand seems at once familiar and profoundly strange. On certain occasions, it seems so close to him as to be part of him; at other times, it seems quite distant and alien. This would seem to be a fundamental human experience, in which I feel myself to be my body, and in the same moment I experience myself as other than my body. Tallis, of course, is not interested in drawing Cartesian conclusions from this. His attempt is to get at some notion of what it is to speak about the experience of being the person that I am. How can I talk about what it is like to be me? As he notes, my being 'here' is my body's being here. 'My body lives my days and sleeps my nights. My body's decay is my decay, its demise my demise.'[27] However, there is an ineradicable ambiguity in this. When I speak of 'my' body, the 'my' connects me to my body, and disconnects me. There is a distance evoked between my body and what I might call my 'self'. This shows itself in an asymmetry between the third and first person usage, inasmuch as I do not as readily separate you from your appearance as I separate myself from mine. None the less, despite this asymmetry and the distance we feel between ourselves and our bodies, there remains the inescapable fact that I am the person I am. This is somehow tied up with the equally inescapable and ineluctable fact that I am in some way my body. The sense of wonder and surprise that are inseparable from this recognition is what drives Tallis's reflections, and provides a route into the issue of the value and meaning of the human person that is central to his work.

One approach to the question of self and body is that taken by P.M.S. Hacker. Hacker begins by drawing a distinction between the role played in our lives by the notion of 'having a body' as opposed to that of 'being a body'. This is a distinction in what Wittgenstein calls the 'grammar' of the two phrases, and it serves to mark the qualitative distinction between the living and the dead, the animate and the inanimate, the sensible and the insensate.[28] As Hacker notes, I may be proud of my body without being proud of myself, and ashamed of myself without being ashamed of my body. It makes sense to introduce myself by saying 'I am N.N.', but to say 'I am this body' is no introduction at all. As he notes, human *beings*, though they occupy space, are not human *bodies*. Indeed, what does it mean to say that I *am* my body? It can't mean that I am *identical* with my body. First, it is not an identity statement to say 'I am my body', any more than it is an identity statement to say 'I am N.N.'. The word 'I' in my mouth does not refer to me: in giving my name I am not picking myself out from others (though of course by so doing I am making it possible for others to do precisely that). Second, I will cease to exist before my body ceases to exist, for at death I will leave my remains behind. Third, though there are a few contexts in which 'I' and 'my body' can replace each other, the very expression '*my* body' presupposes the difference between me and my body and commonly the two expressions cannot replace each other. The fundamental point, for Hacker, as for Wittgenstein, is that only what is alive can be said to 'have a body'. It is not said of machines, or of corpses. 'Having a body, one might say, is a (formal) mark of *sentient life*.'[29] Hanjo Glock and John Hyman have commented on Hacker's (and Wittgenstein's) arguments:

> Suppose that Carter is ashamed of his body because it weighs 18 stone. Carter's body weighs 18 stone if and only if Carter weighs 18 stone. Hence Carter is ashamed of the fact that he weighs 18 stone; therefore Carter is ashamed of himself. However, suppose that Carter is ashamed of himself because he has offended Mary. It does not follow that he is ashamed of his body (of which he may well be proud, if it is beautiful and graceful). For those cases where the mutual implication holds are precisely those which concern bodily characteristics. For what is true of my body is true of me (for as long as I am alive); but what is true of me need not be true of my body (and indeed may make no sense when predicated of my body).[30]

Glock and Hyman go on to note that the substitution of 'Carter' for 'Carter's body' does not preserve truth-value in some cases. From this they conclude that Carter is not identical with Carter's body. In other cases, the substitution results in nonsense, which, they suggest, shows that Carter and his body belong to different categories of particular. Finally, the fact that substitution is permitted in some cases and preserves truth-value indicates that 'Carter is not some other thing, over and above his body, which might survive its (final) destruction'.[31] The conclusion may seem paradoxical: how can Carter not be identical with his body, if Carter and his body are (and must be) in the same place at the same time? Does this not lead straight back to Cartesian dualism? The response is that, while no two *material* bodies can occupy exactly the same place at exactly the same time, a person is not a body, and therefore the objection gets no grip on the concepts of person and body.

Persuasive though these arguments are, I believe they do not quite touch on Tallis's overriding concern, which has to do with the human being's experience of his or her own uniqueness – the fact of my being *me*. What Glock and Hyman are doing is to reflect on the grammar of our language concerning the person and the body, so as to make clear what it is that we take for granted. The result of doing so is to clarify what the confusions are that lie at the root of the many philosophical discussions of the dualism of mind and body. The aim of their approach is to dissolve the problem before it can get off the ground, and to free us from the picture that held us captive, the picture that philosophical language seems to have forced on us. For Tallis, however, the problems attaching to our conceptions of the self cannot be dissolved in this way. He is committed to addressing philosophical questions such as these as if they were not wholly explicable in terms of conceptual grammar. He would want to insist that the appeal to one's own individual experience is something one cannot prescind from or deny. To explore what we mean by the self is, as Tallis presents the issue, inseparable from the consideration of certain kinds of experience, including my experience of wonder at the very fact of my being – the sudden experience that bursts in on me: 'I am me!'

The philosopher who more nearly approaches what is at stake here for Tallis is Heidegger, inasmuch as it is Heidegger who evokes what it is for me to be me – the being of this living body, the subject of anxiety, joy, dread. Heidegger speaks of Dasein, or 'being-there': Dasein is that being whose being is an issue for itself, and which 'bears within itself the task of an explication of an entity which is the questioning itself – the *Dasein* which we, the very questioners, are'.[32] To explore the situation of Dasein requires a shift in the language of philosophy itself, away from deducing propositions and sequences of propositions to 'working out the access to matters from which propositions are to be drawn to begin with'.[33] This leads to statements like ' It is a matter of an entity to which we have this distinctive, at any rate noteworthy, relationship of being: we are it itself – an entity which is only insofar as I am it.'[34] What this order of language (which is everywhere in Heidegger) is trying to evoke is the uncanniness at the heart of our experience of ourselves, of ourselves as human persons, which Tallis noted in his account of the experience of being and not being this body. The experience of the uncanny is the experience of anxiety, and

> in anxiety there lies the possibility of a disclosure which is quite distinctive; for anxiety individualizes. This individualization brings Dasein back from its falling, and makes manifest to it that authenticity and inauthenticity are possibilities of its Being. These basic possibilities of Dasein (and Dasein is in each case mine) show themselves in anxiety as they are in themselves – undisguised by entities within-the-world, to which, proximally and for the most part, Dasein clings.[35]

Dasein is in the world in the mode of having a world, of relating to others, for example, or of knowing one's way about, a mode which cannot be ascribed to objects such as pebbles and rocks, which are simply spatially included within the world. And, as Tallis points out, the fact of my being 'worlded' in this way casts light upon the original self-revelation of the body. Indeed, my being 'worlded' is that through which the body is revealed to itself. I come to my body largely through my interactions with others, interactions which are my being 'worlded', and which constitute me as that being which it falls to me to be. I cannot escape the particularity of my situation by means of thought about that particularity, since my thought about what I am is part of that particularity itself. The anxiety of Dasein is a consequence of my being unable to escape the existential particularity that is my 'ownmost' condition, and the discourse appropriate to the exploration of that condition is, as Tallis, following Gabriel Marcel, insists, far removed from the building of systems, and far even from systematic exposition.

I would add here that the question of the body gets far greater prominence in Tallis than it does in Heidegger. One can get the impression from reading Heidegger, particularly the Heidegger of *Being and Time*, that he drifts between seeing Dasein, on the one hand, as a category of being, and, on the other, as referring to individual human beings. Because of this irresolution, the text seems to afford no place for a sustained consideration of the role and meaning of the body as such, and without the body – its body – it is difficult to see what specific issues Dasein should be concerned about. This may be why, for Heidegger, the key issue for Dasein, uncovered in anticipatory resoluteness, in being-towards-death, turns out to be its own nothingness: its ownmost potentiality-of-being is 'the null basis of its own nullity'[36] – the knowledge delivered by *Angst*. The distance between Tallis and Heidegger is therefore located here, in the weightier emphasis Tallis wants to place on the significance of the body – in order to give Dasein specific issues to be concerned with and to link our lives to the physical constraints in which we live. Perhaps it is these lines that offer a sense of things answering most nearly to what Tallis would seek to describe: 'Now that my ladder's gone, / I must lie down where all the ladders start, / In the foul rag-and-bone shop of the heart.'

IV

This emphasis on the irreducibility of the human person has ramifications throughout Tallis's work, notably in relation to his critique of neurophilosophy and in relation to his account of art. Neurophilosophy has one basic idea underpinning it, namely, that problems in the philosophy of mind may be solved by the investigation of neurology. In other words, the founding assumption of neurophilosophy is that mental phenomena can be explained in terms of processes in the brain. It is further assumed, or believed, that there is empirical evidence for these kinds of explanation, and that the empirical evidence has been supplied by modern neuroscience. Tallis challenges all of this, and his way of doing so is characteristic of his approach to theories of the unconscious more generally. To indicate something of what this approach amounts to, I confine myself to one line of argument, that which he opposes to the so-called identity theory, the theory that neural activity is identical with conscious experience. One might object to the theory, at least as it is posed in these terms, that nerve impulses don't appear to be anything like sensations, feelings or thoughts. This objection has been countered by an argument deriving from the notion that there are different 'levels' of observation or description involved here. One may grant that nerve impulses are nothing like sensations or other more complex experiences, but then the molecules of H_2O are not at all like water. It is therefore wholly possible to explain the great differences between nerve impulses and experiences by way of analogy: the relation between nerve impulses and experiences are analogous to the relation between molecules of water and water itself. Water molecules are nothing like water, lacking as they do shininess, wetness, liquidity, and so on. But no one would be inclined to argue on this basis that water and the molecules that make it up are not identical. H_2O molecules and drops of water are simply the same thing observed at different levels. By analogy, then, it would be perfectly reasonable to say that neural activity and conscious experience are also the same thing observed at different levels.

Tallis points to a number of problems with this argument. The most obvious is that the notion of levels implies levels of observation. Molecules of H_2O and water rushing down a mountain stream correspond to different ways of observing the water. On the one hand, there is water as revealed to a particular method of scientific investigation, and, on the other, there is water as disclosed to ordinary observation. As Tallis makes clear, levels of observation presuppose observation, and observation presupposes consciousness. Levels of observation cannot therefore 'be legitimately invoked to explain the relationship between the seemingly unconscious third person neural activity of the brain and first person conscious experience'.[37] There is a further failing attaching to such a viewpoint, which is that it does not explain why some neural activity has the characteristic of being identical with consciousness while most neural activity – that taking place in the spinal cord, for example – does not. However, the more crucial point for Tallis is that the 'levels' explanation goes no way at all towards explaining what is fundamental and unique to conscious experience: its intentionality, its character of being *about* something. When I am conscious of something I am conscious of something outside of me, outside of my brain. It is completely unclear how the neural discharges inside my brain are supposed to refer back to the object that set them off. If we follow conventional materialistic thinking on the question of perception (a dubious enterprise) we may then think of an inward causal chain leading from the seen object to impulses in the visual cortex. However, there is no way that such a causal chain can work in the opposite direction, whereby the cortical impulses reach out to, or refer to, the object seen. No such processes are to be recognised elsewhere in nature, and there are no grounds for positing them here. There is then a mismatch between the neural activity which the identity theory attempts to describe and the particular sensations and experiences which this activity is meant to explain. There is, beyond this, a complete failure of the identity theory – and of theories like it – to account for 'the organisation of ordinary human consciousness, the infinitely complex lacework of the aims, goals, intentions, notions, ambitions, etc. that comprise our daily lives'.[38] Tallis wants to insist that, even if the identity theory did explain sensations on the basis of a one-to-one correspondence between neural activity and sensations, such a theory would not do us much good. It would not be able to explain the complex unity of conscious experience, let alone the coherence of conscious activity through time which is necessary for the coherence of the understanding self.

This returns us to Tallis's central preoccupation: the origin of the sense of me, here, now. How is that I am a being whose being is an issue for itself? It is no use saying that *my* brain gives me this sense of things, just because it is my brain. Seen from the scientific viewpoint, my brain is just another object amongst others, and possesses no intrinsic ownership. It is therefore unintelligible to say that it can offer me the fundamental sense that I am this person here and now. The fact that things matter to me has simply no place in the materialist world picture of the identity theorist: 'Suffice it to say, there is no basis in the brain for the unified consciousness and the connected fundamental intuition of self: the sense that *I am this thing* and that *I am here*. There is nothing in the brain to make it my brain; it cannot underpin the first person, the viewpoint, the deixis, that make the ordinary moments of life matter to me, here, now.'[39]

It is this sense of what matters to the self, of the intentionality of conscious experience, that Tallis explores further in his discussions of art. He begins from the presupposition that there is an irresolvable tension, in ordinary experience, at least, between two functions of consciousness: 'between moments that pause on the edge of a dancing chaos of contingencies, and the larger projects and ideas, the forms and structures, we pursue through, or attempt to realise in, those moments'.[40] Experience fails fully to instantiate the ideas that bear upon it, and it is itself subverted by the twin distractions of anticipation and memory. This is to acknowledge the incurable wound in the present tense, arising from the almost insuperable difficulty of achieving that unity wherein the intense recognition of the particular and the abstract grasp of it are made one. The unity in question is that of *being*, and Tallis compares it to the religious notion of 'mindfulness' or the mystic's search for absolute self-remembering, in which the unique self is transparent with knowledge, and knowledge made palpable with material presence. The argument that he wishes to advance is that the resolution of this opposition is, at least in the secular West, the single most important function of art. It is in art that we may be able to overcome the problem that seems to lie at the heart of consciousness, the irresolvable tension between experience and the idea of experience. It seems impossible that we should fully experience what we know or that what we know should conform to what we experience. The aim of art, for Tallis, is to allow us to apprehend, if only for a moment, what it is be fully *there* – to experience to the full one's own being there. Tallis seems to have in mind a process not unlike that described (and enacted) in *Little Gidding*: 'We shall not cease from exploration / And the end of all our exploring / Will be to arrive where we started / And know the place for the first time.' It is a crucial effect of the formal features of any art to unify across variety, and by so doing to unify experiences that would otherwise remain disparate. 'Disparate' here refers to what Tallis calls 'the nears and fars of the world; booty from the four corners of the empire of experience'.[41] He argues that the bringing together of these dissonant elements permits an experience arising out of the work that opens out into and fills something larger than that experience – 'something, in short, like what we hope to experience when we seek out experience for its own sake'.[42] It is an experience of the 'mindful'. A work of art gives concrete realisation to an idea, and it does so through an arrangement of parts such that the many may be perceived by way of the one, and unity recovered from diversity: the mutable is perceived by way of what does not change, and the enduring discovered in flux. Art is such that the build-up of form and the physical experience of that build-up do not undermine each other. The paradoxes of vision here are made explicit in lines from *The Dry Salvages*, which Tallis quotes: 'music heard so deeply / That it is not heard at all, but you are the music / While the music lasts'. It is the function of art to bring us to a place where we are completed in an experience that is truly experienced, and where meaning no longer serves any purpose exterior to itself. 'Meaning is at once completed and in process; unfolding and unfolded.'[43] For Tallis, this is to create an idea that is as large as those that wound our consciousness through anticipation and memory, and larger than those realised in ordinary experience. Art addresses what Tallis sees as the intimate tragedy of human consciousness – the failure of ordinary experience to realise the idea of experience in experience itself.

The direction of the argument Tallis is presenting and its larger significance have also received clear expression from Stanley Cavell. As Cavell points out, on this Kantian conception of art, art does not aim to express a specific intention (as statements or assertions do), nor does it aim at the achievement of the particular goals intended by technological skill or moral action.

> [Art] celebrates the fact that men can intend their lives at all (if you like, that they are free to choose), and that their actions are coherent and effective at all in the scene of indifferent nature and determined society.[44]

Cavell takes this to have been what Kant had seen when he spoke of 'purposiveness without purpose'. One can perhaps only more fully take the force of these ideas by way of an exemplification offered by art itself, and in order to develop this point I turn to Wordsworth's 'A slumber did my spirit seal':

> A slumber did my spirit seal:
> I had no human fears;
> She seemed a thing that could not feel
> The touch of earthly years.
>
> No motion has she now, no force;
> She neither hears nor sees;
> Roll'd round in earth's diurnal course
> With rocks and stones and trees.

A critic whose work is expressive of a profound inwardness with the Kantian perspective is F.R. Leavis, and his account of the Wordsworth poem is of immediate relevance here. Leavis notes that the poem undoubtedly emerges out of a profound and involuntary suffering, and yet the experience has been so impersonalised that the effect is one of 'bare and disinterested presentment'.[45] The emotional power of the poem is produced between the two stanzas – she was, and she is not. The poem seems to say something as simple as that, and yet 'once the reading has been completed the whole poem is seen to be a complex organisation, charged with a subtle life'.[46] Part of this subtlety arises from the temporal organisation of the poem, so that it is only when one looks back on it that the first stanza acquires its full force: there seems to attach to 'human' in line 2 a suggestion of the inescapability of the human condition, a suggestion one recognises even as one recognises 'a certain *hubris* in the security of forgetful bliss'.[47] Again, the use of the word 'human' enhances the ironic status of 'thing' in the next line, since in stanza 2 she *is* in truth a thing. 'Roll'd round in earth's diurnal course' with rocks and stones and trees she cannot in reality feel the touch of earthly years and she is immune from death. One might add in relation to the account Leavis gives of it that the poem may be thought as enacting within the complexity of its movement the dynamics of human temporality and being towards death that for Heidegger constitute Dasein. To read the poem is to re-read it, and the revelation of its trajectory is its end and purpose. On this showing, the poem is to be understood not only in terms of movement and stasis, but also in terms of a complex temporality of past, present and future. The poem presents a moment of vision, in which the poet anticipates mortality and is capable of looking back on his former misapprehensions concerning it, while at the same time that moment is placed in a larger scheme of things, a placing implied by 'diurnal' and the context surrounding it. The temporality of our own, living time, of the human world, is set against the impersonal and inexorable movement of the earth, the elusive and mysterious origin on which and in which we have our dwelling. There is a strife between the world that the poem opens up and the earth that displays itself as earth – as something elusive and hidden – and it is the putting of this strife before us that is the poem's achievement.[48]

The purpose of art, for Tallis, has to do with what he calls The Kingdom of Ultimate Ends. Art is not subordinate to some other, non-artistic purpose. It is, like consciousness itself, *sui generis*, and if we need art at all it is in order to be more completely alive. Wordsworth's poem unites the changing world of particulars – of rocks and stones and trees – with the world of ideas, of concepts of life and death, of the human and the non-human, creating out of the events and structures of the poem itself the 'moving unmoved' of form. Art is about experience for its own sake, and because of this it is useless, and yet out of that uselessness it engages us with its own, other purpose: it engages us with that experience perfected. 'So let there be art, rounding off the sense of the world, celebrating the wonderful and beautiful uselessness of human consciousness. Let walking know and perfect itself in dancing.'[49]

Notes

1. Raymond Tallis, *Not Saussure* (London: Macmillan, 1988), pp. 68–9.
2. Ibid., p. 67.

3. F. de Saussure, *Course in General Linguistics*, trans. Wade Baskin (London, 1974), p. 7. Hereafter, page references in the text will be to this edition, given thus: (8), etc.
4. Samuel Weber, 'Saussure and the Apparition of Language: the Critical Perspective', *MLN* 91 (1973): 915.
5. Ibid., 916.
6. Ibid., 922.
7. Tallis, *Not Saussure*, p. 67.
8. Roland Barthes has described the process in the following way: 'The language is an intermediate object between sound and thought: it consists in uniting both while simultaneously decomposing them... . language is the domain of *articulations*, and the meaning is above all the cutting-out of shapes' (*Elements of Semiology*, New York, Hill and Wang, 1980), pp. 56–7).
9. Weber, 926.
10. Ludwig Wittgenstein, *Philosophical Investigations*, trans. G.E.M. Anscombe (Oxford: Blackwell, 1986), §104.
11. Tallis, *Not Saussure*, p. 73.
12. Richard Eldridge, *Leading a Human Life: Wittgenstein, Intentionality, and Romanticism* (Chicago and London: University of Chicago Press, 1997), p. 231.
13. Tallis, *Not Saussure*, p. 226.
14. Ibid., p. 226.
15. Ibid., p. 227.
16. Stanley Cavell, 'Notes and Afterthoughts on the Opening of the *Investigations*', in Hans Sluga and David G Stern (eds), *The Cambridge Companion to Wittgenstein* (Cambridge: Cambridge University Press, 1996): 286.
17. Stephen Mulhall, 'Introduction', in Stephen Mulhall (ed.), *The Cavell Reader* (Oxford: Blackwell, 1996): 9.
18. *The Seminar of Jacques Lacan: Book II*, trans. Sylvana Tomaselli (Cambridge: Cambridge University Press, 1988), p. 46.
19. Ibid., p. 47.
20. *What is Neostructuralism?*, trans. Sabine Wilke and Richard Gray (Minneapolis: University of Minnesota Press, 1989), p. 313.
21. Lacan, *Seminar*, p. 49.
22. Frank, *What is Neostructuralism?*, p. 313.
23. Tallis, *Not Saussure*, p. 216.
24. G.P Baker and P.M.S. Hacker, *Language, Sense and Nonsense* (Oxford: Blackwell, 1986), p. 377.
25. Rush Rees, *Wittgenstein and the Possibility of Discourse* (Cambridge: Cambridge University Press, 1998), p. 192.
26. Raymond Tallis, *On the Edge of Certainty* (London: Macmillan, 1999), p. 156.
27. *On the Edge of Certainly*, p. 158.
28. P.M.S. Hacker, *Wittgenstein: Meaning and Mind* (Oxford: Blackwell, 1990), p. 247.
29. Ibid., p. 249.
30. Hanjo Glock and John Hyman, 'Persons and their Bodies', *Philosophical Investigations* 17:2 (April 1994): 378.
31. Ibid., 379.
32. Martin Heidegger, *History of the Concept of Time*, trans. Theodore Kisiel (Bloomington: Indiana University Press, 1985), p. 149.
33. Ibid., p. 146.
34. Ibid., p. 149.

35. Martin Heidegger, *Being and Time*, trans. John Macquarrie and Edward Robinson (London: SCM Press, 1962), p. 235.
36. Ibid., p. 354.
37. Tallis, *On the Edge of Certainty*, p. 135.
38. Ibid., p. 138.
39. Ibid., p. 145.
40. Raymond Tallis, *Newton's Sleep: Two Cultures and Two Kingdoms* (London: Macmillan, 1995), p. 150.
41. Ibid., p. 154.
42. Ibid., p. 154.
43. Ibid., p. 157.
44. Stanley Cavell, *Must We Mean What We Say?* (Cambridge: Cambridge University Press, 1989), p. 198.
45. F.R. Leavis, *The Living Principle* (London: Chatto and Windus, 1975), p. 73. For a contrasting reading of Wordsworth's poem, see Paul de Man, 'The Rhetoric of Temporality', in *Blindness and Insight: Essays in the Rhetoric of Contemporary Criticism,* second edition (London: Routledge, 1993), pp. 187–228.
46. *The Living Principle,* p. 73.
47. Ibid., p. 73.
48. On this, see Richard Polt, *Heidegger: an Introduction* (London: UCL Press, 1999), pp. 137–8.
49 Tallis, *Newton's Sleep*, p. 208.

Part I
The Explicit Animal

If there is one thought that is central to the many and varied intellectual endeavours that Raymond Tallis has undertaken in the fields of philosophy, the history of ideas, art and literature it is that what above all separates us as human beings from the physical and biological world in which we find ourselves is the fact that we are *explicit* animals. Human beings are that in virtue of which 'That' as in 'That X [is the case]' is imported into Being. It is this quality of explicitness that pervades the human sense of individuality: for Tallis, 'That I am this thing' may be said to lie at the heart of a distinctively human sense of self.

Furthermore, this ability possessed by human consciousness of making states, events, objects and itself explicit is underivable and inexplicable; in particular, it cannot be accounted for in terms of the properties of the material world. (One might say that there is no material X whose properties could explain the transition from X to 'That X [is the case]'.) More specifically, human consciousness cannot be explained by the special properties of the brain. The brain is a piece of the material world, and the neural theory of consciousness, no matter how cunningly it may be elaborated, is therefore always going to be inadequate. Mechanistic explanations, based on biological and/or computational models, seem to promise progress only because they are cast in the language of neuromythology which allows the really difficult questions about consciousness to be bypassed.

Several consequences flow from the failure of neural theories of consciousness and the affirmation of the *sui generis* status of the human mind. Darwinian accounts of human behaviour will always be inadequate: we are explicit human beings and part of what that means is that we act deliberately and at several removes from instinctive and other mechanisms, even in pursuit of our appetites. Evolutionary epistemology – which attempts to explain human knowledge and the nature of truth in terms of adaptation to the environment – is thereby ruled out. To affirm this is to affirm the fact that the liberation of human culture from animal nature is real and capable of unlimited development. For Tallis, such a liberation is what constitutes, in Wittgenstein's phrase, the natural history of mankind: we have limitless possibilities for creating new meanings, new institutions, new relations with the material world and that part of ourselves which is rooted in the organic body.

1
The Poverty of Neurophilosophy

The primary purpose of this reading, taken from *On the Edge of Certainty* (1999), is to make clear the extent to which neural theories of mind – that is, theories that attempt to explain mental phenomena in terms of certain processes in the brain – actually impoverish our understanding of human consciousness and our mental life. This, for Tallis, is particularly clear in the way neurophilosophy fails to give an account of consciousness that is able to do justice to our sense of ourselves and of our conscious lives. In part, this has to do with the fact that the notion of agency is inseparable from that of explicit purpose, from the expression of the rational will, and this in turn requires us to relate to contexts and situations that endure across far greater periods of time than are available to the instant of consciousness. Even the simplest acts involve a huge and complex temporal framework. The challenge to neurophilosophers like Daniel Dennett and Steven Pinker is, according to Tallis, to explain how all the different activities in the brain corresponding to these complex interrelationships can retain their different identities while at the same time these patterns are able to interact with and remain open to each other. All the activity rippling through the brain must come together in the present moment, so that I know where and who I am, but at the very same time it must keep myriads of projects, intentions and actions distinct. The notion that my mind is where my brain is could just as easily be turned on its head: my brain is where my mind is. Without consciousness there is no 'where', no 'here', for my brain to be at. And my brain is ownerless.

Tallis concludes on a more positive note. He is a clinician concerned to understand and ameliorate the effects of neurological afflictions in old age, such as stroke and epilepsy, and therefore he is by no means seeking to undermine or cast aspersions on the efforts of neuroscientists themselves. Even if they are not discovering how the mind works, or how it is constructed, they are, he says, discovering with ever-increasing precision the conditions under which normal experience and volition are possible. It is, however, important to recognise what the limits of science are, and to keep science free of bad philosophy and the malign influence of scientism.

Neurophilosophy

In the last decade or so, there has been a stream of books, both popular and semi-professional and in both philosophy and cognitive neuroscience, purporting to demonstrate that contemporary neuroscience is advancing our understanding of the mind.[1] While none of these books suggests that the mind has yet been fully explained by the neuroscientists, the implicit assumption is that they are, at last, on the right track: it is just a matter of time. It is also suggested that the earlier approaches, typified by the philosopher in the armchair dreaming up hypotheses that are either untested, or more likely untestable, are now simply out of date. A philosophy of mind that is not rooted in, driven by and checked against the findings of the neuroscientists is archaic and empty.

The title of Patricia Churchland's nearly 600-page volume, *Neurophilosophy*, captures the fundamental notion underpinning such books: that at least one particular philosophical problem – the philosophy of mind – may be solved by neurological investigation. Of course, the solution to this problem would have wider implications. It would be a signal advance in our understanding of our own nature and might help us to make progress in other areas of philosophical investigation – for example, understanding the basis of human agency and our apparent free will; determining our place in the natural world and the overall scheme of things; and even solving ethical problems and getting a better understanding of the right way forward for human society. The implicit claims of neurophilosophy are thus even more wide-reaching than their explicit ones.

Some, but not all, neurophilosophers make bold assertions about the extent to which contemporary neuroscience has solved, or shortly will solve, the mysteries that have baffled philosophers for so many centuries. These claims are broadcast in the titles of the books: Daniel Dennett's *Consciousness Explained* (1993) and Stephen Pinker's *How the Mind Works* (1997) are just two extreme examples. While, in the preface to his book, Pinker disavows any claim to understanding how the mind works, this, in the light of his title, is disingenuous to say the least, particularly since he argues that cognitive neuroscience has transformed certain issues in the philosophy of mind from mysteries into problems.[2] I wish to argue here that not only has neuroscience cast no light on how there is such a thing as the mind, how it comes about and how in a fundamental sense it 'works', but also that it is unlikely to do so.

The relationship, or non-relationship, between mind and brain is, of course, a huge subject which has generated a massive bibliography. I myself have contributed to it; in particular, *The Explicit Animal*[3] attacks the notion that biological science helps us to understand the extraordinary nature of human consciousness. I will not attempt a survey of current neurophilosophy. Suffice it to note that there are two theses which may be regarded as central: the belief that consciousness can be explained in biological terms and the parallel belief that it is both appropriate and fruitful to think of the mind as a complex computer or a set of computational functions. The biological dimension of neurophilosophy itself has two elements: the notion that human consciousness can be explained within the framework of evolutionary theory (so that the emergence of consciousness, even specifically human aspects of consciousness, is explicable as a product of natural selection); and the claim that consciousness is somehow accounted for by the neural activity of the brain. Several of these strands are brought together in Pinker's assertion that 'the mind is a system of organs of computation designed by natural selection to solve the problems faced by our evolutionary ancestors' (op. cit., p. 21).

In the present chapter, I shall address the poverty of neurophilosophy. Because I have discussed elsewhere the unsupportable claim that human consciousness can be explained in evolutionary terms, I will not revisit this here: the reader is referred to the relevant chapters (2 and 6) of *The Explicit Animal*. Nor shall I attempt a comprehensive discussion of the computational theory of mind. The language of neuromythology, to which the computational theory owes most if not all of its plausibility, is subjected to an extended critique in Chapter 2 of my *On the Edge of Certainty* and other arguments against the computational theory are set out in Chapter 4 of *The Explicit Animal*, so I shall glance at the theory only in passing here. Nor, finally, will I address the problematic relationship between neural activity and sensations in great depth, though I shall briefly examine the fundamental problems besetting attempts to reduce sensations and other mental phenomena to patterns of nerve impulses.

My primary purpose in this chapter – as will be evident from its title – is to focus on the extent to which neural theories of mind put forward or assumed in cognitive neuroscience, despite their role in raising our awareness of the enormous complexities that are embedded in even the simplest act or the simplest decision, actually impoverish our idea of human consciousness and our mental life. I am, however, not unaware of the major contributions that neuroscientists have made to advancing our understanding of the brain. An additional purpose of this chapter will, therefore, be to try to indicate ways in which neuroscience may contribute to a true neurophilosophy. At any rate I will endeavour to determine the relationship between findings of neuroscience and a true understanding of the nature of the mind. This last question, which is to me the most pressing, will also be dealt with only briefly, not because I have addressed it satisfactorily elsewhere but because I am still unsure how it should be addressed. I will, however, attempt to indicate what is needed if I am to reconcile within myself the believing clinician – whose central interest in medicine is in neuroscience and who in daily practice talks like the most hard-line materialist neuroscientists – and the sceptical philosopher who on a Sunday morning criticises neuromythology.

The case for neurophilosophy

The founding assumption of neurophilosophy is that we can explain mental phenomena in terms of certain processes in the brain; that we have empirical evidence in support of such kinds of explanations; and that this evidence is derived at least in part from the discoveries of modern neuroscience. This assumption is connected with several other theses:

a) that mental phenomena are identical with neural activity (or *patterns* of neural activity – and thereby hangs a tale) taking place in certain parts of the brain;
b) that in the case of perception, this activity is caused by energy (originating from the perceived world) impinging on the brain ('the causal theory of perception');
c) that the brain, in this regard, is like a computer ('mind is the information-processing activity of the brain');
d) that mind/consciousness can be understood in terms of the evolutionary processes that gave rise to the brain.

Irrespective of whether or not the mind really is a computer (or it is correct to think of the mind as the sum of the computational activities of the brain) and whether its emergence can be explained in Darwinian terms, everyday observations seem to give overwhelming support to the notion that there is an intimate relationship between brain and conscious experience. For example, the *content* of my experience is determined by the location of my brain: I am experiencing this room in Bramhall, rather than a room in London, because Bramhall is where my brain presently is. More specifically, I can change my experience by altering the energy that impinges upon my brain via my sense organs; for example, I can alter my visual experience by turning my head in one way or another. I can alter my auditory experience by putting my fingers in my ears. The easiest way of interpreting this is that it modifies the energy reaching my brain in the transduced form of nerve impulses. In other words, my mind is where my brain is, my consciousness is more less *of* where my brain is *at*: in at least one important sense, in waking life, the world of which I am conscious is the world which objectively seems to surround my brain. In contrast, my mind is not necessarily where my leg is: I could leave my leg in London and, so long as I had not bled to death, my mind could still be in Bramhall.

In addition to this compelling evidence of the connection between the brain and consciousness, there are all the many everyday observations that indicate that brain nick and mind nick are closely correlated: a head injury may remove vision, impair memory, alter personality, all of which suggest that vision, memory, personality – everything from the most primitive buzz of sensation to the most exquisitely constructed sense of self – depend crucially on the functioning of the brain.

If these homely observations are thought to cut metaphysical ice, then the more sophisticated ones of science are not required to take us any further. However, on top of this folk database, there is the huge mass of observations made by neuroscientists over the last few hundred years showing close correlations between holes in the brain and holes in the mind, between cerebral dysfunction and abnormalities of consciousness. These observations – which seem somehow more authoritative than what Mrs Smith of Wigan knows from daily life in Wigan or what I observe of myself – range from crude lesion experiments through to the kind of exquisite studies using functional neuro-imaging that currently dominate the literature in cognitive neuroscience.

Importantly, the scientific data include not only negative but also positive observations: certain parts of the brain are seen to be active, to light up, in anticipation of, or during the course of, the discharge of certain mental activities. Magnetic resonance imaging, functional magnetic resonance imaging, positron emission tomography, electroencephalography, magnetoencephalography and other techniques have shown exquisite correlations between activity in certain areas of the brain and mental functions. Under the heading of positive observations, I would also include the effects of brain stimulation, beginning with the famous experiments of Penfield in waking human subjects undergoing epilepsy surgery, in which he observed quite complex memories being switched on by electrical stimulation of the appropriate parts of the cerebral cortex. And then, finally, there are the strong correlations between the pattern and distribution of cerebral activity as recorded by electroencephalography and global states of consciousness: sleep/waking, coma/alertness, attention/inattention.

The problems with neurophilosophy

Everyday life and neuroscientific observations – neurology, neurosurgery, neurophysiology, neuro-anatomy, neuropathology, neurochemistry, neuropsychology, neuroradiology, etc. – would all seem, therefore, to point inescapably to the conclusion that consciousness is due to certain activity in the brain; or that mental activity is neural activity. The confident claim that (for example) 'our sensations are simply identical with, say, a set of stimulation levels (spiking frequencies) in the appropriate sensory pathways'[4] seems close to being unassailable. But actually, there are many insuperable objections to the jump from observing the dependency of mind nick on brain nick to concluding that brain activity somehow explains mind or that consciousness boils down to brain activity.

The first objection is that the way in which the objectively observed neural activity brings about or is in some sense implicated in the subjectively experienced contents of consciousness is far from clear. Indeed, it is profoundly puzzling. There are three front-running accounts of the relationship between nerve impulses and conscious experiences: the dual aspect theory; the causal interaction theory; and the identity theory.

Dual aspect theory

Some have suggested that neural activity and conscious experience – or at least certain 'central' events in the brain and qualia – are two aspects of the same events. However, this so-called 'dual aspect' theory has been largely rejected because most people do not feel happy with the notion of a single event that has two ontologically different aspects – a physical front-side and a mental back-side. It would be a very odd hybrid indeed.

Causal interaction theory

Others have suggested that the neural activity *causes* the mental activity – just as banging on a table causes a loud sound. Under this interpretation, there are therefore two types of events in the brain: on the one hand, nerve impulses which are the material causes; and on the other, the contents of consciousness (sensations, memories, thoughts, etc.), which are the immaterial effects of these impulses. This essentially dualist account runs dangerously close to making mental events mere epiphenoma, digressions from the causal net, ontological diverticula from the material world, which have no role in bringing about other events:

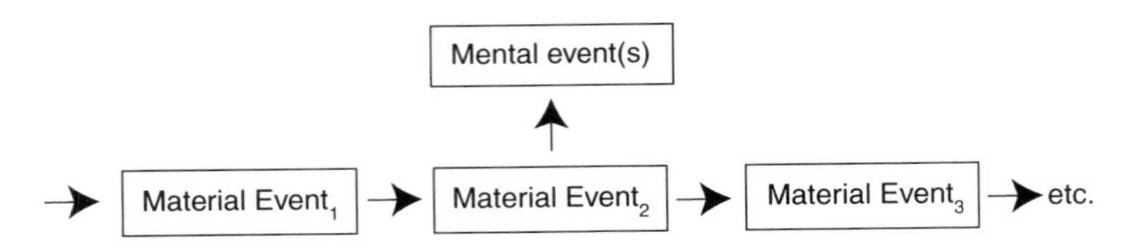

This is obviously unattractive, since it contradicts our firm belief that our conscious experience to some extent drives our behaviour.

If, however, it is claimed, to counter this objection, that the mental phenomena themselves have causal efficacy and are able to bring about material events, in particular the nerve impulses essential for voluntary action, then we have the unexplained situation of a continuous causal chain or net, a material nexus of which we are part, that inexplicably passes into and then out of a mental phase. This is particularly awkward if we believe that material events do, and immaterial events do not, have a location in space. We have, furthermore, to accept the existence of a section of one strand of the causal net – which itself extends indefinitely into the material world of which it is a small inlet – where consciousness inexplicably emerges and initiation, volition is possible; an utterly mysterious area in which the soluble fish of agency and doing somehow crystallise out of the sea of causation and mere happening:

Identity theory

So most philosophers and neuroscientists (when they have a view) prefer to espouse the idea that neural activity is *identical* with conscious experience. This may seem to inherit the difficulties of both the dual aspect theory (one entity, two natures) and the causal theory (an immaterial/material entity embedded in a material causal chain). But it also, of course, raises the objection that neural activity is not at all *like* contents of consciousness. Nerve impulses – waves of electrochemical activity – don't look like sensations. In the wake of this objection comes the further objection that there is nothing in a nerve impulse to explain the specific qualitative features of the sensation it is supposed to be identical with – nothing in, say, impulses in the auditory system to make them specifically the basis of hearing rather than sight. In other words, neither the phenomenal content of consciousness nor the difference between different phenomenal contents of different bits of consciousness has any plausible neural basis. Nerve impulses don't look like sensations and the differences between nerve impulses don't look like the differences between types of experiences.

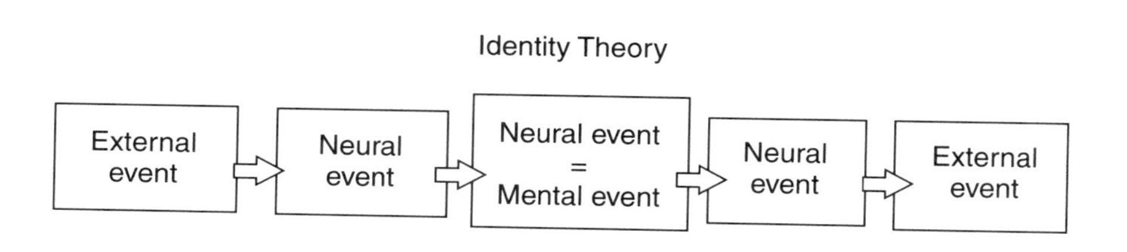

Let me deal with the issue of differences between experiences or mental contents first. Most neuroscientists agree that one lot of nerve impulses looks pretty much like another lot of nerve impulses. The contrast between the monotonous similarity of the nervous system and the infinite variety of the perceived world seems therefore rather puzzling. The argument that *location* of the activity in the brain explains all – that hearings are experienced when the hearing neurones are excited and sights are experienced when the visual neurones are excited – is self-evidently circular. So, too, is the argument that impulses in the visual cortex give sights because they are triggered off by light and those in the auditory cortex give rise to the experience of sounds because they are triggered off by sound. In fact, it is even less helpful than might seem at first sight; for, according to orthodox physical theory, qualities such as brightness and loudness do not exist in nature. There is, for example, nothing in the intrinsic properties of the electromagnetic energy called light that corresponds to brightness or colour. These qualities – secondary qualities – have therefore to be generated in the nervous system – by some unspecified means.

Even if there *were* some way of generating these qualities, how would we account for the discrepancy between their *variety* and the monotonous activity of the nervous system? All nerve impulses are pretty much the same. According to most writers who believe in the identity theory, the basis for the necessary variety is to be found not in the individual impulses but in their *patterns*, the patterns of large numbers of impulses considered together.

The patterns argument says, yes, all nerve impulses are indeed pretty much alike but there are millions of profoundly different possible *patterns of impulses* and it is the variety of these that under-writes the infinite variety of the experienced world. The trouble with this argument, however, is that patterns do not exist in, even less for, the elements that make up the pattern, only for an external observer, a consciousness that extracts the pattern.

Consider, for example, the array in the figure. It could be seen as a single array of nine dots; as an array of six dots on the left and three on the right; or as an array of three dots on the left and six on the right; or as any of a vast number of other possibilities. What this tells us is not that the array contains all these patterns – that it is 'infinitely rich' in patterns – but that it has no inherent pattern; that its patterns exist only in so far as they can be and, indeed, are *extracted*. Unfortunately for the identity theory, they can be extracted only in so far as they are perceived. Likewise there are no intrinsic

An Array of Dots

patterns in the large numbers of nerve impulses that make up brain activity. They do not pick themselves out. The patterns are in the eye of the beholder. If, however, they exist only in relation to a perceiver, and we have to 'send out' for such a perceiver, then the patterns in themselves cannot be the basis either of perception or of its variety.

What about the more fundamental objection to the identity theory that nerve impulses don't seem anything like sensations, qualia, experiences, etc.? This objection has been countered by an argument from 'levels' of description or observation. This argument goes as follows. Granted that nerve impulses aren't at all like sensations or other more complex experiences, but neither are molecules of H_2O at all like water. So we can explain the huge difference between nerve impulses and experiences by thinking of the relationship between nerve impulses and conscious experiences as being like that between water molecules and water. Water molecules are totally unlike water: they do not possess the properties of wetness, shininess, liquidity, etc. But no one regards this difference between water molecules and splashes and dribbles and puddles of water as an argument against the well-accepted belief that water is identical with the water molecules that make it up. Molecules of H_2O are unquestionably identical with drops of water which have phenomenal properties of liquidity and wetness, etc.: H_2O molecules and drops of water are the same thing observed at different levels. Surely, then, it may be argued, by analogy, that neural activity and conscious experience are also the same thing perceived at different levels.

There are, however, many seemingly insuperable difficulties with this solution to the problem of the dissimilarity between neural activity and conscious experiences.[5] The most obvious is that the concept of levels – like that of patterns – implies *levels of observation*: H_2O molecules and water as it is experienced pouring out of the tap correspond to different ways of observing water – water as disclosed to a particular kind of scientific investigation and water with its secondary qualities as disclosed to ordinary perception. *Levels of observation* surely presuppose observation and observations – viewpoints, perspectives, etc. – presuppose consciousness and so cannot legitimately be invoked to explain the relationship between the seemingly unconscious third person neural activity of the brain and first person conscious experience. In addition, the 'levels' argument shares some of the weaknesses of the dual aspect theory, except that, instead of having the same phenomenon seen from the front and the back, as it were, we have the case of a phenomenon seen respectively from the air and from the ground; or a front end which is an aerial viewpoint and a back end which is a view from the ground.

The levels argument, in common with the dual aspect theory, has the additional failing that it does not explain why some neural activity has the characteristic of being identical with consciousness while most neural activity – for example, that which takes place in the cerebellum, the spinal cord, the peripheral nerves, as well as much of the activity recordable in the cerebral cortex – does not. This is rather as if some molecules of H_2O counted as water and others didn't, or as if some had the propensity to add up to phenomenal or secondary qualities such a liquidity and wetness and others did not.

Nor, most crucially, does the 'levels' explanation go any way towards accounting for the fundamental and unique characteristic of conscious experience, namely, its intentionality, its character of being *about* something. For example, my consciousness of the cat refers to something outside of myself, in particular outside of my brain. How do these neural discharges in my brain refer back to the object that triggered them off? This puzzle is set out below:

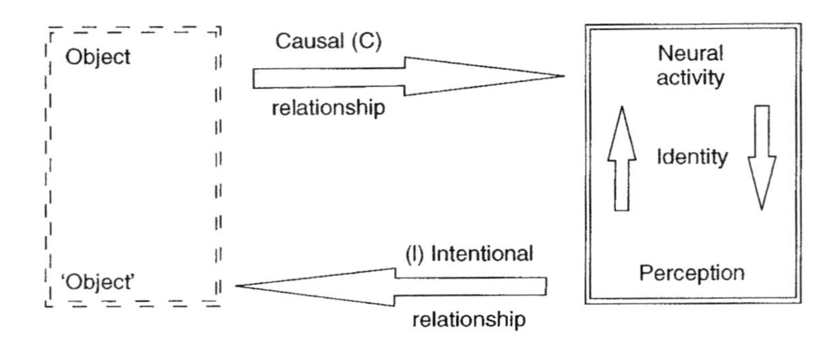

The inward causal chain (C) leading from seen object to impulses in the visual cortex fits with our conventional materialistic scientific framework; but the outward intentional (I) link – whereby the visuo-cortical impulses 'reach out to', refer to, are about, the seen object – most certainly does not. There is nothing else in nature corresponding to this. Moreover, the object they refer to does not itself have the attributes, those secondary qualities of brightness, loudness, etc. that any perceiving consciousness finds in them. Physical objects are odourless atoms that reflect colourless light waves and soundless vibrations in the air. And, moreover, in view of the endless causal chain or causal network of which the brain's activity – according the identity theory – is a small part there is no reason why this reaching back should stop at a particular point – at a so-called object of perception P:

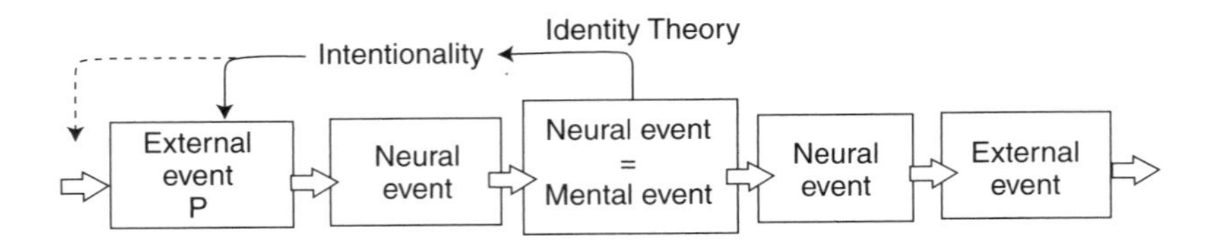

This final point has led some philosophers to abandon the notion of intentionality altogether and suggest that nerve impulses reveal only themselves: that all we know is some of the contents of our brain. This raises the question of how we manage to infer a world from these contents – or rather how the impulses manage to infer a world from themselves; and, moreover, how different brains manage to infer and inhabit a shared, or agreed world – the very world, the public material world, that neurophilosophers believe our brains to be part of. To this there is no answer.

And actually the endeavour to dispose of the problem of intentionality by claiming that impulses disclose only themselves and that all we know is our own brain contents, runs into even bigger problems – as becomes apparent as soon as we ask the question what is the self that the self-disclosing neural impulses would disclose. It is not possible to say what inherent properties they would have. Being physical events, they would have no secondary qualities.[6]

The complexity of ordinary consciousness

These are the particular, as it were technical, arguments against a neural explanation of mental phenomena and, more specifically, conscious experience. Less technical, but equally potent in my view, is the argument advanced by Colin McGinn in a classic paper published in *Mind* in 1989:[7] that it does not seem intuitively satisfying to explain human consciousness in terms of the passage of sodium and other ions across semi-permeable membranes. Neural activity seems the wrong kind of thing to explain consciousness. Of course, neuroscientists – and indeed philosophers – are right to be suspicious of the intuitively satisfying and to remind their critics of the point made so well by Lewis Wolpert[8] that science progresses towards truth by going beyond the intuitively satisfying to the counter-intuitive. More pointedly, philosophers like Stephen Stich have urged us to set aside what he calls 'folk psychology'.[9] However, even if we were to accept this rather special defence of the failure to remain within the intuitively plausible, this would not get the neurophilosophers off the hook. For the failure of neurophilosophy to give an account of consciousness that in any way matches our sense of ourselves and of our conscious lives is profound indeed.

This mismatch is not merely at the 'atomic' level discussed so far – the level at which the neural basis of consciousness fails to explain particular sensations in terms of particular clusters of impulses in particular circuits. The identity theory fails most signally at the higher level, in accounting for the organisation of ordinary human consciousness, the infinitely complex lacework of the aims, goals, intentions, notions ambitions, etc., that comprise our daily lives. I want to argue that, even if the identity theory did somehow explain consciousness, on a one-to-one basis for sensations, such a theory would not take us much further because it would not explain the complex unity of the conscious moment (which presumably involves huge quantities of activity in different areas of the nervous system), nor the coherence of conscious activity over time necessary for the moment of understanding that corresponds to the present self or, even more so, for the coherence of the understanding self. There are impulses here and impulses there but no place where it all comes together in my sense of being someone here now discharging complex plans of the kind that fill most of our ordinary days.

It is worth dwelling on this and reminding ourselves about the long-range, explicit internal connectedness necessary to be the kind of responsible agent who is able to operate effectively in our complicated world. The notion of agency – of the individual as a cause, rather than as an effect – is inseparable from that of explicit purpose, of responsibility, of the expression of the rational will. This requires relating to things across time, to larger situation-frameworks than are available to the instant of consciousness. The temporal framework of an ordinary human agent – you, me – is huge and complex.

Consider the situation, routine for an academic, of giving an invited lecture. (The trigger for this present chapter.) Typically the commitment to speak is undertaken many months, perhaps a year or more, before the appointed date. Fulfilling the commitment – one of many thousands of small- and large-scale commitments in the period between agreement to speak and the actual lecture – connects the moment of that commitment with many other moments: those in which the title of the talk is discussed with the host, those in which ideas are jotted down, the hours in which the text is written and rewritten, the moments in which all sorts of implicit knowledge are deployed in order to find one's way via car and railway and tube and foot to the venue at the right time and in the right place – and all of this, while one is in the grip of a thousand other preoccupations and is floating in a sea of relevant and irrelevant sense data. However much the audience may come to regret the speaker's success in pulling off the feat of getting to speak at the right moment several months after the idea was first floated, it is a remarkable tribute to the complex inner organisation of his life and its extendedness across time. This example illustrates why bursts of electricity in the wetware of the brain don't somehow seem adequate to the exquisitely structured mind that we humans have.

The troubles go deeper than this. There has to be convergence in the unity of the conscious moment, but this must not take the form of a merging of the actions, knowledge and experiences relevant to the dozen macro- and micro-projects in progress at any given time, otherwise these projects would lose their distinct identity. If you think of all the things that would have to be going on in my brain in order to sustain the different levelled activity necessary to underpin my giving a lecture in the right place at the right time you would have the image of a vast number of overlapping circuits supporting a huge ensemble of different functions, and it is difficult to see how they could be kept apart so as not to interfere with one another – while at the same time somehow relating to one another in or through something like a self. Even if we do not have to find space in separate parts of the brain for each of the many different functions or modules of the mind that we may distinguish – for, after all, as Stephen Pinker says, 'the beauty of information processing is the flexibility of the demand for real estate' – we still have problems of keeping them and the separate projects they are engaged in apart. (And we have to remember that one of the major effects of cognitive psychology has been vastly to increase the number of component tasks identified in the seemingly simplest activities, such as reading: trying to design robots to simulate ordinary cognitive functions is, as Stephen Pinker says, 'a kind of consciousness-raising'.)

I used the phrase 'different levelled' just now and it may be worth while spelling this out, to highlight the complexity of ordinary consciousness and the corresponding complexity of the task that would be faced by a cognitive neuroscience that had a clear idea of its object of study. There is the level at which all the elements of the lecture come together. At this level, there is a convergence between the conversations that set up the speaking engagement and the many different moments of thought that contributed to the final form of the lecture. These moments of thought are just as likely to occur while one is thinking of, or busy with, or engaged in, some other pressing task as they are in the set piece hours of composition in the study. An idea for the lecture may come while one is hurrying to catch a train or worrying about the cost of the mortgage, or coming across a word in a book that triggers off a just-connected thought about a better phrasing of a key step in a component argument. The haystack in which needles have to come together is huge. At a lower level, which must always keep the higher-level goals in view, there are the practicalities of writing the lecture – making sure the laptop is working, ensuring a supply of disks, clearing sufficient free time to be able to work on it undisturbed. These practicalities will keep things like deadlines, other commitments, etc. in mind. At a lower level still, there will be the various components of the actions that are necessary to meet the commitment. For example, if the lecture is in another city – London, say – there will be all the elements that comprise the journey and preparation for it. Think of locking up the house in a hurry because one has calculated that one is at risk of being late for the train that will enable one to get to London in good time. 'Locking up the house in a hurry' itself has a vast number of component behaviours whose style will have been radically altered by the knowledge that one is in a hurry. Each of these components in turn will have numerous other components; for example, closing the door and turning the key will involve many elements of ballistic control of the limbs regulated by an overarching sense of their shared goal. Something as seemingly simple as 'getting to the station' will be made up of a myriad of elements, all of them custom-built to the occasion. When, for example, I walk from the car to the ticket office, I will have to take account of the day's particulars: the cars I have to avoid, the person who is coming in the opposite direction, the dog-dirt to be navigated round. And I must take account of these without losing sight of the general purpose towards which the components are directed – that of catching the train – or the singular purpose to which this instance of a general purpose, this train journey, is subordinated: that of giving a particular lecture in a particular place at a particular time. In the meantime, despite the overriding priority of giving the lecture, I cannot afford to be sealed off from either the rest of my life or the rest of the world: the phone will ring, I will remember something I haven't done, I will catch up on my other work on the train, I will remember to get a present I had wanted to purchase opportunistically in London, I will answer the query posed by the person opposite me in the train. Nevertheless – in the sea of relevant and irrelevant events, actions and sensations – I will still keep my overarching purpose alive. Moreover, the lecture engagement itself may relate to a higher level of purpose and goal in my life: my sense of who I am, of what my job is, what I think is important, of where I am going to in my life.

And so we have an immensely complex situation: many elements, at many different levels (ranging from the ballistic control of my arm as I reach for the door handle in my train-catching hurry to the aims and goals of my career), all converging in my continuing sense of what I ought to be doing at any given moment.

This should seem to present overwhelming difficulties to anyone who wished to explain ordinary consciousness in terms of the neural activity of the brain. If it seems to be less of a problem than it in fact is, this is in part because neuroscientists, when they think about neural activity, tend to forget that the abstract logic circuits (which can be multiplied indefinitely) have to be embodied in the wetware of the brain. Information-processing may (to refer back to Pinker) make 'flexible' demands for real estate; but it still does require real estate. After all, the neural theory of mind – even when it has been computerised – requires that all the different mental activities should be embedded in some way in the brain. This inescapable fact licenses us to think of this activity in an ordinary brain as a thousand sets of ripples in a pond created by the impact of a dense shower of hail and to imagine adding all sorts of internal sources of ripples. Neuroscientists are then required to explain how each ripple or a very complex set of ripples – such as those supposedly corresponding to a plan to give a particular lecture on a particular theme on a particular day – retains its separate identity. There seems no way of conceiving how this could be possible. The multidimensional lacework of a vast number of projects with their overarching structures and purposes and their subordinate elements, all of which draw upon a holistic world of interpenetrating meanings, presents a much greater threat to the neural theory of mind even than the 'combinatorial explosion' problem poses to the notion of the brain as acquiring its world through information-processing.

Someone might object that the analogy of ripples interfering with one another is unfounded because the neural circuits are insulated by myelin. But we can't appeal to electrical insulation when we talk – in the way, as we have noted, cognitive scientists do talk – of *patterns* of activity. It seems even more impossible if we remember that, ultimately, the nervous system will have to allow everything to come together in the moment of present consciousness, steeped in present meaning, but retaining its relation to a highly structured near and distant past and protending into an equally structured future of expectation, responsibility, timetable, ambition and life plan: so that the ballistic control of my arm in trying to lock the door in a hurry ultimately relates to my ambition to get my ideas accepted as true by a wider community of people.

The bluffing by people like Daniel Dennett who are wedded to computer analogies (of which more presently), which license them to talk of the functioning brain as sustaining a multiplicity of simultaneous virtual machines and nascent modules, clearly cannot answer this problem of the ultimate unity of the intelligent conscious moment: unity and distinctiveness. In this moment everything has to be brought together – so that I know where and who I am – but in it vast numbers of projects, programmes, duties, unscheduled reactions to unforeseen events, etc. must be kept distinct. To make things even more difficult, those distinct projects must be intelligently connected with many others as each contributes to the others' framework of possibility or acts as a constraint. My giving a lecture that I perceive as important explains my not getting drunk the previous night to celebrate – as I would most naturally do – Manchester United's failure to win the Premier Division.

The challenge to the neurophilosophers, then, is to explain how the distinct identity of a vast number of patterns of ripples could be retained while *at the same time* those patterns have to interact with and be open to one another. And this is the killer: my ordinary consciousness has to retain its global openness in order that I can enact my planned activities in a setting which will be effectively a sea of unplanned contingencies: for example, avoiding the bicyclist who might have killed me as I crossed the road in Manchester on my way to accomplishing the timetabled complex task of giving my lecture in London. A multitude of overarching and subordinate intentions, large- and small-scale, ranging from the micro-level of co-ordinated movement to the macro-level of life plans have to coexist and interact without merging into mush and at the same time be able to take account of the huge kaleidoscope of the unforeseen particulars of every actual moment during which real plans are enacted.

I gave already indicated how complex and subtle these interactions are. But let me illustrate with a real-life example just how much more complex they may become. When, the other week, I had some difficulty getting the key to turn in the front door and I was indeed anxious about missing a train taking me to London to give a lecture on consciousness, I thought of this as an example I might use of the interaction between the micro and the macro and here I am using it. I wanted to note this example down as soon as I thought of it and the only quiet place was the station buffet. I didn't want to buy a coffee as my train was due in a couple of minutes. However, I was conscious that the buffet was quite full and I would have to legitimise my use of a table in the eyes of the rather large assistant who had some months before expressed concern about my occupancy of a seat when I had not purchased anything to be consumed on the premises. I therefore bought a packet of biscuits which I did not want but which I could carry away. I then thought of presenting this packet of biscuits during the lecture as (to quote the jotting on the Post-It I wrote on in the buffet) 'a startling tribute to the exquisitely organised, but open to the winds, structure of my consciousness and to the fact that my ordinary intelligence is quite unlike, and unimitatable by, the co-operation of automata portrayed in contemporary neuropsychology'.

There is a problem, therefore, of modelling, in electrical ripples, the fact that we bring together, and yet keep separate and apart, so many things. Compared with the extraordinary openness of my consciousness necessary for me to enact even a relatively simple task in the real, unpredictable outside world of our multitudinously engaged minds, even the most powerful all-purpose SuperCray seems almost laughably narrow in its dedication. Everything has to be brought together in this moment – so that I know where (in the widest sense) and who (in the deepest sense) I am – but something must *at the very same time* keep myriads of projects, actions, micro-projects, micro-actions, distinct.

We tend to overlook the complexity of our own lives when we think about the neurophysiological basis of consciousness. I would go further: neurophilosophy seems half-way plausible only if it is predicated on a desperately impoverished account of our many-layered, multi-agenda-ed, infinitely complex but wonderfully structured and organised selves. Dementia is salutary in this regard by being an indirect reminder of the fact that to be human is to be explicitly extended in and across time; and this connectedness over time has to be *sustained across an extraordinary interdigitation of preoccupations, themes, locations, situations.*[10] We do not require continuous summative recall to secure psychological connectedness and preservation of identity but we do require sufficient recall to give a context to the present, to give it temporal depth – the implicit depth of recognition and the explicit depth of specific reference back. It is impossible to imagine how this could be embodied in the ripple-tossed pond of the brain, and how, in addition, this brain could sustain the act of deliberate recall of an episodic memory – housing the recaller, the act of recall and that which is recalled.

The mystery of the first person

This question of the open but ring-fenced unity of consciousness itself opens on to an even deeper problem: that of accounting for the fact that there is such a thing as the first person – the me, here, now – to which the boundless variety of experience is ultimately referred. Without such a unifying element – based upon what Kant called the unity of apperception, and rather unfortunately described as 'the I think that accompanies all my perceptions' and which linked the moments through some kind of transcendental ego – the brain would simply be a colloidal suspension of not-quite-haunted modules – which is how the cognitive scientist seems to present it. The third-person neural activity of the brain as seen by neuroscience can provide no explanation for the unified Tallis who is putting together this critique of the neuroscientific explanation of the consciousness of Tallis and his conspecifics.

I have raised the question of the first person in the context of the mystery of the coherence of my consciousness – of my world and of myself as an agent in it. But this in its turn connects with a deeper mystery: the origin of the sense of me, here, now; of the suffering agent, the responsible creature who is a viewpoint on the world. It is no use saying that *my* brain gives me the sense of me here now because it is *my* brain and it is here and now: looked at through the third person materialistic eyes of conventional neuroscience, the brain is just an object in the world, like a brick or a pebble, and it has no intrinsic ownership and therefore offers no basis for the fundamental sense that I am this thing here and now. The difference between the ionic activity in the brain and the atomic jigging in the pebble does not yield this ownership out of which arises the sense of being this thing here and now. And yet this sense is required if I am to have the feeling that I am here now, that I am, to use Heidegger's phrase, a being whose being is an issue for itself. The fact that things matter to this brain cannot be accommodated within the neurophysiologist's account of the brain. More generally, mattering has no place in the materialist world picture of the identity theorist.

These are very deep waters and the thoughts they give rise to are elusive. Suffice it to say, there is no basis in the brain for the unified consciousness and the connected fundamental intuition of self: the sense that *I am this thing* and that *I am here*. There is nothing in the brain to make it my brain; it cannot underpin the first person, the viewpoint, the deixis, that make the ordinary moments of life a matter of me, here, now. Such indexicality has no place in the materialist world-picture of the identity theorist. And this connects back with something that I alluded to at the beginning of this chapter: the folk observation that I (my consciousness, my mind) am where my brain is. This 'where I am' cannot be taken for granted as a given. There is nothing in the brain, as neuroscientifically construed, to provide a foundation for this 'where I am', for the viewpoint that results in my brain (or at least my body) assuming the position of the 0, 0, 0 point in the Cartesian grid or the 0, 0, 0 point of personal or hodological space. The third-person world of science offers no basis for the first-person viewpoint; in short for viewpoint *per se*. The folk observation I alluded to at the outset – that my mind is where my brain is – could just as well as be turned on its head: my brain is where my mind is. For without consciousness, there is no 'where', no 'here' for my brain to be 'at'. And my brain is ownerless.

The fugitive thoughts that arise from here seem to me to be thinkable about once a fortnight. To return to slightly shallower waters, it is interesting to gauge just how far we are from comprehending the ordinary fact of the coherence of self in neural terms – a coherence back-lit by its disintegration in dementia. This is betrayed by the eccentricity of some recent theories advanced by some extremely respectable people. One of the frontrunners is the idea that the global nature of consciousness is made possible by the microtubules in neurones which, because of their peculiar biophysical properties, are able to host quantum coherence (Bose-Einstein condensates) which, it is conjectured, can extend across an appreciable part of the entire brain.[11] Unfortunately, this model – in which an entire system containing a large number of particles behaves like a quantum state of a single particle and thus provides the basis for the unitary sense of the self – would, even if it were coherent itself, fall foul of two facts: that microtubules are present in many human and non-human biological tissues that are not conscious; and that quantum coherence occurs outside of living tissue.

The language of neuromythology to the rescue

All of this would seem to force us to the conclusion that ordinary, intelligent consciousness cannot be due to activity in the brain; or, to put it at its most charitable, neural activity is an inadequate explanation of mental activity. And yet this is a message that has certainly not got through to many neuroscientists and their neurophilosophical fellow travellers. Why is this? Because they speak to themselves in a language that conceals from them the barrenness of their explanations. The language of neuromythology is what permits the neurophilosopher to cross the mind/brain barrier without solving the problems that I have alluded to.

The key step is to redescribe the mind in mechanical terms – and so remain within the materialist and even biological framework of neuroscience – but to think of its mechanisms as operating like a machine (which has purposes and functions) and, moreover, a very special sort of machine – a computer – which can be readily spoken of in highly anthropomorphic, or mindly, terms. Brainy minds and mindly brains meet in the idea of the computer; the mind is the computational activity of the brain; or brain is to mind as hardware is to software.

Computers are very obliging models because, for a long time, it has been traditional to use anthropomorphic terms in describing their functions, however humble they are. For example, we talk about a pocket calculator having a memory, or executing a series of instructions or mobilising its logic. This is fine, because it is not likely to lead us to believe that it also experiences nostalgia, is subserviently obedient or wonderfully rational. In short, the transferred epithets – transferred from the human users to the small plastic object they use – are harmless. They are not harmless when they are used in neuroscience, because then we start taking the terms in both literal and metaphorical senses.

In order to get across the mind-brain barrier, all you have to do is take two easy steps:

a) describe the activity of the brain in terms of the functions of a computer;
b) describe the computer in 'mindly' terms.

The oscillation of terms between the mental and the physical realms lies at the root of the myth that modern neurological science has somehow explained, or will explain, or has advanced our understanding of, what consciousness truly is. Of all the terms that straddle the mind/brain barrier, the most important is 'information'. When Stephen Pinker preaches the Official Doctrine that mind is the 'information function' of the brain, he has solved the mind-brain problem without making one discovery or conceptual advance. Janus-faced words like 'memory' and 'information' – which look in the direction of both man and machine – dissolve the very problems that philosophically are most interesting. In truth, neurologically-based, biological and computational explanations of consciousness begin beyond the point where the real questions are to be found.

I believe that the progress neuroscientists imagine that they have made across the mind/brain barrier – so that the brainy mind and the mindly brain merge into one another – has nothing to do with any empirical observations and everything to do with the presuppositions, half-hidden because embedded in the terminology they use, that inform their discourse about those observations. A truly illuminating account of the relationship between mind and brain would not be one that had 'information' on both sides of the mind–brain barrier: it would explain how physical energy (which is all that there is in the material world of which the brain is a part) was transformed into information, knowledge, consciousness: how light energy became the object of sight; how light (which does not know itself) became the seen, the visible world.

Provisional conclusion: cognitive science does not and cannot explain mind

In the absence of such an explanation, one has to stand firm and say that there is as yet no satisfactory account of the relationship between brain and mind and that current research and the current neurocomputational framework for research are not taking us anywhere. Indeed, the complexities thrown up by cognitive psychologists' own analysis of relatively simple mental functions compound the challenge by revealing the massive complexities that stand in the way of materialist or computational accounts of mind – complexities that, even at a surface level, are evident to anyone who reflects for more than a minute or two on the way we have to function in ordinary life. For my money, no multiplication of automata forming co-operatives will be able to replace the conscious human being knowing what he or she is doing: there is something called 'conscious understanding' that goes beyond a mass of modules, notwithstanding that being able to do what one intends – and even formulating intentions – requires, is built upon, the smooth working of various automatic systems which lies beyond the reach of consciousness. That conscious understanding is necessary not merely to meet our need for an intuitively satisfactory account of the process underlying ordinary behaviour but also to get the outputs that are needed. Some neurophilosophers – Pinker, for example – aware that we cannot explain qualia, would like to separate 'cognitive functions' such as intelligence from sentience because they recognise that sentience is not yet explicable in neural terms:

> At least for now, we have no scientific purchase on the special extra ingredient that gives rise to sentience. As far as scientific explanation goes, it might as well not exist. It's not just that claims about sentience are perversely untestable; it's that testing them would make no difference to

> anything anyway. Our incomprehension of sentience does not impede our understanding of how the mind works at least.
>
> (p. 147)

While this is better than Dennett's attempts to deny the reality of subjective experiences, or at least of qualia, dismissing them as cognitive illusions, it is still somewhat unsatisfactory. Though Pinker's position is consistent with, indeed necessary to support, the extraordinary claim that 'Thought and thinking ... are mechanical processes that can be studied' (p. 131), its inadequacy will be apparent from what has already been said. Not only is to leave out qualia, effectively, to omit the contents of consciousness – and so reduce the mind to a set of mechanical functions – but it also makes it impossible to see how the typical activities of conscious human beings are achieved. We cannot make sense of intelligent behaviour without assuming that intelligent behavers are conscious of what they are doing. From which it follows that we cannot 'park up' trying to understand sentience for the present (because it is too difficult) and proceed to investigate intelligence without it.

The observations made earlier strongly suggest that on the contrary we cannot begin to get a handle on intelligence without assuming, and hence explaining, sentience: in short, intelligent behaviour requires *knowing what one is doing*. (Only to a neurophilosopher could that seem disputable and reasserting it a revelation.) All the computing power in the world, any number of mysteriously co-operative automata, would be insufficient to stand in for the necessary sense of 'knowing what I am doing' – which, at the very least, would require that intelligence was informed by sentience. Sentience is the first and not the last requirement of intelligence and to try to understand the latter while not taking into account, never mind understanding, the former, is like trying to build a house by starting at the second floor. It may be desirable, methodologically, to set aside the problem of sentience because it seems more difficult in principle to investigate neuroscientifically; but this does not reduce the problems that arise out of having done so.

Sentience, is the first, not the last, problem (or mystery) of psychology. It is not merely the most difficult of the problems of consciousness or mind; it is also the pivotal one and addressing it cannot be postponed until one has solved the 'easier' problems such as those pertaining to 'cognitive functions' like intelligence, memory, thinking, etc. When we humans deploy our intelligence, we do so in a wider context, in a complex framework which may be captured by the phrase, 'knowing what we are doing' (or trying to do). It is impossible to explain how the automata that are mobilised in the service of those ends are requisitioned without reference to that context.

It would seem, therefore, that nothing of what we know about the brain, or, indeed, of what we are likely to discover about it using present research paradigms, would account for the status that it enjoys among neuroscientists as that in virtue of which we are conscious; its unique status as a piece of matter in virtue of which matter discloses itself and becomes the contents of the consciousness of the individual identified with the brain. Nor is there anything in neural activity that would explain how all this disclosing is organised into the unified moment of consciousness. Nor is there anything that can account for the extremely elaborate, unified, many-layered multiplicity that is the necessary substrate of and background to the ordinary acts of the ordinary human agent, acts which relate to numerous hierarchies of overarching and sub-ordinate frameworks of intention. Nor is there likely to be.

Neurophilosophy: separating the neuroscience from the neuromythology

And that would seem to be that. And yet, and yet, I, too, am a neuroscientist of sorts and a humble toiler in the field where many individuals much more talented than myself are working, thinking, speculating and experimenting. And the truth is, I don't *really* – or fully – believe either that the mind has nothing to do with the brain or that scientists have made no progress in understanding the physical conditions of the mind.

How, then, am I to reconcile the warring views within me? Or am I condemned for ever to have a split mind over the nature of the relationship between brain and mind, with my left hemisphere believing that the brain is the basis of the mind and that our advancing brain science is helping us to explain mind, and my right hemisphere saying that mind cannot possibly be explained by the neural activity of certain parts of the brain and that we are no nearer to understanding the nature of mind or consciousness than we were when Descartes suggested that mind and matter were connected through the pineal gland.

Is there a way out of this neuro-antinomy? One escape route would be to propose that, while neural activity cannot explain why there is consciousness, it can explain the shaping of consciousness, or even the fact that consciousness has specific contents and what those contents are. While my brain being in London does not explain why I am conscious of anything at all, perhaps it does explain why, given that I *am* conscious, my consciousness is of a bit of London rather than, say, of a bit of Manchester.

This escape route leads straight into yet more difficult problems. For example, it requires us to accept the notion of contentless consciousness which is, as it were, coloured in by the activity of the nervous system. This is somewhat difficult to grasp. Moreover, it does not explain how the nervous system interacts with this blank, general, consciousness-of-nothing in particular, this uncommitted awareness, to commit it to particular sentient experience. Nor, most damagingly from the viewpoint of those who are serious about trying to understand consciousness, does it suggest how this interaction might be investigated.

Another, seemingly slightly less vulnerable escape route is to invoke the distinction between a necessary and a sufficient condition. A necessary condition of something happening is the set of circumstances that has to be present in order for it to take place. In the absence of those circumstances, it will not take place. The presence of those conditions, however, will not guarantee that it will take place. It is necessary for me to be in a particular street in order to be knocked down by a bus in that street. But being in that street is not a sufficient condition of being knocked down by a bus, even by a bus in that street. A sufficient condition, self-evidently, is the sum of those circumstances which, if present, will guarantee that the event will take place. One could use this distinction to argue that a normally functioning brain, producing certain ('normal') neural activity in response external stimuli or as a result of normal quasi-endogenous activity is a necessary condition for mental phenomena, for normal consciousness, but it does not of itself produce that consciousness in the sense either of causing it or of being identical with it. To connect this with our earlier discussion about the relationship between where the brain is at and where the mind or self is at: my brain has to be in London for me genuinely or directly or truly to experience being in London; but this is not a sufficient condition of my experiencing London. The closest analogy would be with a radio: a normally functioning radio is not enough to ensure the reception of programmes; there has to be a radio station within range transmitting programmes. (The same escape would seem, incidentally, to apply to some aspects of the evolutionary theory of mind: of course, mental activity has somehow to be adapted to support the activities necessary to ensure survival in a hostile natural world. Evolutionary forces and the demands of the natural world do not, however, explain how consciousness could have emerged in the physical world. Evolutionary advantage, therefore, is a necessary but not a sufficient condition to explain the structure and functions of mind.)

But this escape route is actually fraught with difficulties, even dangers. First of all, while it might account for lesion (negative) experiments, it does not seem to account for stimulation (positive), Penfield-type experiments, in which the active nervous system seems able to work nicely on its own in producing consciousness; where, in other words, neural activity seems to be both a necessary and a sufficient condition of consciousness. It might be argued that such false experiences are – like hallucinations – parasitic upon and depend upon a track record of normally produced experiences arising out of encounters with real external things. In other words, that they have as it were parasitic or borrowed mentality or intentionality. Stimulation experiments, for example, can re-evoke memories of experiences had by a normally functioning brain, but they could not implant properly formed experiences – with all their holistic links – in a brain that had been totally deprived of experiences through the normal routes. I am not clear how strong this argument is.

A more worrying concern is prompted by the very analogy that is used to illustrate the difference between a necessary and a sufficient condition – that of the radio receiver. This would seem to suggest that the nervous system is merely a tuned device to receive consciousness from elsewhere – from some kind of 'within' in the case of volitions and from without in the case of perceptual experience. The former would be a return to a homuncular kind of thinking that we all shrink from, the latter to a kind of mystical thinking that would bear a rather unnerving resemblance to the lunatic new age ideas of certain thinkers (I shall withhold their names for the sake of their families) who have argued that, for example, memories are picked up by 'morphic resonance' between the brain and a kind of ether in which the impressions of the past are held. One of the reasons why such mystical notions are unattractive is that they do not suggest any kinds of research programmes, even less specific experiments. They can only be dogmatically asserted or equally dogmatically rejected. Perhaps making sense of the relationship between the brain and consciousness will require an epistemological and ontological rethink.

The requirement for an epistemological rethink – for a new theory of knowledge that goes beyond the idea that knowledge itself is based upon experiences arising out of energy impinging upon the excitable tissue in our bodies – is, surely, not surprising. All the things that neuroscientists have discovered about consciousness, or think they have discovered, have been based upon observations that amount to a very small sample of our consciousness. It would be extremely surprising if this small part of consciousness were able to dig beneath (all) consciousness to discover the basis of the latter; or if, on the strength of a relatively few perceptions (even high-quality expensive, specialised ones such as are enjoyed in neuroscience laboratories), we were able to find and understand the basis of all perception. The belief, underpinning the neurophilosophical expectation that the basis of mind is amenable to empirical investigation with our minds, is intuitively implausible for all its tenacity. And it is connected with the assumption – which I hope by now will be recognised as ill-founded – that our world, ourselves as viewpoints sustaining personal worlds, could be housed in, and explained by, the functioning of a small something in that world.

As for an ontological rethink, in *The Explicit Animal* I expressed the view that we would need a new ontology to make sense of the relation between matter and mind, or between brain matter and consciousness; that we should abandon not only dualism (which leads to all the problems of Cartesian epistemology) but also materialism (which is the implicit framework of much contemporary neuroscience and in particular the neural theory of consciousness). As others have done before me, I floated a third possibility: a neutral monism that took as ontologically foundational the category of *presence* (which spans both subject and object, perceiver and object of perception). I also, regrettably, made the routine, facile appeal to the new physics (in which the ghost of mind haunts even the microphysical world, being the necessary condition of the wave-pocket collapse of otherwise indeterminate quanta).

None of this is very satisfactory. Nevertheless, I do feel sure that the founding myth of neuromythology – that conscious experience is created out of the impingement of various sorts of physical energy upon the excitable transducers of the sensory system and that the evoked neural activity is identical with that experience – must be set aside. That, in other words, our whole approach to the consciousness of embodied creatures such as human beings must be radically revised. And this is all to the good; for neurophilosophy seems to require a drastically impoverished account of our own nature as wholly mysterious animals, at once a part of nature and at the same time uniquely distanced from it – as reflected in our ability to articulate it.

But all is not doom and gloom. While thinkers are trying to formulate the new framework for thinking about perception, etc., neuroscientists may be reassured that what they are doing is far from worthless or unilluminating. Even if they are not discovering how the mind works, or how it is constructed in the brain, they are defining with ever-increasing precision the conditions under which normal experience and volition are possible: the necessary but not the sufficient conditions. And, for my money, as a clinician concerned to re-create or encourage those necessary conditions in patients from whom they have been withdrawn, that is good enough. Metaphysics it is not; supremely worthwhile it certainly is. It just needs to recognise its limits, so that good science is not discredited by bad philosophy and scientism causes scientists to be accused of 'single vision and Newton's sleep'.

Notes

1. The best of these are: Patricia Churchland, *Neurophilosophy* (Cambridge, Mass., MIT Press, 1986); Paul M. Churchland, *Matter and Consciousness: a Contemporary Introduction to the Philosophy of Mind* (Cambridge, Mass.: MIT Press, rev. edition, 1988); Daniel C. Dennett, *Consciousness Explained* (Harmondsworth: Penguin, 1991); Steven Pinker, *How the Mind Works* (Harmondsworth: Allen Lane, Penguin, 1997).

2. The curious mixture of claims and disclaimers in Pinker's Preface is worth noting:

 > When we face a problem, we may not know its solution, but we have insight, increasing knowledge and an inkling of what we are looking for. When we face a mystery, however, we can only stare in wonder and bewilderment ... I wrote this book because dozens of mysteries of the mind, from mental images to romantic love, have recently been upgraded to problems (though there are still some mysteries, too!)

3. Raymond Tallis, *The Explicit Animal: A Defence of Human Consciousness* (London: Macmillan, 1991).
4. Paul Churchland, op. cit., p. 149.
5. See also the entry LEVELS in Chapter 2 of my *On the Edge of Certainty* (Basingstoke: Macmillan, 1999).
6. Discussed in Raymond Tallis, 'The Impossibility of Neurally-mediated Disclosure: Why Neural Theories of Consciousness Will Always Fail', submitted for publication.
7. Colin McGinn, 'Can We Solve the Mind/Body Problem?', *Mind* (1989), 350–66.
8. Lewis Wolpert, *The Unnatural Nature of Science* (London: Faber, 1992).
9. Stephen P. Stich, *From Folk Psychology to Cognitive Science: the Case against Belief* (Cambridge, Mass.: MIT Press, 1983).
10. Discussed in Raymond Tallis, 'A Dark Mirror: Reflections on Dementia', *News from the Republic of Letters* (1997), 12–16.
11. See Roger Penrose, *Shadows of the Mind: A Search for the Missing Science of Consciousness* (Oxford University Press, 1994), pp. 367–9.

From: *On the Edge of Certainty* (Macmillan, 1999), pp. 127–54.

2
On the Edge of Certainty

The question of the explicit is given a rather different focus in this second reading, also from *On the Edge of Certainty*. Here, Tallis considers the reflections on knowledge and certainty that Wittgenstein wrote during the last days of his life in 1951 in Cambridge, and which appeared as *On Certainty*, first published in 1969. The book is a consideration of G.E. Moore's defence of common sense, as exemplified by his assertion 'I *know* that that's a tree'. Wittgenstein was not happy with formulations of this sort; out of their usual contexts statements like 'I know that that's a tree' or 'I am certain that I have two hands' seem to have no sense. For Wittgenstein, doubt does not come in here: in our daily lives we make statements about our hands and we use the word 'hand' without hesitation. In addition, we act, and when we act we almost always make use of our hands: we wash ourselves, including our hands, we fix things, we cook, we clean, we write, and so forth. As Wittgenstein has it: in the beginning was the deed. It is not knowledge and certainty that lie at the basis of how we use language: it is the presuppositions built into a way of life. Freedom from doubt in this context is not based on reasoning or proof. As Norman Malcolm has noted, in a lecture on the relation of language to instinctive behaviour, this freedom from doubt is too fundamental to be either 'unjustified' or 'justified'. In fact, this way of being with language is so fundamental that there seems to be no way of describing it in language at all: it is no good calling on expressions like 'knowledge', 'belief', 'certainty', or 'acceptance', since these have their appropriate usage within specific language-games, and what Wittgenstein was trying to get at is something that lies beneath all language-games. But as he addressed this question, the ground was constantly shifting under his feet, and in the last days and hours of his conscious existence Tallis believes him to have been suspended between his own intuitions of chaos and an ordered world – the world of concepts and linguistic practice – that had no way of acknowledging what lay outside itself. He argues that during this time Wittgenstein experienced anew the mystery that had been with him all his life – the irreducible mystery of explicitness that is the consciousness of man, the irreducible mystery of meaning. Tallis hears in Wittgenstein's last words – 'Tell them I've had a wonderful life' – an echo of an intuition of 1916: 'The aesthetic miracle is that the world exists. That what exists does exist.' The theme fundamental to Wittgenstein's thought, that concerning the limits of language, is also that which unveils the fundamental wonder and mystery of our being. As he remarked in 'A Lecture on Ethics': 'Now I am tempted to say that the right expression in language for the miracle of the existence of the world, though it is not any proposition *in* language, is the existence of language itself.'

It is so difficult to find the *beginning*
Or, better: it is difficult to begin at the beginning.
And not try to go further back.

I

(1)

In December 1949, after several months of illness, Wittgenstein was discovered to have cancer of the prostate gland. At the time of diagnosis secondary deposits were already present in his spine, so there was no hope of cure. A palliative treatment in the form of hormones, however, had recently become available and he was started on Stilboestrol. For the next thirteen or fourteen months, while he was 'letting the hormones do their work'[1] he found himself quite unable to think:

> My mind's completely dead. This is not a complaint, for I don't really suffer from it. I know that life must have an end once and that mental life can cease before the rest does.[2]

His inability to think during this period is not altogether surprising. For a real thinker, thought is not merely a response to what others have said and written, but has endogeneous roots; it takes its rise from a region, neither entirely sensual nor wholly verbal, where articulate consciousness merges with bodily awareness. In a profound intellectual impulse, the urge towards clarity and the perspicuous view is inseparable from an ache for sharper self-presence. The sense that the world has a deeper, secret meaning to yield up – which transforms technical problems into matters of the utmost personal urgency and makes the thinker willing to suffer and to protract the intolerable tensions of inconclusion, to cultivate active uncertainty – originates in an excitement, an agitation, a curiosity, that may borrow some energy from sexual desire. In the absence of pain, nausea, malaise, fear or confusion, certain disease states may displace the thinker from his familiar self and deepen the active dislocation that makes original thought possible. A treatment such as hormone therapy, however, must switch off the springs of delight and consequently the creative astonishment that formulates itself into questions and the intuition of possible answers. Linked to the world, presented to himself, through the mediation of an alien body, he may cease to think.

If it is not too difficult to understand how Stilboestrol rendered Wittgenstein's mind infertile, it is hard to accept his claim that he did not *suffer* from this loss of intellectual libido, that he accepted it as easily as he implied in his letter to Norman Malcolm. Did he really not mourn a lost self-taste or the vanished drama of intellectual tension and its resolution? Surely he felt empty when so much of his essential self had dissolved into vagueness, absence, generality? Surely he resented the perpetual sea-fog intervening between him and himself, the permanent mist over the mirror of self-articulation? Or was he already only half-alive, buried beneath both hope and despair and reconciled to the ending of himself?

There is, of course, no way of answering these questions with certainty. One writer, not always regarded as reliable, speaks of Wittgenstein's 'almost constant' depression during the last year.'[3] Anyway, in February 1951, when it was obvious that his illness was beyond even palliation, he stopped taking the hormone tablets. His ability to think at his accustomed depth returned soon after. On 16 April, thirteen days before his death, he wrote to one of his ex-pupils:

> An extraordinary thing happened to me. About a month ago I suddenly found myself in the right frame of mind for doing philosophy. I had been *absolutely* certain that I'd never again be able to do it ... Of course, so far I've only worked for about five weeks and it may be all over by tomorrow, but it bucks me up a lot now.[4]

His physical well-being had returned:

> ... apart from a certain weakness which has constant ups and downs I'm feeling very well these days.[5]

To Mrs Bevan (the wife of his GP, in whose house he was living and dying), he said:

> I'm going to work now as I've never worked before![6]

The final period of thought lasted just under seven weeks. Its fruits comprise over half of the posthumously published volume titled *On Certainty*, compiled by two of his ex-pupils.[7]

On 10 March, he noted:

> Not all corrections of our views are on the same level.[8]

This seemingly banal observation inaugurates an intense, polyphonic, obsessional meditation on topics that had engaged him for most of his thinking life. During these seven weeks he was 'apparently in the best of spirits';[9] and the pages of *On Certainty* bear out von Wright's claim that 'as late as two days before his death he wrote down thoughts that are equal to the best he produced'.

The poignancy of the philosophical quest of *On Certainty* is heightened by scattered autobiographical reflections. They are not given paragraph numbers and are severely cordoned off in square brackets. On the same day as his jubilant letter to Norman Malcolm, he observed:

> [I do philosophy now like an old woman who is always mislaying something and having to look for it again: now her spectacles, now her keys.][10]

Four weeks earlier he had written:

> [I believe it might interest a philosopher, one who can think himself, to read my notes. For even if I have hit the mark only rarely, he would recognise what targets I had been ceaselessly aiming at.][11]

And on 5 April, he reflects sadly:

> [Here there is still a big gap in my thinking. And I doubt whether it will be filled now.][12]

The final entry, No. 676, was dated 27 April 1951 – the day he lost consciousness and two days before his death.

(2)

Immediately after the melancholy remark about 'the big gap' in his thinking is an entry which gives succinct expression to something that had from the outset lain at the heart of his philosophical views, attitudes, styles and inconclusions. It summarises his entire philosophical struggle; and illuminates why philosophy should have been so much more of a *struggle* for him than for others much less gifted than himself:

> It is so difficult to find the beginning. Or better, it is difficult to begin at the *beginning*. And not try to go further back.[13]

This was the burdensome insight he had lived with – or inside of – since he had first come to philosophy.

The traditional itinerary of the Western European philosopher was given its classical form by Descartes who set out in his *Meditations* from total doubt and thought he had ended at absolute certainty. Universal doubt, Descartes claimed,

> delivers us from every kind of prejudice, and sets out for us a very simple way by which the mind may detach itself from the senses ... and makes it impossible for us ever to doubt those things which we have once discovered to be true.[14]

Philosophy begins with the cultivation of a radical scepticism trained upon the deepest presuppositions and habitual assumptions of everyday life. Nothing is immune from this doubt – not even the belief that there is an 'outside' world independent of my mind, or that I am sitting here at my desk writing. Everything that can be questioned, everything that is known with less than total certainty, is burnt away until there remains only that which cannot be doubted without self-contradiction. When the demolition job is complete, the unassailable truths that remain form the basis for reconstruction. The philosopher builds upon the self-evidently given, the primitive, the axiomatic, unpacking a new world by means of impeccable arguments constrained by an iron logic. This new world is either a radically revised, 'truer' world than the old one; or – more commonly – the old, unchanged everyday world with its foundations, its truth, made explicit. The philosopher passes through doubt to certainty; and his scepticism, which destroys mere prejudice, clears the way for 'absolute' or 'true' knowledge.

The legitimacy of the recovered certainty on the far side of doubt had often been challenged since Descartes. 'Scepticism', David Hume observed, 'is a malady which can never be radically cured but must return upon us every moment, however we may chase it away.'[15] And F.H. Bradley had sardonically characterised the metaphysician's attempt to place his world picture upon a firmer footing as 'the finding of bad reasons for what we believe upon instinct'.[16] Once radical doubt has been admitted, things can never be the same again. No 'thinking certainty' can feel as secure as the unthinking certainty destroyed by critical reflection. Wittgenstein's originality lay not in his scepticism about the happy ending of the philosophical journey but in his questioning the validity of the doubts from which it set out. It was not merely the solutions philosophers found to their problems that he regarded as questionable but the problems themselves.

Like Kierkegaard – whom he deeply admired ('Kierkegaard was by far the most profound thinker of the last century'),[17] though he found him too 'long-winded' – he considered most philosophical questions to be inadmissible on existential grounds. Philosophical doubting was largely a charade – a matter of 'writing *de omnibus disputandum* and at the same time being as credulous existentially as the most sensuous of men'.[18] And he was influenced by Moore who found it absurd that a man should doubt (or worse, deny) the reality of space and time while confidently planning to have his breakfast before his dinner and to eat it in one place rather than another. But it was his dissent from traditional philosophy on logico-linguistic grounds that gave rise to some of his most original and interesting and once notorious contributions to twentieth-century philosophical debate.

You cannot, he said, really ask most philosophical questions since they cannot be formulated without suspending the conditions in which utterances make sense. If, for example, there were any real doubts about whether or not there was an outside world, then this could not be *discussed*.

> Scepticism is not irrefutable, but obviously nonsensical, when it tries to raise doubts where no questions can be asked.
>
> For a doubt can exist only where a question exists, a question only where an answer exists, and an answer only where something *can be said*.[19]

The conspicuous unanswerability of many philosophical questions is, therefore, merely the obverse of their overlooked unaskability. To reach as far back as the places where most philosophical discussion starts out is to go too far back. For a proposition or an utterance to be true (or even false) it must make sense. Only when an utterance meets sense-conditions – so that it can have meaning and secure reference – can it have truth-conditions and be either true or false.

> Most of the propositions and questions to be found in philosophical works are not false but nonsensical ... [They] arise from the failure to understand the logic of our language ...[20]

In *Tractatus*, the grounds for denying sense-conditions to most philosophical questions and answers are linguistic rather than existential – 'the failure to understand the logic of our language'. Philosophical questions

> belong to the same class as the question whether the good is more or less identical than the beautiful.[21]

In later years, however, logical and linguistic objections to traditional philosophy became interwoven in a more complex way with existential dissent. It was no longer sufficient to assert that many propositions of philosophy often contravened 'the *logic* of our language' and transgressed the boundaries of the sayable. For there is no single logic of language: the limits of the sayable are not internally determined, functions of the intrinsic properties of language. What is sayable cannot be inferred from the general features of the relationship between signs (or propositions) and the objects (or situations) that they signify (or propose). The meaningfulness of particular utterances is determined less by whether or not they have a particular structure (so that they are logical pictures of the reality they speak of) than by the customary use to which their component signs and their combinations have been put. It is not only the *structure* of an utterance that determines whether it is meaningful but the context in which it is uttered. Sense-conditions are existential as well as logico-linguistic:

> A proposition has meaning only in the stream of life.[22]

Life and language cannot readily be extricated from one another. Contrary to what had been implied in *Tractatus*, everyday speech does not have a formal symbolic system (with an unsayable grammar) at its heart; rather, it is composed of an indefinite number of heterogeneous language-games that serve the purposes of the moment.

Language has an enormous number of grammatical rules; there cannot be a single *philosophical* grammar describing the fundamental features, the logic, of language. Moreover, all its grammars are local: no grammar can be complete without reference to the differential existential settings in which language is used. The existential conditions that make utterances intelligible are inevitably local; so no universalising or philosophical grammar is possible. Philosophical discourse is often senseless, not because it contravenes 'the logic of our language', but because it uproots expressions from the specific contexts in which they have meaning and so deprives them of the existential conditions for complete sense.

To ask the question 'What time is it?' is to participate in a particular language-game which is deeply rooted in a certain form of life – our own. To ask the apparently similar question 'What is Time?' is to remove 'time' from the settings that give it a completed sense – rather like asking 'What is five o'clock on the sun?'[23]

Failure to recognise that the meaning of words is inseparable from the local contexts in which they are usually used also results in the error of confusing grammar with ontology; of inferring, for example, from the fact that the word 'time' is a noun in the question 'What time is it?', that 'time' refers to a 'substance' or a 'thing' or a 'medium'. Much philosophy consists in taking words and utterances out of the contexts in which they are usually used – and make sense – and subjecting them to abnormal scrutiny. Drawing ontological conclusions from accidents of grammar is in some respects analogous to studying the moves in football to determine the Laws of Motion.

Philosophers are especially prone to draw invalid universal conclusions from local grammar because they tend to concentrate upon a handful of utterances that have a particular kind of structure.

> A picture held us captive. And we could not get out of it, for it lay in our language and language seemed to repeat it to us inexorably.[24]

The interplay of existential and linguistic grounds for Wittgenstein's objection to conventional philosophy is vividly expressed in his assertion that

> Philosophical problems arise when language goes on holiday.
>
> The confusions which occupy us arise when language is like an engine idling, not when it is doing work.[25]

(3)

Wittgenstein's repudiation of traditional philosophy had nothing to do with the easy scorn of the non-philosopher who has never been touched by the mystery of the world. Nor was it the shallow and lazy irrationalism of a man pleased to point to the limitations of logical thought as a pretext for turning his back on the rigours of hard thinking. He lacked neither the amazement which is the precondition of true philosophy nor the intellectual willpower to pursue an argument or a train of thought over hours, days, weeks, years ... As Russell said of him:

> He has the theoretical passion very strongly ... He doesn't want to prove this or that, but to find out how things are. It *hurts* him not to know.[26]

'It *hurts* him not to know.' If he was so consistently an original thinker, it was because he was one of those rare spirits possessed of the strength of mind to begin each day's thinking as if the world had not already been thought about the day – or the millennium – before. He refused to become a mere echo or imitation of himself; to decline in response to the pressures to publish from a thinker into a journalist; to freewheel through middle age on the intellectual momentum generated by the terrors and appetites of his youth. Nothing, therefore, could have been more unjust than Russell's diagnosis of the posthumously published *Philosophical Investigations* as the work of 'a man who is tired of thinking'. He never tired of thinking and his objection to traditional philosophy and its attempts to reconstruct a world razed by doubt were not shallowly anti-philosophical. They were deeply philosophical: they gave birth to much of what was most original in his thought.

Nevertheless, he knew that philosophical doubt was perfectly justified: the intelligibility of the world is incomplete, its structure and meaning only partly revealed and its purpose (if any) concealed from us; there are contradictions at the heart of consciousness itself; and we cannot even identify with certainty which things we are entitled to be certain of. At every level, in every direction, in every dimension, the sense of the world is incomplete, provisional. Wittgenstein never ceased to feel this and to suffer from a correspondingly fierce appetite for certainty. He knew the vertigo of the metaphysical moment, the panic-stricken hunger for absolute knowledge. And yet he could not ignore the implicit critique that ordinary life and ordinary discourse applied to the profound doubts and revolutionary conclusions of such moments.

> My *life* consists in my being content to accept many things.[27]

His entire philosophical life was discoloured by an unresolved conflict between valid *felt* doubts (which opened on to astonishment) and the inadmissibility of most expressions of those doubts and (*a fortiori*) of expressed solutions to those doubts. Philosophical doubt cannot be made public without self-contradiction. I may genuinely *feel* as if I am now dreaming; but I cannot seriously *debate* it publicly. Philosophy that begins with the possibility that 'it might all be a dream' or that 'I may be deceived in my belief that there is a world outside of me' – indeed, uses it as an official or traditional starting point – begins too far back, outside of the existential sense-conditions of language. Philosophy that starts out from universal doubt must, at the very least, doubt its own intelligibility. Its making its questions a matter for public debate must undermine its authenticity.

He was held in stasis by the conflict between the doubts that moved him to grapple with philosophical problems and his perception that most philosophical debate took place outside of the conditions in which any utterance could have sense. For him there was no escape from metaphysical vertigo into the community of discussion. In his early youth, he at least had the hope of breaking that solitude with those whose intellectual powers he respected – Frege, Russell, Moore. But that hope evaporated. Frege steadfastly pursued his thoughts into a labyrinth of technicalities: he was a mathematician rather than a philosopher and gave the philosophy of language – and his attempt to make language into a kind of mathematics by means of a logical calculus – priority over epistemology. Even when Russell pointed out the contradictions in his system, Frege did not yield to the epistemological temptation. He died a heartbroken technician, shipwrecked on the Russell paradox, but determined not to draw its metaphysical conclusions. Russell himself remained brilliant and prolific long after he had suffered what Wittgenstein considered to be 'a loss of problems'. Russell's quickness, lucidity and fluency seemed to him the mark of a fundamental shallowness; and the latter, exasperated by Wittgenstein's refusal to deal with conventional philosophical problems in the direct manner to which he was accustomed, described the later Wittgenstein as a man 'tired of thinking'. Moore, who was closest to sharing his second-order scepticism, confessed to never having suffered from philosophical problems in the first place:

> I do not think that the world or the sciences would ever have suggested to me any philosophical problems. What has suggested problems to me is things which other philosophers have said about the world or about natural sciences.[28]

Moore's second-order scepticism, superficially akin to Wittgenstein's, was inseparable from the almost child-like honesty that struck all who knew him, including Wittgenstein. But it was also part of his second-order (though not second-rate) philosophical impulse. Nothing could have been more alien to a man possessed by the philosophical daemon than Moore's admission that it was not the world that prompted him to philosophise but philosophy books. Of the other thinkers whom he could respect as equals or near-equals, Sraffa was an economist who, like Keynes, turned his incomparable intellect upon philosophical matters only as a kind of recreation; while F.P. Ramsay, who had sought out Wittgenstein in Austria and had been one of the earliest admirers as well as co-translator of *Tractatus*, had died of leukaemia at the age of twenty-six in the year of Wittgenstein's return to Cambridge.

(4)

Almost, but not quite, paralysed by the conflict between felt doubt and the inadmissibility of philosophical discussion, he continued to tread a path between philosophy and anti-philosophy. Sometimes in total physical isolation, mentally in almost constant solitude, he moved away from the positions of his peers and contemporaries and yet was reluctant to turn back to expound his views to them in the systematic way that they expected of a philosopher. This was in part because he could not systematise his views:

> After several attempts to weld my results together into such a whole, I realized that I should never succeed. My thoughts were soon crippled if I tried to force them on in any single direction against their natural inclination.[29]

Behind this incapacity was a stubborn refusal to order his thoughts along conventional curricular lines or around standard problems. And behind this again was a heroic scrupulousness – a refusal to abandon thinking to himself in order to think to or for others. His list of completed works, of thought-objects for public consumption – one short book published in his thirties, a brief article in his forties – was absurd for an academic; next to Russell's torrent of books it is almost laughable. And yet the posthumously published evidence of his unceasing activity makes it clear that the scantiness of his bibliography was the direct result of his valuing the process of thinking over mere products of thoughts. Like Valéry, he was intensely conscious of the opposition between the latter and the awareness necessary for true thought; of how one has to stop thinking at the deepest level in order to arrange one's thoughts into something that can be published, to turn them into an item in one's bibliography. With a scrupulousness rare even amongst great thinkers, he did not allow himself to be diverted from the pursuit of truth by a wish to *make* something – to build a book, an *oeuvre*, a reputation. He lived perpetually in his current account and did not permit himself the luxury of a deposit account – a body of published work – to fatten or to insulate his self-esteem.

He never ceased thinking to and for himself and yet it seems as if the dreamed of dialogue and someone with whom he might engage in discussion as an equal eluded him. His later books and notebooks contain snatches of dialogue and, though both voices are always his, they suggest that if he was not tired of thinking he was tired of being condemned to think always to himself. He could not find anyone amongst his few peers to bend his mind to the peculiar grain of his thought or to respond to the unremitting urgency of his approach to philosophical problems. And with others he so dominated any discussion that it became effectively a monologue: he grew impatient as they toiled over ground he had already covered. Moreover, to differ from him, to fail to understand him, was to be wilfully stupid, to show hostility. He could not tolerate those who did not, like him, think continuously, the 'tourists' who were not really troubled by the problems and thought about philosophy only when they talked about it. A philosopher was 'one who can think for himself'.[30] In the end he had to settle for disciples recruited from amongst pupils who accorded their teacher the status of a prophet. Inevitably he had (in the words of one of them) an 'inhibiting effect':[31]

> I feared his judgement and admired in silence: I accepted that most of what he said was beyond my then comprehension but hoped that some day understanding might dawn ... I was ... diffident about myself and my opinions and nervous of making an ass of myself in the rarefied atmosphere in which I now found myself, and I had already burned my fingers.[32]

Wittgenstein was uneasy with this authority, especially as the nervous awe with which he was held was at least as much a product of his failures as a man (his impatience, his intolerance) as of his power as a thinker.

He suspected that he was a bad teacher; and by all the usual criteria he was. He induced panic in his pupils so that they could not think in his presence and tended to ape his intellectual mannerisms in his absence. And yet he may have been a bad teacher of philosophy for good philosophical reasons; for to teach philosophy is to take one step deeper into the pragmatic self-refutation that is almost inescapable in philosophical discussion. If a teacher is someone who is senior to his pupils not only in years and office but also in virtue of the knowledge, experience, wisdom, maturity he has to impart to them, then the idea of a teacher of philosophy is absurd: how can one be 'senior' to another in the matter of raising, holding, handling, resolving or doubting the legitimacy of our belief in the existence of an external world? How can one *seriously* entertain the possibility that the whole of one's life may be a dream while at the same time engaging unquestioningly in organising tutorials (tutorials in which to doubt the outside world), planning timetables, devising curricula, assessing pupils – involving oneself in all the paraphernalia of the pedagogic enterprise? What would be an appropriate way to discipline a pupil who failed to attend a seminar in which 'our knowledge of external reality' had been subjected to critical and inconclusive examination? How can one commend a pupil's intellectual capabilities if they have been demonstrated in a discussion which failed to resolve doubts about our knowledge of other minds? From the metaphysical standpoint, all men are equal, none is more senior in knowledge than any other, there are no objective tors on the collective consciousness.

This may have been one of the many reasons why he did not give formal lectures. (Though there was also his disinclination to dismount from thought to put its products into conventional form or to engage in mere scholarship. He was unscholarly and unreliable as a reporter on other philosophers.) Instead, he thought out loud and (occasionally) engaged in dialogue. Since he had ceased to believe that he had solved any of the problems of philosophy by the time he had become a professional philosopher, he did not think that he had any *results* to impart. All he could offer was a method of philosophising that had developed out of his ceaseless dialogues with himself. His 'lectures' were an invitation to his pupils to engage with him in the process of thought. In practice, however, his impatience got the better of him and he cowed them out of thought into submissive silence, into abject pupilhood.

The conflict between the metaphysical equality implicit in the radical sceptisicm of philosophy and the hierarchical arrangement of individuals in a university reflected the conflict within him between his impulse to speak (to lay down the law, to assert the unassailability of his viewpoint, to dominate with monologues) and his conviction that, because they suspend the space in which utterances have sense, there is simply nothing to say about philosophical questions and certainly no experts available to answer them. Even *Tractatus* – the only book he published in his lifetime – was explicitly not a textbook:

> Perhaps this book will be understood only by someone who has himself already had the thoughts expressed in it – or at least similar thoughts. So it is not a textbook. – Its purpose would be achieved if it gave pleasure to one person who read and understood it.[33]

In the posthumous *Philosophical Investigations*, one has the sense of overhearing Wittgenstein talking to himself; or of a dialogue between him and an ideal interlocutor whose absence made him tolerable and spared Wittgenstein the need to assert his authority. In this book, too, we are aware of being presented not with the products of thought but with the process of thought, with understanding developing through conflict with itself. He did not envisage his readers receiving his results as termini of the thought process:

> I should not like my writing to spare other people the trouble of thinking. But, if possible to stimulate someone to thoughts of his own.[34]

Nevertheless, the *Investigations* still implicitly carried the authority that accrues to something so thoroughly worked over. It is in the posthumously published notebooks that one has texts that are freest from being textbooks. And it is above all in *On Certainty* – especially in the last fifty pages or so where there is no hope of completion – that one gets the sense of being in the presence of a man truly thinking to himself, at ease in articulate self-presence, engaged in utterly free enquiry. The audience – real or imaginary – has attenuated to a faint ghost. In so far as there is an addressee, it is his equal, 'one who can think himself'.

> [I believe it might interest a philosopher, one who can think himself, to read my notes. For even if I have hit the mark only rarely, he would recognise what targets I had been ceaselessly aiming at.][35]

Someone to whom he could admit:

> Here I am inclined to fight windmills because I cannot yet say the things I really want to say.[36]

(5)

To the end, however, he remained uneasy: hungering for the kind of truth and certainty that the older philosophers cultivated doubt in order to reach; while conscious that philosophical discourses were largely nonsensical. He still could not determine the sense-conditions that would make *expressed* philosophical doubts as legitimate as the felt doubts that prompted them.

In the pages of *On Certainty*, we see him coming to question even the second-order scepticism that countered philosophical doubt – to dissent from the 'robust common sense' that was Moore's characteristic stance. He was suspicious of Moore's protestation that he *knew* that there was an outside world because he knew these were his hands or that this was a tree. There is something dubious in asserting what is usually taken for granted (even if the assertion is intended to counter the absurdities of the sceptical position). It is 'like saying "Good morning" in the middle of a conversation'.[37]

> I am sitting with a philosopher in the garden; he says again and again 'I know that is a tree', pointing to a tree that is near us. Someone else arrives and hears this, and I tell him: 'This fellow isn't insane. We are only doing philosophy'.[38]

And the illegitimacy of Moore's defending the common-sense certainties by saying 'I know there is a hand in front of me' goes deeper:

> It is as if 'I know' did not tolerate a metaphysical emphasis.[39]

While there are sense-conditions for the assertion 'I know that there is a train from Cambridge to London at 5.00 pm', there are no such conditions for the assertion 'I know that there is a hand in front of me' intended to carry the metaphysical conclusion that there is an outside world. I cannot 'know' that there is a hand in front of me in the metaphysical sense or a world outside of me because I could not (accidentally) not *know* it; I could not be simply mistaken about it. I could imagine a situation in which I might be emphatic about my knowledge of train times – because it is easy to imagine doubt being cast upon it or even upon the likelihood of my being well informed on the matter. It is less easy to imagine reasons for others doubting my assertion that this is my hand, especially when the assertion is meant in a metaphysical sense. If an assertion is indubitable (and its indubitability is bound up with the metaphysical weight it is intended to carry), then it does not really count as a claim to knowledge, because I could scarcely be mistaken over it.

> Can one say 'Where there is no doubt there is no knowledge either?'[40]

> Doesn't one need grounds for doubt?[41]

Where there are no such grounds, there can be no doubts – and hence no knowledge either.

The claim to certainty cannot, therefore, be made – or it cannot take the form of a claim to certain knowledge. When Moore says 'I know that that is a tree' he is mistaken in thinking that his absence of doubt is based upon certain knowledge. He is merely brushing away the grounds for doubt:

> I really want to say that a language game is possible only if one trusts something (I did not say 'can trust something').[42]

> If I wanted to doubt whether this was my hand, how could I avoid doubting whether the word 'hand' has any meaning?[43]

> To say of man, in Moore's sense, that he *knows* something; that what he says is therefore unconditionally the truth seems wrong to me. – It is the truth only inasmuch as it is an unmoving foundation of his language-games.[44]

Moore, by countering the sceptical position with claims to have absolutely certain knowledge of at least some things, falls into the sceptical trap of overlooking that

> My *life* consists in my being content to accept many things.[45]

In other words, overlooking the existential grounds for rejecting the sceptical position. Moreover, doubt itself rests only upon what is beyond doubt.[46]

> A doubt that doubted everything would not be a doubt.[47]

So, even Moore's refusal to accept the validity of scepticism 'begins too far back'. Meeting the sceptics on their own dubious ground he is lured into poor arguments, mere protestation that 'of course' he knows that this is his hand, etc.

> What is the proof that I *know* something. Most certainly not my saying I know it.[48]

> And so, when writers enumerate all the things they *know*, that proves nothing whatever.[49]

Second-order scepticism – scepticism about the validity of philosophical scepticism – then, is going to be a much more complex and subtle position than a 'robust' or 'stubborn' defence of common sense, especially since metaphysical certainty seems to have little or nothing to do with the things that in practical daily life cannot be doubted:

> Why is there no doubt that I am called L.W.? It does not seem at all like something one could establish at once beyond doubt. One would not think that it is one of the indubitable truths.[50]

The existential and linguistic sense-conditions for admissible doubts, or for metaphysical certainty, prove impossible to define. But if it is not possible to determine what may be doubted, or known with certainty, there can be no way of knowing how or where to begin. This was 'the big gap in his thinking' which he noted so near to his death:

> [Here there is still a big gap in my thinking. And I doubt whether it will be filled now.][51]

Unlike Moore, he could entertain the possibility that he had got everything wrong, that he had no basis for his common-sense confidence.

> Is my understanding only blindness to my own lack of understanding? It often seems so to me.[52]

But how was he to respond to that intuition and find the beginning from which to move forward? How to remove what he thought to be uncertain without transgressing common sense, to build only upon what had seemed irrefutable without talking nonsense? How to speak when he could no longer endure the silence he enjoined upon himself?

Again and again, he had felt the ground shift beneath his feet but this had not justified his questioning, in the traditional philosophical fashion, the very existence of the ground. And now, in the last few days of his conscious existence, he continued his mental itinerary along the catwalk between philosophy and anti-philosophy, suspended above his own intuition of chaos in a superficially ordered world inhabited and run by people who knew nothing of that chaos and had no way of acknowledging it. To the last he struggled with his problem, his metaproblem and himself, fulfilling his vow

> that as long as I live and as often as my state of mind permits I will think about philosophical problems and try to write about them.[53]

(6)

He continued thinking and writing almost to the edge of his life, remained a consciousness still trying to make sense of itself as senselessness and coma approached. Even as he used the *Nachsommer* of his intellect to investigate the grounds of the confidence enjoyed by fluent, unsurprised daily awareness and to define the scope of legitimate doubt, he was encircled by many-layered uncertainty: he had no confidence in the value of his thoughts, or the direction they were taking; his mind did not know when it would cease to think ('it may well be all over by tomorrow');[54] and he did not know when he would cease to live.

There is an intense poignancy in the note that opens his last day's thought.

> We might speak of the fundamental principles of human enquiry.[55]

Yes, we might speak of them; but he knew now that if there were such principles they would elude him forever. His ceaseless endeavour to get to the bottom of things had resulted only in one short, systematic treatise, which he himself had rejected, and a huge wake of penetrating but scattered observations that scholars would comb over minutely for generations. The lure of complete but self-transparent understanding that had led him from mechanics to physics, from physics to mathematics and from the foundations of mathematics to philosophy had ended only in 'the big gap in his thinking' which he no longer believed would be filled. Again and again he had been deflected from the targets 'he was ceaselessly aiming at'. Between him and the fundamental questions lay language – language, without which there might not be such questions. And though he had once thought he had seen into the heart of language with a gaze before which the fundamental questions evaporated, he had subsequently come to understand that language had no heart – only an endless and unfolding surface upon which no perspicuous view was possible. And so he was twice removed from the fundamental principles; and yet ... these seven weeks had witnessed a kind of return to the mystery, to the riddle which, despite the anti-metaphysical stance of the author of *Tractatus* did, after all, exist,

He returned on this, his last day of thought, to the topics that had obsessed him over the previous weeks, the preceding decades.

> If someone believes he has flown from America to England in the last few days, then, I believe, he cannot be making a mistake.
>
> And just the same if someone says that he is at this moment sitting at a table and writing.[56]

If my belief that I had flown from America to England over the last few days had proved false, I could not be merely *mistaken*. Likewise, my belief that there is an external world, or that the world has existed for more than five minutes, or that others are not products of my imagination, could not turn out to be mere mistakes resulting from my happening to be ignorant of my own life – even allowing for the fact that, as he had said at the outset,

> Not all corrections of our views are on the same level.[57]

So it is odd, even perverse, for me to pretend to regard such beliefs as (mere) matters of knowledge. No experience, giving rise to information, could ever count as grounds for them or evidence against them. Indeed, it is probably wrong to describe them as convictions at all, as if they could be something personal, something I hold, positions I have arrived at (as a result of experience): they are too fundamental. The framework, the presupposition for all knowledge, conviction, belief, they are hardly things I can be *merely certain* about. Even less can I be *uncertain* about them to the point of calling them into question.

> If I don't trust *this* evidence why should I trust any evidence?[58]

Nevertheless, there are seemingly fundamental things which can be doubted. As he had reflected a few weeks earlier:

> But what men consider reasonable or unreasonable alters. At certain periods men find reasonable what at other periods they found unreasonable. And vice versa.[59]

And now he writes:

> Is it not difficult to distinguish between the cases in which I cannot and those in which I can hardly be mistaken? Is it always clear to which kind a case belongs? I believe not.[60]

In the last few hours of his writing life, he admits to his uncertainty as to what can be – must be – regarded as unshakeably certain. It is no longer clear to him where empirical fact ends and the rules of grammar or metaphysical frameworks begin. There starts to emerge a third-order scepticism which modifies his own radical critique of the philosopher's radical doubt. The boundaries of legitimate doubt are ill-defined; and so, correspondingly, are the boundaries of justified certainty. The balance between philosophical doubt and existential certainty begins to tip towards doubt ... But the movement is arrested:

> There are, however, certain types of cases in which I rightly say I cannot be making a mistake, and Moore has given a few examples of such cases ...[61]

However,

> I can enumerate various typical cases, but not give any common characteristic.[62]

The argument then takes another, astonishing, turn:

> And, even if in such cases I can't be mistaken, isn't it possible that I am drugged? And if I am and if the drug has taken away my consciousness, then I am not now really talking and thinking. I cannot seriously suppose that I am at this moment dreaming. Someone who, dreaming, says 'I am dreaming', even if he speaks audibly in doing so, is no more right than if he said in his dream 'it is raining', while it was in fact raining. Even if his dream were actually connected with the noise of the rain.[63]

These remarks take the reflection of a month earlier –

> The argument 'I may be dreaming' is senseless for this reason: if I am dreaming, this remark is being dreamed as well – and indeed it is also being dreamed that these words have any meaning.[64]

abruptly, vertiginously, deeper.

The obvious target is the artificial doubt that had led Descartes by so many false steps to the 0, 0, 0, point of Cartesian philosophy:

> At the same time I must remember that I am a man, and that consequently I am in the habit of sleeping, and in my dreams representing to myself the same things or sometimes even less probable things, than do those who are insane in their waking moments.... At this moment it does indeed seem to me that it is with the eyes awake that I am looking at this paper; that this head which I move is not asleep, that it is deliberately and of set purpose that I extend my hand and perceive it.... But in thinking over this I remind myself that on many occasions I have in sleep been deceived by similar illusions, and in dwelling carefully on this reflection I see so manifestly that there are no certain indications by which we may clearly distinguish wakefulness from sleep that I am lost in astonishment. And my astonishment is such that it is almost capable of persuading me that I now dream.[65]

'*Almost* capable of persuading ...' In this respect, at least, Descartes was honest; but the rest of the paragraph is riddled with inauthenticity, with pragmatic self-refutation. We are asked to believe that the writer almost believes he is dreaming (to a degree sufficient to justify the doubt that sets his philosophy in motion); but since the writing is cast in the present tense, we must believe that he is capable of suspecting that he is dreaming and, at the same time, of communicating this suspicion. Wittgenstein has already pointed out that it is inadmissible to start by arguing 'I may be dreaming' because if I *am* dreaming when I say 'I may be dreaming' then my utterance lacks sense-conditions. So the proposal would have to be false for me to propose it. It cannot therefore be seriously entertained. And it certainly cannot be used to inaugurate a public debate. Even less can it be taken as the *traditional* starting point for philosophical discussion. Or, rather, there is something almost grotesque in the fact that it is.

'I cannot seriously suppose that I am at this moment dreaming.' Without a fully conscious communicative intent, my utterance would be merely a set of sounds: a material event, but not a speech-act. A dreamer cannot intend to communicate the fact that he is dreaming without moving outside of this dream state. And if 'we are close to waking when we dream that we are dreaming',[66] we must needs be wide awake to *assert* that we are dreaming – especially if we assert it with the explicit purpose of initiating a philosophical debate.

If it so happens that I *am* dreaming when I mutter 'I am dreaming', this does not make the sounds I produce count as a true statement. Before a vocalisation can qualify as a true statement, it has to be a statement; before it can be true, it has to make sense. A dreaming man mumbling 'I am dreaming' is no more making a true statement than a dictaphone located inside a corpse playing 'I am dead' is *someone* pronouncing himself dead. Nor would it be so even if the tape were a recording of the ex-man's own voice. The mere coincidence between a series of sounds and the truth-conditions of the utterance that would use those sounds is not in itself sufficient to make the sounds a true statement because it is insufficient to make it a *statement*. (Failure to appreciate this point has played a large part in the recent proliferation of fallacious computer analogies in the theory of mind; if it had been understood, the fifty-year cul-de-sac of AI theories of mind, opening up at about the time of Wittgenstein's death, might have been avoided.)

(7)

The very last sentence he wrote takes his argument further, deeper:

> Even if his dream were actually connected with noise of the rain.

Statement S may be about state of affairs A but a causal relationship between the occurrence of S and the occurrence of A is not in itself sufficient to make S be 'about' A; and *a fortiori* it is insufficient to make S a true statement of or about A. Without the mediation of a communicative intention (so that the sounds corresponding to S are being deliberately used to communicate 'that A'), S does not count as a statement; and as such it can neither be true nor false. The words coming from the dreamer's mouth amount to a speech-act only if they are interpreted as such by someone else overhearing the words; and even then they amount only to an apparent speech-act. They become such only in another consciousness whose act of interpretation releases their potential meaning – a meaning that is, curiously, not actively meant by the producer of the words; a meaning that has a consumer but no producer; a meaning that is not meant.

This is analogous to the situation with natural signs where, for example, causes may signify their effects. Whereas I may infer from the clouds in the sky that it is probably about to rain, it does not follow from this that every cloud in the sky is a permanent statement to the effect that 'It is probably going to rain'. For this to be true (and for natural signs to be true statements of future or actual states of affair) the clouds would have to intend the inferences that are drawn from their presence; which, of course, they do not.

If states of affairs caused the statements that are 'about' them and thereby made those statements to be 'about them' and to be true, we would be witness to a curious convergence of causation and tautology, of causal and logical necessity. But Wittgenstein recognised (and this was what he was concerned to emphasise in this, his last written thought) that for an utterance to have sense, it must be explicitly meant. So the utterance 'I am dreaming' cannot make sense since, if true, it could not have an addressee and so could not be *meant*. In a dream there can be no one to talk to – not at least *about* the dream – so there can be no speech. The intrinsic properties of the utterance or even its relations – causal or otherwise – to that which a waking onlooker might regard it as 'being about' would be insufficient to fulfil the conditions for its having sense.

He had arrived back at the concerns that had occupied most of his philosophical life. And he recognised, perhaps, at last, precisely what was behind his twenty-five year quarrel with *Tractatus*. The author of *Tractatus* had believed, or wished to believe, or to prove, that the sense of a proposition and its meaning content could be guaranteed by a relationship between its structure and that of the state of affairs 'depicted' in it. A structural identity, a coincidence of logical forms, was sufficient to ensure that proposition P meant the state of affairs A. In this way the having of sense (by utterances) could be automated; and the inexplicable acts of intention (of meaning) and comprehension (of meaning) could be bypassed. Meaning could be transmitted without its being explicitly meant or explicitly grasped. Not long after his return to philosophy, ten or more years after the publication of *Tractatus*, Wittgenstein came to the conclusion that the structure of a proposition was insufficient to determine its meaning, even less to guarantee that it had a meaning. The same picture could be used to depict or illustrate different things; nothing in it could determine what it was a picture of – its intentionality. Structure was insufficient to fix, to generate fully determinate sense. The more radical conclusion of *Philosophical Investigations* was that a proposition had no intrinsic sense, being meaningful 'only in the stream of life'. He now touched the furthest point of the long journey from *Tractatus*, perhaps reaching in his last thoughts a mystery that he had intuited all his life: the irreducible mystery of explicitness (itself most explicit in speech) that is the consciousness of man – the explicit animal.

As he ended, the beginning was at last once more in sight and new horizons were opening up. Whether it was a beginning from which he could have moved forward, whether it opened on to a development in which his consciousness might have come closer to completing its own sense, moving from chequered doubt and certainty to the serenity of self-transparent mystery, is uncertain. We do not know what he might have written on 28 April 1951 because coma intervened. By 29 April he had re-entered the organic world from which the supreme explicitness, enjoyed or suffered by a philosopher of genius, had uniquely distanced him.

II

(1)

On the afternoon of 27 April, neither drugged nor dreaming, Wittgenstein took what proved to be his last walk. It was a cold gusty day with spells of dazzling sunlight between the showers. So far as one can tell, he was alone as he made his way through the streets of a town in which, more than any other, he had worked out his destiny. In Cambridge, his inner chaos – that 'constant, indescribable and almost morbid state of excitement'[67] – had taken shape as the career of a philosopher; an external form part-willed part-resisted but ultimately acquiesced in for lack of a more tolerable alternative.

A walk with Wittgenstein was 'very exhausting':

> He would walk in spurts, sometimes coming to a stop while he made some emphatic remark and looking into my eyes with his piercing gaze. Then he would walk rapidly for a few yards, then slow down, then speed up or come to a halt, and so on. And this uncertain ambulation was conjoined with the most exacting conversation![68]

His companions were not encouraged to relax. They were not at liberty to open themselves up to their non-verbal surroundings in order to contemplate the beauties of nature. They were caught up in the inner tensions of a man who almost from childhood had driven his intellect relentlessly. And that intellect had, equally relentlessly, driven him. From this inner pressure, it was hard to escape:

> Often he would rush off to a cinema immediately after the class ended. He insisted on sitting in the very first row of seats, so that the screen would occupy his entire field of vision ... He wished to become totally absorbed into the film no matter how trivial or artificial it was in order to free his mind temporarily from the philosophical thoughts that tortured and exhausted him.[69]

While the blaring crudity of the cinema might shout down or anaesthetise the lucid delirium of his thoughts, the spectacle of nature seemed unable to penetrate him:

> In his youth Ludwig showed great interest in technical things, unlike Paul (his brother) who was drawn overwhelmingly to nature by flowers, animals and landscapes.[70]

A walk was less an escape from philosophy than an occasion for peripatetic dialogue – with others or with himself. He could not lose himself in things that lay outside of his primary preoccupation unless he could actively engage them. He read widely in literature – for that required an interpretative response on his part: more words, more thoughts. He took a deep interest in architecture when he himself was occupied in building – and rebuilding – his sister's house. Music he could appreciate because the passivity it demanded was relieved by the analytic attention to structure that it invited; and because he could play or whistle or (in imagination) conduct it. I know of no record of his being interested in painting. It is not unreasonable to assume that the natural world lay at the distal end of his fierce scrutiny, prevented from entering him by the outward pressure of his unremitting self-awareness. He lacked that 'negative capability' which would have permitted him to dissolve, howsoever little, into the spring day surrounding the last walk of his life.

Spring can be seen as having four phases: the return of the songs; the return of the light; the return of the green; and finally the return of the heat. The last phase was late that year, as it always is. Although there had been a mild, sunny spell in mid-April, the weather from the 26th onwards was chilly, windy, showery. On the 29th there was a hail storm, brought to Cambridge by northerly winds emanating from a depression over Scandinavia. The light, of course, continued lengthening irrespective of the usual 'unreasonable' weather; and, although records of birdsong and greenery are not available, it may be assumed that blackbirds and thrushes were rejoicing the chilly air with their carols and that everywhere the dehiscent buds were starting to blur the stark winter outlines of the Cambridge trees.

In his depression in the autumn of 1949 when the cancer was first diagnosed, he must often have woken early and heard the robins singing on the lawns and among the crisping leaves of Trinity College. Those chilly rills of sound could only have deepened the despair that haunts the intersolvent edges of thought, fatigue and sleep. The final period of thought had begun when birdsong had returned: the blackbirds were singing from their lodging places on the tops of the budding trees and on pinnacles of carved stone. It seems unlikely that their gleaming ribbons of song incising the April air could also slice through the fog-and-phlegm befuddled darkness and the endocrine glooms of the winter past. Unlikely that they had gladdened his heart as he struggled to formulate criteria by which to separate admissible from inadmissible doubt. Equally unlikely that they unpeeled the husk of summer memories as he walked towards Midsummer Common or along the Cam, brooding over something that someone had said about him or his work, attending to his body for signs of improvement or deterioration, or thinking in a moment of brilliant sunlight of the losses he was living beyond. For he had no such memories.

The South had never called him:

> of this I am certain: that we are not here in order to have a good time.[71]

From his Catholic-Jewish-Protestant background he seems to have derived only a Calvinistic inability to relax; a guilty conviction that we are here to work and not to enjoy ourselves. (The iron will of his father – the great industrialist and patron of the arts – may have driven three of his brothers who had found it too burdensome to suicide.) Thought was not delight but labour and suffering, proof of a ruthless and unremitting integrity.

No, it was not the South but the North – the far North – that attracted him. In October 1913 he had left England to winter in the north of Norway, first on a farm and then in a yet more remote ski hut which he had built for himself, to concentrate on logic. There he passed his days 'between logic, whistling, going for walks and being depressed'.[72] He returned to Norway repeatedly, his last visit as late as autumn 1950. He scarcely found peace of mind there:

> Everyday I was tormented by a frightful Angst and by depression in turns and even in the intervals I was so exhausted that I wasn't able to think of doing a bit of work. It's terrifying beyond all description the kinds of mental torment there can be! It wasn't until two days ago that I could hear the voice of reason over the howls of the damned and I began to work again.[73]

> I often think I am going mad.[74]

> Sometimes things inside me are in such a ferment that I think I'm going mad: then the next day I am totally apathetic again.[75]

But at least he was spared the company of others:

> Being alone here does me no end of good and I do not think I could now bear life among people.[76]

There was perhaps a bitter satisfaction in the correspondence between the barren landscape of his mind, as he sought illumination in total darkness, and the glacial solitude of this dark and deserted Ultima Thule.

> If a blackbird could talk we should not understand him.[77]

No, the blackbird's song was unlikely to gladden his heart; or even, by reminding him that this might be his last spring, to sadden it either. As for the flowers, the leaves, the buds unclenching despite the chilly weather – it is doubtful whether he paid them much attention. He could not permit himself to become lost in looking. Compared with thought, sight – being irredeemably particular – is stupefaction. If he exhorted philosophers caught up in paradoxes not 'to think but to look' (as he did in *Philosophical Investigations*), he meant not to look at *things*, to break out of language into wordless reality, but simply to look and see how words were actually used rather than talking about them from within blind preconceptions. He himself could never have suspended his thoughts long enough to permit the seen to enter and possess him. True looking, pure seeing, requires a tranquillity and an ability to become passive; and this was beyond him. At a superficial level, the assertion in *Tractatus* that

> *The limits of my language* mean the limits of my world[78]

might be interpreted as being less a description of how things are in general than an acknowledgement of his own imprisoned state; of the coextensiveness for him of wakefulness and words.

Upwelling words pressed back nature, sealed him off from the new-leafed spring: if he ever escaped his own voice down his senses it was into mind-cancelling banalities of the cinema screen and not into the electric yellow of the daffodils and the forsythia, the transfixed hail of the white-green buds, or the newly lengthened evenings and the mystery of the returned light.

(2)

On the night of 27 April 'he fell violently ill'.[79] Precisely what form this sudden deterioration took is not disclosed in Norman Malcolm's *Memoir*. There are many possibilities: haemorrhage due to the thrombocytopenia which may occur with widespread secondary cancer in the bones; a urinary tract infection giving rise to septicaemia and gram-negative shock: heart failure consequent upon a heart attack to which a period on Stilboestrol would have made him prone. He at first remained conscious, so that Dr Bevan was able to tell him that he did not have long to live. His response to this information was characteristic:

> ... he exclaimed 'Good!'[80]

Mrs Bevan stayed with him throughout the night.

There is no record of how he passed the hours that remained to him between his collapse and the loss of consciousness. It seems improbable that he should have prayed in any formal or conventional sense. Many years earlier, when he was a soldier moving (by choice) up to the front line, he had written:

> To pray is to think about the meaning of life.[81]

In that sense of the word 'pray' he had never ceased praying since childhood. There are no reports of discussions about the possibility of a 'future life' or 'a next world'. As he had admitted to Drury a few weeks before:

> Isn't it curious that, although I have not long to live, I never find myself thinking about 'a future life'. All my interest is still in this life and the writing I am still able to do.[82]

Yes, it was curious. There was a strange dissociation between the certainty and doubt that he was exploring in his thoughts and the vast uncertainty that encircled him. Perhaps his inability to address himself to the existential situation that was closing around him, the death that was moving towards him, poised to extinguish his thoughts and the ground on which they stood, was part of 'the big gap' in his thinking which he now doubted would ever be filled. His inability to connect his thoughts with his life – with the things that deeply disturbed him and still defined him however much he dedicated that life to the process of thought, was curiously a part of his unassailable integrity. He knew that the two – his thoughts, his life – were connected, but that the connection lay unimaginably deep. It was for the shallow philosophers, for Russell and Joad and their like, to move easily between technical discussion and the Wayside Pulpit.

When as a volunteer in the First World War, deliberately choosing the firing line, he had been close to death before, he had found it difficult to continue philosophising:

> I've had time and quiet enough for working. But nothing stirs me. My material is far away from me. It is only death that gives life its meaning.
>
> Only one thing is needed: to be able to contemplate whatever happens to one; *collect* oneself.[83]

Now that he was being pressed, involuntarily, to the firing line, he no longer, it seems, felt the need to collect himself, to gather up his consciousness into the kind of summarising reflexion, triggered by the nearness of death in battle, that had entered the repudiated *Tractatus*. He simply continued to reflect as often and as deeply on the topics that seemed to him most fruitful. His material was close to him.

His final weeks were not filled with theological discussion. As he had confided to his notebook in 1916:

> To believe in God means to understand the question about the meaning of life.
>
> To believe in God means to see that the facts of the world are not the end of the matter.[84]

This, rather than trying to address oneself to a chimera in which metaphysical and moral categories were inextricably fused. The essence of the religious sensibility lies in its appreciation that the sense of the world is open, indeterminate, provisional, and not rounded off, or completed in, or encompassed by, our everyday knowledge or understanding or even by the more general descriptions and interpretations of the scientist.

> It is not *how* things are in the world that is mystical, but *that* it exists.[85]

The inexplicable fact of the world's being there undermines the completeness of any attempted explanation of its specific character and properties. About the former, he was sure, there was nothing to say. Theology that aimed to define the mystery, to articulate the aesthetic miracle of the world's existence, to enclose it in the characteristics attributed to God, could not have meant anything to him. Moreover, he had already ruled out a death-bed conversion by revelation:

> An inner experience cannot show me that I know something.[86]

It seems probable, then, that in those hours between collapse and coma, while he was waiting for the world 'not to alter, but to come to an end'[87] there was no prayer, no discussion of a future life, no commending of his soul to God. (This last his friends performed for him after he had died – and one of them has 'been troubled ever since as to whether what we did then was right'.[88]) And yet, he seems to have awaited death without fear.

> Fear in the face of death is the best sign of a false, a bad life.[89]

His end, like his father's, was exemplary – free of pain as well as of fear.

In 1913, he sat by his father's death-bed and had written about the experience to Russell, the philosophical father he was soon to repudiate:

> My dear father died yesterday in the afternoon. He had the most beautiful death I can imagine; without the slightest pain and falling asleep like a child! I did not feel sad for a single moment during all the last hours, but most joyful and I think that this death was worth a whole life.[90]

And the wish he had expressed as a soldier over thirty years before:

> May I die a good death, attending myself. May I never lose myself[91]

seems to have been fulfilled. Just before losing consciousness, he said to Mrs Bevan:

> Tell them I've had a wonderful life![92]

And with this, his voice, his mind, and the language that was himself, his world, came to an end. The sense-condition of all utterances evaporated. He passed into coma, that most savage of all critiques of certainty. The explicit sense of the spoken word, the implicit unsayable sense manifested in his life, the gaps in sense that provoked him into thought and the senselessness intuited outside of sense, all went out. The inexpressible distances that his consciousness constituted and his language had stabilised imploded. He left behind only a wake of words: propositions that others would have to find sense in and utter for him. He was silent – with a silence that lay an immeasurable distance from that which he had enjoined upon others and tried to find without success within himself.

> Tell them I've had a wonderful life!

Norman Malcolm, who reported these last words, found them 'mysterious and strangely moving':

> When I think of his profound pessimism, the intensity of his moral and mental suffering, the relentless way in which he drove his intellect, his need for love together with the harshness that repelled love, I am inclined to believe that his life was fiercely unhappy. Yet at the end he himself exclaimed that it has been 'Wonderful!'[93]

They were sad as well as 'mysterious and strangely moving'; for Wittgenstein's native language was German and he was talking to an English woman. The voice of this solitary man without wife or child or brother or sister, had ended in a language foreign to him. To utter your last words on earth in a foreign tongue and to someone whom a few months before you scarcely knew is to die far, far from childhood. But then anyone who has outlived his youth has lived long enough to have become remote from whatever as a child he had imagined himself becoming. He has lived long enough to lose sight of himself – although, in one sense, Wittgenstein had perhaps travelled less than most: he had kept faith with and close to more of himself than had the average man; there is a clear thread of tenacious self-adherence connecting the ten-year-old child who had astonished his family by constructing a sewing machine with the sixty-year-old philosopher bidding the world farewell.

There is no account of Wittgenstein's condition at the time of his last words. We are told only that he spoke them 'before losing consciousness'. Since his respiration is not reported, we do not know whether the sentence was gasped out or uttered without difficulty; whether it was articulated clearly or whether it was unclear what he actually said. We don't even know if his conscious state was such as to permit us to assume that the utterance had the necessary sense-conditions to carry a truth-value. The imagination, provoked by these missing details, reaches out to places where others, equally crucial, are lacking; until the utterance, uprooted from the stream of Malcolm's narrative, seems encircled by doubts, and to reverberate in an enormous silence. For example: Was this an isolated remark? Had it been preceded by a long pause? Was it a response to a question? Had he looked at Mrs Bevan as he uttered it? Was she holding his hand? What expression did he have on his face? Were there tears in his eyes or emotion in his voice? Had the dawn begun breaking and was there daylight on his face? Were the birds singing outside – reminding him of the spring and of the coming summer, the first one for sixty-two years he would not know? And whom did he mean by 'them'?

'By "them" he undoubtedly meant his close friends,' Malcolm assures us.[94] But who were they? Was anyone close to him? Were the close friends few or many? Mrs Bevan, at any rate, could not possibly have had any conception of the extension of 'them'. She may have been aware of a small, nearby, recent sector of them; but the further reaches – the far away, the long ago, the secret, the incidental, those many acquaintances (lost in the recesses of his failing consciousness or the corners of a devastated and changing Europe) in whose lives he had been an unparalleled occurrence – would have lain outside of her knowledge. The catchment area from which they were drawn spanned a nineteenth-century childhood in Vienna and a late middle age in postwar Cambridge. Friends and enemies had been made in Vienna, Salzburg, Linz, Berlin, Manchester, Cambridge, Skjolden, Cracow, Olmutz, Monte Cassino, Schneeberg, London, Newcastle, Wicklow, Galway, Dublin, Ithaca, Oxford ... The reference of 'them' ranged over the eminent and the unknown, the ageing and the still young, the living and the dead. Did he believe, as he spoke, that his message, his concluding unphilosophical postscript, would percolate through the near-them to the middle-them and so to the far limits of the living them? And was there – among that widely scattered crowd (scattered both sides of the grave) of acquaintances, pupils, admirers, readers, colleagues, friends, adversaries, fellow soldiers, teachers and fellow teachers, relatives, lovers – one person, a face, a voice, a heart that had once seemed like the wavering image of home, to whom above all this final statement was addressed?

Of one thing we can be certain (a cornerstone perhaps of the language-game): his final utterance was fashioned out of expired air. We are permitted, therefore, to imagine his body appropriating for the last time a portion of the formless atmosphere, giving it audibility as a cry sculpted by his larynx, his palate, his tongue, his teeth and lips and conferring sense upon it by his presence and his communicative intent. Thus was it spoken by the man and heard by the woman; and thence it passed, from lip to ear, along radiating lines of speakers and listeners until, in Norman Malcolm's *Memoir*, it reaches the printed page to be propagated in a thousand, ten thousand, hardbound and paperback copies and read decades after the sounds had faded, after that long night had passed and the mouth that had spoken it had dissolved in the rain.

This, then, was his final enactment of the mystery that he had devoted so much of his thoughts to elucidating; the mystery that had at some times seemed to intervene between him and The Mystery and at others had seemed itself the source of all mysteries, real and contrived: the mystery of verbal meaning. In his youth, this mystery had been hard-edged; as he grew older, it lost its sharp edges and melted into the larger, more elusive, less articulable mysteries of everyday life. How he had suffered as, in his middle years, the perspicuous view had escaped him and language had changed from the autonomous sign system of his earlier vision into a complex *instrument* that could not be extricated from the boundless rule-governed chaos of human sociality!

Perhaps it was appropriate, then, that his last utterance should have been precisely the kind of complex speech-act whose analysis would have been beyond the scope of the philosophical grammar of the *Tractatus*. Appropriate, too, that his last words should have been a command: 'Tell them ...' There could have been no more characteristic way for that small, spare man with 'deep, often fierce, eyes' to have closed his account with language.

Embedded in the command, however, was a statement:

> I've had a wonderful life.

Was this a legitimate assertion? A permissible move in the language-game? Even *Tractatus* would have made short work of this: in order to evaluate our lives, we must step outside of them:

> The sense of the world must lie outside the world.[95]

And since my world and my life are coterminous, the sense of my life must lie outside of it and, what is more, outside of my language. The value of my life is precisely one of those things that cannot be summed up and said. If it was strange that, in spite of his depression and guilt, his isolation and the ugly quarrels that had disfigured so many of his relationships with others, in spite of the unbearable tension of thought and his ultimate failure to arrive at a final illumination, his last utterance before dyspnoea or coma dictated silence should have been in praise of life, it was surely stranger still that he, of all men, should have chosen to end his life uttering words evaluating that life. His younger self, the author of *Tractatus*, who had touched death in his thoughts, would have judged the last statement of his final self, reaching death in his body, rather harshly. The conditions under which an utterance makes sense do not widen just because someone is dying – even if that someone is oneself.

In his defence, he could perhaps have cited another of the propositions of *Tractatus*:

> Death is not an event in life: we do not live to experience death.[96]

Conclusions about life must be drawn by the living; after death, there is nothing to be said:

> At death, the world does not alter but comes to an end.[97]

If we wait until the end to conclude, we shall have waited too long.

(3)

Had he ended, then, as he had lived, struggling against pragmatic self-refutation? Throughout his life he had longed to speak things that elsewhere he had established as belonging to the unsayable or meaningless. Sometimes he had spoken them: he had found it impossible to remain silent about the mystery of things that he denied himself the right to speak about. He longed for a general solution to the puzzling fact of being alive; and longed, too, to feel more deeply, more continuously, puzzled by it:

> We find certain aspects of seeing puzzling because we do not find the whole business of seeing puzzling enough.[98]

Anything less than the forbidden metaphysical enquiry was too local, too superficial, in short too trivial, to have a legitimate claim on his thoughts and to answer to his needs. And so he remained arrested in indecision, in the borderland between two deeply conflicting views of life: as a problem to which there might at least be partial answers; and as an inviolable mystery which could be neither analysed nor explained – nor even spoken of. His mission was consequently in conflict with itself. Like Beckett's artist, Wittgenstein had lived inside

> The expression that there is nothing to express, nothing with which to express, nothing from which to express, no power to express, no desire to express, together with the obligation to express.[99]

And the tireless thinker, who began each day's thinking as if the world had not been thought about the day, the millennium, before could have taken Molloy's conclusion as his motto:

> I can't go on. I'll go on.[100]

Did he die, then, with self-contradiction on his lips? Did he say farewell to himself, and to the world, gripped by self-refutation? Writing in 1916, shortly after he was taken prisoner in battle, he reflected:

> The aesthetic miracle (*Wunder*) is that the world exists. That what exists does exist.[101]

And now, thirty-five years later, at death's edge, he did not say that his life had been happy, or that it had been worthwhile, or good, or even that it had made sense – only that it had been 'wonderful'. And on this, his younger self and his dying self, all his many conflicting selves, would have met in agreement.

Seeing his life, reflected in the black mirror of death as an unaccountable fact, and the world as 'a limited whole',[102] what else could a truly profound man feel but the simple wonder that had visited him so rarely throughout his life but which had perhaps lain deeper than, and prompted all else? Is it surprising that, knowing he had only a few hours or minutes to live, he should have been overwhelmed by astonishment at having been given such a self to live, such a world to live in? What else but wonder should he have felt (since he was not crushed by pain or drowning in nausea, malaise or confusion) on the threshold of unbeing, of the coma, of the death where the dialectic of speech and silence, doubt and certainty, would resolve itself?

(4)

And what of the beginning he had found so difficult to begin at? Was he to die, to end, without ever having reached it? A few weeks earlier, he had copied Faust's famous words into his notebook:

> *Im anfang war die Tat.*[103]

In the beginning was the *Deed*. So, at the beginning, there is not philosophy with its puzzles, its problems, its first- and second- and third-order doubts. For the beginning was not the Word but the Deed – the deed that had brought about the strange fact of the world. And philosophy should begin not with doubt or certainty nor with questions or disputations – they must come later. In the beginning, there must be astonishment – at the huge and beautiful fact of the world, at what the poet called 'the million-petalled fact of being here':[104]

> There is nothing more wonderful than the *true* problems of philosophy.[105]

Philosophical problems are true when they are prompted by astonishment. To begin at the beginning (and not to begin too far back) means not to go further back than one's astonishment dictates or can penetrate.

Early in his career as a soldier, he had written:

> Perhaps the nearness of death will bring some light.[106]

It seems it had. At the very limit of his life, when familiar, differentiated daylight had become the edge of undifferentiated eternity, where words were only the spindrift of breaking silence, he had glimpsed the strange truth that, to 'one who sees the world aright'[107] all lives that are not terrible are wonderful.

In the beginning was astonishment. And so it was with a cry of astonishment, of wonder, perhaps even of joy, that he passed over into silence.

On 29th April 1951 there died at Cambridge, England one of the greatest and most influential philosophers of our times, Ludwig Wittgenstein.[108]

Notes

1. Letter from Wittgenstein to M. O'C. Drury, quoted in *Ludwig Wittgenstein. Personal Recollections*, edited by Rush Rees (Oxford: Blackwell, 1981).
2. Letter from Wittgenstein to Norman Malcolm, quoted in *Ludwig Wittgenstein. A Memoir* (Oxford University Press, 1958), p. 98.
3. William Warren Barkley III, *Wittgenstein* (London: Quartet Books, 1974), p. 130.
4. Letter to Norman Malcolm, 16 April, 1951, quoted in Malcolm, op. cit., p. 99.
5. Malcolm, ibid., p. 100.
6. Malcolm, ibid., p. 100.
7. Ludwig Wittgenstein, *On Certainty*, edited by G.E.M. Anscombe and G.H von Wright. Translated by Denis Paul and G.E.M. Anscombe (Oxford: Blackwell, 1974).
8. *On Certainty*, paragraph 300.
9. G.H. von Wright, *Ludwig Wittgenstein: a Biographical Sketch* (Oxford University Press, 1958), p. 18.
10. *On Certainty*, between paragraphs 532 and 533.
11. *On Certainty*, between paragraphs 387 and 388.
12. *On Certainty*, between paragraphs 470 and 471.
13. *On Certainty*, paragraph 471.
14. R. Descartes, *Meditations on First Philosophy*, translated by Elizabeth Haldane and G.R.T. Ross, in *The Philosophical Works of Descartes*, Volume I (Cambridge University Press, 1967).
15. David Hume, *A Treatise of Human Nature* (New York: Dolphin Books, 1961), p. 199.
16. Quoted in John Passmore, *A Hundred Years of Philosophy* (London: Penguin, 1968), p. 61.
17. Wittgenstein's remarks on Kierkegaard are quoted in M. O'C. Drury's contribution to Rees, op. cit., pp. 102–4.
18. S. Kierkegaard, *Concluding Unscientific Project*, translated by David Swenson and Walter Lowrie (Princeton: Princeton University Press, 1944).
19. Ludwig Wittgenstein, *Tractatus Logico-Philosophicus*, translated by D.F. Pears and B.F. McGuinness (London: Routledge and Kegan Paul, 1963), 6.51.
20. Ibid., 4.003.
21. Ibid., 4.003
22. Quoted in Malcolm, op. cit., p. 93.
23. Ludwig Wittgenstein, *Philosophical Investigations*, edited and translated by G.E.M. Anscombe (Oxford: Blackwell, 1963), p. 111.
24. Ibid., p. 115.
25. Ibid., p. 132.
26. Quoted in Ronald Clark, *Bertrand Russell* (London: Penguin, 1975), p. 211.
27. *On Certainty*, paragraph 344.
28. G.E. Moore, *Autobiography*. Quoted in John Passmore. *A Hundred Years of Philosophy* (London: Penguin, 1968) p. 201.

29. Preface to Wittgenstein, *Philosophical Investigations*, op. cit.
30. *On Certainty*, between paragraphs 387 and 388.
31. Desmond Lee, quoted in Rhees, op. cit., p. 85.
32. John King, quoted in Rhees, ibid., p. 85.
33. Ludwig Wittgenstein, Preface to *Tractatus Logico-Philosophicus*, op. cit.
34. Ludwig Wittgenstein, Preface to *Philosophical Investigations*, op. cit.
35. *On Certainty*, between paragraphs 387 and 388.
36. *On Certainty*, paragraph 400.
37. *On Certainty*, paragraph 464.
38. *On Certainty*, paragraph 467.
39. *On Certainty*, paragraph 482.
40. *On Certainty*, paragraph 121.
41. *On Certainty*, paragraph 122.
42. *On Certainty*, paragraph 509.
43. *On Certainty*, paragraph 369.
44. *On Certainty*, paragraph 403.
45. *On Certainty*, paragraph 344.
46. *On Certainty*, paragraph 519.
47. *On Certainty*, paragraph 450.
48. *On Certainty*, paragraph 487.
49. *On Certainty*, paragraph 488.
50. *On Certainty*, paragraph 470.
51. *On Certainty*, between paragraphs 470 and 471.
52. *On Certainty*, paragraph 418.
53. Malcolm, op. cit., p. 97.
54. Malcolm, op. cit., p. 99.
55. *On Certainty*, paragraph 670.
56. *On Certainty*, paragraph 657.
57. *On Certainty*, paragraph 300.
58. *On Certainty*, paragraph 672.
59. *On Certainty*, paragraph 336.
60. *On Certainty*, paragraph 673.
61. *On Certainty*, paragraph 674.
62. *On Certainty*, paragraph 674.
63. *On Certainty*, paragraph 676.
64. *On Certainty*, paragraph 383.
65. Descartes, in Haldane and Ross, op. cit.
66. Novalis, in *Pollen*, collected in *Hymns to the Night and Other Selected Writings*, translated by Charles E. Passage (Liberal Arts Press, 1960), p. 70.
67. Hermine Wittgenstein, quoted in Rhees, op. cit., p. 1.
68. Malcolm, op. cit., p. 31.
69. Malcolm, op. cit., p. 27.
70. Hermine Wittgenstein, in Rhees, op. cit., p. 1.
71. Quoted by Drury, in Rhees, ibid., p. 103.
72. Ludwig Wittgenstein, letter to Russell, collected in *Letters to Russell, Moore and Keynes*, edited by G.H. von Wright, translated by B.F. McGuinness (Oxford: Blackwell, 1974), p. 45.
73. Letter to Russell quoted in von Wright, op. cit., p. 47.
74. Letter to Russell quoted in von Wright, ibid., p. 57.

75. Letter to Russell quoted in von Wright, ibid., p. 57.
76. Letter to Russell quoted in von Wright, ibid., p. 43.
77. Cf. *Philosophical Investigations*, op. cit., II, xi.
78. *Tractatus Logico-Philosophicus*, op. cit., 5.6.
79. Malcolm, op. cit., p. 100.
80. Malcolm, ibid., p. 100.
81. Ludwig Wittgenstein, *Notebooks 1914–1916* translated G.E.M. Anscombe (Oxford: Blackwell, 1969), p. 73.
82. Drury, in Rhees, op. cit., p. 183.
83. Rhees, in Rhees, op. cit., p. 216.
84. Ludwig Wittgenstein, *Notebooks* 1914–1916, op. cit., p. 74.
85. *Tractatus Logico-Philosophicus*, op. cit., 6.44.
86. *On Certainty*, paragraph 569.
87. *Tractatus Logico-Philosophicus*, op. cit., 6.431.
88. Drury, in Rhees, op. cit., p. 184.
89. Quoted in Rhees, op. cit.
90. Letter to Russell quoted in von Wright, op. cit., p. 21.
91. Quoted in Rhees, op. cit., p. 214.
92. Malcolm, op. cit., p. 100.
93. Malcolm, ibid., p. 100.
94. Malcolm, ibid., p. 100.
95. *Tractatus Logico-Philosophicus*, op. cit., 6.41.
96. Ibid., 6.431.
97. Ibid., 6.431.
98. *Philosophical Investigations*, op. cit., II, xi.
99. Samuel Beckett, *Proust* and *Three Dialogues with Georges Duthuit* (London: Calder and Boyars, 1970.)
100. Samuel Beckett, *The Unnameable* (London: Calder and Boyars, 1959).
101. Quoted by Rush Rhees, op. cit.
102. *Tractatus Logico-Philosophicus*, op. cit., 6.45.
103. Quoted in *On Certainty*, paragraph 402.
104. Philip Larkin, 'The Old Fools'. In *High Windows* (London: Faber, 1974).
105. Letter to Russell, quoted in von Wright, op. cit., p. 14.
106. Quoted in Rush Rhees, op. cit., p. 214.
107. *Tractatus Logico-Philosophicus*, op. cit., 6.54.
108. von Wright, op. cit., p. 1.

From: *On the Edge of Certainty* (Macmillan, 1999), pp. 189–227.

3
Man, the Explicit Animal

This reading, taken from *The Explicit Animal* (1991, 1999), addresses the question of what it is for human beings to be aware of themselves as human, which is inseparable from the question of how to characterise human consciousness. Man has repeatedly defined himself as a kind of animal, but one with special qualities, as an animal who in certain vital respects is not an animal at all. There is in effect an irreducible distance between the human and the animal and it is a distance that for Tallis derives from the fact of human explicitness. Man is the being who questions his own being. Man has been defined as the rational animal, the moral animal, the metaphysical animal, the tool-making animal, the spiritual animal, and so on. However, explicitness, or the power to make things explicit, is something deeper and wider than any mere faculty, such as reason. It is that in virtue of which the faculties themselves develop to the degree that they do. What makes us unique is the fact that we know what we are doing. Tallis makes it clear that the evolutionary explanation of the development of the human *body* is not in question; but none the less, he insists, the emergence of explicitness cannot be explained in terms of the Darwinian picture. He returns to his central point: the power of explicitness is *sui generis*, underivable. It cannot be reduced to anything else, nor can the existence of consciousness be explained. And to grasp this fact is to provide a further level of defence against the all too pervasive temptation to explain consciousness as though it were a machine.

> Man need not be degraded to a machine by being denied to be a ghost in a machine. He might, after all, be a sort of animal, namely, a higher mammal. There has yet to be ventured the hazardous leap to the hypothesis that perhaps he is man.
>
> Gilbert Ryle[1]

Introduction: Defining man or remembering what we are

I have described how consciousness has been emptied by much modern thought (see figure, p. 68). The purpose of the present chapter is to begin the process of restoring human consciousness, by drawing attention to its *difference* and its *all-pervasiveness*. Consciousness is rather tricky stuff to get hold of and even more to display. In order to succeed in convincing anyone of its substantive reality, one must proceed by indirection and 'come at' consciousness via that which it is not. One such approach is to show what *human* consciousness amounts to by contrasting the creatures that possess such consciousness with those that do not. And this is the strategy of the present chapter: to compare man with the animals; or (since man is neither machine nor angel) with the *other* animals.[2] It is necessary to emphasise at the outset that I am not denying that other, non-human, animals are conscious; only underlining the unique degree to which consciousness is developed in humans. That, however successful philosophers and others may think they have been in reducing animals to the status of soft machines, of automata driven by the wetware of a nervous system, this apparent success cannot be transferred to humans.[3]

Man, the self-defining animal

The human species, it seems, has a predilection for pithy descriptions of itself. The history of written thought is marked by the species' repeated attempts to seize hold of itself in a handful of words – as if to enable it to hold itself up to the light; or to catch sight of itself as from a great distance; or to strain towards a self-recognition so cold it may pass for objectivity. The comparison with other animals is its favoured way of getting at its own nature; or at its distance from Nature and from simpler natures. We get to know ourselves through our differences from things which are different from us, but not so different as to make comparison unilluminating. Animals seem to be our nearest ontological kin; and so their natures seem to hold up a mirror to our own. Animals are (to use Lévi-Strauss's term) *bonnes à penser* – things that are good for thinking about ourselves with;[4] they are (according to Foucault) that Other through which we can encounter the Same which is ourselves.[5]

And so man has repeatedly defined himself as a kind of animal – but one with special qualities; or, since those special qualities are not to be found anywhere else in the animal kingdom, as an animal who is not, in certain important respects, an animal at all: an animal at an irreducible distance from animality. Animal but not animal; a very special kind of animal: this is the perspective from which the present chapter is written.

Man has called himself (among other things): the rational animal; the moral animal; the consciously choosing animal; the deliberately evil animal; the political animal; the toolmaking animal; the historical animal; the commodity-making animal; the economical animal; the foreseeing animal; the promising animal; the death-knowing animal; the art-making or aesthetic animal; the explaining animal; the cause-bearing animal; the classifying animal; the measuring animal; the counting animal; the metaphor-making animal; the talking animal; the laughing animal; the religious animal; the spiritual animal; the metaphysical animal; the wondering animal ... Man, it seems is the self-predicating animal.

Some of these definitions are obviously far too specific, far too narrow, to capture all that importantly distinguishes man from other animals. Others seem too close to the kind of self-admiring evaluation that invites cynical scorn: defining man as 'the rational animal' or 'the moral animal' elicits shallow mockery or profound, sorrowing dissent. Moreover none of the definitions gets to the bottom of things – to the primordial difference between man and other animals; indeed, between man and all other forms of matter. The epithets pick out striking characteristics that seem or seemed (to certain men) to distinguish men from their ontologically closest neighbours; but they do not pin down what it is that lies behind or encompasses these differences. As definitions, they may answer to a focal surprise but not to the rounded and total astonishment that should mark our profoundest encounters with ourselves. The primary argument of this chapter is that these epithets identify only secondary or symptomatic differences and that there is a more fundamental difference from which they are all derived.

* * *

Some human self-definitions

The rational animal

This is the most celebrated definition of man, traditionally attributed to Aristotle, though, as Mary Midgley points out, Aristotle himself did not give this definition. Behind it is recognition of man as a creature whose behaviour is explicitly linked with its specific goals or larger purposes. 'I did this because ...' Human acts are propelled by reasons rather than being brought about merely through material causes operating on organ systems or being driven by unquestioned instincts. Behaviour is defended on general grounds, even universalised. Moreover, the form of actions is modified by general considerations concerning the most effective way of bringing about desired outcomes. Means and ends are explicitly identified and the ways of connecting them crystallised in method. General methods are established for extending knowledge and power; for passing from ignorance and uncertainty to knowledge and control; and for deriving the future from the past.

This definition has become the target of much shallow derision. So much for 'man, the rational animal', people will say, after having seen newsreel pictures of a massacre or, on a smaller scale, having watched a political argument degenerate into a punch-up. The fact that people sometimes, or often, behave in ways that are at odds with their best interests, or that of

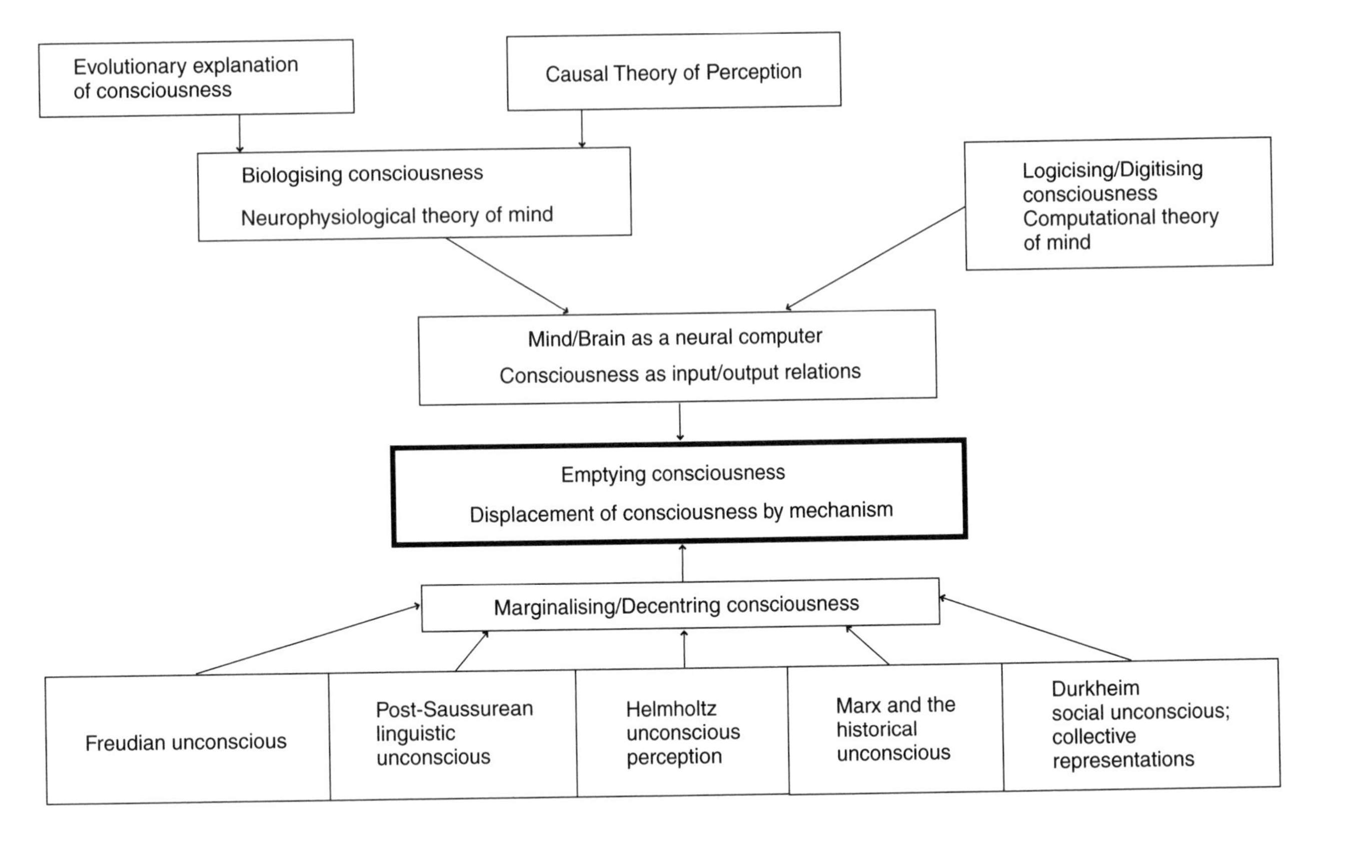

Emptying Consciousness

humanity as a whole, in no way reduces the extraordinary domination of reason in human life. Even the conduct of all-out war – that paradigm of unreason – requires the deployment of immensely complex reasoning (think of the logistical problems of getting the troops to the places where they are to slaughter one another, of keeping them fit enough and sufficiently well fed to make sure they are on top slaughtering form, and so on).[6]

Reason itself seems, moreover, to be rooted in something even deeper than itself. As Midgley points out, rationality is not merely a matter of cleverness, but also of integration, the latter meaning 'having a character, acting as a whole, having a firm and effective priority system' (p. 262). Nor is it a question of an abstract logic, a series of syllogisms, operating in, and directing, human behaviour, rather as the simple laws of physics operate in, and direct, the movements of material objects. Logic is only the skeleton of understanding, of realisation and recognition, and is no more identical with them than axes or dimensions are identical with experienced space. Reason is not an external force acting, as if from without, as a control upon passions, an alien presence within the soul. For reason is not primarily abstract ratiocination: its primary home is among the passions, the emotions; it is these latter that give reason the substrate upon which it can work, the soil from which it can arise. Reason and passion are united in *motivation*; in the practical reasoning that makes purposeful action possible.

Reason then is not an isolated faculty – it is rooted in so much else, it pervades so much of what we are, it is a fundamental attitude of the human psyche. Nor is it a single faculty, but a nexus of faculties: practicality; sensibleness; reasonableness; abstract reason using general laws, symbols and calculations; and, finally, its own skeleton, logic. And these are not monometric, arranged on a single scale.

What is special about reasoning in man is the extent to which it *can* be made explicit; that it can be uprooted from the practical needs of the moment to such a degree that the question of its integration with other faculties is raised and that it may seem at times to be (in Midgley's words) regarded as a colonising force. Man, uniquely, has identified reason as a *faculty*; has made reason conscious of itself; talks of general principles and identifies the rules of inference; even produces accounts, albeit conflicting, of logic, its skeleton. Man often specifically discriminates between behaviour he describes as being in accordance with reason and that which he thinks is unreasonable – and gives reasons for doing so.

In short, man reasons about reason; and reasons about his reasoning about reason; and so on. None of this kind of activity is observed in animals. And it is not a minor, second-order, development: the distances between an animal seemingly reasoning about how to escape from a trap in which it is caught and the hunter reasoning about how to set better traps (in the light of what has been observed about the animal's usual patterns of behaviour) are enormous. And there are further enormous distances between the hunter's reasoning and, say, Aristotle reasoning about the essence of reason and the rules of inference. And they illustrate the extent to which reason in man is not implicit, not entirely embedded in individual situations. Human reason rises above individual situations – in general laws and principles and rules of inference – in order to deal better with them. It is *explicit*.

The variousness of human reason – it encompasses the sensibleness embedded in practical activity and arguments conducted in symbolic logic about the adequacy of Fregean logic – stems from its explicitness. Explicitness permits a proliferation of the forms of reason beyond its narrow identification with, say, logic or mathematical reasoning, or with degrees of reasonableness in behaviour that could be arranged monometrically on a single scale.

The economic animal

For Marx, man is fundamentally a producing animal:

> Men can be distinguished from animals by consciousness, by religion or anything else you like. They themselves begin to distinguish themselves from animals as soon as they begin to *produce* their means of subsistence, a step which is conditioned by their physical organisation. By producing their means of subsistence, men are indirectly producing their actual material life.
>
> This mode of production must not be considered simply as being the production of the physical existence of the individuals. Rather it is a definite form of activity of these individuals, a definite *mode of life* on their part. As individuals express their life, so they are. What they are, therefore, coincides with their production, both with *what* they produce and *how* they produce.[7]

These are striking thoughts; but they do not seem to get to the heart of the matter, which lies in the unique *relation* of humans to their productivity. For it is out of this relation to, and attitude towards and awareness of, productivity, that *homo economicus* and much of human history have emerged. At the root of this distinctively human relation to productivity is an explicit awareness of the connection between needs and the objects that will satisfy them. This is the *sine qua non* of the transformation of objects of need (or objects that will satisfy need) into commodities.

Let us go back to the beginning, to the gathering and storing of naturally occurring foods. We can regard this as the most elementary form of productivity. Although the materials gathered (nuts, fruit, etc.) are not produced in the sense of being processed, the activity of gathering can be plausibly treated as a primitive form of labour and its results as products. What makes this count as 'labour' (while grazing does not) is the clear temporal separation between the process of obtaining the object of need and the actual satisfaction of the needs. The storing animal is concerned with the satisfaction of *future* needs. This does not, however, make non-human animals into producers in the way that humans are. Man is distinguished from other animals by the degree to which the future of need, implicit in the storing of food, is explicit. Human need has an *explicit* future tense: I want this now, but I will also need (more of) this in the future. Moreover, items of need are not only stored up for the future; they have the explicit character of commodities that will serve *any* comparable need; not only my future needs but those of any other creature who has a similar need.

At the heart of the transformation of objects of need into commodities (and so of the emergence of *homo economicus*), then, is the clear separation of the object of need from the moment of its satisfaction, and, increasingly, of the object of need from the experienced need itself and from the individual who experiences it. In the case of hunting and gathering, the need-related activity is not clearly separated from a need-driven one. With storage, we have the beginning of a separation of the two and the recognition of the future tense of need.

This becomes more fully explicit with the emergence of farming whose complex activities manifestly relate to future, rather than present, needs. The things needed to maintain life are grown (rather than merely found growing); are herded and tended (as opposed merely to being bumped into or chased after). The sheep being tended will not serve the present hunger experienced by the shepherd. The future tense of need is yet more explicit in agriculture (as opposed to animal husbandry) where man genuinely does 'produce the means of his own subsistence'. He not only stores the objects of need, but is in a large part responsible for their existence: gathering and storage are only a small part of an overall picture of complex need-related activities that will serve not present but future needs. Agriculture marks the full transformation of need-related activity into *labour* and the objects of need that result from that activity into produce.[8]

Agricultural man is thus at a decisive distance from animals – even from those animals such as squirrels whose instinctual storage of food seems to imply an inchoate recognition of the future tense of need, of needs distinct from actual sensations associated with need. The scene is now set for further major transformations in the field of need-related activity. *Labour* in the service of future rather than present needs dominates existence; and the objects of need acquire a life and status of their own. They are ripe to evolve into *commodities*. This latter change – which will open the way towards a collective life based largely upon cooperative manufacture – will be closely connected with the changing context of labour. In agricultural communities, it will become obvious that many people working together will better serve the needs of all than each working individually for himself.

The first collective will, one may surmise, base itself upon the natural occurring collective of the family. Within that unit, one individual will dominate over others: the women and children will work not only with, but also for, the father. As larger collectives form, so the scene will be set for the hierarchical differentiation into those for whom work is done and those who do the work, those who own the means of production and those who have only their labour to sell, into bosses and workers. The occasional war and the capture of slaves will expedite the emergence of this idea. The early collectives will also provide the context in which different talents can emerge: the strong, the shrewd, the skilful will come to the fore in different situations, in different crises. Upon this naturally occurring differentiation will be based a future division of labour – a horizontal differentiation in addition to the vertical one already mentioned. Finally, the collective will make explicit something that is implicit in mere loosely cooperative activity: the collectivisation of need.

The hunger faced by the collective as a result of the failure of their collective activity in a poor harvest is an explicitly collective hunger. The emergence of such a hunger marks a giant step in the socialisation of initially physiological needs and their liberation from the uncommunicated experience of the individual body. The equivalence of need – my hunger is the same as your hunger, as any hunger – has, through the provision of general, collective solutions, led to the objectification and generalisation of need. This is reinforced by the increasing interdependence of individuals upon one another; even in an inhuman slave camp, the masters have to recognise the reality and equivalence of the needs of the slaves in order that the slaves shall remain alive and productive. The collectivisation of need as (acknowledged) *scarcity*, described by Sartre as 'the fundamental but contingent relation of man to Nature'[9] is a most remarkable distancing of man from animality, from the organic state in which it is, of course, rooted. Scarcity is felt need projected from the physiological to the social plane, from the hypothalamus to the public domain. And out of this recognition of others' needs, of how others share the needs that one has oneself, out of this universalisation of one's own needs, many other things develop.

The transformation of the objects of need into *commodities* and the collectivisation of need into *scarcity* set the scene for the next step: the emergence of the explicit notion of the *value* of the object of need. This value will become increasingly uprooted from its primary source in experienced need; it will cease to be measured by the intensity with which the object appeals to the appetites. Traditionally, the explicit value of an object of need is thought to have been first quantified in terms of other objects serving other needs. The value of a sheep could be expressed in terms of the number of bushels of corn to which it was thought to be equivalent, in terms of its exchange value. And then exchange value itself underwent a gradual transition into, or was superseded by, *price*. As strangers met strangers and needs multiplied – for utensils as well as corn, for utility goods such as clothes as well as meat, for instruments of labour such as ploughs as well as for the products of labour, for luxuries such as jewellery as well as salt – it became impossible to quantify the exchange value of objects of need in terms of other objects of need. Currencies were developed as the universal measure of value – or at least as the universal bearer of exchange value – and increasingly money reflected *market value* rather than an *intrinsic value* that could be measured in the stomach or on the pulse, in hours or days free of physiological need.

With the transformation of objects of need into commodities and the displacement of exchange value by market value and prices,[10] labour was less frequently rewarded by a share of the products of the labour. These were anyway frequently too specialised to satisfy all the needs of the labourer. More often, labour was rewarded with the means of purchasing the fruits of others' labour. The common crop of those who laboured was money, the passport to all objects of need. With the further differentiation of labour, it was possible to be rewarded for activities which were only remotely connected with meeting physiological need. The early service industries – the priesthood, medicine, professional soldiering and so on – emerged.

The above sketch is not intended as a factual account of the early steps of human economic history nor even a rational reconstruction of the embryology of *homo economicus*. It is simply a device for drawing attention to, and annotating, the huge distances that separate perfectly ordinary human need-related activity from the need-driven behaviour of even the highest animals. Cash payment for non-productive activity within the service industries stands at an extraordinary distance from animal servicing of physiological need. Salaried man is at the far end of a vast journey, of an astounding distancing of need from itself resulting in the increasing liberation of need from its organic origin and from implicitness. Although I have described the components of this journey as if they followed naturally from one another, there is in fact neither logical nor mechanical necessity driving the species down this track. The story I have outlined is one of continuous progression into the unprecedented and the underivable. Why *should* one species, uniquely among the many millions of others, toil to satisfy needs that he will have in several years' time? Why should man be the only site in the planet where the fruits of labour are transformed into commodities? Why should he, alone among all the others, inhabit a world of wages and prices? Why should man alone be able to degrade the life of his conspecifics into a condition of living-for-others in which he is (to use Marx's phrase), 'personified labour-time'? Why should man, uniquely among the animals, be able to place such vast distances between himself and his needs so that he is able to serve them with such awesome efficiency? How did he get such insight into his needs, how did he get to know himself thus?

To suggest that human economic institutions have their origins in instinctual, animal behaviour is to deepen, not to reduce, the mystery and to make the gulf between man and animals more, not less, unfathomable, as I shall discuss presently.

The moral animal

We have already noted how human – and indeed much animal – behaviour is moved at least in part by reason rather than merely being 'energised' by drives or, at a lower level of organisation, driven by reflex mechanisms primed to respond stereotypically to stereotyped aspects of external events or objects. Of course, there are certain universal characteristics and stereotypical features of human behaviour, as there are of animal behaviour. But the universality and stereotyping is not as tight-meshed as in the case of animals; and, moreover, humans, unlike animals, recognise the universality. The behaving human's knowledge of what he is doing is pitched at a certain level of generality. Activity is related to explicit purpose, to explicit outcomes. The effects of behaviour are also explicitly available to the behaver; and this explicitness encompasses not only those effects that relate to the desired goal but the incidental effects on other humans, the equivalence of whose needs (similar content, equal importance) is recognised in principle, even if it is neither felt on the pulse nor acted on in practice. The respect for others which this presupposes is itself based upon a capacity to generalise oneself – to appreciate that, fundamentally, 'he' is like 'me' and has an existence that goes beyond his interactions with me. It is rooted in an intuition that those who enter my world themselves have worlds that I enter.

This explicit generality – which generalises not only the actions but also the actor and others upon whom the actions impinges – is the foundation of a distinctly human morality. If physiological need and instinctual drives energise behaviour, explicit generality, itself not derivable from physiological need or drives, makes it possible for behaviour to be shaped, mediated, even driven, by social pressures expressed in and transmitted through moral precepts and formal codes. These extend and elaborate the recognition, at the root of morality, of the other as equivalent to oneself.

Other things arise out of this. The moral animal feels the need for recognition. Recognition is, as Hegel emphasised, a fundamental human need, essential to a self-conscious and rational creature seeing himself as living in a coherent world with other creatures like himself. The moral animal can pass judgement on his own or another's behaviour, and his need for recognition (and so for the approval of others) can make such judgements – or even the possibility of them – influential in shaping behaviour. Most important from the point of view of the distinctively human morality, man can experience strong emotions about behaviour that does not directly impinge on himself.

The liberations of emotions separate from proximate occasioning events enables them to grow in complexity. This may be why man, the uniquely moral animal, is also uniquely the consciously evil animal – as a product, perhaps, of an unsatisfied need for recognition and the thwarting of attempts to acquire it.

To suggest that humans are unique among the animals in having a fully developed morality – in the sense of an explicit codified morality – is to run the danger of seeming to claim that humans are uniquely well behaved. Nothing could, of course, be further from the truth. Midgley marshalls sufficient evidence to suggest to a dispassionate observer that man is uniquely ill-behaved. No other animal destroys its conspecifics on such a mass scale; no other animal routinely tortures, unjustly imprisons and tyrannises over other animals; and so on. Man seems unique in the extent of his conscious evil. Midgley's argument that the wickedness of beasts is a projection of humans' sense of their own wickedness is persuasive: once the gods had been redefined as good and divine possession could no longer be blamed for human atrocities, the burden of guilt had to be made bearable by blaming the crimes on something else. The Beast Within, or beastly possession, provided the necessary scapegoat. Swinburne's claim that 'men ... have an awareness of goodness and moral obligation lacking in animals'[11] begins to seem rather odd. Surely, after Auschwitz ... But to react in this way is a sign that one has misunderstood the argument that is being advanced. The essential point is that human morality (and immorality) is qualitatively different from the constraints that regulate other animals' dealings with their conspecifics.

Just how easy it is to underestimate this difference is illustrated by Midgley's suggestion that human morality is derived from a rather weak but genuine instinctive inhibition against killing his own species, an inhibition very similar to that which controls the behaviour of other species. She then adds that 'Conceptual thought formalizes and extends what instinct started' (p. 41). This would seem fine if it did not seem to imply that the role of conceptual thought in developing a specifically human morality were a comparatively minor one – a question of giving final shape to something whose essential content has already been fixed; *merely* a question of formalisation and of extension. To see the difference between human morality and the instinctive constraints that regulate animals' behaviour towards their conspecifics in this way is to bypass the great mystery of human morality and to overlook a gulf between man and animals; to leap over, or diminish the huge gap between, say, the operation of instinctive inhibition on the one hand, and reading or writing a treatise on comparative morality on the other. It misses an essential difference between humanity (and inhumanity) and animality (and beastliness) in a fundamental area of life.

One way of reminding oneself of the size of this difference is to think of the transitions from tropisms to ethological traits; from ethological traits to customs; from customs to statutes; and from statutes to contracts. Man has undertaken the greatest part of the journey from ethological traits to contracts in isolation.

The political animal

Both humans and animals form groups. The simplest groups are spatial aggregations, but in both man and animals groups may take the form of complex social formations rather than mere spatial aggregations. In some animals, for example ants, the complexity is stereotyped, role differences being reflected in bodily structure; in others, such as many birds (e.g. geese, jackdaws), carnivores (wolves and wild dogs), elephants, whales and dolphins, and the higher primates, complexity of social grouping is based on rather open instincts and there is considerable room for improvisation. Leaving aside these differences in styles of grouping, we can say that most animals form groups and that these groups are social. They are not, however, political; and this is a crucial distinction between human and animal groupings. Man is, uniquely, a political animal.

What is meant by 'political'? Let me try to elucidate the term in its widest sense by looking at certain features of human groupings. The collectivisation of need into scarcity is related to the explicit recognition of common interests. Many animals act in a cooperative fashion, but this is highly stereotyped and is not based on, nor does it require, this recognition of common interests, a conscious pact. It occurs but is not affirmed: social behaviour has evolved biologically rather than being based in an historical social contract. In contrast, human groupings, which extend outside of natural groupings – such as those based on kinship or geographical accidents – are, and need to be, explicit. They cannot depend on natural inertia to maintain them. They will, for example, typically be reinforced by insignia underlining belonging; by oaths of loyalty and other explicit bonding procedures. Hence clans gathered under totems, teams, clubs, professional organisations, nations. Group identity is *asserted*; and this will emphasise the threat represented to common group interests in the context of scarcity (a permanent possibility of human life) by the interests of other groupings. Groupings will therefore be not only internally cooperative but externally adversarial. They will have the appearance of concentrations of power opposed to other concentrations of power.

Although there is a hostile relationship between conspecific animal groups, the reason for that hostility is not explicit. That is why what I have said so far is only the beginning of the political story. Despite the benefits of cooperation, and though groupings are founded on the basis of an explicit equivalence of 'your' need and 'my' need, the individual human's interest cannot be totally absorbed into the common interest. In consequence, there will always be the possibility of conflict. This is especially likely as groups are functional or beneficial only with respect to certain needs or certain aspects of their satisfaction. Two individuals may cooperate in the collective cultivation of a field but will be in conflict when competing for the attentions of a particular woman. A group – and the power structure within a group – may have legitimacy with respect only to particular goals.

In order to maintain the stability of the group even when cooperation is not clearly of benefit, power will have to be invested in an individual, or group of individuals, to whose authority the group as a whole submits. This will be necessary to ensure that individuals conform to group needs even at the cost of their own temporary disadvantage. Indeed, the stabilisation of the group and the emergence of a hierarchy, and a ruling class, will create a sub-population of permanently disadvantaged individuals; or individuals who put more into the group than they get from it. There will, moreover, be a tendency to extend the legitimate power of the authority to areas other than those in which it maintains the coherence of the group in cooperative activity. Sub-groups will work together to maintain that illegitimately extended power; the power structure within the group, embodied in certain acknowledged hierarchies, will become self-legitimating, with the mobilisation of religious, moral and rationalising and material forces.

This, at least, is one of the most popular explanatory paradigms of political philosophy. At any rate, it sets the scene for power struggles between sub-groups which will have all the character of the external conflicts between one group and another. Factions will emerge, expressing the feelings of disaffected individuals that the power of the Authority is alien to them. Such factions, expressing collective grievances, a complex sense of rights and duties and obligations, are central to politics. They are totally absent from animal group in-fighting, at the very least because animals do not have the means to express complex grievances, even less to turn them into slogans, manifestoes and political parties.

In arguing for the uniquely political nature of human groupings, it is not necessary to deny the complex reality of animal ensembles – either of the transient groupings of creatures that may hunt in packs or more permanent groupings maintained for less narrowly defined ends, including companionship. As Midgley points out, several groups of animals

> have independently 'invented' fairly advanced forms of social life. They are, that is, not 'anonymous herds' whose members stay together and take no notice of one another. They can *do* things together, help and look after one another to some extent, and have individual friendships. (p. 335)

At the root of many animal groups is 'attachment; a bond of affection constantly fed and maintained by friendly attentions' (p. 338). Peacemaking is an important feature of animal social life: 'The positive social bond consists of friendly gestures that arise from the need to consider an existing possibility of aggression.' Group stability is maintained by a dominance hierarchy which is far from tyrannical; indeed,

> rank is very closely linked with the behaviour typical of parent and child. Those of lower rank defer to those they respect in the same way that they did to their own parents, and where conflict looms, one participant has often only to make infantile gestures to appease the other, who responds with parental ones. (pp. 335–6)

The complexity of animal groups, then, is not in question; and, as in the case of humans, animal groups answer to a collective need that is inchoately collectivised. Animal groups too may acquire a strengthened solidarity in response to the threats posed by other groupings, either within or outside of the index group. The groups, however, are not explicit in the sense of being liable to develop anything like a constitution, a codified law or a myth of their own origin and legitimacy. There are no formal rights, duties or obligations and no appeal to them or rhetoric of them. Such codified, explicit laws, laid down in permanent documents, enable human groupings to be formed and maintained which are not defined or limited by spatial cohabitation: between individuals who have never met one another; between large numbers of individuals who could never, because of their numbers, encounter one another; and across continents and centuries. The manner in which I can be treated by the group corresponding to Great Britain has been decisively influenced by the signing of the Magna Carta. Such are political groupings; and in this very important and wide-ranging sense, animal groupings are not political groupings at all. Man is, uniquely, a political animal.

The historical animal

All species change with time but the vast majority of these changes are mediated through species-wide alterations in bodily structure and composition, themselves a reflection of changes in the genetic blueprint. The human animal changes at an astonishing rate and, in contrast with other animals, most of these changes are mediated by changes in collective knowledge and skills, themselves embodied in rapidly evolving artefacts and in the huge accumulations of knowledge housed outside of the body. The quickening pace of change is beautifully summarised by John Maynard Smith:

> About 400 million years ago the first aquatic vertebrates evolved; at least two million years ago man's ancestors first chipped stones to make simple tools. Less than ten thousand years ago, in the neolithic revolution, animals and plants were first domesticated. If a film, greatly speeded up, were to be made of vertebrate evolution, to run for a total of two hours, tool-making man would appear only in the last minute. If another two-hour film were made of the history of tool-making man, the domestication of animals and plants would be shown only during the last half-minute, and the period between the invention of the steam engine and the discovery of atomic energy would be only one second.[12]

With the emergence of *homo sapiens*, it would seem that history has broken free of evolution. As Maynard Smith (p. 312) observes, 'we can be fairly confident that the "nature" (i.e. genetically determined capacities) of human beings has not greatly changed since the neolithic revolution, since 7,000 years is too short a period for major evolutionary changes'; yet during this time the life of human beings has changed out of all recognition. Moreover, especially since we have started planning for our remote descendants as well as for ourselves and our contemporaries, the human species advances towards its own future with its eyes at least partly open.

Of course, individual organisms can adapt to changed circumstances and some of these behavioural adaptations can be transmitted directly without the mediation of genetic change. Tits learn how to open milk bottles, macaque monkeys acquire the habit of washing their sweet potatoes before they eat them. These new behaviour patterns are culturally transmitted from generation to generation; their emergence is an historical and not an evolutionary event. But in all animals apart from man, they contribute in only a minor way to species change; they are merely sporadic events. In the vast majority of cases, human advances are transmitted to future generations by cultural and not by genetic means. Maynard Smith again:

> There is no need to wait for the genetic assimilation of a new adaptive advance made by an individual. Such advances are transmitted to future generations by cultural and not by genetic means; children do not inherit a 'racial memory'; they learn what their parents teach them. ... It is this change from genetic to cultural transmission which determines the differences between evolutionary and historical processes, and is responsible for the greater rapidity of the latter. (p. 313)

In animals, by contrast, 'instead of one historical event leading directly to another, as in human history, ... each such event has been followed by long periods of genetic evolution' (p. 314).

The opposition between Nature and History has been an important rallying point for political and social theorists – especially self-styled progressives and conservatives. Marxists and other left-wing thinkers are irritated by writers who attribute the Order of (Human) things to the work of Nature, when it is, in their opinion, clearly historically derived; for this eternalises the way things are and consequently obstructs changes that would benefit society as a whole. The appeal to Nature – and consequently to unchangeability – is, they argue, very much in the interest of those who are benefiting from the status quo. Conservatives not only naturalise the social order but also the individual's position in it: our 'proper stations' correspond to our own intrinsic properties, rather than being the product of conflict and historical accident and stabilised by self-legitimating activity of the privileged. An aristocrat, the naturalising, essentialist, conservative argument goes, is intrinsically aristocratic; his point of origin confers certain properties upon him that befit him for his high station. The opposite viewpoint, espoused by those of a progressive and melioristic turn of mind, is that, far from there being a fixed individual and general human nature, human nature is culturally or historically determined and will vary from culture to culture. Likewise, an individual's nature is culturally determined or conditioned by his own history, by the social experience to which he has been exposed since birth.

One could reconcile the warring viewpoints of the 'naturalists' and the 'culturalists' or the 'naturalists' and the 'historicists' by saying that it is human nature to be historically determined and to encounter nature mediated by culture. This is not, however, to deny the innate or the genetic element in human nature. Although humanity has changed out of all recognition independently of any change in the human genome, that genome still crucially shapes what we are. We are not determined by, say, our physiology but we are embedded in it; it is the ground upon which we stand, the natural pitch upon which we play our cultural games, the coordinates with respect to which our history unfolds. And this is true at the psychological level as well. There is a legitimate analogy between the jealousy one animal may feel towards another that has secured a large piece of meat and the jealousy one individual may feel towards another because he can afford to go to an expensive restaurant. The two situations are analogous, yes; but there is an enormous distance between them, a distance I marked out in the Economic Animal section.

To fail to see this distance – and more generally to fail to notice the extent to which evolving culture, rather than fixed nature, determines the content of human lives – is to overlook a profound difference between man and animals. As history unfolds, we do not lose our roots in nature – our embodied state ensures that we remain a piece of nature – but we diverge more and more from other pieces of nature. Man is a living creature whose evolution has forked off from the general evolutionary process. His environment is increasingly a man-made one and his preoccupations distinctively human.

Since we are talking about Culture and Nature, a word or two about Structural Anthropology may be in order here. Consider Lévi-Strauss's meta-myth about cooking.[13] Man discovered that food could be transformed from its natural state, while still retaining its edibility and nutritional value; this, according to Lévi-Strauss, was a crucial moment in the establishment of an explicitly human culture set off against Nature. The functionalist explanation of cooking can be set aside: the food probably didn't taste any better cooked (the preference for cooked over raw food is acquired) and the microbiological advantage of cooking was probably not evident at the time that cooking entered the human scene. No, behind the preference for the cooked over the raw was a desire to set oneself off from nature: Man, the Cooking Animal, reaffirms his difference from, and superiority to, the beasts and asserts his distinctive species being. From this initial difference unravelled a thousand distinctions and distances from the other beasts and the world of nature in general.

This somewhat flippant account of the thesis of *The Raw and the Cooked* is offered only because it provides another example of a tendency to overlook, by rather taking for granted, an extraordinary property of human beings: their ability to *elaborate* differences and out of them create enormous multi-dimensional distances. The cooking story is not sufficient to account for the origin of culture or of the culture–nature divide; for what it leaves unexplained is the propensity *to make so much out of a difference*. This propensity is an *ability*; it is possible only because, for humans, differences are explicitly appreciated, so that their implications can be elaborated. Animals and men are different; but the 'we are different from them' is different for animals than for man; we are conscious of, and make much of, this difference. Without *this* difference – this different attitude to difference – no amount of happy or astounding accidents could account for the emergence of a vast proliferating culture increasingly separating man from other pieces of nature.

The technological animal

> Men make tools, and so can change their environment to suit themselves instead of evolving new, genetically determined adaptations to new environments.[14]

Man, according to Benjamin Franklin, is The Toolmaking Animal. In a sense this definition begins too far along the road taken by organisms in manipulating their own environment to ensure survival, to bring out the full strangeness of man. To see what he is, you have to step back a little further.

Begin at the beginning. Think of a simple multicellular organism moving, by virtue of a tropism, in the direction of an area of different pH in the fluid medium in which it happens to be. The purpose of this behaviour is to keep it in an environment most favourable to survival, i.e. in an environment least likely to overthrow the polyphasic dynamic equilibrium that describes the conditions under which the organism counts as being alive. The organism is unaware of its need to move towards the more favourable environment, cannot anticipate what may happen to change its environment and has no strategy to cope with changes in the pH outside of those which it can correct by tropism-driven swimming. In contrast, a human animal recognises a vast number of the conditions necessary for its life and comfort and is constantly taking steps to ensure that not only present but also future comfort and safety are ensured. The maintenance of, or the bringing about of, conditions directly, indirectly or remotely related to pleasure, comfort and survival, is an abiding preoccupation of the human animal. It is tempting to claim that, in this respect, man is no different from many other animals. But there are important differences that can be highlighted by using the tropism-driven primitive organism as a zero point to measure how far man has travelled into self-consciousness – and, indeed, to make the road along which he has travelled visible.

Human survival-related activity takes the form of solving problems by means of artefacts using *methods, rules and techniques*. The solutions sought involve the application of principles, conceived at different levels of generality, to particular circumstances. Underneath all man's problem-solving is this intuition of *a general principle with particular application*. The here-and-now is always an *instance*. The development of enduring artefacts with certain general properties designed to enable them to deal with whole classes of problem-situations exemplifies this extraordinary, inexplicable intuition apparently denied to other animals.

Man is the tool-making animal, *homo sapiens* is *homo faber*; whereas at best certain animals may be tool-finding animals. Animal tools are neither manufactured, nor are they preserved and stored against future uses on future occasions. The early human artefacts were extensions of the body, and modelled on the body's powers, to magnify those powers. With the advent of the wheel, the search for technical solutions to the problems of living was liberated from the implicit and severely limiting metaphor of the body. Technology woke into itself and tools began their long evolution to the kinds of gadget we now take for granted: artefacts designed in accordance with abstract solutions provided for generalised problems. The means to satisfy needs became quite separate from the activity of the needing body or even the form of that activity.

The development of distinctively human tools has been associated with an increasingly clear appreciation of both the nature of need and of the relationships between the events that will bring about their satisfaction. Tools are the most powerful possible testimony to the self-knowledge of human need. It is in technology that, above all, the explicitness of the human condition to humans is made apparent. Technology demands explicitness; it is explicitness embodied. This is vividly illustrated when the satisfaction of a need is reduced to a path between two explicitly defined states and that path is redescribed in the form of a computer program. (This is not to say that the computer is itself explicit. Rather, it embodies explicitness. Just as the sounds of language are not themselves meaning, but the embodiments of meaning that are 'cashed' elsewhere. The explicitness is in the technologist not the technology.)

The fact that in the early stages of tool production, the underlying principles were not made fully explicit is illustrated by the extraordinary constancy of the size (some 9 inches) and shape of hand axes over 100,000 years across several continents. As Maynard Smith points out, 'this wide distribution in space and time of a particular type of tool implies a process of meticulous copying for many generations' (Maynard Smith, p. 315). The value of 'try it and see' and the search for the underlying principles, which lie at the root of modern technological advance were not recognised until the Renaissance, whose exemplary – indeed emblematic – figure is Leonardo da Vinci. This late entry of the fully developed experimental method is a tribute to the egregious character of the method. In Maynard Smith's two-hour film of tool-making man, 'try it and see' has been around only for between two and three seconds.

The differences between the tools used by animals – stones for throwing at enemies, sticks for getting at food that would otherwise be out of reach – and those used by man are not merely differences of degree. That man makes his own tools; that those tools are not mere extensions of his body or modelled on his body; that he stores tools for future use; that the tools have been designed with reference to stated general principles; that they may be enormously complex (as in the case of the robots used in car manufacture) – these are all symptoms of a fundamental underlying difference. To suggest that a chimpanzee picking up a rock to scare off an intruder is in the same business as an individual calculating the necessary quantities of radioactive material to make an atomic bomb, determining the size of the explosion it would cause, pondering how big an explosion would be necessary to demoralise the enemy sufficiently to make it surrender, thinking about the dangers presented to his own side by failing to meet certain storage conditions, is to stretch credulity to the limit.[15]

The classifying animal

There is a (somewhat tendentious) sense in which all animals classify the contents of those parts of the world they come into contact with. A primitive multi-cellular organism that moves towards a life-sustaining type of substance and away from another, life-threatening one – for example, the flatworm moving towards food and away from strong light – could be described as *behaviourally* classifying the contents of the world into 'good' things and 'bad' things. But these 'behavioural classifications' are only implicit and really exist only in the organism – man – that observes and describes the organism's behaviour. Any labels we give to the two types of item have specific content only in so far as the labels belong to a much wider system of classification – namely the system of language – the use of which it would be absurd to attribute to a primitive organism.[16] To suggest that such an organism has the concepts 'good' and 'bad' – with the meanings these terms have for us, with the work they do for us – would be no less implausible than to suggest that it has the concepts 'Good for me' and 'Bad for me'; or 'Liable to improve my chances of survival' and 'Liable to cause me harm'; and so on.

The claim that man is uniquely 'the classifying animal' is easy to sustain when the only rivals are primitive multi-cellular organisms. It is less easy to sustain when one considers the higher animals. In order to do this it is necessary to look more carefully at the nature of classification.

First of all, true classification deals in universals. The classes corresponding to terms – 'dog', 'green', etc. – are infinite and open-ended and encompass a whole universe of possible instances. Secondly, it is systematic: classification does not operate through a heap of isolated terms. The terms are closely interrelated; they belong to sets ('green', 'blue', etc.); they have logical relations to one another (synonyms, hyponyms, admissible combinations, appropriateness of application); and they are comprehensive, in the sense that they cover all possibilities in a defined range. Thirdly (and this follows from the first two points), classification cannot be embodied in, or reduced to, or dissolved in, discriminant behaviour directed towards the classified objects, but involves the use of symbols specific to the purpose. These symbols will be explicitly symbols: they will not be mistaken for the things classified; they will stand off from the world whose contents are being classified.

Only man is a classifier in this sense. For only he is explicitly – that is to say separately – aware of the labels of the classes into which things are classified and is able to distinguish the classes from the things classified. In human consciousness, the classes, and their labels, have a separate existence. Generality has a home of its own. And because of this, objects can not only be classified but, since the classes are distinguished from their members, *re*-classified. The real nature of human classification – as opposed to any animal analogue based on discriminant behaviour or upon signalling – is revealed in the fact that man is the re-classifying animal. Unlike creatures 'classifying' objects by discriminant behaviour, man does not assimilate the objects entirely into the categories to which they are assigned. The objects remain distinct from their classes; and so they are available for indefinite re-classification.

Nothing could be in more complete contrast to this than the 'behavioural classification' thought to be implicit in, for example, the response of a robin to a red patch painted on a brown background. The robin attacks objects that conform to this pattern and it is argued that the robin has effectively placed such objects in a general class – that of 'rival robins' or 'enemies'. The fact that we cannot confidently say what that class is, or that the class will vary in accordance with how *we* describe the robin's behaviour, should make it clear that, so far as the robin is concerned, no such class exists. Stimulus generalisation, such that an organism will exhibit a conditioned response not only to the conditioning stimuli but to other stimuli which share with it certain characteristics, has also been taken to be an animal equivalent of classification. The animal, it is argued, by behaving towards a range of similar stimuli as if they were the same, is effectively classifying those stimuli together. Unfortunately, this would seem to base classification on *failures* behaviourally to discriminate between similar stimuli. And it would follow from this that all entities which elicit the same behaviour are being classified together. This would suggest that animals have access to very abstract categories indeed, such as 'air', 'enemies' and even 'walkables', 'barkabilia', 'space', etc.

All true classification is explicit; that is, the class label is distinct from the class members. In behavioural 'classification', the label does not exist except in the mind of the spectator – the human being – observing the behaviour.

The talking animal

The feature most commonly invoked in attempts to pinpoint the differences between man and other animals is, of course, man's possession of language, and discussion of classification brings us naturally to this. Much of the debate revolves around whether man is unique in having language (in other words, whether the other animals, which assuredly have communication systems, really have language at all) or whether his uniqueness resides only in certain features of his language.[17]

It is important not to get side-tracked into secondary issues. My own position is that human language has certain fundamental differences from all other animal communication systems (or rather one fundamental difference from which many others follow; or a fundamental difference which determines the entire character of human language). Whether we should conclude from this that only humans have 'true language' is a mere matter of definition and therefore of little interest.

So in what sense is human language unique? One has first of all to consider its scope and consequences. Language ranges over the entire experienced universe, penetrating every aspect of reality at every level – at the level of the atom, of the cell, of the leaf, of the tree, of the forest, of the nation, of the planet, of the galaxy. And language has a multitude of types of levels. For example, I can talk about what you did; about your feelings about what you did; about my theory about your feelings about what you did; about your attitude to my theory about what you did; about my feelings about your attitude to my theory; and so on. Talk, moreover, is not confined to the actual. Our ability to refer to that which is absent is only the beginning; we can refer not only to the absent actual but also to the absent possible (and language has given birth to vast, proliferating worlds of the possible that enormously outnumber and out size the unimaginably large actual one); and to the impossible. To quote George Steiner, '*Anything* can be said and, in consequence written, about *anything*':

> Only language knows no conceptual, no projective finality. We are at liberty to say anything, to say what we will about anything, about everything and nothing (the latter a particularly striking and metaphysically intriguing licence). No deep-lying grammatical constraint, if any such can indeed be shown to obtain, abrogates the anarchic ubiquity of possible discourse ... Language need halt at no frontier, not even, in respect of conceptual and narrative constructs, at that of death ... Inside grammar, future tenses, optatives, conditionals are the formal articulation of the conceptual and imaginative phenomenality of the unbounded.[18]

The possibilities of language are unconfined by the physiological constraints that limit other human activities. As Steiner has said elsewhere, 'Man has talked himself free of organic constraint.'[19]

So much for the scope of human language. What of its consequences? These are so enormous that it is impossible to see them whole: language is the air in which our minds breathe, the very space in which our consciousness is deployed. There is, consequently, no place outside of language from which we can see it. As a result, some thinkers have focused on relatively small, though telling, consequences of man's being the talking animal. Nietzsche and Marcel,[20] for example, were sufficiently struck by one linguistic activity peculiar to man – that of promising – to see it as a defining characteristic. Man was 'the promising animal'. What excited them was the fact that promising – and, more particularly, the keeping of promises – involved the individual in committing his own future. This in turn presupposed an explicit sense of one's own future and a belief in one's own continuity. If I promise to do something (or sign a contract, or undertake certain responsibilities), I bind at least part of my future self. I am working on the assumption that my future self will feel itself to be bound by my present self, that it will recognise it as the same as *its* self. Promising makes the future and the extension of a unified self over time, explicit. It is, however, but one aspect of language-mediated explicitness, albeit an important and exemplary one.

One could think of virtually every aspect of civilisation, and of humanity as opposed to animality, as a consequence of the curious gift of language. But placing language at the root of all that divides man from the rest of the animal kingdom and opposes civilisation to nature will be unilluminating unless we consider the phenomenon itself and try to identify what it is about language that accounts for its scope and momentous consequences.

Every attempt to pinpoint features unique to human language seem doomed to refutation by counter-examples. Let us consider some such attempts:

1. Human language refers to that which is absent

Whereas animal cries usually refer to (or, strictly, are triggered by) present dangers, prey, etc., human talk is not so restricted.

Counter-example: the bees' dance, referring to pollen supply which is absent in the sense of being outside of the current sensory field of both the sender and recipient of the message. Of course, such absence is a restricted absence. The dance could not refer to a future, or a remote past, or a never-existing supply of pollen. Even so, reference to the absent does not seem to be a sharply distinguishing feature of human language as opposed to animal communication systems.

2. Human language uses arbitrary, conventional, rather than natural signs

Counter-example: again the bees' dance. The elements of the dance bear no natural relation to the things they signify. There is, for example, no physical similarity between the waggle dance and the locations it is used to signify.

3. Human language has a complex syntax not evident in animal signalling systems

Counter-example: yet again, the bees' dance. One could regard the different components of the dance and the relationships between them as being analogous to different parts of speech and their syntactical ordering. Certainly, there are rules of combination that seem essential to the message. Grammar, however, is very much in the eye of the beholder. It is possible to describe animal languages in terms of complex rules that, under the most objective definitions of grammar, seem grammatical – just as one can describe animal behaviour as belief-driven and these beliefs in propositional terms.

The point is that to look for specific distinguishing features between human language and animal communication systems is misconceived. It will be obvious, of course, that whatever features are considered, they will be developed to an unimaginably greater degree in human language. But this will not capture the fundamental difference between human and animal language. For one can always redescribe animal communication systems in terms that make them seem like human language; as if, for example, they were based on a system of arbitrary signs organised grammatically and capable of having reference to absent as well as present objects, to particulars as well as generalities. It will be more fruitful to ask ourselves why human language has its unique capacity for development.

Let us consider arbitrariness. This, according to Saussure, is the 'primordial' fact of language; and yet it is a feature arguably shared by the signs used in non-human communication. The arbitrary sign is not a mere index, causally related to that which it signifies, as clouds are to rain. Nor is it an icon, signifying 'naturally' in virtue of replicating some aspect of the significate. Arbitrariness thus sets off the sign, separating it from a causal net or a mere mirroring of reality. The arbitrary sign is an explicit sign; it could not be mistaken for the significate, or an effect or consequence or symptom of the significate, or another instance of it. Arbitrary signs are signs that wear their status – the fact that they are signs – as signs on their sleeves. And yet man is the only animal who has appreciated this and exploited its possible consequences. If the sign is uprooted from the significate, it may not only be able to signify a present significate or one that is absent but actual; it may also be used to signify the possible (but non-existent) and the impossible. Signifying, moreover, may not only be uprooted from the significate but also from the context in which the significate is usually signified. It may, finally, be uprooted from the natural processes of signifying: from utterance. These developments seem inevitable; but their inevitability is an effect of hindsight and their non-inevitability can be inferred from the fact that no other animal has used its communication system in the way that humans have. The consequences are momentous.

The most important consequence results from the separation of the processes of signifying from the act of signification, from utterance. This is the emergence of writing – often, though dangerously, thought of as: the storage of communication outside of the moment of its being communicated; the storage of information outside of the body; or the transformation of communication-events into enduring objects. With writing, the transmission and preservation of knowledge no longer depends on the frailty of the human body and, in particular, the limitations of memory and attention. It is on writing, and on comparable systems of written communication, more than on anything else, that the divergence of human history from bodily evolution, and the astonishingly rapid cultural evolution from physiological change, have depended. Without writing, the process by which accumulated knowledge and expertise is handed down from one generation to the next – so that each generation is the beneficiary of the experience and collective genius of all who have gone before – would not have been possible.

The most important and most distinctive features of human language are consequences of its having the explicit status of being a language. The uniqueness of human language is that it is a communication system that knows what it is. Humans are not alone in having a language composed of arbitrary signs; but they are alone in seeing that arbitrariness and exploiting the possibilities that flow from it. Of course other animals may sometimes play with signs. They may, for example, produce warning cries in the spirit of fun and mischief, suggesting that they have some dim sense of the status of signs as signs. But that sense is at best nascent and transient and never unfolds even to the extent that would justify one in thinking that the animal was explicitly aware that its signs were a way of bringing about a belief in another animal – a belief based on the second animal's recognition of the intention of the first. In contrast, the sense of the other person trying to say something is elementary in humans. It is part of the basic structure of ordinary communication. The entry into human language (as opposed to the acquisition of mere competence in signalling) involves recognition of signs as signs. Understanding mediated through arbitrary signs has to be based on an appreciation that the signs are signs. Speech, because it has to be understood in order to have its effects, can fail to have those effects. Signs operating through the causal mechanisms of natural association cannot fail in this way.[21]

The distinctive nature of human language is not, then, based in the objectively demonstrable complexities of the system. Any system can be redescribed in such a way as to seem enormously complex; it can have complexities and sophistications foisted upon it. So we can, if we like, find grammars and parts of speech and propositions in the language of bees. But the proof of the pudding is in the eating and, if the bee language has these properties, the bees do remarkably little with them. They certainly haven't used them to improve pollen-finding over the millennia in which they have been using their language. Whereas man, if he does indeed have only the same means at his disposal as bees, has made much, much more of them. He has (to borrow von Humboldt's phrase) 'made infinite use of finite means'. This is because in using language we are conscious of language itself; when we speak, we are explicitly aware of what we are doing or trying to do. It is this that has enabled us to do almost anything with our language – to the point where discourse has developed an unlimited complexity.

The most telling sign of this consciousness – that language is language, that signs are signs – is the all-pervasive presence of metalanguage. This is evident from the earliest years. Tiny children relish the sound of words in parallel with appreciating their meaning. They play with language as well as use it. Punning, rhyming, etc. are early, not late, forms of linguistic behaviour. And the metalinguistic dimension remains a major presence in human discourse. We quote what other people say; and so do toddlers ('Man said "No!" to doggy'). We imitate (and mock) how they say it, we ask for the meaning of words. We are taught the grammar and general characteristics of language. We do exercises to improve our powers of self-expression or to modify our accents or our tone of voice. We are aware of how others may be differently aware from ourselves of certain features in our own speech. We learn others' languages and dialects. And so on, through the innumerable layers of consciousness and self-consciousness of talk and writing and talk about talk and talk about writing and writing about writing and writing about talk about writing. Metalinguistic awareness reaches from the top to the bottom of language. Man may not be uniquely the talking animal; but he is uniquely the metalinguistic animal.

At the highest level, we should note that he is the only animal who is astonished by his language, is intrigued by it and has theories about it. His is the only species that communicates theories of communication. *Homo linguisticus* may be a small sub-population of *homo sapiens* but he is a symptomatic one. He is, of course, a sub-species of *homo theoreticus* (if the macaronic may be forgiven), a character whom we shall discuss presently.

Am I arguing that man is, after all, The Talking (or meta-talking) Animal? Is it language, then, that lies at the bottom of everything, of all the differences between humanity and animality? No. The uniqueness of human language, and in particular of its metalinguistic dimension, is itself only a symptom of a deeper difference; of the uniqueness of man the explicit animal. What language does is to make explicitness itself explicit: in language, the sense of material objects, for example, is embodied in events – words – that are independent of those things. (I have developed this point of view in more detail elsewhere.[22]) Language makes explicit sense itself explicit: it lifts it off the specific material objects in which for non-human animals it is entirely embedded or embodied and for human animals is primarily embedded or embodied. The arbitrariness of linguistic signs distances them from that which they signify.[23]

The sense-making animal

We have only glimpses of how other animals see the world whereas we have first-hand knowledge of how humans (or at least ourselves and those we know or know of) see the world. It is easy, therefore, to exaggerate the differences between man and animals; in particular, to overlook the faculties animals share with, but are unable to communicate to, us. How much idea does a dog watching me type this chapter have of what I am doing or thinking? Probably more than he could tell me. Even allowing for this lack of access to the inner life of animals, however, it seems as if humans have impulses that take them far beyond the animal world; at the root of these impulses seems to be the desire to make general sense of things.

For Lichtenberg, man was 'the cause-bearing animal'. This is striking but too narrow to capture man's great theorising impulse. Theorising has two major sources: the practical need to make things go better, to meet one's needs more effectively (goal-orientated theorising); and impractical wonder. The second of these sources is often overlooked because, in the mythology of early man (i.e. the myths we late men have about our ancestors) the technical and the theological seem to converge. The role of the theologian, we are told, was to determine the attitudes and wishes of the gods and to promote those ritual behaviours which would make them favourable to man and his purposes. A Rain Dance is both a recognition of Higher Beings and a practical technique for bringing about that desired end. Nevertheless, the sense that there are Higher Beings is based upon an ultimately impractical wonder, whose supremely impractical expression is the intuition that this life and this world are only a small part of what there is and one that, moreover, may not be all that important.

This theorising or, more generally, *sense-making* instinct carries man through specific solutions to specific problems to the greater problems. Man is an explaining and explanation-seeking animal. The faculty has several components: the impulse to classify and generalise; the need to control the world in accordance with the purposes and goals related to need; and a feeling that there are further purposes operating in, and more powerful controls operating on, the world. The intuition that there are gods and that there are laws of nature has the same ultimate source; and it converges in the concept of necessity, fate, destiny or The Law. Their continuing close relationship is dramatically demonstrated in the way in which, according to A.N. Whitehead, the Principle of the Uniformity of Nature derived from the unification of the gods into One God in Christian culture.[24] The quest of the explaining animal is a protracted one and carries him a long way: it begins with the casual classification of experience had in the open field of everyday life and advances towards the testing of explicitly formulated hypotheses under controlled conditions. He starts out from the attempt to make low-grade practical predictions, and so sharpen expectancy to particular expectations, and advances to the search for laws of the widest scope. In the course of his journey from the one to the other, man woke out of his status as a creature simply finding the most convenient and efficient and safest ways round the world and started seeing the world as a theatre for investigations. A crucial step was the intuition of, and consequently the search for, *general* solutions; his seeing that a particular problem is but an instance of a whole class of similar problems and that the right sort of solution to the problem would be a solution to a whole class of problems.

Man, then, is to a unique degree a sense-making animal. And the kind of sense he makes, or tries to make, of himself and of the world he finds himself in, is unique. Granted, all animals make some kind of sense of the world. They 'sus out' the ecological niche in which they find themselves. And they try, in some cases, to extend that sense by exploratory and even experimental behaviour. But their need for sense is satisfied, even saturated, by outcomes that satisfy physiological need. Art, science, philosophy and religion are all manifestations, to a greater or lesser degree, of a hunger for more, or more complete, sense, activated by a feeling that the deliverances of experience are an incomplete account of what there is, and of what it means.[25]

And so man is an art-making animal, creating artefacts that serve no clear practical purpose; creating images of himself – in words, in pictures – in order to know himself better; creating images of the world, to impose order on felt chaos; 'cultivating the emotions for their own sake' (Whitehead) to escape the insufficiency of ordinary experience. The peculiar character of art and what it implies about human distinctiveness is often not fully appreciated. In her discussion of behaviour suggestive of dancing observed by Jane Goodall in chimpanzees, Mary Midgley suggests that this 'throws a sharp and sudden light on the origin of human sport and dancing'. 'Naturally,' she adds, 'this sort of thing is not just what goes on at the Bolshoi Ballet. But it does something to indicate on what bush, growing out of what soil, ballet is a flower.'[26] We have only to consider what distances separate the guileless brief ritual of the chimpanzees (seen by Goodall only three times in ten years of observation) from the complex and self-conscious procedures of ballet to doubt this claim. If the chimpanzees had a Rain Dance correspondent, then I might start considering this claim as plausible. Midgley's suggestion, discussed earlier in relation to human morality, that 'Conceptual thought formalizes and extends what instinct started', is, as I expressed it then, to encapsulate the entire miracle in an aside and so overlook it.

Man is also the scientific animal, driven by a sense that the sense of the world is incomplete though it may be completable – in, for example, discoverable laws of nature. And he is the metaphysical animal, a wondering animal, whose sense of the incompleteness of the sense of the world is less focused, more hungry, and drives his attempts to reach a vision that unifies the scattered occasions of experience. He is the religious or spiritual animal whose sense that the sense of the world is incompletable – because life terminates in death and we are finite beings set down in infinity – leads him to postulate a Supreme Being or a Next World beyond this world where the sense of this world and of himself is completed. He is the death-discovering animal; and, uniquely aware that his own existence is not securely grounded, he transforms his abstract, unfocused fears, his awareness of the continual possibility of suffering, into the image of One who will answer all fears, who can control all suffering; and turns death from a terminus into a gateway and 'the world' (itself a concept produced by very high-level synthetic activity of consciousness) into '*this* world', a limited whole, set off against a Next World. Physical, moral, existential and spiritual uncertainty converge in the dream of a benign all-powerful Being; or the rival dream of a benign all-powerful science that will permit complete control over the universe and bring an end to death, suffering and all that conflicts with human desires.

Man, driven by an active, *cultivated* uncertainty, uniquely comes face to face with the irremediably incomplete intelligibility of the world and the inexplicability of the fact that the world is intelligible at all. Here, at the boundaries of sense, in his astonishment at the senseless fact that the world makes partial sense, the sense-making animal is at an infinite distance from all other creatures.

Spelling out the distances

We could summarise most of what has been said so far in a sentence: *Man knows what he is doing*. To assert this, however, is not adequate to our purpose of making consciousness so *visible* that it cannot be denied, eliminated, assimilated into the properties of matter or simply overlooked. For this purpose, it has been essential to unpack the various ways in which human consciousness is elaborated and to show the great spaces that have opened up between man and other forms of matter, including his closest ontological cousins, the non-human animals. Those great spaces still remain even when it is conceded that human consciousness is deeply interpenetrated by unconsciousness (or 'the Unconscious') and that most animals have some degree of consciousness, that they seem to have some notion of what they are doing. Nevertheless, the twin claims that the heart of human consciousness is occupied by various forms of the Unconscious (the Id, the political Unconscious, the linguistic Unconscious, etc.) and that animal consciousness is very similar to the human variety, act like a pincer movement making the distinctive miracle of human consciousness more difficult to see. For this reason, in order to secure the ground that has been gained so far, it is worth, at the risk of some repetition, adopting a different approach to the task of making human consciousness visible and undeniable and of demonstrating the many different ways in which we have to modify, or distance ourselves from, the concept of animality in order to arrive at that of humanity.

Let us therefore imagine a thought experiment in which someone tries to derive man as we know him from that of 'other' animals. In the course of that derivation, a succession of transformations or displacements would be required, a multitude of huge gaps would have to be crossed. Some exemplary gaps are seen in the table that follows.

Animals	*Man*
Instinctive behaviour	Rational action
Appetite-driven activity	Behaviour according to a written code
Corporeal evolution	Historical development
Spatial herding	Self-legitimating grouping
Object-needing	Commodity-wanting
Need-driven behaviour	Salaried labour
Extensions to bodies	Complex autonomous machines
Responses to changing reality	Behaviour planned in response to complex, predictive accounts of actual and possible reality
Tropisms	Systems of classification and re-classification
Reacting to stimuli	Seeking out ways of finding new and more complex pleasures.

The same point is made in the next table through more specific instances:

Some Exemplary Distances Between Man and Animals

	Typical Instance	
Observed Parameter	*Animals*	*Man*
Feeding behaviour	Hunt for food Chase prey	Plans a restaurant meal Chooses a cheaper main course that will not financially embarrass host
Grouping behaviour	Form spatial herd	Identifies with group who have similar interest in stamp collecting
Species development	Change bodily form	Legislates over nutrition, education, etc.
Object of need	Prey	Sufficient income to pay mortgage
Tools	Stick	Machine to assist the manufacture of surgical instruments
Response to unknown event, object	Startle	Classification, explanation, metaphor
Learning	Undergo operant conditioning	Organises babysitter so that can attend next year's course of evening classes

I shall presently argue that all that is distinctive about man may be gathered up in the fact that he is *the explicit animal*. In preparation for that conclusion, let me tease out some of the dimensions of human explicitness as they relate to the fundamental categories of needs, means, communication, time, sense and sense of self. This will involve going over some ground already covered but those readers who are already convinced of the point I have been endeavouring to make may wish to regard the next few pages less as an analysis of a difference than as a celebration of a mystery.

Needs

For man, uniquely among the animals, the objects of need are transformed into commodities whose value is quantified not physiologically (with the subjective aspect of intensity of appetite) but in monetary terms. Need-related activity takes the form of labour: access to the objects of need is indirect, via activity that is usually quite unrelated to them (for example, a doctor tends more sick people in order to pay off his gambling debts; a bricklayer works overtime to fund his interest in philately). In addition, needs are measured not by their moment-to-moment felt intensity but in terms of predicted requirements over time. There is stockpiling and storekeeping; and not only at an individual but at a collective level.

Means

In the simplest case, an animal satisfies a need by moving towards or chasing after its object. When, as in man, needs are made explicit to the needer, pursuit of their satisfaction involves increasingly complex, increasingly indirect, increasingly conscious means. The means and the needs they serve become generalised: the means take the form of a general solution. Modern technology is the culmination of such explicitness. Without explicitness, technology would not have been liberated from the model of the body-as-means; wheels would not have displaced legs; electrical or electronic solutions replaced mechanical ones. Once means are made explicit, their refinement is not constrained by accidental features of the first, the 'natural' solutions. Fire can be supplanted by light bulbs and radiators. Technology is means that know themselves, connecting explicit goals to present states by the application of general principles; it is therefore free to evolve by internal growth, by self-refinement.

Communication

Man consciously deploys signs to convey propositional sense. He recognises his signs for what they are: signs. He quotes, and reflects on, what has been said. Within his sign system, he distinguishes the possible from the actual and can separately assert possibilities and actualities. He distinguishes also the particular and the general (without a complex sign system, neither the particular nor the general has explicit existence).[27] He is able to assert that something (a predicate) is true of something (a subject): he can dismantle and reassemble the world in thought. He can refer to what is the case and so transform material reality into the truth-conditions of statements. At the level of object language, he consciously classifies and re-classifies; and at the level of metalanguage he uses, plays with and mentions signs. And in writing he stores his signs not only outside of his own body but also – and here the extreme case would be the reference library – outside of the situations and occasions in which they might signify. All of these extraordinary developments depend upon the explicit recognition of signs as signs.

Time

Man not only ages, and suffers time as duration, but also divides time up and measures it. An individual consciously projects himself into a future related to the present and consciously reflects on the past in which he distinguishes the general past from his own past and that of others. He binds himself to the future and to the past by taking on commitments and by acknowledging responsibility for certain past events. Commitment to the future may sometimes be quite detailed, as in a timetable that reaches for months ahead. He knows his own age (and so is positioned in his life), and his own probable span and his own certain finitude. He is aware that his life is a temporal process among other temporal processes that will out-endure him and have been present before him. He situates his own time, his lifespan, in History which out-spans his own history.

Sense

The world does not merely impose its patterns on man. He identifies patterns and transforms them into laws which he uses to refine expectancy and to increase the power he has in ordering his affairs. He induces, abducts, conjectures, infers. Expectation is refined into, and by, reasons and hypotheses. Man's expectations are so refined that he is able to experience higher-level surprises that are far remote from mere startle responses: he can be astonished at unexpected patterns in a cloud chamber. He has strategies for finding explanations, adopts discovery procedures. He is capable of the active uncertainty of thought and cultivates doubt in order to deepen his understanding. Behind all of this is a sense that the world makes sense, even a partially unified sense. This intuition is itself most explicit in science with its assumptions of uniformity and its regulative idea of a unified explanation of all things. Underlying this is a further intuition that the fact that the world makes sense itself is quite inexplicable, indeed senseless – an intuition that brings science to the edge of religion.

Sense of self

Man entertains complex ideas of who or what he is. He sees himself as different from or similar to other individuals, groups, types or species. He locates himself with respect to colleagues, friends, relatives, teams, clubs, nations, historical predecessors. He contrasts himself with or derives his self-image from other entities – things, animals, people. He locates himself on a thousand maps of varying scope. He proposes horizon after horizon against which he cuts a silhouette. He finds himself in society, in history, and in an intuited schema that transcends society and history.

Conclusion: man, the explicit animal

Philosophy, Wittgenstein once remarked, 'consists of assembling reminders for a particular purpose'.[28] I quote this in defence of my method of proceeding in this chapter and the devotion of many pages to describing features of ourselves with which we are all familiar. I do not apologise for stating the obvious at such length because it is precisely the obvious that gets taken for granted and consequently overlooked when we consider our own nature and compare ourselves with the other species inhabiting this planet. In consequence, although we take this for granted in our behaviour towards, and the way we think about, non-human animals in our everyday life, we seem to forget, when we philosophise upon our own nature that we are utterly and absolutely different from them. It would be absurd to deny that we have much in common with other animals: we, too, have physiological needs and also share some of their socialising instincts. Nevertheless, all of these things have been utterly transformed in us *because they are explicit in us*.

In emphasising our distinctiveness from the other animals, I am not trying to downgrade them, to suggest that they are unconscious automata, that they lack purposes or intentions or even lasting character traits. Even less, as I have already made clear, would I wish to suggest that they are incapable of suffering, to justify our treating them badly or to diminish our responsibility for treating them worse than is necessary for our own survival. We do not have to downgrade animals to back up our claim to uniqueness. We simply have to hold on to an undistorted view of ourselves. Such a view inescapably reveals us as an animal whose distances from other animals is many-dimensional, whose cultural divergence from the rest of nature is infinitely elaborated.

I am not, of course, denying that we are in very important senses natural; that we have natural needs; or that culture is rooted in nature. Nor am I trying to suggest that in us intelligence has wholly replaced instinct (a position that Midgley forcibly and convincingly refutes). Our needs are, in many places, analogous to those which we discern in animals: for food, shelter, affection and so on. But, although the general framework of instinct has not been supplanted, the instincts themselves have been utterly transformed. Yes, there is a distant analogy between the nesting behaviour of a chaffinch and my purchase of a house; but the closer we look at the details of my behaviour (for example, the row I have with the solicitor about the time the conveyancing is taking; or my guilt over a decision to postpone filling in yet another form because I am feeling lazy) the more remote the analogy seems. We often say of a woman who decorates a bedroom just before she goes into labour that she is 'nest-building'; but the decision as to whether to have one coat of paint or two and the discussion as to whether to buy the paint from B&Q or Texas shows just how far the analogy, even in this particularly compelling case, can go: not very far. Of course, our culture must have some kind of givens – physiological needs, for example – to work on. However, in so far as there is a distinctive human nature, it is institutional and conventional rather than, say, physiological; or, rather, it is one in which the expression of the physiological has been transformed by institutions, customs, conventions rituals and statutes. And this transformation is the result ultimately not of the emergence of a collective human unconscious – Society, History, Oedipal forces or whatever – but of the operation of consciousness, of explicitness, and their free play within the ordinary behaviour of individuals.

The passage from natural needs and drives to human institutions and patterns of behaviour – let us say from mating to marriage, from mating calls to love letters – is predicated upon an infinitely developable explicitness. The lover who writes a carefully calculated letter to put himself in the best possible light is not merely enacting a variant of a bird singing a stereotyped song. *He knows what he is doing*[29] – is awake to his goal, his methods and to the object of his attention – in a way whose difference is a matter not merely of degree but of kind. This wakefulness is one that is continually waking up to itself, reflecting on itself, seeing what it is, what it wants. We have no evidence that it is shared by the singing blackbird.

Even in such 'beastly' areas as sexual behaviour (according to Kant, 'Sexuality exposes one to the danger of equality with the beasts'), human beings operate at an immense distance from animals. To refer to behaviour that surrounds mating in both humans and animals by the same terms (e.g. 'courtship rituals') is at least as misleading as it is illuminating; as liable to lead to a serious distortion of both human and animal behaviour as it is to show up valid analogies.

As I have suggested, the greater part of the contents of this chapter should be superfluous since the reminders it assembles are sufficiently obvious; nevertheless, it is necessary to state, and to reiterate, these things because they are forgotten by many philosophers thinking about human consciousness.

The fact that human beings share many properties with animals – for example, bodies that run on very similar principles – has led to our assimilating animality to humanity rather too easily, to regarding man as some kind of (admittedly rather special) animal. Of course, we are more like animals than we are like machines or angels; but we are not 'just', 'at bottom', animals or unimportantly different from the other animals. All of the characterisations I have discussed above – the rational animal, the moral animal, the sense-making animal, etc. – capture only single dimensions of the multidimensional distance between man and the animals. To assert this infinitely complex difference by adding a single predicate to 'animal' – to see man as an animal with a particular faculty – is to close the gap, or to make shallow the unbridgeable gulf, that lies between humanity and animality. For these predicates, these isolated faculties, are all *symptoms* – of man's utter otherness from animality. The unbridgeableness of the distance is owed to explicitness, itself the very essence of human consciousness, which permits indefinite autonomous development. Explicitness turns difference into a multi-dimensional infinity.

It must be emphasised that when I characterise man as 'the explicit animal', I am not talking of just another faculty. Midgley has demonstrated the vacuousness of single faculty accounts of man. The main weakness of such accounts is that it is impossible to think of a faculty that one could not *read into* the behaviour of other animals, no feature that could not plausibly be claimed to be echoed in some animal or other.[30] Even leaving one's spraint on the ground could be taken, by someone desperate to assert the continuity between man and animals, as a primitive form of writing. And other faculties, that animals do not possess, such as that of drawing up timetables, seem too specific to mark our difference from the beasts. Explicitness, or the power of making explicit, is deeper and wider than any mere faculty, such as reason; or, if it is to be thought of as a faculty at all, we may think of it as that faculty in virtue of which our faculties – which indeed may be analogous in their embryonic forms to animal faculties – may develop to an extraordinary degree. Or as 'the faculty-making faculty'.

The power of making explicit seems to answer the requirement for a 'mark of man' that would not fall foul of the criticisms I outlined at the beginning of this chapter. The problems in identifying distinctively human characteristics setting off man from other animals included: the danger of a partial view of animals and an equally partial view of ourselves; the need for the chosen characteristic to be a structural, rather than a focal, surface, feature – one that affected the whole organisation of the life of the species rather than being just 'an isolated miracle'; and the need to take account of the fact that man, to a unique degree perhaps, is self-defining and self-transforming. The characterisation of man as 'the explicit animal' seems to meet these problems and requirements.

The definition also, I think, helps us to deal with the question of the relationship between animal faculties and human ones. Is the difference between human language and animal communication systems simply one of degree of complexity? Is animal intelligence similar to but simply less well developed than human intelligence? Are the ape dances described by Jane Goodall embryonic or primitive versions of the Bolshoi ballet? In other words, is man just a creature who has travelled along the same road as other animals but has simply gone much further? Are animal and human achievements points along the same axis? Are we dealing with differences of degree or of kind? The answer is that we are dealing with enormous differences of degree that have been made possible by a different route of development of the faculties – which are, therefore, in a sense, of a different kind. Human faculties have achieved their present advanced state by different means – by progressive and successive application of the power of making explicit. As a result of this, their development has been so extraordinary that they have evolved into things of different kinds. In their mode of development and, less convincingly perhaps, in the destinations they have so far reached, they are different in kind. We may think of the power of making explicit as the faculty that permits faculties that have animal origins to be transformed to the point where their relationship to animal faculties is purely notional or even metaphorical. Consider the ape rain dance and the Bolshoi ballet. The complex booking system, the notices in the newspaper, the competitiveness between career ballerinas – these are all secondary developments, yes; but they symptomatise what happened to dancing once it entered the life of the explicit animal.

My vision of the relationship between human and animal faculties may be captured by imagining the animals fighting their way through a wilderness near to the beginning of a motorway that humans are travelling along at sixty miles an hour. The animals may move in the wilderness parallel to that motorway for a few yards but cannot drive on it. With a few exceptions, each generation of animals, moreover, begins at the same point in the wilderness as the last and there is no cumulative progress – not even painfully slow progress – except in so far as the animal's body changes over vast periods of time. The power of making explicit, the explicitness inherent in human consciousness, is what makes motorway travel possible for humans and lack of it that denies animals such travel. The analogies between human and animal faculties deceive us into thinking that we and they are travelling along the same road, that they are on the same road as us, only further back. In fact, animals are not even on the road; only at a parallel location corresponding to a point just beyond the beginning of the road. Thus the relation between animal tool-using and human technology; or between animal communication and human language.

My method of delineating the differences between man and animals has been to take certain characteristics and show how they have unfolded in human life; or how many folds, how much complexity and elaboration, they have acquired. My description has no pretence to being an historical or genetic account of the evolution of human faculties and institutions. It is merely a way of showing how far we are from the animals, and not a way of describing, even less explaining, the road we have taken in getting from animality to humanity. My ultimate purpose is to show how remote we are from automata or machines; to underline the unique extent to which we know what we are doing. (If tomorrow someone were to show me that animals did, after all, have as complex and elaborated and self-conscious a consciousness as ours – so that, for example, there were animal analogues for human learning techniques such as organising babysitters so that one can go to an evening class – I would not be too upset, though I would be *very* surprised. I would simply transfer some of the distances I am currently assigning to the gap between man and animals to that between man and machines. The distance between man and machines would remain undiminished. The *size* of consciousness, and the importance of deliberate conscious behaviour and of the mediations of consciousness, would still be as great.)

My account of the difference between man and animals leaves the relationship between them deeply puzzling and the transition from the one to the other almost inexplicable. It may be argued that this is the result of the techniques of analysis I have used. Is it not possible that each step in the unfolding of *homo economicus*, for example, seems to be underivable from the starting conditions, and the overall trajectory unprecedented, only because I have taken faculties in isolation? That in other words, *homo economicus* would seem less of 'an isolated miracle' (to use Midgley's phrase) if the evolution of human language were considered at the same time. That we can understand the development of the parts only if we understand the development of the whole. To understand the whole without understanding the parts seems to be a tall order, though I am sympathetic to this. It is my position, after all, that all of these developments do have a single precondition and motor: the power of explicitness. The particular trajectories I have traced, however, do not distort explicitness or exaggerate its mysteriousness; they merely uncover its multifarious working and show its mysteriousness.

I am not, of course, denying the evolutionary explanation of the origin of the human *body*: morphologically, physiologically, biochemically, neurobiologically, etc. it is clear that that body has evolved from the bodies of non-human predecessors. I have no doubt that, in this sense, the primates are our immediate ancestors. But the emergence of explicitness – which created the gulf between man and the other animals – does not seem to fit into this story about bodies.

Ought I to apologise for this failure to accommodate the explicitness story into the evolution-of-bodies story? Not at all. It is better to have an unsolved problem than a false solution. We have grown accustomed to the idea that human development takes place outside of the evolutionary process. We shall have to accustom ourselves to the related idea that the origin of this capacity to evolve outside of the genome also fails to fit into the evolutionary scheme. In his essay 'Truth and Lie in the Extra-Moral Sense',[31] Nietzsche suggested, with masterly sarcasm, that man was a clever animal who simply 'invented knowledge'. This is an absurd suggestion but it is about the best explanation we have so far of this curious state of affairs whereby man, uniquely, enjoys a capacity to make explicit that can unfold without limit.

The power of explicitness seems to be *sui generis*, underivable. And for this reason it shares with consciousness an inability to fit into the evolutionary scheme. This correspondence is not surprising; for explicitness is the essence of human consciousness. And it is to consciousness that we must now return. The ultimate purpose of the present discussion of the difference between man and the other animals has not been to downgrade animals but to protect man from the downgrading that begins with seeing him as 'only an animal'. Those who animalise man use this as a first step to machinising him; for they downgrade animals as well and tend to reduce them to the status of machines. They dislike seeing the obvious and recognising that, unlike machines, animals have purposes, intentions and affections and in many instances, as Midgley repeatedly emphasises, enduring character traits that organise their behaviour over long periods of time and across many settings. In short, those who are practised in the art of overlooking the obvious traits of human beings will be past-masters when it comes to overlooking the obvious characteristics of animals. The perverse skill necessary to reduce humans to animals will take the reduction of animals to machines in its stride. By drawing attention to the distances between man and animals, I have hoped to make the visible impossible not to notice. Once the nature of man as the explicit animal is grasped and explicitness is understood as the essence of consciousness, it becomes much more difficult to overlook the all-encompassing nature of consciousness, to eliminate, marginalise or underplay its role in behaviour, to reduce it to a focal property of a creature similar in essential respects to non-conscious entities such as lower animals and machines – so that the difference between an event's happening and something being done is minimalised or denied. The purpose of this 'assembly of reminders', then, has been to draw attention to the inadequacy of current popular views about consciousness; to enable us to approach with the requisite critical spirit the recent attempts we have discussed to explain, or explain away, or to downgrade, or to denature, consciousness. The importance of my claim that man has a fundamentally different type of consciousness from the animals is that it provides a further layer of defence against the temptation to see humans, or human consciousness, as machine-like.

Notes

1. Gilbert Ryle, *The Concept of Mind* (Harmondsworth: Penguin, 1967), p. 310.
2. I owe this point (and this way of putting it) to Mary Midgley whose excellent *Beast and Man. The Roots of Human Nature* (London: Methuen, 1980) I read after the first draft of this chapter (which goes a long way back in my own thinking) had been completed. The present version has been enormously influenced by her passionate, witty, erudite, lucid and, above all, sane book. Reading Midgley saved me from some of the naiveties that beset philosophers when they find themselves – somewhat reluctantly in my own case – having to become armchair zoologists; and she has sharpened my appreciation of the mines with which the field of man–animal comparisons is sewn. *Beast and Man* has made me aware not only of my own prejudices about animals (her insights felt their way into the basement of my preconceptions) but also of the venerable historical tradition of which they are a part. In addition it has furnished me with many thought-provoking examples of animal behaviour analysed in such a way as to force me to modify, or at least to disambiguate, the fundamental point I was trying to make and the use to which I was putting animals (or my conception of them). The numerous references to *Beast and Man* will give only an incomplete account of my debt to it.
3. The apparent success in describing animals in machine terms is almost certainly due to our ignorance of what goes on in them – as Midgley has so eloquently argued.
4. For a discussion of this, see E.R. Leach, *Lévi-Strauss* (London: Fontana, 1970).
5. This view is developed in *Madness and Civilisation*. The madman, too, provided rational, civilised man with an image of his opposite, to iterate his sense of being rational and civilised. The connection between madness and animality in Foucault's thought is well expressed by Alan Sheridan (*Michel Foucault: The Will to Truth*, London: Tavistock, 1980, p. 30):

   > madness was perceived by the eighteenth century as a relapse into animality. In the first case, man had lost the use of reason and had sunk into the innocent, amoral condition of the animal; in the second, man had deliberately chosen to rid himself of the guidance of reason, of his very humanity. The 'furious' lunatic was seen and treated as a wild beast. Many accounts of madmen in confinement attest to their extraordinary resistance to extremes of hunger, heat, cold and pain. This was regarded as further proof of the animality of the mad.

6. The relationship between reason and unreason in 'irrational' behaviour is rather analogous to that between consciousness and the unconscious in the enactment of neuroses. Just as the successful enactment of neuroses in irrational behaviour requires the full resources of rational daylit consciousness, so the pursuit of irrational ends (ends that seem against the best interests of the agent or at cross-purposes to his real goals) requires unremitting rationality.

Consider this example, drawn from my own experience, of a patient who exhibited neurotic behaviour (a situation in which the unconscious and its manifestation in irrationality should be at its most dominant). The case will demonstrate how, while the basis of the neurotic's behaviour is unconscious and irrational, the behaviour itself is fully conscious and pervaded with rationality. Or, rather, how unconsciously driven, irrational behaviour has to be enacted through a medium of consciously chosen, rational acts.

The patient in question was a woman in her late twenties who developed a neurotic anxiety about breast cancer. She repeatedly found, or thought she had found, lumps in her breast. Whenever she detected such a lump, she could not prevent herself rushing off at once to her general practitioner to be examined. After examination, she would be reassured for a few days; but she would soon find another lump and would request another emergency appointment with her doctor. The anxiety about breast cancer was, of course, a symptom of a deeper anxiety – traceable to the death of her father, by suicide, when she was aged twelve and the conscious motivation of her behaviour was quite different from its real, unconscious, motivation. While it was apparently motivated by a rational fear of breast cancer triggered off rationally by the observation of a breast lump, it was really driven by a need for security, fatally undermined by the sudden death of her father, and for a father's love denied by her father's decision to remove himself from her life. She needed the kindly father-substitute general practitioner to palpate her breasts, literally and metaphorically to soothe her bosom, and tell her that she was all right, that all was well and that she was loved and cared for.

A clear example, then, of an apparently rational action driven by motivations of which the actor is apparently unconscious. Even so, the complex behaviour is still conscious even where it is most obviously driven by unconscious forces. In examining herself, in ringing up for an appointment to see the doctor, in planning to catch a particular bus to take her to the surgery, in waiting her turn, in going into the consulting room when her name is called, in telling her story to the doctor, she is fully conscious and deploying a good deal of extremely complex reason. (Try programming a computer to do a thousandth of what the patient achieves in getting to see the doctor.) In short, the unconsciously driven act is still a conscious act – or a complex suite of conscious acts – and the patient's engagement in it is not an intermission in consciousness or reason.

Consciousness of a high order and rationally-driven activity are essential for the unconscious to be enacted in apparently irrational behaviour. Moreover, that consciousness, unlike coma or dream, has the openness of ordinary consciousness; it is still able to take account of and respond to data that are quite irrelevant to the enactment of the neurosis. Even neurotics have to eat, and plan supper for the kids and remember to get mother-in-law's books from the library and to ring up the department store to complain about the problems with the vacuum cleaner. On her way to the doctor's, the patient is still able to recognise and to greet and to converse with her next door neighbour whom she happens to encounter; she is still able to take note of the weather, to avoid the unexpected car bearing down on her as she crosses the road, to note that the price of potatoes is lower in the greengrocer's than it was last week and act on that knowledge when, on the way back from the doctor's, she decides to buy her potatoes there rather than in the supermarket.

The neurotic patient is thus neither unconscious nor is she somnambulating, even in that small proportion of her daily life when she is acting out her neurosis, in the hours when she is in the grip of behaviour that is clearly driven by unconscious needs rather than the conscious agenda it thinks it is enacting. Consciousness, and even rationality, still dominate in this paradigm of unconsciousness-driven, irrational, behaviour. This is manifest not only in the patient's ability to continue ordinary life and make ordinary observations and take ordinary steps to bring things about and in her continuing responsiveness to the accidental, contingent details of the outside world through which she has to act out her neuroses; but also in the present anguish she feels. The domination of the present external world by the internal one of the past is only partial; and where she is possessed by the past, the experience is still a present conscious experience. The present, conscious experience of the feelings and motivations, howsoever they are interwoven with self-deception, are the reason the neurosis matters and so desperately needs treatment.

In order to enact our dreams, as opposed to dreaming that we enact them, we have to be fully conscious: to be manifestly possessed by the night, we have to be daylit. The unconscious does not operate like epilepsy or blot out the conscious like a coma. And it operates through reason: it is through the unremitting use of reason that neurotics reinforce the validity of their fears. Phobias and other manifestations of the unconscious and the irrational do not prove that either consciousness or reason is any sense marginal. Just as false consciousness is still consciousness, so even the patient, even in those moments when she is most clearly in the grip of irrationality beyond rationalisation, is unremitting in her reasoning.

7. Karl Marx and Friedrich Engels, *The German Ideology*, edited and introduced by C.J. Arthur (London: Lawrence & Wishart, 1974), p. 42.
8. According to some authorities, the transition from hunter-gathering to farming may not have been beneficial. It is as if the advance towards explicitness has a momentum of its own that is not only not driven by practical benefit but may be at cross-purposes to it.
9. Jean-Paul Sartre, *Critique of Dialectical Reason*, translated by Alan Sheridan (London: Verso, 1982), p. 260. Sartre's enormously long discussion of the extraordinary capacity of human beings to generalise themselves, to see themselves as terms in a series and equivalent to other terms in the series, is intermittently illuminating.
10. 'The value of a commodity is expressed in its price before it goes into circulation, and is therefore a precedent condition of its circulation, not its result', Karl Marx, *Capital*, vol. 1, translated by Samuel Moore and Edward Aveling (London: Lawrence & Wishart, 1970).
11. Richard Swinburne, *The Evolution of the Soul* (Oxford University Press, 1986), p. 2.
12. John Maynard Smith, *The Theory of Evolution*, 3rd edn (Harmondsworth: Penguin, 1975), p. 311.
13. Lévi-Strauss's views are accessibly summarised in E.R. Leach, *Lévi-Strauss* (London: Fontana, 1970). An interesting and entertaining critique of Lévi-Strauss is by his erstwhile pupil J.G. Merquior in *From Prague to Paris: A Critique of Structuralist and Post-Structuralist Thought* (London: Verso, 1986).
14. Maynard Smith, op. cit., p. 313.
15. Man the weapon-maker is a rather too obtrusive subdivision of man the toolmaker.
16. Attributing classifying behaviour to primitive organisms on the basis of their discriminant behaviour is a particularly obvious example of misplaced explicitness. Less obvious, but much more widespread, is the tendency to attribute propositional attitudes to non-human organisms. A belief, say, is inferred from an animal's behaviour. Well and good. But that belief is then cast in propositional form in the language of the observer. Not so good. To suggest that a

dog believes that his master is kind is not as absurd as attributing a belief to a thermostat. But it implies that the dog has the concepts 'master', 'kind', etc. and also that it operates with subject–predicate relations. This fallacy – which combines inappropriate propositionalisation with misplaced explicitness – is very widespread indeed and accounts in good part for the extraordinary extent to which the difference between man and animals has been overlooked. It is more dangerous than anthropomorphism because it is more subtle.

17. This has caused much impatience amongst certain cognitive psychologists, for whom belief in man's uniqueness seems to represent an unwarranted mysticism and a barrier to serious investigation. For example, Christopher Longuet-Higgins in a review article in *London Review of Books*: 'Why are theoretical linguists so infernally sensitive about the linguistic uniqueness of *homo sapiens*?' ('Mental Processes', 14 August, 1988, pp. 13–14).
18. George Steiner, *Real Presences* (London: Faber, 1989), pp. 53–4.
19. George Steiner, *After Babel* (Oxford University Press, 1975).
20. See Gabriel Marcel, *A Metaphysical Diary* (available in *Being and Having*, London: Fontana, 1965), pp. 47–63.
21. See Raymond Tallis, *The Explicit Animal* (London: Macmillan, 1991), Chapter 7.
22. Raymond Tallis, *Not Saussure* (London: Macmillan, 1988), 'Reference Restored' in this selection.

    One point perhaps worth making here is that animal calls are neither 'merely general' (as some writers would claim), referring to general concepts or categories such as 'danger'; nor are they explicitly particular, referring to particulars, such as a particular danger (or 'that predator over there'). They are intrinsically neither general nor particular. That is why under our linguistic descriptions they can be glossed as either. The co-emergence of the explicitly particular and the explicitly general is one of the many features peculiar to human language.
23. Midgley (*Beast and Man*, p. 249) suggests that the great leap forward may have been a mutation that enabled better control of the larynx but that this alone is insufficient:

> To compel a general change as strenuous as learning to use conventional instead of natural signs, it is not enough for an exceptional individual or two to be born capable of starting the game. All must take the trouble to join in ... What we need to make the origin of speech intelligible, in fact, is a line of hominids which does not just have a lucky mutation, but has in general the right temperament – is exceptionally cooperative, persistent, and thorough in using what it gets. They must not just be lucky opportunists; they must be stayers ... sheer stout-hearted persistence could be the crucial distinctive factor that led the species to out-distance and eventually put out of business all its near relatives and competitors, thereby leaving itself in that strange isolation which has made it so deeply confused about its status. (pp. 250–1)

This is thought-provoking; but I do not think it cuts down far enough: it fails to recognise the depth of the problem. Persistence would not solve anything if the animal did not have the vision – the conception, at any rate – of what it was persisting at. The opportunity to become civilised would not present itself to an animal that was not on the lookout for civilisation. Even together, laryngeal mutation and a certain dogged determination towards self-betterment could not explain the transition to an infinitely expandable discursive self-awareness.

24. A.N. Whitehead, *Science and the Modern World* (New York: New American Library, 1925). See in particular the opening chapter on the origins of modern science:

    > In the first place, there can be no living science unless there is a widespread instinctive conviction in the existence of an *Order of Things*, and, in particular, of an *Order of Nature* ... [The] scientific mentality instinctively holds that all things great and small are conceivable as exemplifications of general principles which reign throughout the natural order ... the faith in the possibility of science, generated antecedently to the development of modern scientific theory, is an unconscious derivative from medieval theology. (pp. 4, 5 and 10)

    The entirety of this chapter by Whitehead could be seen as a brilliant meditation on the theme of 'man, the sense-making animal'. Whitehead, however, is concerned with the extent to which man woke up from his earlier self, rather than the much greater and even more mysterious distance of human from animal consciousness.
25. It might be worth noting at this juncture a minor symptom of the sense-making animal, namely is that he is the laughing animal. According to Hazlitt, 'Man is the only creature that laughs and weeps; for he is the only animal that is struck with the difference between what things are, and what they ought to be' (*Lectures on the English Comic Writers*). How true this observation is, I should not like to say. Midgley (p. 228) suggests that non-human primates also laugh.
26. Midgley op. cit. p. 248.
27. See Tallis, *The Explicit Animal*, Chapter 6 and chapters 4 and 7 of *Not Saussure* (op. cit.) for further discussion of this point.
28. 'The work of the philosopher consists in assembling reminders for a particular purpose', Ludwig Wittgenstein, *Philosophical Investigations*, translated by G.E.M. Anscombe (Oxford: Blackwell, 1953), p. 50e.
29. Curiously, this is recognised even by that hardline machinist Skinner: 'Only humans can not only see things, like rats, but also see that they are seeing them. That is, humans become aware or conscious of their own behaviour, in a way that is true of no other animal species' (B.F. Skinner, 'The operational analysis of psychological terms', *Behavioural and Brain Sciences*, 1984; 7:547–81). It is difficult to know how Skinner can be so sure of the lack of self-consciousness in rats, but it is extraordinary to encounter him acknowledging the existence of second-order consciousness in humans.
30. The tendency to read humanity into animal behaviour is part of a larger tendency to import explicitness and self-consciousness into places where it simply does not exist. This sometimes results from equating perceptual experience with information and regarding the latter as equivalent to the words that encapsulate it. See, for example, Daniel Dennett, 'When Frogs and Others Make Mistakes' in *The Intentional Stance* (Cambridge, Mass.: Bradford Books, 1987) and, in particular, the discussion beginning on p. 112 with the remarkable statement that 'the frog is bathed in sensation but we are bathed in information'. Most of the difficulties Dennett addresses so engagingly in that chapter arise from a misplaced explicitness that fails to distinguish between tacit and explicit beliefs. For example, contradictory tacit beliefs can exist side by side without the person being fairly described as irrational (or not wilfully so, anyway). Only when beliefs are uttered can you start looking at their entailments, their consistency with other beliefs, etc. *Any* attribution of a belief to an animal couched in human language runs the risk of being over-explicit;

and the further we go down the evolutionary scale, the more absurd that over-explicitness becomes.

31. F. Nietzsche, 'Truth and Lie in the Extra-Moral Sense'. This is available widely in numerous translations; for example, Geoffrey Clive (ed.), *The Philosophy of Nietzsche* (New York: Mentor, 1965), pp. 503–15.

From: *The Explicit Animal* (Macmillan, 1991, 1999), pp. 17, 161–3, 168–209, 281–7.

Part II

The Nature of Language

The most striking, pervasive and elaborate manifestation of a distinctively human consciousness is language. Human language is unlike animal signalling systems, for example, inasmuch as the signs of a human language are explicitly signs. They are not, for example, symptoms, embedded in a causal chain passing through transmitters and recipients, nor are they remotely analogous to natural signs such as the signs that connect clouds with rain. Tallis insists that linguistic signs are arbitrary, in the Saussurean sense of that word. (There is no natural connection between signifier and signified within the sign, and signs are the signs they are in the system by virtue of their differences from all the other signs in the language system.) For Tallis, the true significance of the arbitrariness of the sign lies here: linguistic signs are signs that display their status as signs explicitly. This is another way of saying that the auditory and written signs of language are used in the full understanding that they are signs and that, in order to discharge their signifying function, they have to be understood as signs by a recipient who is aware that the producer of them is relying upon their being understood in this way. Human language, and its numerous derivative codes, is uniquely an instrument by which meaning is *meant* in order to occur. It is riddled from top to bottom with metalanguage and exhibits throughout much of its usage elaborate patterns of self-consciousness and self-referral, both in serious communicative activity and in play.

Tallis sees the arbitrariness of the linguistic sign as lying at the heart of the distinctively human linguistic activity of reference. Reference utilising arbitrary signs has several features that distinguish it from the communicative function of signals emitted by non-human animals. For example, reference is distanced in several rather special ways from the object referred to – the latter is merely an instance of a general possibility; or, to put this another way, reference is achieved through general meanings. Indeed, Tallis believes that human discourse – in contrast with animal responses to present actualities – is predominantly about *possibility*: possible states of affairs which may or may not be realised. It is this, he argues, that makes language the supreme means by which explicitness may be elaborated and new meanings created.

4
Reference Restored

This reading is taken from *Not Saussure* (1988, 1995), the first of Tallis's books to address the errors and confusions of post-Saussurean literary theory. His aim here is to defend a notion of reference in order to defend realism – not only the so-called 'classic realism' of the nineteenth-century novel and mainstream Hollywood feature films, but also subsequent 'experimental' realism – against the attacks launched on it by theorists such as Colin MacCabe, Stephen Heath, Catherine Belsey and Terry Eagleton in England, and Roland Barthes, Jacques Derrida and Julia Kristeva in France. One ground for this attack from the theoretically inclined generation of the 1970s and 1980s derived from the notion that there is no outside to language: everything is text and there is no outside to the text. Lacan went so far as to assert that it is the world of words that creates the world of things. These kinds of idea have their basis in the belief that Saussure had shown that language does not mirror a reality that pre-exists it and that meaning arises as a consequence of the internal relations holding within the language system. To the theorists, this inevitably meant that the attempt to let reality into the novel was misconceived. Realism can only be a way of passing off what seems real, the verisimilitudinous, as what is real: realism is therefore no more than a fake, the mere creation of an '*effet du réel*'. Furthermore, if one links realism with the tastes of the dominant class, the bourgeoisie, it follows that the fate of the nineteenth-century novel, and indeed any form of narrative pattern that resembles it, such as Hollywood narratives were thought to do, is sealed. Tallis wants to say that while one may indeed agree that language does not correspond to the world, in the sense of mirroring it or providing a window onto it, it does not follow that reference and realism are thereby impossible. A plausible account of language must recognise that, while discourse does not mirror the world, precise reference and accurate description are nevertheless a central part of the way we ordinarily use words.

---

1 The problem

The anti-realist case thrives on myths about realism. One such myth is that those who write, or attempt to write, realistic fiction imagine they can do so only because they believe that language is a reflecting mirror or a transparent window – at any rate, a passive surface that effaces itself before an extra-linguistic reality which it undistortingly reflects or reveals.[1]

In point of fact, we have little evidence bearing on beliefs the great realistic novelists may have had about language. Tolstoy did not write any treatises on the philosophy of language; and Zola, while he had a marked preference for fiction based on fact rather than upon fancy, and for observation over fabulation, did not derive these preferences, so far as we know, from a consideration of the nature of words.

More specific information is available about the beliefs of one or two minor figures. Perhaps the most simplistic view of the relation between language and reality is to be found in the opening passage of Christopher Isherwood's *Goodbye to Berlin*: 'I am a camera ...'. And there are naïve contemporary novelist-critics too. Some interesting names appear under this heading. William Gass, who elsewhere attaches himself to the non-referential school, is one example: 'Wittgenstein believed for a time that a proposition, in the disposition of its names, pictured a possibly equivalent arrangement of objects. This is a pleasant fancy, and plainly must be true ... of fiction.'[2] Some whole-time critics are equally naïve. Todorov, for example, sometimes holds views on the relations between language and reality that, for a structuralist, are really rather surprising: 'Words are to things as desires are to the objects of desire.'[3] But Todorov – like Benveniste – is, as we have seen, prone to startling lapses from structuralism.[4]

One realistic novelist commonly thought to have espoused a mimetic theory of language and hence of the aims and possibilities of the novel is Stendhal. In practice, however, many of the chapter headings in *Le Rouge et le Noir* make fun of the idea that the novel can capture reality wholesale, that it can *replicate* a whole world, mocking what Barthes calls 'secretarial realism'. (See, for example, *Men and Manners in 1830*.) As for the famous description of a novel as 'a mirror passing down a road', yes, this is cited by Stendhal – it originates from Saint-Réal; but, like many of the epigraphs, is quoted at least in part with irony.

Apart from the examples of one or two minor novelists and a few novelist-critics and isolated major figures misinterpreted by critics, there is little to support the notion that writers of realistic fiction believe in a naïve 'window' or 'mirror' model of language. Nevertheless, it is almost invariably assumed that the realistic novelist must, either consciously or unwittingly, believe that words stand proxy for things; that the relationship between words reflects the relationship between things; or that there is a one-to-one correspondence between language and reality. If, so the (usually unspoken) argument goes, a writer *must* hold these views about language in order to want to write realistic fiction and if, as is surely the case, these views are untenable, then realism itself, as an aim or a particular method of realising that aim, is invalid. If Saussure has shown that language does not mirror a reality that pre-exists it, then the endeavour to let reality into the novel is misconceived and any apparent success must be consciously or unconsciously faked – the creation of a mere '*effet du réel*'.

The linguistic argument is rarely spelt out as baldly as this but it is the heart of the post-Saussurean case against realism. We must therefore ask ourselves whether, since language is not (as assuredly it is not) a mirror of reality, and there is no one-to-one correspondence between the elements of a description and the components of the described, it follows that realism is impossible. If language is not structured like extra- or pre-linguistic reality, if there is no isomorphic mapping between words and the world, can texts (including fictional ones) be 'about' or 'refer to' the real world? Can one concede the non-correspondence (in the windowing or mirroring sense) between discourse and the world without being forced to abandon belief in the possibility of reference or realism? Is there a theory of language that can reconcile these apparently inconsistent facts: (i) discourse does not by any stretch of the imagination mirror the world; and (ii) precise reference and accurate description is a normal part of everyday life?

A plausible account of language must take a middle course between the implausible idea that language 'passively' reflects reality and the equally implausible idea that reality is produced by language; between the naïve view that discourse merely replicates the form and content of the pre-linguistic reality and the equally simplistic view that reality is differentiated only post- or intra-linguistically. It must be able to accommodate the fact that meaning is articulated (in the sense of being divided up and joined together) by language without making this fact a springboard to the belief that meaning is *created* by language. It must recognise that while the category of 'the edible' does not correspond to a pre-formed natural grouping of objects, to a 'natural kind', nevertheless the ineluctable truth that the difference between 'edible' and 'non-edible' (and so between eating one's fill and starving to death) is not merely a matter of binary oppositions between two values belonging to a language system, is not an internal affair of language.

An adequate philosophy of language must neither aim to correlate words with pre-existing natural kinds (a 'labelling' theory) nor ignore the very real constraints that are placed by extra-linguistic reality upon the manner in which things are linguistically classified. Reality and language are not two rigidly correlated matrices existing in the relationship of, respectively, master and slave; nor is language the only shaper of perceptual reality and the sole determinant of empirical truth; nor, again, are words scattered randomly over extra-linguistic reality. A satisfactory account of language will, at the very least, acknowledge that language stabilises, and to some extent organises, our world in so far as the latter is intelligible, even though it does not itself generate the meanings into which we find ourselves plunged; that linguistic meaning refers us in the end to experiences that go beyond or, more strictly, lie beneath, language.

2 Theories of universals

One time-honoured approach to the mystery of the relationship between words and the world is through the problem of universals – of the functioning of general terms (usually nouns and adjectives) and of the nature of reference. Solutions to this problem are traditionally classified into essentialist (or realist), nominalist, conceptualist and resemblance theories.

At the heart of *essentialism* is the belief that common nouns correlate with natural kinds and that material objects are naturally or inescapably classified into those kinds. Essentialists, however, find it difficult to accommodate the everyday observation that an individual object can be classified and reclassified under a multitude of different names; that the same entity, for example, can validly be called 'a brick' or 'a weapon'. They also have trouble explaining the fact that there appears to be no common set of properties linking all the objects correctly made to bear a given name. Nor can essentialists deal with words (such as 'the economy') that seem not to correspond to pre-existing natural kinds, nor to have instances occupying determinate stretches of space–time or to be capable of non-linguistic encounter or ostension. The fundamental problem of essentialism is that it proposes too tight a correlation between types of tokens and types of extra-linguistic objects.

Nominalists take account of the facts that the same term may collect objects that have no evident common property and that a given object may be referred to by a wide variety of terms – of the double dissociation, in short, between words and objects. They have no difficulty with words such as 'or' and 'nevertheless' which do not correlate with objects at all. The trouble with nominalism, however, is that it seems to carry the implication that anything may be called by any name whatsoever and that there is no extra-linguistic basis for the grouping of objects under general terms. In practice, there *are* obvious constraints upon the choice of words by which I refer to an object; and these are not purely a matter of linguistic convention. I cannot, without prior special agreement, call a cat 'dog'. Except for certain special purposes – which require separate explanation (as when, for example, it is decided that a piece of wood shall be called 'The King') – I cannot refer to a brick by the word 'balloon'. The non-random distribution of words over things seems to be a necessary condition of successful verbal communication.

Many of the 'entities' corresponding to words do not seem to have independent material existence outside of language – for example, abstract objects. This observation seems to be the main inspiration for *conceptualism*, which sees universals as essentially *mental* entities and correlates common nouns and adjectives not with types of material objects but with types of perceptions – with, that is to say, *conceptions* abstracted from a multitude of similar perceptions. One of the many problems of conceptualism is that it cannot cope with nouns whose referents could not have originated in an ensemble of percepts (e.g. Africa), with abstract nouns not even remotely rooted in perception or with words that function differently from nouns. It is a genetic theory in so far as it looks at universals through the processes by which knowledge of them is acquired by an individual. It is not surprising, therefore, that it places insufficient emphasis upon the relations between one word and another – upon the *systematic* aspect of language. Empiricist–associationist language *is* 'a word heap'. Conceptualist accounts also face the difficulty of correlating highly variable, accidental, ill-defined concepts with a public language. Language could not be reliably related to public reality by means of essentially private experiences: denotation would be continually threatened by private connotation.[5]

A fourth theory sees universals as inhering in the correspondence between words on the one hand and, on the other, the feature or property by virtue of which the members of the group of objects gathered under the word *resemble* one another. So 'red' is that in virtue of which all red objects resemble one another. Apart from the obvious unsatisfactoriness of a tautological definition, and the fact (pointed out by Russell) that 'resemblance' itself remains as a universal irreducible to resemblance, there is the further problem of non-artificially or non-tautologically finding resemblances between all the members of the class defined by a certain word. In virtue of what property do all 'todays' resemble one another? Even Wittgenstein's conception of family resemblance hardly covers the case which it was introduced to deal with, that of games. To say that 'Ring-a-ring-a-roses', the Olympic games, poker and what a cat does to a mouse are all 'games' by virtue of a family resemblance between them is extending the idea of a 'family' somewhat.

Wittgenstein himself appreciated this:

> I can think of no better expression to characterize these similarities than 'family resemblances' ... 'games' form a family.
>
> And for instance the kinds of numbers form a family.
>
> And we extend our concept of number as in spinning a thread we twist fibre on fibre. And the strength of the thread does not reside in the fact that one fibre runs through the whole of its length, but in the overlapping of many fibres.
>
> But if someone wished to say: 'There is something common to all these constructions – namely, the disjunction of all their common properties – ...' I should reply: Now you are only playing with words. One might as well say: 'Something runs through the whole thread – namely the continuous overlapping of those fibres.'[6]

Resemblance theories are really variants of essentialism – essence being sought in resemblance – and they share the latter's difficulties. The error common to both is that of trying to define the semantic catchment area of a word solely in terms of the properties of extra-linguistic objects and without reference to the relations between one word and another – the error, in short, of treating language as a heap of separate words; of trying to explain the relations between words and the world without regard to the *value system* that makes specification of reference possible. And this criticism could, as we have already said, be advanced against conceptualism – which claims that words ultimately owe their meaning to the unstable, private, inner objects with which they are correlated. The opposite mistake of post-Saussurean nominalism is to deny that any correlation exists at all or that it has any pre-linguistic basis, so that the shape of described reality is merely a reflection of the system of the language in which the description is cast.

'The problem of universals' is only one way of approaching the enigma of the relation between language and reality. Most theories of universals, apart perhaps from post-Saussurean system-nominalism, have problems in dealing with language as a *system* and in accommodating terms to which the contrasts particular/general, class/member, type/instance do not apply. It makes intuitive or pre-theoretical sense to talk about the (external) relation between the type 'dog' and the class of entities that are dogs; or between the token 'dog' and a particular dog such as Rover. It makes considerably less intuitive sense to think of the type 'or' as not only being instantiated in tokens used on particular occasions but also as being correlated with a general class of 'ors' whose members are referred to by token-instances of the word.

All theories of universals take hold of one aspect of language, or approach language from one (admittedly very important) direction; but they inevitably fall short of giving a comprehensive account of the relationship between language and extra-linguistic reality. They seem most appropriate in dealing with individual terms and in particular those that appear to have specific reference but less so for those that cannot be said without a good deal of Pickwickianism to have reference. To anticipate distinctions discussed later in this chapter, theories of universals seem to bear more directly upon the referential than the value pole of language – though this distinction is clouded by the fact that reference is achieved, directly or indirectly, only through value. Clearly, the idea of point-to-point correlation between words and world has more intuitive appeal when one is using nouns or nominalised forms of adjectives and verbs.

Another limitation common to all theories of universals is that they tend to treat individual words as if they were typically encountered in isolation. In practice, words occur in strings and even point-to-point reference involves the co-operative activity of many terms, including function words, such as articles, that no theory of universals could accommodate. Moreover, reference is impossible without mobilising the context of the discourse. All reference is situation-dependent and without the implied deixis of the present speaker or the surrounding text (and sometimes the surroundings of the text), reference is at best virtual. So, although the burden of specification, of classification-related meaning, is carried by forms such as nouns that theories of universals treat (and to a lesser extent by adjectives and verbs), these are able to operate only in the context of an actual or implied complete sentence; and the latter is itself a communication act possible only in the context of extra-linguistic life.

I am not pretending, therefore, that a satisfactory theory of universals would solve the mystery of the relationship between language and reality. Nevertheless, an anti-nominalist (and, incidentally, anti-essentialist) theory such as will be presented here is a useful corrective to the extreme – and extremely naïve – nominalism of post-Saussurean theory, typified in the Lacanian claim that 'it is the world of words that creates the world of things'.

3 Words, senses, objects

With few exceptions, all parties to the debate about universals are agreed that words do not stand proxy for material objects in a simple point-to-point fashion. Or at least that words do not secure reference to individuals by virtue of standing proxy for them. Words are not merely 'deputy things'. There are many reasons why this must be so. The most obvious is that, in so far as a token has a meaning, that meaning is general; material objects, on the other hand, are particulars occupying specific regions of space–time. The *meaning* of a word cannot be a particular object. So the relation between word and object when the word is used to signify a particular object cannot be a direct correlation. The relation between word and object must be mediated.

In the model I wish to present here, reference to an object is secured by materialising in a sign *one (general) sense* that the object has. The token (or more precisely the referring expression which may be composed of one or several tokens) acts as proxy for *a sense of the object*. A given object may have any number of senses and whether or not the linguistic materialisation of one of the senses secures reference to it will depend upon the context in which the referring expression is used. The context will include what has just been said, what can be assumed in the shared world of the communicants, and the actual physical surroundings of the utterance. Because an object has an indefinite number of possible senses (corresponding to the different relations speakers may have to it, the different ways they may see it, the different uses they may have for it, and so on), then there is room for repeated classification and reclassification.

In reference, word and object meet in the identity of the general meaning of a particular token with one of the (general) senses of an intelligible object. Under this analysis, the sign, or the chain of signs constituting a referring expression, acts as an alternative materialisation of one of the general senses of the object, and 'reference' is the coincidence between the sense of the linguistic sign(s) and the sense of the particular object.

This model makes a clear distinction between the signified on the one hand and the referent of a sign on the other – in contrast to post-Saussurean theory where the two are persistently confused. In most cases, we referentially take hold of objects in the world via the general senses that they have. Reference resides in the coincidence between the sense of a particular token or group of tokens and one of the senses of an object. The linguistic signified is not the referent; and, outside of the particular occasions when its parent sign is used to secure reference, it is not even a meaning; it is a value, which is best thought of as a 'virtual meaning' realised only when the word type is materialised in a token *in use on a particular occasion*. Correlation between a particular token and a particular object is possible only when the textual and physical co-ordinates of the utterance have been mobilised to secure reference. The relevant noun or noun-phrase – the referring expression – then takes all the credit for what has been a co-operative effort of many linguistic elements as well as involving the implied or explicit deixis of the extra-linguistic situation of the speaker or writer.

This model is consistent with there being constraints upon the choice of general terms by which we refer to an object. These will not be so tight as to imply a rigid correlation between verbal types and natural kinds. The senses of an object – which are potential lines along which it may be classified and narrow the range of expressions that may be used to grasp hold of it linguistically – are determined to a great extent extra-linguistically. But they are not fixed solely by physical properties or by some other 'natural' classifying feature. The sense of an object is potentially as variable as its significance; it is certainly relative to the situation of the individual observing or talking about it. The sense of the object will have historical and social as well as physical determinants. Selection within the range of possible senses of the object will be influenced by the current needs and the past history of the observer. There will be certain circumstances, for example, in which I may be inclined to see a brick as a weapon and so to call it a 'weapon'. Conventions of linguistic behaviour will also be influential on their own account: intertextuality operates even in the most casual conversation; though at the level of particular conversations it is never the sole and rarely the dominant determinant of how things are named, any more than it legislates over what it is that is said. It is not textual forces alone but also the particular circumstances in which I refer to the animal that make me call it 'That bloody canine' rather than Rover or 'the dog'. All three expressions may be stereotyped – they need to be if they are to be used successfully in reference – but the choice of one in preference to another will be influenced by the unique features of the particular situation of my utterance.

The theory shares the virtues both of essentialism – which takes account of the extra-linguistic constraints upon the choice of the general terms by which we refer to objects – and nominalism – which emphasises that these constraints do not always operate along natural or (even less) physical lines. Physical composition is not the sole arbiter of the *sense* of an object; the theory can accommodate what nominalists point out against essentialists and resemblance theorists, namely that there are few natural kinds based purely on common properties. Physical features alone are insufficient to determine the linguistic classification of an object or, more generally, the emergence of universals. Objects may, for example, be viewed in terms of their uses; in such a case, a log, say, or a boulder, may become a 'seat' though they will bear little physical resemblance to an armchair. Cases like this provide the strongest attraction of nominalism – on the mistaken assumption that if there is no common property shared by all the objects gathered under a given general term, then there is no basis for classification outside of language itself and that anything may be called anything once the appropriate conventions have been set up. But the variability of the application of words to objects (and the influence, that is sometimes apparent, of language on the division of the world into individuals), the differences between objects collected into a single linguistic class and the freedom we have to reclassify objects under different categories, do not license the assumption that there is a total arbitrariness in the relations between words and things. The reasons that we are more likely to classify one balloon with another balloon (even though there are no two balloons precisely alike) rather than to classify one particular balloon with other objects classified as bricks are not intra-linguistic. One obvious extra-linguistic reason is that it is possible to substitute one balloon for another in a practical activity but it is rarely possible to replace a balloon with a brick. (Use of course is not the only extra-linguistic basis for the classification of reality.) In summary, the theory fits with the facts: there are constraints upon the manner in which one assigns individuals to classes; they may be very loose but they are real; and they come from outside of language.

It may be thought that the 'object-sense' theory advanced here is merely a variant of conceptualism. This is not so. The senses of the object are external to the psyche of the language user in two respects: first, they are tethered to a particular object rather than being abstracted as a result of repeated encounters with supposedly similar objects; and secondly, they owe their independence, their separate and distinct existence, such as it is, to the position they have come to adopt in the language system. It is language, not the psyche of the individual, that confers the edges upon the senses. For this reason, the theory I have put forward is in no way a return to psychologism. The 'sense' retains its attachment both to the public object and to the public language: it is not a private entity. This is worth considering in more detail.

Let us conduct the thought experiment of considering an object being encountered alinguistically. It has a significance which we may characterise as a nimbus around it. This nimbus of unstable or nascent meaning becomes differentiated into stable, denumerable, discrete, hard-edged senses only when they are picked out linguistically. The word freezes one sense of the object from a shifting cloud of significance. Until the relevant terms pick them out, the senses are really 'sense ions' whose distinct or separate existence is only notional.

It must not be thought that language creates or generates either the senses of the object or the object itself. Rather, it confers an *aseity* upon senses that, prior to their secondary materialisation in the signifier of the sign, are confused with other senses. Language does not create differences of meaning; rather it stabilises senses that are pre-linguistically fused in the significance of an intelligible object.

The most important advantage of this model is that it obviates the apparent need for an isomorphism between language and reality. A verbal account of a piece of physical reality does not need to be shaped or structured like reality in order to be true of or to it; for what get expressed – and hence referred to – are not lumps of raw matter but the *senses* of material objects as they appear in particular situations. These senses are not the physical properties of the objects; nor do they necessarily correlate clearly with those objects; for while physical properties place limits upon plausible senses (for example, feasible uses), they do not fix those senses completely. The sense of a piece of matter will, as we have already remarked, be highly variable, even when its physical properties remain macroscopically constant. It will depend upon the interests, moods, physiological states and personal history of the individual taking notice of it, as well as, more remotely, upon the history of the society in which he lives. Conversely, the characteristics of all the objects that answer to or materialise a certain sense – let us say that embodied in the word 'table' – cannot be specified in physical terms; we cannot draw a continuous line around the group, class or cluster of properties that would determine whether or not an object could fulfil or carry that sense or not. There is thus a *double dissociation* between senses and physical properties.

One could not therefore hope to embody extra-linguistic sense linguistically by somehow replicating the physical properties of the objects that carry that sense. The sense of things cannot be signified by physical resemblances – one-to-one correspondence of components, for example – because sense is not tightly correlated with physical characteristics. A mirror gives the visible appearance of objects but does not replicate or indicate or express their senses. *Sense* cannot be mirrored; so the non-mirror-like nature of language does not have any bearing upon its capacity or otherwise to express reality.

4 Value, meaning and reference

In some cases it appears to be possible linguistically to isolate objects that could not otherwise exist on their own. Outside of language, 'green', 'haste' and 'smile', to take three examples at random, could not enjoy the spatially separate existence they have in written texts or the temporally distinct existence they enjoy in speech. But this must not be taken to mean that discourse deals with or refers to an autonomous realm populated exclusively by linguistic objects. Though it points to the inadequacies of a naïve realist theory of universals (whether of the transcendental Platonic variety or the immanent Aristotelian type), the existence of smiles, hastes and greens as referents of words does not license the conclusion that verbal meaning is internal to language; even less that verbal *reference* is to intra-linguistic referents. The smile is out there even if it is separated from the smiling face only by and in the statements that describe smile and face as two mutually external relata. Outside of language, we cannot pick up, or even physically point to, the quality green without picking up or pointing to other qualities of a green object at the same time. But green, none the less, remains extra-linguistic; it is a *quale* which is not reducible to its opposition to other colours. It is a positive reality, not a purely differential value. 'Green' may be a verbal type that has token instances; but green itself does not have realisations but spatio-temporally located instances. If this were not the case, it would be difficult to see how language could be used (as it is sometimes used) to redirect someone's attention without physically pointing – as when we say 'Look at that gorgeous green!'

Reference, which is the coincidence of one sense of the object with the sense of a linguistic sign brought down from generality of meaning by tokenisation and the mobilisation of deictic co-ordinates, connects, as we always thought it did, the linguistic and the extra-linguistic realms. The sharp edges of the emergent separate senses are due to the mutual pressure of rival signifieds, as described by Saussure. The sense itself, however, is not intra-linguistic: it still remains tethered to the object as *a sense of that object* and that object comes armed with its own, spatio-temporal rather than semantic, edges, which language cannot supersede or obliterate. The theory shows, moreover, how the *division* of meaning is not the same as the *generation* of meaning: it is values, not meanings, that are purely differential and negative; and it is values, not senses, that are pure form without content.

In so far as language *is* in places an autonomous realm, with its own 'objects', then we are dealing with value rather than reference. Whereas complete statements must, if they are fully intelligible, have reference, individual words may be almost pure value terms, having no other reference than their contrast with, or their effect in modifying the meaning of, other words. We may, if we consider words in isolation, assign them places upon a notional line leading from 'pure value' to 'pure reference' (see Figure 1).

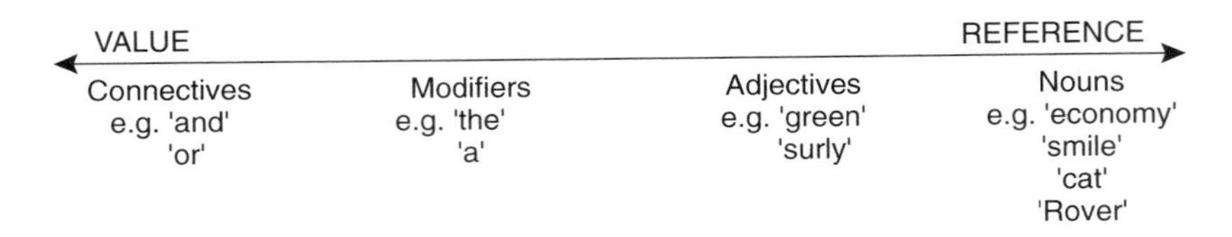

Figure 1

(This metaphorical line must not be taken literally. It is not my intention to ape structuralist scientism.)

'Meaning', of course, spans the whole spectrum, encompassing value at the one end and reference at the other. At one end of the axis are connectives, such as 'and' and 'or' that have value with little plausible reference;[7] at the opposite end are the proper names of real objects which may be said to have reference but little value, in so far as they do not belong to a system of oppositional terms.[8] Within these grammatical types, some words are closer than others to one or other end of the spectrum (for example, we could assign nouns different places – see Figure 2). The nearer the term is to the left of the spectrum, the more it will seem to conform to the structuralist conception of a word as a value; or rather, the more plausible the structuralist reduction of words to values appears. But even in the case of terms at the far left of the spectrum, the structuralist account does not apply in full because such words do not have definite meaning in isolation. If they appear to do so, this is only because we are used to finding them in the context of other words where they do contribute to meaning, and it is natural to think that that meaning would be preserved even if the words in question alone constituted the vocabulary of a single-term language.

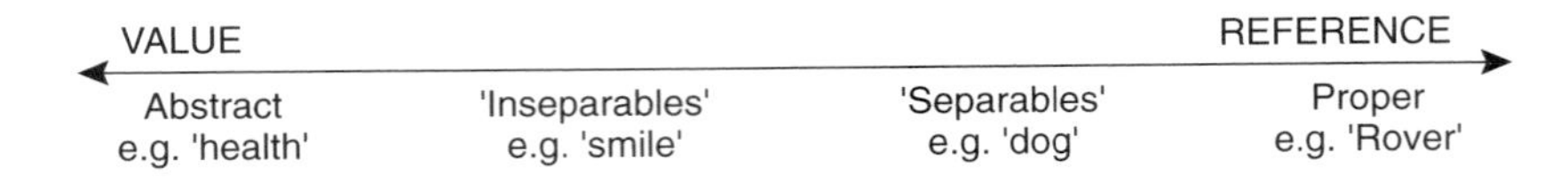

Figure 2

Once the distinction between value and reference is grasped, it is easy to see why there need be no one-to-one correlation between verbal meanings and extra-linguistic objects, or between the elements of language and the elements of reality. Even where there does sometimes appear to be such a correspondence (sufficient to give mirror or picture theories a momentary plausibility),[9] this is only apparent. In the statement 'The dog is in the street', there appears to be a one-to-one correspondence between the (two) components of the described situation (dog, street) and the components of the description ('dog', 'street'). This correspondence, however, operates only in the context of a whole sentence, which itself contains several non-corresponding components and is composed of seven, rather than two, words. There is at best a three-and-a-half-to-one correspondence; and the apparent correspondence is parasitic upon non-correspondence. So there are no *purely* referential terms since all terms have to co-operate with others in order that something can be done with or through them. No word is an island. Even the baldest of referring expressions, such as proper names, are only syncategorematically so; indeed, we could say that, ultimately, proper names are as referentially syncategorematic as determiners such as 'the' and 'a'. No intrinsic grammatical property of a term is sufficient of itself to determine that that term shall count as a referring expression.

Behind the many fallacies of post-Saussurean literary theory may be the assumption that if there is no simple (e.g. numerical) correlation between terms and pre-linguistic entities, then there can be no reference to, or veridical account of, extra-linguistic reality. The post-Saussurean critique of realism may be rooted in the belief that a truly referential language should consist if not entirely of pictures at least of proper names set out in a manner that reflects the arrangement of their referents. The arbitrary nature of individual signs and the systematic features of language are then taken to imply the impossibility of realistic reference. In a sense, post-Saussurean literary theory espouses an error opposite to naïve isomorphic theories: instead of seeing all terms as being like proper names and located at the right hand of the value–reference spectrum, it sees all words as if they were function terms, as pure values located at the other end instead.

5 The triadic theory of signification

The theory of reference advanced in this chapter is triadic and shares many features with the traditional account of linguistic signification which also employs three terms – the sign, the concept and the significatum.[10] It might be thought that these terms could be directly mapped on to those used here and the corresponding entities mutually reduced (see Figure 3). There are important overlaps; but the differences are important, too. The present theory

Traditional account	**Present theory**
Sign	Referring expression
Concept/signification	Sense (ion)
Significatum	Object/referent

Figure 3

is specifically one of reference rather than of signification as such. This is not simply because reference is what is most at issue in the post-Saussurean attack on realism but also because it is only in reference that one can legitimately separate the three elements. Away from the reference end of the spectrum, concept and signification tend to merge in 'value'; meaning and the thing meant are difficult to extricate from one another.

The most important difference between the traditional and the present theory relates to the middle term. In the traditional triadic account of signification,[11] 'words signify [things] by means of mediating concepts'. Now 'concept' is ambiguous. As Lyons points out 'The term "concept" could be used, therefore, in two senses; not only for what we now call mental concepts ... but also for postulated extra-mental entities that were apprehended by the mind in its knowledge and perception of the external world.'[12] Lyons uses 'objective concept' to cover both senses of 'concept'. Such a term suggests the possibility of convening the three partners to the classifying enterprise – the mind, language and extra-mental reality. There is a tendency, as we have already discussed, to interpret 'concept' in a narrower sense, as an intra-psychic entity built up out of recurrent experiences. As the immediate signification of a word, 'concept' in this narrower sense would seem to be far too unstable to mediate between language, reality and the individual language user. Alternatively, 'concept' may be used in such a way as to suggest 'mind amongst things' and to imply a mentalistic, and yet realist, account of universals. A doctrine of natural kinds with the linguistically competent mind as a passive mirror or in miraculous pre-established harmony with the natural world would seem then to lie dangerously close at hand.

The theory I have outlined tries to avoid these difficulties. Sense ions remain tethered to individual objects (though the latter are generalised by virtue of being intelligible as 'such-and-suches'); but they are extricated from the significance field of the object and separated out only as a result of the activity of a linguistically competent mind. The present theory, in other words, gives all three elements – language, the individual psyche and the specific object – their due. If, as a result, it only clarifies the traditional triadic account of signification and, in particular, reforms the idea of 'the objective concept' so that it can no longer be used in support of essentialism, nominalism or psychologistic conceptualism, I should be content.

6 'A picture held us captive'

Although the signifier and the signified are values, the sign as a whole *in operation* on a particular occasion is not a pure value. Even so, most referring expressions contain terms that are not themselves explicitly or intrinsically referential: reference is the result of the co-operative activity of a number of elements. There could not, therefore, be a one-to-one correspondence between the components of statements and the components of the realities they are purportedly about. The linguistic capture of an object takes place through one or other of its senses and the latter do not have, nor do they correlate rigidly with, physical properties. There are thus reasons on both sides of the language barrier for regarding the arbitrariness of the linguistic sign and the systematic nature of language as being irrelevant to the question of whether there can be genuine discursive reference to a genuinely extra-linguistic reality.

To put it more bluntly, the presence or absence of physical resemblance or numerical correspondence between discourses and realities does not bear on the question of whether or not the former can really be 'about' or be true of the latter. Physical resemblance between word and object (or the lack of it), or isomorphism between statements and states of affairs (or the absence of it) is quite irrelevant to the truth, the precision or the power of verbal signification. That language does not mirror reality – discourse does not look like, it is not structured like, what it is supposed to be about – is scarcely surprising when we consider that what it is about is the *sense* the world makes to us (rather than the dumb materiality of bits of matter) and sense is not something that can be mirrored. If sense were susceptible of mirror imaging, every puddle in the road would be a continuous source of hyper-realistic discourse.

All of this should be sufficiently obvious. Why then has the opposite view held such sway amongst literary theorists over the last few decades and been so crucial to the contempt in which realistic fiction is held? It is almost certainly because many writers on literature and language have been bewitched by a misleading image of the nature of reference, description and linguistic expression. 'A picture held us captive ...'[13] as Wittgenstein said – with particular reference to his own theories of verbal meaning. The picture in question derives from the idea that the mechanism and the goal of signification is to *replicate* or to *reproduce* reality in part or in whole – so that to talk or to write realistically about anything is, in some sense, to copy it. Since copying is not possible, then realism (so the, usually unspoken, argument goes) is impossible and descriptions and stories – true or fictional – will seem realistic only as the result of a kind of fraud. Behind this extraordinary prejudice is, curiously, the belief that reality is ultimately pure matter and that the only legitimate, accurate and truthful way of speaking of it would be to deploy an array of signs whose material properties, or at least structural relations, in some degree *replicated* that physical reality. The fundamental belief, 'the picture that held us captive', is that true signification is *physical synecdoche* – that reality is matter and to report on it is to copy it. In the light of this fallacy, spoken or written language, whose signs and sign combinations are arbitrary with respect to the physical properties of the realities referred to, must appear to be a shabby and unreliable instrument of communication.

The 'physical synecdoche' prejudice is well illustrated by Edmund Gosse's century-old argument against the ambitions of the realistic novel and his reference to 'the inherent disproportion which exists between the small flat surface of a book and the vast arch of life which it undertakes to mirror'.[14] This rather literal interpretation of the supposed ambitions of realism is, of course, intended ironically. Nevertheless, the fact that the discrepancy between the physical characteristics of a book (small, flat) and that of extra-literary reality (vast, curved) should count as any kind of argument at all is a symptom of the way in which the project of realism is often conceived. It is as if the aim of realism were a neutral transcription of essentially material reality; and the asymptote of realism were *chosisme*.

A more recent example comes from the prominent anti-realist critic Robert Scholes. Scholes has swallowed many of the standard structuralist reasons for rejecting realism and the implicit claim of realistic writing that it is 'about' something.[15] But he also believes, paradoxically, that literary realism has had its day because it has been superseded – by cine-realism:

> The cinema gives the *coup de grâce* to a dying realism in written fiction. Realism purports – has always purported – to subordinate words themselves to their referents: to the things words point to. ... But when it comes to representing things, one picture is worth a thousand words, and one motion picture is worth a million. In face of competition from the cinema, fiction must abandon its attempt to 'represent reality' and rely more on the power of words to stimulate the imagination.[16]

Realistic literature is assumed to consist essentially of the 'representation' of reality understood as literally re-presenting or reproducing it. The reality in question is also assumed to be physical reality; or, more specifically, picturable or visual reality, because that is what pictures, even moving ones, are restricted to depicting. This is what the 'competition' from the cinema must be all about.[17]

Scholes is a highly respected writer on the novel. So my critic who believes that realistic writers want simply to reproduce the physical world inside the covers of their books – and who therefore seem to succeed in fulfilling the aims of realism only by means of a rather pathetic fraud – is no straw man invented for my polemic purposes to distract attention from the real opposition and the real arguments. Moreover, as I have already indicated, it is not only recent critics who seem to imagine that realism is a matter of the replication of reality; or that to do justice to reality one should attempt to duplicate it. The early twentieth-century writer T.E. Hulme suggested that poetry should aim at 'the bodily handing over of sensations'. Poetry would seem to be a remarkably inefficient way of doing this: visual sensibilia could be better delivered by the cinema; and as for the rest, sexual intercourse, tourism and the provision of *ex gratia* cash payments to permit the audience to obtain the sensations first hand themselves would seem to be more efficient ways of bodily handing over sensations. At best, language can be an invitation to recall or to imagine experiences (at the level of perception rather than sensation): no amount of fiddling with words and meanings could make the word 'itchy' itself itchy – or not, at least without a good deal being provided by the reader. Of all activities, the consumption of words is the most remote from pure or bodily sensation. This would not, of course, count against language as an instrument for presenting reality were it not for the fallacious belief that all art should aspire to the condition of the cinema or that in order to report truthfully on a part of the world one must duplicate it.

This misconception – wrong both as to the means and the ends of language – has misled many a poetaster into dreary attempts to exploit the physical characteristics of written and spoken words in the hope of making the referents more vividly present and so of intensifying the meaning of the discourses in question. Onomatopoeia is cited as an exemplary poetic technique in classrooms, despite the fact that it rarely – if ever – guarantees a closer resemblance between expression and expressed. Actually, onomatopoeia should be classified along with other devices, such as alliteration, assonance, rhythm and rhyme, which serve to draw attention to the material properties of words so that a poem may become what Valéry said it should be – a discourse that hesitates between sound and sense. Such hesitation is, in fact, only an unimportant aspect of most verse (even Valéry's verse) and is certainly not central in the way that those who follow Jakobson assert that it is. Be that as it may, a poem *never* hesitates between *sight* and sense: words make rotten pictures. This explains why so-called Concrete Poetry, in which the visible surface of the written text is supposed to replicate to some extent the visible surface of the referred-to reality, is so uniformly unsuccessful. Since Apollinaire used it to crack a few literary pleasantries, Concrete Poetry has been extensively promoted; it remains, nevertheless, about as poetic as concrete. A picture indeed held us captive: it was the picture of a picture.

7 Referential realism and fiction

The theory I have outlined above is not intended to revive a Platonic or even an Aristotelian realism. I do not wish to suggest that universals are real extra-linguistic entities: I am a 'referential realist' not a realist *vis-à-vis* universals.

For verbal meaning to result in successful reference, deictic co-ordinates must be mobilised: the spatio-temporal context of the utterance is crucial to the process of identifying the referent and pinning the necessarily general meaning to the necessarily particular object. Only under such circumstances are complete reference, and consequently true or false statements, possible.

The emphasis on deixis may seem to raise insuperable barriers against (realistic) referential *fiction*. The difficulty is not, however, as great as it might seem at first sight. For the situation of realistic fiction is not qualitatively different from that of non-fictional written texts and even non-fictional stories told in everyday life. In the written text or even the spoken tale, the role of deixis may be played by anaphora or the intermediate form of textual deixis.[18] Body-, person- or situation-relative identification is supplanted by text-relative identification. Many referring expressions employed in everyday life are (to use Strawson's term) 'story-relative'.[19] Strawson gives the example of a speaker beginning a story as follows: 'A man and a boy were standing by a fountain.' The story continues: 'The man had a drink.' In the first sentence the article linked to 'man' is indefinite; in the second it is definite, indicating that the second occurrence of 'man' is co-referential with the first. The text establishes a restricted universe of discourse and within this universe the definite article is sufficient to establish unique, numerical identity because no entities of the same type have been referred to and consequently brought into question. Under such conditions, numerical and type identity converge. 'A man' and 'the man' can be assumed, without further evidence, to be co-referential. Since the first encounter was via reference, identity is indistinguishable from the means of identification and repeat reference is the equivalent of reference to an entity that has already been identified by non-referential encounter. Story- or text-relative identification is an essential part of the true telling of ordinary events in everyday life – even of the simplest kind. 'You know that dog that I have been telling you about? Well, he was back in our garden today.' And in fiction, where the object referred to remains absent throughout the reader's textual encounter with it, things are not so different. Just as in the ordinary reporting of true events, encounter followed by reference, followed by repeat reference is replaced by reference followed by co-reference and repeat co-reference.

Novels are usually written rather than spoken, and it may be argued that the situation of a text is different from that of a conversation. For speech offers the possibility of at least a remnant of person- or situation-deixis. In practice, this difference has the opposite implication and works to the advantage of fiction. If the story or report is about something that is not in the vicinity of the speaker, his body will offer no spatio-temporal deictic co-ordinates to help pin down reference to particulars. The only restriction upon the universe of discourse will be then the sum of what the speaker is likely to refer to and this must be co-extensive with his knowledge or experience. In the case of a novel on the other hand, the universe of discourse will be restricted to the contents of the book or of the series of books to which the novel belongs. There is only one Emma in *Madame Bovary* so that we can always safely assume that all references to 'Emma Bovary' are co-referential with all other references to 'Emma Bovary'.

This raises another problem regarding fiction, however. If the referents of the expressions used in a novel belong entirely to a space that is outside of the spatio-temporal nexus of reality, how can what is said about them be true or false? No experience could confirm or refute what is said by Shakespeare to be true of Hamlet. If Hamlet does not even exist, how can it be true that Hamlet is a man and untrue that he is a woman? The answer is that this is what consistency demands of us. The list of characters at the beginning of *Hamlet* tells us that he is Prince of Denmark and from this we infer that he is male. This inference is supported by his being referred to as 'he', 'my good lord' and so on, and by many aspects of his behaviour – for example, his swordsmanship and his courtship of Ophelia. It is not possible to be both wholly male and wholly female, and since there is no evidence in the play to suggest that he is androgynous we conclude that it is untrue that he is a woman.

For a fictional statement to be true, it must, at least, be consistent with the statements considered to be basic or foundational in the fictional universe of discourse. But this is not all. There is also the question of plausibility. Now plausibility is not sharply distinguished from consistency. Whatever is inconsistent at the level of logic ('not[$p \bullet$ not p]'), must also be implausible. It is relatively easy to decide that it is inconsistent for Hamlet to be literally a woman as well as literally a man because most people are one or the other and, as already noted, there is nothing in the play to suggest that he belonged to one or other of the intersexes. Likewise, we would have no difficulty in defending the claim that it was implausible that Hamlet had four legs, even though there is no point in the play where the number of Hamlet's legs is specifically stated; for being four-legged is inconsistent with being a human being. This is an empirical rather than a logical observation because being two-legged is an extensional rather than an intensional property of human beings. A race of four-legged, one hundred per cent human beings is thinkable in the way that a race of female, one hundred per cent males is not. We would, however, have more difficulty in establishing the implausibility of a critic's claim that Hamlet spent a good deal of his time mending roads and that (although Shakespeare suppressed this fact) he used to say 'Yer know' at the end of his every statement. Our objection to these claims would be based on the idea that there should be an empirical as well as logical consistency between the founding statements about Hamlet and any other claims about what he was or did. The appeal to probability would be based on that automatic cluster analysis which takes place as a part of the acquisition of experience of the world. We would then argue as follows:

(i) People of Hamlet's sort (princes) do not usually behave in this way.
(ii) This behaviour is therefore inconsistent with what we have been told about him and which has established the kind of person he is.
(iii) We therefore judge the character of Hamlet (as presented by Shakespeare or developed by a subsequent writer) to be implausible, incoherent, *untrue* to the way people usually are.

In other words, we judge fictions as true or false (or statements made about fictional characters or events as true or false) on the grounds of plausibility, which encompasses logic at one end ('not [p•not p]') and our general experience of the world at the other. We judge fictions, in short, rather in the way that we judge true stories told to us in everyday life; and this is not surprising, since we are not often in a position to test the supposedly true stories told to us directly against experience. We do not experience most facts; and so we deem supposedly factual reports false if they are internally inconsistent or they are externally inconsistent, in the sense of not conforming to the way we have directly or indirectly experienced things usually to be. Enough will have been said to make it clear that the line between internal and external consistency, between *a priori* impossibility and *a posteriori* or empirical improbability, is not sharply drawn and the indications for the invocation of the law of the excluded middle are not precisely defined or definable.

Our assessment of the plausibility or the consistency of a fictional story, therefore, is similar in important respects to the way in which we assess these things in a true story or an ordinary report. There remains a sense, however, in which the referents of fictions are virtual referents. They depend upon us, the readers, to provide the world into which they can be inserted. For, despite what many critics say to the contrary, novelists rarely create worlds – only (if they are very good) plausible tracks through the world the reader brings to his reading. But this dependency is not a matter of the relationship between language and reality; only if the empirical fact that fiction happens to be factually untrue and that, even in the case of true stories, we can invoke a world by referring to it but not replicate it. The trajectory that the story takes through the world (or rather – and this is an important qualification – *a* world) will be new to the reader (as may the world itself, or the level at which the journey takes place); and in this way, fiction may act as a critique of the fossilised world picture, the fixed angle of vision and the calcified conceptions implicit in what the reader brings to the novel. Even so, the worlds in which realistic novels operate are continuous with extra-fictional realities, just as the world of a true story is a real world. For all stories – true or fictional – *make sense* only by virtue of implicit reference to a real world. The latter is the 'horizon', in the phenomenological sense, of the fictional events.[20]

8 The mystery of reference

A lack of physical resemblance – both at the level of the individual elements and at the level of their structure and organisation – between discourse and extra-discursive reality does not in any way preclude the former being 'about' the latter, except under the erroneous assumption that all signification must take place by replication of that which is signified. We have, I think, given adequate reasons for maintaining that neither reference nor description[21] could operate through *duplication* of material reality. Reference, far from being made less likely or more difficult by the arbitrariness of linguistic signs and the lack of isomorphism between discourse and reality, is probably dependent upon them. It is precisely the non-naturalness of the relationship between language and reality that establishes the distance which enables sense ions to be dissected out from a significance field and, ultimately, makes language a means by which man can step back from physical reality in order to refer to and express it and so, in George Steiner's words, 'to talk himself free of organic constraint'. Non-arbitrary signs such as reflections or causal chains, would not embody the wakefulness or the explicitness that, in the last analysis, is what is given expression in language.

Enough has been said to support the claim that it is possible to develop a view of language that adopts a plausible middle way between implausible alternatives: either that language is totally responsible for the differentiation of reality; or that reality is differentiated completely independently of the manner in which it is spoken of. I have further argued that the concept of 'reference' presents no greater difficulties when applied to fiction than it does with respect to the recounting of true events or the production of true descriptions in everyday life.

'Referential realism' would seem therefore to be a tenable position. Nevertheless, I do not pretend that what has been said here amounts to a satisfactory theory of reference. Reference remains one of the great mysteries of language and hence of human consciousness. One, not uncommon, response to the mysterious is to deny that it exists and this refusal to accept the reality of the inexplicable, or the as yet unexplained, may be in the end what lies behind the post-Saussurean denial of the possibility of genuine reference to extra-linguistic reality. Since we cannot yet comprehend how a sculptured puff of air can refer to some object or state of affairs an indefinite distance away, one rather natural response is to deny that the distance is crossed and to assert that the object is either intra-linguistic or the reference is only apparent.

A comparable temptation faces those who are vexed by the mystery of perception; and, indeed, there is an analogy between the denial of reference to discourses and the denial of the objective reality of the intentional objects of perceptions. I offer the following tentative analogy:

SENSATION:PERCEPTION::VALUE:REFERENCE

Since perceptions are not miniatures of the external world, it is argued that they tell us nothing about extra-cerebral or even extra-mental reality. As with language, there is a tendency to think that perceptions would be more accurate and easier to understand if they somehow replicated the reality they are supposed to be 'about' – if there were an isomorphism between percept and object. In accordance with this argument, the best way of constituting a perception of a cup or creating an accurate description of it, would be to place another cup next to it. The analogy between epistemological idealism and the structuralist view of the world is apparent in the parallel between the views that reality is a verbal construct and that material objects are *illogical* constructs out of perceptions. Both views reflect a reluctance to admit to the reality of something that it is difficult to understand. But the fact that we do not understand something is not sufficient grounds for denying its existence unless we adopt the Hegelian principle that the real is always intelligible. Without that evidently false principle, there can be no rationale for denying the existence of things that are beyond the reach of our understanding. Reference is a mystery; but it is not, for that reason, an illusion.

Scepticism about the referential possibilities of language has, of course, a venerable tradition reaching back at least as far as classical times. Cratylus, believing that it was impossible to use words without being misunderstood and without misrepresenting apparent referents, espoused aphasia. For reasons that are fairly obvious, he did not record his own views; they have come down to us through Plato, who tells us that Cratylus declined to use words in philosophical discussion, confining himself to wagging his finger. A discussion with him must have been a rather dull, not to say one-sided, affair; but at least his silent gesticulations were more consistent than the profuse outpourings of his modern successors. Even so, one wonders how Plato came to know of Cratylus' reasons for retreating from language. Cratylus himself must somehow have expounded them at some time and it is difficult to conceive how he could have done so without using words. Finger wagging does not readily lend itself to the expression of complex, abstract and general doubts about language.

One suspects that then, as now, the metalanguage used to criticise language was itself granted a mysterious dispensation from the general condemnation. It is, to put it mildly, rather implausible that language should be available to refer to itself and, in particular, to its own limitations *and to no other referent in the world*. Nevertheless, it is usual for those who profess radical doubts about language to suspend those doubts when it comes to using language to express them. But metalinguistic statements that put the expressive power of language in doubt should not themselves be allowed to pass without critical scrutiny. If discourses cannot reach to a reality outside of themselves, if they cannot be truly 'about' anything, then they certainly cannot be used to comment on the relationship between themselves and reality.

Nor can they be used to pass harsh judgement upon those highly elaborated, ambitious and ordered expressions of parts of reality that we term (realistic) novels. Even if we were to accept the much narrower thesis that it is only literary discourse, uprooted from immediate practical needs, that is self-referential, this would still not release the literary theorist from the charge of pragmatic self-refutation. Barthes, for example, tells us that in (literary) 'writing': 'a fact is *narrated* no longer with a view to acting directly on reality but intransitively, that is to say, finally outside of any function than that of the very practice of the symbol itself'.[22] If 'writing' consists only of the practice of the symbol itself and if the symbols in question consist of signifiers inexplicably uprooted from signifieds (according to Hawkes 'prised utterly free of signifieds'), then writers are condemned to spending their days spinning chains of signifiers that are only meaningless – and certainly referenceless – marks on paper. These are two large and fortunately counterfactual ifs. If, however, these were not counterfactual, then we would have to accept Barthes's claims that when a fact is narrated without a view to 'acting directly on reality', the writer is merely inscribing signifiers without signifieds. And this must cause some embarrassment to literary theorists. For if literature *is* divorced from practical need, so too is literary theory; for the latter is at best second-order or meta-literature. What, therefore, are we to make of apparently realistic literary theory that talks referentially about literature in a way that the theorist forbids the novelist to talk about the world? Is post-Saussurean literary theory merely an '*effet de la théorie*'? I leave the reader to draw his own conclusion, though he may be assisted in his deliberations by considering this passage from Terence Hawkes:

> 'New' New Criticism would thus claim to respond to literature's essential nature in which signifiers are prised utterly free of signifieds, aiming, in its no-holds-barred encounter with the text, for a *coherence* and *validity* of response, not objectivity and truth.[23]

How is it possible to distinguish a 'valid' response from an invalid one, once one has repudiated *both* objectivity and truth, especially when the thing one is responding to consists only of marks on paper that have been severed from reference and meaning and especially when, as Barthes says, no reading of a work is *wrong* and Racine, for example, consists only of what has been said about Racine?

What seems to be lacking in those who deny the reality of reference is a willingness to recognise the existence of something that they cannot explain. And this is connected with the inability of the structuralist and poststructuralist *terribles simplificateurs* to respond to the inexpressible mystery of language and to see that language cannot be simply modelled. Because words do not mirror the world, it does not follow that discourse is cut off from the world. The correct observation that language is not a heap of labels corresponding to a heap of extra- and pre-linguistic objects does not license the opposite conclusion that it is a closed system. It does not follow from the fact that language is not a mirror that it must be a self-sufficient crystal. It is more likely to be analogous to a heap of spaghetti on a plate or a pile of string vests. More likely still, it cannot be modelled at all: it is a mystery that is exceeded in depth only by that of consciousness itself.

It is possible to subscribe to the aims and hopes of realism while still retaining a sophisticated conception of the relationship between language and reality. The radical nominalism of post-Saussurean literary theory leads directly to a self-defeating linguistic idealism. If in our narratives (or our statements), in our fictions (or our facts), we are confined to the inside of anything, it is not of language but of the sense we make of the world, of consciousness. But to be confined to the inside of consciousness is not to be inside at all, nor to be confined.

Notes

1. The myth gains a good deal of support from the use of that unfortunate ambiguous word 'mimesis'. It is often stated that realism aims at mimesis, where mimesis is understood to mean at least metonymic *replication* of reality. The 'mimetic fallacy' is, however, a fallacy *about* realism, not the fallacy *of* realism.
2. 'Philosophy and the Form of Fiction', in R. Scholes (ed.), *Fiction and the Figures of Life* (New York: Alfred A. Knopf, 1970), p. 12.
3. Quoted – without protest – by Jonathan Culler in *Structuralist Poetics* (London: Routledge & Kegan Paul, 1975), p. 109.
4. The phenomenon of 'lapsed structuralism' is discussed in Raymond Tallis, *Not Saussure* (Basingstoke: Macmillan, 1988, 1995), section 3.4.
5. Saussurean linguistic theory incorporates a modified conceptualism. The signified is a concept. The latter does not, however, pre-exist language as a psychological entity. A word is not a pre-existing sound associated with a pre-existing object; on the contrary, one does not start 'from the terms and construct

the system by adding them together'; rather, 'it is from the interdependent whole that one must start and through analysis obtain its elements' (Saussure, *Course*, p. 113). Their co-presence in the linguistic *system*, their mutual pressure, stabilises the concepts and gives them more definite edges. They are consequently 'objective concepts' in the sense to be discussed below (see also *Not Saussure*, section 3.1).

6. Ludwig Wittgenstein, *Philosophical Investigations*, trans. G.E.M. Anscombe (Oxford: Basil Blackwell, 1953), p. 32.
7. Several philosophers (notably Russell) tried (unsuccessfully) to give reference to certain logical connectives, correlating 'or', for example, with a feeling of hesitation. Such psychologising of function terms would require identifying a mood or other psychological state to correspond to each of the grammatical features of a language – an artificial and implausible exercise.
8. Traditionally, proper names are said to have reference but no sense; but the situation, as John Searle and others have shown, is not as simple as this: see, for example, John Searle, *Speech Acts* (Cambridge University Press, 1969), section 7.2, 'Proper names'.
9. So that talk of equivalent logical multiplicity between a state of affairs and the proposition that describes it (in the style of early Wittgenstein) could seem to make sense.
10. See John Lyons, *Semantics* (Cambridge University Press, 1977), vol. I, ch. 4.
11. Ibid., pp. 96–9, 109–14.
12. Ibid., p. 111.
13. '*A picture* held us captive. And we could not get outside it, for it lay in our language and language seemed to repeat it to us inexorably' (Wittgenstein, *Philosophical Investigations*, p. 115).
14. Edmund Gosse, quoted in Damien Grant, *Realism* (London: Methuen, 1970), p. 15.
15. 'Criticism has taken the very idea of "aboutness" away from us. It has taught us that language is tautological, if it is not nonsense, and to the extent it is about anything, it is about itself' (Robert Scholes, 'Fictional Criticism of the Future', *Triquarterly* 34 (Fall 1975)).
16. Robert Scholes, *The Fabulators* (New York: Oxford University Press, 1967).
17. Raymond Tallis, 'The Realistic Novel versus the Cinema', *Critical Quarterly*, vol. 27, no. 2 (1985), pp. 57–65.
18. The interested reader is referred to John Lyons' lucid, subtle and comprehensive review of deixis in *Semantics*, vol. II, pp. 636–724. His definition of deixis: 'a function of personal and demonstrative pronouns, of tense and a variety of other grammatical and lexical features which relate utterances to the spatio-temporal coordinates of the act of utterance' would be difficult to better.
19. P.F. Strawson, *Individuals: An Essay in Descriptive Metaphysics* (London: Methuen, 1959). See especially pp. 18, 23, 24.
20. A truthful realistic fiction should be not only consistent (allowing, of course, for diametrically opposed viewpoints of the characters within the fiction) and plausible but also *representative*, so that the novel is a metonym for a larger reality than that which it describes. The metonymic claim of fiction is more problematic and will be dealt with in another work.
21. Where reference ends and description begins is not easy to establish, except in grammatical terms, when 'reference' captures that which falls under the subject and 'description' encompasses the predicates applied to the subject. This over-simple account does not accommodate the fact that reference may be achieved through

description, a referring expression being a 'definite description'. A theory of reference, as Russell found, tends to pass into a theory of description.

22. Roland Barthes, *The Death of the Author*, in *Image–Music–Text*, selected and trans. Stephen Heath (London: Fontana, 1977), p. 142.
23. Terence Hawkes, *Structuralism and Semiotics* (London: Methuen, 1977), p. 156. The passage from which this phrase is taken (quoted a little further on in my text) is of great interest to the pathologist of modern literary theory.

From: *Not Saussure* (Macmillan, 1988, 1995), pp. 100–27, 258–60.

5
Language and Consciousness

In this brief extract, from *The Explicit Animal* (1991, 1999), Tallis considers why attempts to naturalise language won't do. Behaviourists like B.F. Skinner have tried to see language as a form of communication that is essentially the same as that taking place between animals. Signs signify by stimulating behaviour identical to that which would be stimulated by the object itself. Tallis is critical of these kinds of conception – basically because they bypass what is essential about language, its quality of explicitness. The very notion of meaning something depends on intention, and meaning transmitted through signs makes this explicit. Linguistic signs are meant, and for us to understand them depends on us seeing that they are meant. Brief though this extract is, it sums up much that is at the heart of the way Tallis sees language and human consciousness.

I have characterised human language as that in virtue of which explicitness is made explicit. It is the main medium of higher-order explicitness and opens the path to the endless elaboration of explicitness: of consciousness of consciousness; and consciousness of consciousness of consciousness; and so on. Language is not, of course, the only medium in which reflexive self-consciousness can unfold; but it is a matrix in which higher-order unfoldings most typically take place; in which, for example, I become most elaborately aware of your awareness of my awareness of me; or I consider the reason you tried to indicate that your handshake was not as sincere as it might have been, given normal behaviour and expectations.[1]

The signs of human language are radically arbitrary. At the most obvious level, they do not look like, sound like, etc. the objects that are signified through them. They are not, that is to say, iconic and their formations do not signify in virtue of replicating a piece of reality. More importantly, they are arbitrary in the sense of being uprooted from their context: they are not causally related to that which they signify. Natural signs such as clouds signify rain because they cause it. Other natural signs may be effects of what they signify: for example, a scream may signify pain or fear or danger. Both kinds of signs may be seen as symptomatic or, at least, synecdochic; the sign and the significate are parts of a single whole – a causal process or sequence. Natural signs are embedded in the same context as their significates. Linguistic signs are not.

Attempts to naturalise human language have, consciously or unconsciously, been directed towards undermining or denying this arbitrariness or, conversely, reading into natural signs properties – grammar, reference, etc. – that are in fact dependent on arbitrariness. At the very crudest level, it has been suggested that the emission of signs is triggered by the objects they signify and that the meaning of the sign is its effect on the recipient. The presence of the object, for example, is communicated from one individual to another as follows:

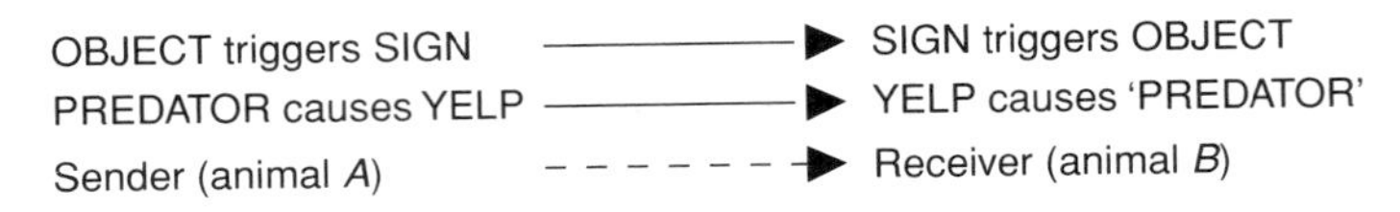

For example, animal *A* encounters a predator and emits a yelp; animal *B* hears the yelp and behaves as if it had encountered a predator; it, too, runs away. The fact that it runs away is taken to be the cash value of the communication 'There is a predator in the vicinity'; it is regarded as the behavioural interpretation of the communication. For the receiver, the sign (the yelp) stands for the object (the predator); it signifies in virtue of stimulating behaviour identical to that which would be triggered by the object itself. Communication between the two animals, therefore, takes place automatically in virtue of a single unbroken causal chain passing through the two organisms. One could take the analogy further – as writers such as Skinner have done – by describing the stimulus producing the yelp as the 'referent' of the yelp: the 'yelp' refers to the predator.

What is wrong with this view of language – a view that bypasses explicitness and consciousness and reduces the transmission of information to the transmission of stimuli by proxies? Pretty well everything, if it is offered as an account of human language. It is wrong empirically and it is, more importantly, wrong conceptually.

First of all, the facts. The production of signs by human beings is not always, or even typically, a triggered response to stimuli; even more rarely are the stimuli the objects signified by the signs. There are a few occasions – as when the sight of fire may trigger the scream 'Fire!' – when the object triggers its name but these are rare. Even on such occasions, the sight of fire may lead to a quite different shout – for example: 'Get the children out!' We more often talk about absent objects or abstract objects. And our talk of (absent or present) objects does not itself consist of emitting the signs corresponding to them: we talk *about* them, predicate things of them; we do not merely enumerate them. Conversation does not consist of yelp-strings, yelp-lists.

(And there are numerous problems in thinking of yelps and other vocal responses as 'names'.) Moreover, we talk about possible objects and impossible ones as well as actual concrete and abstract ones. The truth is that the occasions and referents of our discourse are extremely complex and it is not even slightly plausible to suggest that our talk-emissions are responses to stimuli. Even the talk of a five-year-old ('When we get home from holidays, I'm going to practise my yo-yo until I'm an expert') could not be subsumed under any kind of stimulus–response model. There is equal implausibility in the attempt to reduce to a behavioural response the recipient's understanding of the communication. We often do not respond outwardly to what is said to us; equally often, our outward response is a further piece of discourse which may or may not be what the sender expected and may, anyway, be only remotely occasioned by what he has said. Finally, the suggestion that we routinely behave towards the sign-stimulus as we would towards the significate is, of course, nonsense. The responses towards signs (and the complexes of signs that constitute ordinary discourse) are as complex as the occasions, and relations to the occasions, that prompt their emission.

So much for the facts that are against stimulus theories of meaning. But what of the conceptual muddle behind them? The fundamental error is that of trying to naturalise linguistic signs, incorporating them into a causal nexus that passes through in animate objects and organisms alike. This, in turn, results from a failure to understand what lies at the bottom of arbitrariness. Arbitrary signs are, precisely because of their arbitrariness, manifestly *signs*. They are visibly signs because they lack all occasion apart from the intention to signify; and this creates the distances from the causal net that have then to be crossed by meaning and reference. True reference is inseparable from the *intention to refer*, just as information cannot be understood, except metaphorically, independently of the intention to inform. My understanding what you are saying depends on my understanding *that you are saying*. I consume your meanings because I understand that it is meaning that you are producing.

Since Grice[2] pointed this out – that being affected by an utterance depends on understanding its meaning and that understanding its meaning in turn depends on understanding the speaker's semantic intention (what he intends you to believe) – the stimulus theory has had little credibility in philosophical circles. Human meaning is an act as well as an influence; there is producer-meaning as well as consumer-meaning. Natural signs may mean things in one sense ('Spots mean measles') but not in another important sense (as when I mean to inform you of something – i.e. to bring about in you a certain belief). Spots may be informative but they are not informants.

Human linguistic meaning – the business of meaning things with words – is an act, not merely a link in a chain of causes and effects passing from an object through a speaker to a receiver. This act requires, utilises arbitrary signs; signs that, being uprooted from a nexus of natural associations, from the chain of causality, display themselves as signs, as human interventions. The appearance of a cloud signifying rain is primarily an event and only secondarily a sign; the arbitrary sign, by contrast, occurs *in order to* signify and so signifies its status as a sign. The acquisition of metalinguistic awareness early in the process of language acquisition and the ubiquity of metalanguage in everyday discourse emphasises the way in which linguistic signs are explicitly signs to their users.

* * *

This should bring out the difference between a sign that signifies through being part of the causal chain – being caused by the object or entity which it signifies, and having the effect of acting proxy for that object or entity – and an arbitrary sign; between a natural and a genuinely linguistic sign. A cloud does not have to be conscious to signify rain; the consciousness necessary for it to count as a sign is provided by the consumer. Natural signs mean things; but the meaning is engendered in the consumer and in the absence of the consumer there is no meaning. Linguistic signs, on the other hand, are *meant* and their interpretation, as Grice has repeatedly emphasised, depends upon seeing that they are meant. As Bennett has put it,[3] the very notion of meaning (of meaning something) depends essentially on intention and belief; and meaning mediated through linguistic signs makes this explicit: my appreciating the meaning of what you are saying depends on my understanding that you are trying to communicate something to me; more specifically, that you are intending to make me believe something. By contrast, a natural sign such as a cloud is not a statement; for example, a standing assertion to the effect that 'it is probably going to rain'. Clouds do not intend the inferences that may be drawn from their presence in the sky. They are not 'about' rain, or the probable occurrence of rain, even though they may cause us to expect rain. It is we, not they, who provide their 'aboutness'. In themselves, they – and other natural signs – are not about anything. The very fact that they rely upon natural association with their significates – similarity of appearance, spatio-temporal association – denies them the distance necessary for fully explicit 'aboutness'; the distance necessary for the intentionality of linguistic signs that forms the basis of the reference they alone can sustain and the truth values only assertions composed of them can carry.

The stimulus theory of meaning incorporates illuminating errors which serve to bring out the true nature of language and its relation to explicitness. The deficiencies of the theory show us what is implicit in the emergence of linguistic meaning. The unnatural sign which creates and maintains, even when it is signifying, its distance from the significate, facilitates the emergence of ever more explicit meanings. It transforms the contents of the world into referents, things of which other things can be predicated. More than any other human faculty, arbitrary sign language elaborates the distances out of which truth about existents can emerge out of existence, so that existence can be transformed into truth and existents become truth conditions. The stimulus theory of meaning, which tries to assimilate meaning, reference and truth into the causal nexus that passes through objects and organisms alike shows us, by its failures, the true miracle and mystery of language.

It is worth emphasising that the genuinely consistent stimulus-response theories of signs – such as those of Skinner[4] – are ultimately physicalist rather than biological. They deal in causal, rather than specifically behavioural, chains. To assimilate the meaning to a stimulus or to response, and both of these to parts of a causal chain to be understood ultimately in physicalist terms as 'energy transfer', is to undermine their status as 'meaning', 'stimulus' and 'response'. Skinner, in particular, seems to want to have the world of meaning, of language, and of human beings anthropomorphically, while eating reality in exclusively physicalist terms. Physicalism does not strictly allow 'meaning', 'stimulus' and 'response'. The stimulus theory of meaning has physicalism as its final goal; and yet, if that goal were achieved, 'meaning' would be an inadmissible category. The theory, like the causal theory of perception, assumes a world picture it is trying to demolish.

Notes

1. Of course, we can make *any* signs – linguistic or non-linguistic, conventional or natural – carry higher-order, complex consciousness. For example, the fact that I am wearing new shoes may, in a first-order way, indicate that I am trying hard to please and/or impress. Or I may use this fact to give the impression that I am trying hard to please or impress. Or I may use this rather obvious sign that I am trying hard to please/impress as a way of signifying my naivety in order to disarm someone. Or I may use this sign of my trying to disarm that person ironically as a way of signifying my sophistication. And so on. It is not so much the means or medium that distinguishes the operations of explicitness but what is done with it. That is why Mary Midgley's reference to the fact that human language is rooted in para-linguistic phenomena such as gestures as an argument in favour of a closer relationship between human and animal language is misconceived. (See Mary Midgley, *Beast and Man. The Roots of Human Nature* (London: Methuen, 1980), chapter 10, especially pp. 239 *et seq.*) It is not the material that we use for our communications but the kinds of uses we make of it that distinguishes us from animals.
2. See for example, H. P. Grice, 'Meaning', *Philosophical Review*, 1987, 66:377–88. His views have been developed by others, notably Jonathan Bennett, 'Stimulus, Response, Meaning', *American Philosophical Quarterly*, 1975, 9:55–88. Fred Dretske (*Explaining Behaviour: Reasons in a World of Causes*, Cambridge, Mass.: MIT, 1988) has argued, against Grice, that natural signs *do* intrinsically carry information and that

they indicate even in the absence of a consciousness to indicate to: 'there is something *in* nature (not merely in the mind that struggles to comprehend nature) some objective observer-independent fact or set of facts, that forms the basis of one thing meaning another or indicating something about another', p. 58). He claims that denying that natural signs indicate in the absence of consciousness is 'merely a specialised version of the more general and even more implausible idea that nothing is true unless it is true for someone' (p. 55). I would turn Dretske on his head by saying that the belief that natural signs signify in the absence of any consciousness to signify to is merely a specialised version of the more general superstition that meaning, reference and truth can inhabit material objects, a superstition that is more compatible with panpsychism than materialism. The belief that truth inheres in material things is also criticized in my *Not Saussure* (London: Macmillan, 1988, 1995).

If Dretske's belief that natural objects and events could signify in the absence of consciousness were true, the problem would arise as to determining which sub-group of objects would count as signs, which as significates and which neither; presumably all objects and events would have equal claim to the status of signs. All cats would be iconic signs of all other cats; every object would be an iconic sign of every object like itself. Every effect would indexically signify its causes and every cause its effects. And so on. Dretske's natural world would be a place of total self-indication, an horrendous unbounded endlessly iterative pandiculation.

3. Bennett, 'Stimulus, Response, Meaning'.
4. Skinner's views are summarised in B.F. Skinner, 'The Operational Analysis of Psychological Terms', *Behavioral and Brain Sciences*, 1984, 7:547–81. This is a revision and reprint of his classic 1945 paper, usefully combined with twenty or so responses from experts and Skinner's own response to these responses.

From: *The Explicit Animal* (Macmillan, 1991, 1999), pp. 230–3, 235–6, 290–2.

Part III

The Centrality of the Conscious Human Agent

Tallis is convinced that an overriding aim common to much twentieth-century thought has been the displacement of the conscious human agent from the centre of things. The attack on the human agent has been from two directions. First, the physical and biological sciences have been deployed to suggest that human consciousness, self-consciousness and behaviour are explicable in mechanical terms, the particular mechanisms being rooted in the drives and instincts that were necessary for our animal forebears to survive. Hence the self is not master in its own house: it is in the grip of and (unknown to itself) acts out forces and dramas that are derived from the remote past. Second, anti-humanist human sciences – Marxist historiography, sociology, psychoanalysis, structuralist anthropology, post-Saussurean linguistics – have been cited to support the notion that we are the playthings of various modes of cultural unconscious; that, far from being originators of our actions, even of our utterances and the meanings we wish to express through them, we are merely nodal points in a variety of systems – usually systems of signification – whose full nature is hidden from us, and it is these that drive our actions and confer their meaning on them.

It need hardly be stressed that this notion of the unconscious dominating over consciousness is profoundly at odds with the idea of 'man, the explicit animal' that Tallis has been propounding. The thrust of a substantial part of his argument has been to expose the self-contradictoriness of most of the arguments of those who would 'marginalise consciousness' and deny the fundamental differences between contemporary human society and animal communities or pre-historic cultures.

6
Recovering the Conscious Agent

In this reading, from *Enemies of Hope* (1997), Tallis argues that a major problem with theories that downgrade the significance of consciousness is the extent to which such theories themselves embody higher levels of consciousness than they would seem to allow. This implies that anyone convinced of the truth of such theories is going to be involved in a high degree of self-deception about their nature and origin. Unless one accepts that the very existence of theories like those of Freud and Marx is evidence of high levels of disinterested consciousness – and of our ability to get at truths that are not ruled out by their ultimate roots in unconscious processes – such theories must undermine their own credibility. *The Interpretation of Dreams* is evidence of the domination of a high order of consciousness over the unconscious. Explicitness is manifest everywhere in its pages. Furthermore, there is an unacceptable sense of helplessness induced by theories that displace consciousness to the margins. Post-Saussureans, like Derrida and Lacan, believe that language can never express intentions, wishes, feelings and aspirations because the system dominates over the speaker, producing effects that are signs of nothing other than the operation of its own rules. To adapt a remark of Lacan's, representation represents nothing other than the lack of the function that engenders it. One must despair of effective intervention in the life of the world since language is the site only of error, exile and loss. Tallis seeks to reassert the reality of the self and by so doing to reassert the centrality of individual experience and individual agency as expressed even in the most commonplace actions and off-the-shelf utterances such as saying 'hello'. Our own actual and unique experience is proof of the distance between us and the systems for whose domination over us too many in the twentieth century have argued.

The theories I have discussed [in *Enemies of Hope*] have, directly or indirectly, had an enormous influence on contemporary thought about what it is to be human. They have in common a tendency to discredit the notion of the self-possessed individual choosing at least some aspects of his or her life, and to downplay the role of conscious decision-making, deliberation, and indeed consciousness itself, in everyday life and behaviour. A specific consequence of this is a sceptical attitude towards the role of reason in personal and public life – in behaviour *tout court*. My avowed reasons for actions or beliefs or principles are taken to be rooted in self-deception or self-misrecognition: they are mere rationalisations of behaviour whose true origin lies in some place hidden from me. According to Marxist thinking, the hidden hand that shapes my behaviour – my political beliefs, my sense of morality, my choice of ends in life – is a largely unconscious, historically determined class consciousness, created by the objective conditions of production. For Durkheim and his sociological successors, the hidden hand is the society to which I belong and whose larger outline and deepest tendency is concealed from me. For the Freudians, the ultimate source of my behaviour is to be found in the asocial instincts refracted through the ancient repressive structures of civilisation – an origin I could not fully acknowledge, even if it were revealed to me. Much of my most reasonable, civil, practically useful activity is in fact the enactment of buried damage sustained in the battle during my infancy between the warring imperatives of natural instinct and cultural constraint. For the post-Saussureans, it is the system of signs that gives my behaviour its meaning; and this is so deeply buried that only the smallest part of it has been revealed even to semiologists. And so I am simply unconscious of the true significance of what I do, say or think.

The cumulative impact of these theories – which have assigned reason, deliberation, the conscious, retrievable intention and finally consciousness itself, an increasingly marginal status – has been to suggest that human beings are to a greater or lesser degree automata acting in accordance with laws of which they are unaware. While not all these theories impinge with equal directness on the question of the reality of consciousness *per se*, they all contribute to an intellectual climate in which ordinary consciousness is granted at best a relatively minor part in the drama of ordinary private and public life.

Although it is obviously counter-intuitive to deny the centrality of consciousness and deliberate choice in everyday life – to deny, for example, that there is any fundamental difference between falling down a cliff and going shopping or between formulating a treatment plan for a patient with epilepsy and having an epileptic fit oneself – it is not easy to rebut the overall tendency of these revised accounts of what it is to be a conscious human being. After all, not even the most passionate defender of consciousness can ignore the ever-present background of *mechanism*, against which even voluntary action based on full consciousness takes place. Much of what we do and most of what happens in our bodies, during the course of carrying out ordinary actions, is not accessible to introspection; below a not very deep level we do not have control over our activity. The goal towards which I am moving, or in accordance with which my actions are taking place, is only a small part of what is going on in me when, for example, I rush down stairs to answer the doorbell. It is an even smaller part of what is going on when, missing my step, I make a series of lightning adjustments to prevent a nasty fall. We have no way as yet of describing, or even conceptualising, the dialectic between mechanism and conscious choice in actions that are ordinarily seen as free. Moreover, it is very difficult to underline the autonomy of consciousness without seeming to espouse a naive, unreformed Cartesian vision of a transparent, auto-regulating self. The best one can do, perhaps, is to reassert the obvious – the centrality of consciousness and deliberate choice in everyday activity – and then show why the theories that question this are mistaken and how the general project of finding reasons for marginalising consciousness is ultimately self-contradictory.

As regards the latter, it is necessary only to consider the status of the theories themselves: they manifestly exceed the very limitations they place on consciousness. Freud's own works – his act of writing them, others' acts of reading them with something approaching comprehension and assent or disbelief – justify the observation that humans in their waking life are so far from being in the grip of dreams that some of them, at least, are able to formulate theories of dreams and of their relationship to, and significance for, waking life. The many pages of *The Interpretation of Dreams* are evidence of the domination of consciousness of a high order over the unconscious. And what more potent counter-argument to Marx's claim that the social existence of men determines their consciousness and that their ideas, views and conceptions passively reflect the material conditions of their existence, than the pages of this petit bourgeois's *Capital* or the spectacular transformation of his own views in the 1840s and 1850s? (The very fact that *Capital* has been so influential is itself a tribute to the independent power of the superstructure. Marxist theory is not only unable to explain why the Marxist revolution began in Russia – this is a point that has often been made – but is also unable to explain why there is such a thing as Marxism and why Marx was such a major force in history rather than being simply a wild footnote to intellectual history, like Bakunin.)

The problem, in short, with any theory that wishes to curtail the importance of consciousness is that such a theory itself embodies higher levels of consciousness than the theory would seem to allow. For Freud, Marx, Durkheim and some other (though by no means all) apostles of the unconscious, this must mean, if one believes their theories to be true, that those very theories entrain the greatest measure of self-deception about their own nature and origin. To put this another way: unless the very existence of these theories is accepted as bearing witness to the reality of higher, disinterested reaches of consciousness – and of our ability to get at truths that are not invalidated by their ultimate roots in unconscious processes – they seriously undermine their own credibility. There is an additional irony in the fact that those theories which have most radically questioned the originality and innovativeness of the individual, which have, indeed, undermined the whole idea of the *individual* as a *source*, have as their own source immensely fertile, innovative individuals. To the unprejudiced mind, Freud, Marx, Durkheim, Derrida et al. are clearly defined individuals not anonymous voices arising out of history, society, the Unconscious or the language system.

It may seem odd to choose something as narrow and specific as the theories themselves to counter their claims about the nature of consciousness and to use the theories to reinstate consciousness in the middle of ordinary life. The choice is not, however, mere polemic mischief. For what the theories exemplify, despite themselves, is the general tendency of human beings to become ever more self-conscious, and the seemingly unlimited capacity human consciousness has for becoming ever more explicit. None of the 'unconsciousnesses' discovered – or allegedly discovered – by the theorists can, despite what is claimed, either deny or account for the fundamental and inescapable fact that explicitness, consciousness, deliberation, lie at the heart of human life. The actual process of discovery of the various brands of the unconscious – political, social, psychological, linguistic, perceptual – itself underlines this capacity of human consciousness for unfolding explicitness. It is, therefore, no minor or insignificant observation that consciousness can even bring its own unconscious to consciousness! Moreover, as I pointed out in the discussion of Freud, when we consider the characteristic examples of the operation of the unconscious in the naive subject – the invocation of reasons that turn out, on more sophisticated inspection, to be mere rationalisations – we still do not diminish the presence of explicitness, the role of consciousness. It is difficult to think of anything less machine-like or more remote from automaticity than the ability to produce a flattering but untrue reason for some action one has performed. Or the ability to show that that reason is flattering but untrue.

The thinkers I have discussed are united in their rejection of the world-picture that Lucien Goldmann identified as underpinning the Enlightenment hope of progress:

> all the leaders of the Enlightenment regarded the life of a society as a sort of sum, or product, of the thought and action of a large number of individuals, each of whom constitutes a free and independent point of departure.
>
> (Goldmann, *The Philosophy of the Enlightenment*, p. 32)

Our contemporary anti-Enlightenment figures see society, or one of its proxies such as history, socially mediated instincts or language, as being anterior to, and transcending, the individuals that make it up. Consequently, they deny those individuals any space outside of society from which they could engage it as 'free and independent points of departure'. The vision, promoted by these Apostles of the Unconscious, of the individual as helpless, blind, self-ignorant has undermined the notion of agency and relativised the Enlightenment's most trusted weapon against ignorance: the reason deployed by men of honour, justice and common sense. For Marx, the individual is a cork swept along in the sea of history, her consciousness and self-consciousness being shaped by the laws of social development of which she is unaware, except through the distorting lens of ideology. *Homo politico-economicus* has no personal or private space outside of, or transcending, the collective dream. As Camus expressed it:

> To put economic determinations at the root of all human action is to sum up man in terms of his social relations. There is no such thing as a solitary man, that is the indisputable discovery of the nineteenth century. An arbitrary deduction then leads to the statement that man only feels solitary for social reasons.
>
> (Camus, *The Rebel*, p. 167)

Durkheim, too, had uncovered society – unobserved social forces – at the heart of individuality. Freud had found the self to be rooted in a collective past, instinctual and mythical, and the ordinary intercourse between individuals to be deeply influenced by the damage sustained during forgotten prehistoric battles between nature and culture. The post-Saussureans (many of whom had also incorporated the pessimistic messages of Marx, Durkheim and Freud into their thinking) saw selves vanish completely into nodes in sign systems or soluble fish in a boundless sea of discourse.

In placing these thinkers under the single rubric of 'marginalisers of consciousness', I have overlooked important differences between them. And in focusing on their contributions to contemporary *Zeitgeist*, I have most certainly been guilty of simplifications and, in some cases serious injustices. I have already made clear that Saussure cannot be blamed for the influence his ideas have exerted through the post-Saussureans. And it would be most unfair to lay the misconceptions that vitiate much thought in cognitive psychology at the door of Helmholtz. It is unlikely that Durkheim would have accepted the elaboration of his functionalism into the wild speculations of Lévi-Strauss. On the other hand, Freud surely is to blame for some of the ideas – not to speak of the practices – of the post-Freudians; and attempts to distance him even from the 'abuses' of psychoanalysis by the 'recovered memory' therapists in contemporary America require a good deal of active forgetting of Freud's own clinical methods and the grotesque irresponsibility of his means of obtaining and interpreting 'facts' supportive of his theories. Even Freud, however, is capable of being misrepresented and his message distorted; for example, Lacan's 'structuralising' of psychoanalysis produced results that The Master would have resisted. The transformation of his view that 'the ego is not master in his own house' to the dissipation of the ego altogether into an illusion that is kept alive through the constant pursuit of itself through the generalised absence of language is a travesty of Freud's travestying account of human nature. Likewise, although Marx did not advocate the evils done in his name in, say, the Soviet Union, his theory rationalised the abuses of human rights and the crushing of free speech that Lenin made a matter of policy. Marx inaugurated 'the hermeneutics of suspicion',[1] which made generosity to those who disagreed with one's own views merely a sign of lack of revolutionary will. The connection between the totalitarian practice and the Marxist theory is set out very clearly by Isaiah Berlin:

> What Lenin demanded was unlimited power for a small body of professional revolutionaries, trained exclusively for one purpose and ceaselessly engaged in its pursuit by every means in their power. This was necessary because democratic methods, and the attempts to persuade and preach used by earlier reformers and rebels, were ineffective; and this in turn was due to the fact that they rested on a false psychology – namely the assumption that men acted as they did because of conscious beliefs that could be changed by argument. For if Marx had done anything, he had surely shown that such beliefs and ideals were mere 'reflections' of the condition of the socially and economically determined classes of men, to some one of which every individual must belong.[2]

Another important difference between the thinkers I have discussed is the different extent to which they undermined the notion of the autonomous, rational self as agent. (What subsequent writers made of them is, as I have indicated, another matter entirely.) Marx and Durkheim focus less on everyday life than on political actions and collective beliefs. It is arguable that neither saw ordinary human beings as going about in a kind of daze when pursuing their daily business. Men would be capable of pursuing their ends rationally. However, those ends might be seriously misconceived. For Marx, the bourgeois is simply unable to see the naked rapacity behind the respectable business of commerce and industrial production and the way the law and morality are so ordered as to ensure the reproduction of the conditions of production and the perpetuation of the ruling elites. And for Durkheim, the pious man freely expressing his deep and private religious sentiments, his intimations of transcendental otherness, is unaware that he is simply affirming the greatness of society. Once such major misconceptions have been conceded, of course, then the way is open to questioning the rationality of all behaviour; and, although Marx and Durkheim did not do this, they did make it easier for others to take this step. Marx's and Durkheim's views, that is to say, were ripe for transformation into a more radical critique of the notion of individual agent. As we have seen, 'structuralised' Marxism deeply undermined the notion of autonomous action on the basis of transparent reasons; for Althusser, Marx had shown that the unified self crowned with consciousness was a bourgeois illusion. In Lévi-Strauss's hands, the insights of Durkheim could be married to those of structural linguistics to create a structuralised social anthropology which saw all behaviour as being subservient to the fulfilment of unconscious structures reflecting the fundamental structures of the human mind.

Freud's undermining of the rational self was more thorough than that of Marx or Durkheim (prior to radicalisation by their followers); after all, in his view irrationality, indeed psychopathology, pervaded everyday life; and it was that much easier for his followers, inspired by his hints of the ubiquity of the Unconscious, to see behaviour as largely symbolically driven: whatever I do, I am not really doing what I think I am doing; whatever I feel, my feelings are not what I think they are. Smoking a cigarette, arriving late, on time or early for an appointment, getting angry with someone who has stolen something from you, becoming a doctor, playing tennis, eating a meal, writing a book: these are all motivated by drives that I cannot be aware of and would deny if they were pointed out to me. (The passion and sincerity of my denial is, of course, a measure of the truth of the ascription.) The apparent function and rationale of an action has nothing to do with its true reason.

There is, as we have discussed, a serious problem with this irrationalist view of the springs of human behaviour: in order to bring about the set-piece irrational actions, numerous subsidiary rational actions are necessary. The means to the irrational ends have to be composed of rational actions; the latter are rationalised in only one sense. In order to act out my irrational anxiety about my health, I have rationally to fill up my car with petrol or, even more rationally, make sure that the garage has repaired the engine fault to meet the standards required by the Ministry of Transport. The arias of Freudian irrationality and magic thinking are, in short, embedded in a recitative of rational activity driven by non-magic thinking; the acting out of neurotic symptoms requires the support of a densely woven canopy of non-neurotic behaviour and calculation. Freud's vision of the nature of the human animal cannot accommodate this difficult notion of a plain of rationality sustaining a few peaks of irrationality. For once we accept the ubiquity of hidden, unacknowledged forces and motives in behaviour, then it is difficult to see how even dysfunctional behaviour can get off the ground. Why, in short, there should be any kind of limit to the operation of irrational forces in our everyday life; why we should be able to wake up out of the nexus of potent symbols that is supposed to have us in its grip. Irrationality should infect everything that we do, since the forces that drive it seem to have such powers of penetration. Why, since everything we think of, say or do is at such a small remove from the dark forces that are supposed to motivate us, does the tongue not always slip, do angers not always possess us in a seemingly inexplicable manner, and so on?

Of course, Freud the metapsychologist and metaphysician of the Unconscious was generally much more radical than Freud the clinician; the latter, therefore, could not base himself in the former. The healer of suffering souls should have had nothing to do with the prophet of the Unconscious. Nevertheless, the influence of the prophet has been the more potent and widespread. The radicalism inherent in his thought has been picked up by many writers and the claims of his more lunatic followers – people like Groddek and Lacan – that they have drawn out of his writings no more than what was implicit or inherent in them are justified.

As for the post-Saussureans, they have emphasised rather than denied the extremity of their attack on the rational, conscious individual capable of undeceived self-awareness and purposeful agency in private and public life; indeed, they have celebrated 'the death of the subject' and the myth of actions informed by the intentions of agents.

In some respects, the project (and the assumptions) of cognitive psychology – with the computerisation of mind, or its reduction to unconscious mechanisms, culminating in the elimination of difficult elements such as qualia – should have seemed a yet more radical undermining of the rational self and marginalising of consciousness. But cognitive scientists are themselves instinctive believers in rationality and do not have the courage of their convictions. They recover consciousness in the places where it should not be[3] and they feel that the mind is obliged, for biological reasons, to be rational: rationality is built into the very structure of the brain to ensure the survival of the human organism.

It is poststructuralism – or, more widely, postmodernism – that has brought to a climax the anti-rationalist, anti-individualist and, indeed, anti-humanist strains in the Counter-Enlightenment thought of the present century. 'Postmodernism', as Edward Said asserted, 'stresses the disappearance of grand narratives of emancipation and enlightenment.'[4] Although there has been a good deal of discussion as to whether Marx and Freud are simply more radical *aufklärer* underneath – after all, Marx believed in a universal human nature, a 'species being', and Freud shared the Enlightenment vision that man was a part of nature and understandable through science, and both Marx and Freud hoped to shed the light of human reason even on irrational human behaviour[5] – there is no room for doubt about the attitude of those postmodernists who cite these marginalisers as the grounds for their anti-individualist, anti-liberal, anti-humanist discourses – and their 'hermeneutics of suspicion'.

The collective impact of the marginalisers, as gathered up in postmodern thought, is to induce a sense of helplessness in anyone who would wish to help bring about improvement in the world. Foucault rejected the very idea of progress in the treatment of criminals and regarded as baseless the belief that Enlightenment ideas had led to a humanisation of the law and, specifically, of punishment. So far as he was concerned, the pre-Enlightenment live dismemberment of Robert-François Damiens was not morally different from the regulated life of the prisoners recommended in 1838 by prison reformer Faucher. The difference between the two modes of punishment – the one unspeakably barbaric, the other relatively humane – is, for Foucault, merely one of style, a change in the discursive formations gathered about the notion of punishment. Post-Saussureans are equally pessimistic about the future of politics. Language can never express purely human intentions, wishes, feeling, aspirations because the system dominates over the speaker and it produces effects which are not signs of anything other than the operation of its own rules. It follows from this that, according to Paul de Man, 'the political destiny of man', which is 'structured like and derived from a linguistic model' does not lie in his own hands:

> 'society and government' are neither natural nor ethical nor theological, 'since language is not conceived as a transcendental principle but as the possibility of contingent error'. Hence, de Man concluded, political activity is 'a burden for man rather than an opportunity'.
>
> (Lehman, *Signs of the Times*, p. 219)

Even those who turn to postmodern thought as an instrument of liberation are not very certain about its power to foster desirable change. Take Joel Handler's 1992 Presidential Address to the annual meeting of the Law and Society Association – a bastion of Critical Legal Studies and of the anti-establishment semiotic approach to the law. He begins with some cheerful noises:

> And what does postmodernism have to do with society and the law? The major theme that I emphasise is subversion, the commitment to undermine dominant discourse. The subversion theme – variously described as deconstruction, radical indeterminacy, anti-essentialism, or antifoundationalism – whether in art, architecture, literature or philosophy – seeks to demonstrate the inherent instability of seemingly hegemonic structures, that power is diffused throughout society, and that there are multiple possibilities for resistance by oppressed people. The postmodern conception of subversion is a key part of contemporary theories of protest from below and the new social movements. ... Deconstruction ... seeks to destabilise dominant or privileged interpretations.[6]

The Kingdom of the Instantaneous is at hand! However, the cheerful noises are soon drowned by cries of despair, which recognise the consequences of accepting the postmodern world-picture. In the very same lecture, Handler quotes Rosenau who points out that since 'Post-modernism questions causality, determinism, egalitarianism, humanism, liberal democracy, necessity, objectivity, rationality, and truth. ... [It] makes any belief in the idea of progress or faith in the future seem questionable' (Handler, p. 726).

Questionable indeed, especially since those who espouse the belief that we are the helpless playthings of discursive systems, of a society composed of semiotic formations, of an unconscious that is structured like a language, are deeply suspicious of those systems, those formations, that language. All discourse – even liberal discourse – is, Foucault would have us believe, about power and, in particular the retention of power by the powerful. There is no difference, it seems, between a drunken bully imposing his views on a helpless and weak opponent and John Stuart Mill arguing for tolerance in *On Liberty*. It is all simply a matter of the exercise of power – though it remains unclear as to where the power is. (At times, the drunken bully, John Stuart Mill and the helpless opponent seem equally powerless before the all-powerful, autonomous activity of the discursive formation.) Semiotic formations are committed, according to Barthes, to the misrepresentation of History as Nature and so support the process by which ideology conceals itself, with the inevitable consequence that, again, the dominant and the powerful may pass unchallenged. The very language we use in ordinary life, we learn from Barthes and the thousand writers imitating his easy omniscience, wears jackboots: it is fascist because, 'even in the subject's deepest privacy, speech enters the service of power' (Barthes, Inaugural Lecture, p. 460).[7] Our selves are socialised without residue; our sociality is deposited in the systems of signs that is language; language, which speaks us, is either opaque (or its signs are totally indeterminate as to meaning) or malign ('fascist'); and so we are helpless to choose, to change ourselves. We are caught up in a net of all-powerful forces and unreliable signs. Thus does pessimism become totalised and, with the assumption that the totalitarian state is already in place within us, does the return of totalitarianism come a little nearer. Or would, if anyone took this kind of stuff seriously.

There is considerable evidence that nobody, least of all those for whom they have brought tenure, jet travel and adulation, truly believes in the ideas that have so much currency amongst humanist intellectuals. When de Man asserted that it was never possible to determine the meaning of a text because all meaning was indeterminate, he did not therefore stop writing, or give up trying to mean one thing rather than another. Nor did his official position of total doubt about truth, meaning and reference prevent him (as Lentricchia has pointed out) from having sufficient command of 'the rhetoric of authority' to say what literature – and indeed the world-text – has been, is and must always be:

> Even while, in *Blindness and Insight*, he was telling us that there was no truth, or if there was, that it could never be known, he spoke transcendentally of 'the foreknowledge we possess of the true nature of literature'.[8]

And while Barthes was confident that language (including that of Roland Barthes, presumably) was 'fascist', he saw the role of intellectuals (wordsmiths like himself) as 'taking action against *powers*' (p. 459) – a difficult task, one would think, if what he said about language were true – like trying to dry up a stream by adding water to it or cleaning out the Augean stables with a few buckets of liquid manure.

Foucault, likewise, could not see any way out of the nexus that bound together power and discourse. Nevertheless, he too saw his works as unmasking the mystifications of power, even if they abjured 'the grand narratives of emancipation and enlightenment'. And he certainly seemed to believe that his own writings were less oppressive than the dossiers produced on suspects by the Gaullist police. Foucault's deeply pessimistic and anarchistic views – his profound suspicion of order and authority of all sorts – did not prevent him from scheming to be elevated to a prestigious Chair; nor did it make him very tolerant of any breakdown of order that might adversely impinge on his ability to pursue his scholarly pursuits. His biographer (Macey, p. 413) notes that this savage critic of bureaucratic, rational society became increasingly frustrated 'with increasing delays in the book delivery service' at the Bibliothèque Nationale and that this resulted in bitter personal quarrels with the library's director. (Luckily he found a cosy billet in a very well-appointed private library.)[9]

In many cases, postmodern ideas are anyway literally unthinkable, if only because of their limitless scope (cf. 'Language is Fascist') and, related to this, their failure to respect or even to retain the kinds of distinctions that not only critical intelligence but also common sense would demand. Yes, there is a sense in which speech is in the service of power – or quite a lot of the time. But there is the world of difference between the performative, persuasive, manipulative use of speech to soothe a frightened child or to raise help for someone who is drowning, and its use by a bullying gang directing humiliating taunts at a victim, by an interrogator in a police state or by Joseph Goebbels furthering the cause of state-sponsored anti-Semitism.

Nor are these ideas greatly helped by being, as has repeatedly been pointed out, self-contradictory.[10] Perhaps this is why they do not, in everyday life, seem to influence the behaviour even of those who profess them. Perhaps it is a bit much to expect that the moral outrage you might feel when someone infringes your person, property or rights – taking your parking slot, overcharging you in a restaurant, clapping you in gaol without due cause, or threatening the life of your child – should be dissipated by thinking that you and he are simply corks floating helplessly on the stream of history or soluble fish in a sea of discourse. And it is understandable that, despite earning their living and world-wide renown for denying the difference between magic and scientific medicine (merely rival discourses propagated by different power groups), post-Saussureans prefer to have a ruptured appendix abscess treated by conventional surgery (which has advanced enormously over the last few decades) – supported by antibiotics and the recent generation of anaesthetics and intravenous fluids – and so (usually) survive, than by a witch doctor who, barring a miracle (or a lucky misdiagnosis), would supervise the patient's avoidable metaphysical translation to the sunless realm.[11]

Trilling's observation is again apposite: 'it is characteristic of the intellectual life of our culture that it fosters a form of assent which does not involve actual credence.' The mitigating plea that post-Saussurean and, more widely, post-modern, ideas have little effect, that they are totally insignificant in the real world outside the Academy, that they are harmless fun, should not, however, be upheld, in order to let the post-Saussureans and other posties off the hook. They may have long-term adverse consequences in muddying the waters, in their anti-educational effects on students who are force-fed on them and in the resources they consume elsewhere. The overriding concern must be that this 'form of assent' and these glamorously pessimistic ideas undermine others' efforts to see things differently; to see, for example, that an even relatively autonomous thinking agent might contribute actively to a process of change – the necessary condition for individuals deliberately trying to bring about progress – or, if this sounds too grand and too global, to try to improve things. The communal trances in which individual consciousnesses are supposedly dissolved allow no room for individual initiative or even for change that anyone actually wills. The marginalisers of consciousness deny the possibility that human beings might be able to reform human institutions in order to ensure the more efficient production of goods and a more equitable distribution of power in society. They foreclose the future and say that, if the latter is different from the past, it will not be the result of individual's efforts or of deliberate collective effort. Where there is unequivocal evidence of progress, the totalising pessimism of the marginalisers of consciousness will oblige them to deny this evidence: it was not simply a spirit of perversity that moved Foucault to maintain that penal reform was merely a change of style aimed at inserting social control deeper into the criminal's soul and that the reformed prisons of Faucher were therefore no advance on the public dismemberment of criminals. The anti-individualistic and anti-humanist works upon which his fame had been built required that he should take this position – as well as other anti-progressive positions, such as preferring the theocracy of Iran to the democracy of France.

The system-trance theorists are not able to explain change; even less are they able to explain beneficial change; and even less still are they able to explain beneficial change brought about by the will of individuals. The subject is simply the effect of a nexus of signs or power relations. And this makes science and science-based technology a particularly hard nut for the marginalisers to crack. For science has brought about the most dramatic changes in the nature and conditions of human life (including the conditions and forces of production); it has been the result of willed effort (technology is the most effective application of will and intelligence in the pursuit of generalised goals); and many of the advances can be attributed to the genius of named individuals. Although the ant-heap of anonymous toilers has supported and developed the great advances contributed by those individuals, the latter have formatted the disk on which the rest of us have written. Newton, Ampère, Faraday, Clerk Maxwell, Boltzmann and Einstein cannot simply be read as nodes in discursive systems, as soluble fish in the seas of language, even though they were steeped in the languages and notions of their time.

Let us take a particular example. The observation of the relationship between electricity and magnetism, which has transformed the world in the century and a half since Faraday made his crucial experiments and surprised himself with the results, was not simply the sign system acting out its eternal tunes. The first demonstration of electromagnetic induction by a changing magnetic field was a specific event that took place on a particular day – 29 August 1831. Following up its practical and theoretical implications was an heroic ten-year effort, which brought Faraday close to breakdown.

Nor is it valid to claim to recover the system within the individual by sociologising away science, seeing its results as simply the emergence of a dominant herd rhetoric about 'nature', itself understood as a term mobilised by an interpretive community to support their claim to having captured objective truths. Scientific knowledge cannot be merely a matter of fantasies induced by social or economic or depth psychological forces because its technological applications *work*. A computer that reliably executes its routine miracles of data-handling proves the differences between group fantasy and natural reality. Technological success is the proof of the non-historicist basis, the extra-human truth, of science; evidence of the difference between the methods of the scientist and of the public relations man. Contemporary system-trance thought denies that margin of freedom which makes the willed future, so evident in the internal progress of science, possible – the freedom in virtue of which 'L'homme surpasse infiniment l'homme'.[12]

Many of those thinkers who, with varying degrees of sincerity, deny that an autonomous agent may make an independent contribution to society, do so because they are prone to a rather simple fault: a propensity for gross exaggeration. More specifically, they share a tendency to unpack the whole truth about man and society from a few grains of truth about both. Without those grains of truth, their implausibilia would not have generated so much excitement, would never have been so widely accepted. Let us look at some of these grains of truth. It is true, for example, that the most seemingly altruistic of us may have political views, which, although they are sincerely held, and seem to promote the general welfare, are to our personal own advantage and to the advantage of those with whom we are most likely to identify. In short, we are sometimes likely to present our interests to ourselves as if they coincided with the general interest. This does not, however, mean that the origins of our political views are buried away from us in an historical unconscious sealed into our souls. And it is also true that we – our thoughts, our feelings, our attitudes, our convictions, our 'deepest' sense of self – are more socially determined than our adolescent selves, intensely aware of the distances that separate us from others and acutely conscious of our differences from them, would readily acknowledge: things that seem most personally chosen may well merely reflect the implicit social framework within which our presuppositions operate. But this does not mean that we are entirely dissolved in society. It is, further, true that we may sometimes do things for reasons that are objectively different from those that we ourselves give for our actions. But it does not follow from this that we are ordinarily irrational, or that the true reasons for our actions are usually hidden from us. Finally, it is true that there is a good deal that is automatic in our speech, and individual linguistic responses in certain circumstances may show a high level of predictability; but it does not follow from this that we are simply sites where language speaks itself through us. As I have already discussed, even the use of a predicable phatic word – a linguistic near-reflex – such as saying 'Hello' is rarely if ever 'the system speaking itself' through the mouth of the speaker. The decision to say 'Hello' is very often calculated, as is the tone in which it is said, not to speak of the endless elaborations of 'joky' consciousness that may be expressed through it. We may summarise the process by which thinkers marginalise consciousness, the individual agent, the rational self as follows: grains of truth are expanded into the whole truth. And when a small part of the truth is jacked up to the whole truth an untruth results.

What, then, is the truth about the self, about individuality, about rational agency, and about the relationship between the subject and society? The first – and most important – truth is that there is not going to be a *single* truth about these things. To forget this is to replicate precisely the error of those thinkers we have been criticising who have, as we have said, strayed into untruth by elevating part of the truth into the whole truth. There are, however, important truths (in the plural) about the self, society and rational agency that need to be reaffirmed in order to correct the unbalanced and deeply pessimistic account of humanity and society that contemporary Counter-Enlightenment thinkers seem to delight in.

Any credible attempt to restore the notion of the individual, the subject, the self as in some sense the centre of a world in which she/he acts as a rational, self-present agent must take account of some obvious limitations on freedom, self-presence and unity. It is worthwhile setting these out, if only to avoid the charge that one is naively unaware of them:

1. *Human lives are enacted within certain physical and biological limits*. There are the laws of physics under whose sway we fall, as do other pieces of matter. Most of the time these laws are implicit – as the framework within which our lives are enacted – but they may come to the fore under certain circumstances – as when we engage in physically strenuous tasks or fall down stairs or are involved in a car crash. On top of these physical limits, there are the biological constraints placed upon our performance by our species characteristics. These latter are represented not merely in, for example, our inability to fly without the assistance of an aeroplane or run at 100 m.p.h. They are also reflected in the biological determinants of our needs and of the means that our body provides for satisfying them. These needs give rise to reflexes, tropisms, instincts, appetites, etc., which to some extent regulate our behaviour. The biological constraints are most dramatically illustrated in the almost total absence of control we have over the developmental processes by which we unfold from the potentiality of the gamete to the actuality of the adult human being: we are, for the most part, the passive site of this process rather than enactors of it. Moreover, we carry within us, as important influences on our behaviour and experiences, the particular vicissitudes that we have as individuals experienced during this journey. Intra-uterine growth retardation, an early injury, malnutrition will irreversibly influence our feelings and be major biological limits added on to the general physical and species-specific constraints upon our range of self-choice that we share with our conspecifics.

This natural 'facticity' will, in the very broadest sense, determine the agenda our lives will be obliged to address. Nevertheless, this is a very loose determination. The entirety of cultural evolution, the distances between humans and nature (set out in my *Explicit Animal*)[13] measure the extent to which (in Steiner's words), 'man has talked himself free of organic constraint'. This is widely appreciated and there are relatively few sincere biological determinists for whom the self is simply dissolved into a sea of physiological events or waves on such a sea. Yes, we are animals inasmuch as we indulge in feeding behaviour; but in human animals such behaviour undergoes extraordinary transformations – for example, into concern not to embarrass one's host (especially if one perceives him to be less well off than oneself) by ordering an expensive dish when one is dining out at his expense. And, yes, like other animals, humans learn. But the 'bump-into and explore' learning of animals is a long way from the kind of way we learn. To appreciate this, it is only necessary to think of a mother planning to gain some points in the babysitting circle this year so that she will be able to attend an evening class next year without having to worry about childcare arrangements.

2. *There are (more or less local) cultural constraints on one's experiences, feelings and behaviour.* Our desires, our sense of what we ought to do, want to do and can do, are multiply determined by the macro- and micro-environments within which we were born, have developed, are enjoying (or not enjoying) our lives, and will decay. What is expected of me will influence what I do; what 'they' think will influence what I think; what 'they' want will influence what I regard as desirable and so desire. The scope of 'they' will vary – ranging from the history of my culture (itself influenced by the history of preceding and surrounding cultures); through the implicit and explicit pressures applied by the groups within which I have landed or with whom I most closely identify; to the individual examples set by, and the approval sought from, the specific 'significant others' who have been co-actors on the stage of my particular life. A cultural constraint may arise from sources as disparate as the transient disapproval of a friend or the Judaeo-Christian tradition of which I am a late product.

No one, then, in his or her right mind will deny the potency of biological and cultural constraints on the self, the individual. Our self-possession is limited by our deepest selves being to some extent in the keeping of forces, fields, influences of which we are incompletely aware. I do not invent myself; to an extent, the self I live out is implanted in me by things I am not fully aware of. For this reason, the notion of the individual as an utterly transparent Cartesian self, and as an absolute point of origin in the world, is unsustainable. Once the Cartesian self had lost its theological support (the truth of rational thoughts was underwritten by a non-deceiving God so the mind could rise above any formative influences such as custom and tradition and gain access to the truth by the pure operation of reason) and once it had lost the backing of epistemological idealism (the Cartesian self could always master its own world once it shed the other partner in the duo – the material world), there remained only the transcendental *cogito* of the phenomenologists, which ultimately required the absurdly exaggerated claims of existentialism to keep it viable.

For Sartre,[14] the self – in the form of the pure current account *pour-soi* – is not only utterly self-possessed and transparent, but enjoys absolute freedom. The only constraint on its freedom is its obligation to avoid the bad faith of denying its freedom. Otherwise it is in charge, inserting into a world of not-quite-fact the very values by which it lives and which comprise the agenda of its existence, making of its circumstances (such as they are) what its freely chosen values wish to make of them. The pure current account *pour-soi* is not even limited by its own history; it is not cluttered with the baggage of permanent characteristics (these latter are the alibis of the scoundrel wishing in bad faith to escape from the responsibility of the *pour-soi*, into the inert condition of the *en-soi*); and in so far as it is affected by (biological or cultural) history – its own or that of the collective to which it belongs only electively – it is marked by it but not determined by it.

This is manifestly false – as Sartre himself recognised eventually (though his recognition was so deeply buried in his *Critique of Dialectical Reason* that he managed to execute his U-turn without anyone, least of all himself, feeling the centrifugal force). We do not choose that we should exist at all; we do not choose our date of birth or (usually) our date of death; we do not choose the kind of families we are born into, the talents or disabilities that we have – to mention only the coarsest of the meshes in the net that constrains us. And although it may be argued that we freely choose to evaluate painful stimuli negatively and pleasurable ones positively, we do not choose that it is easier to enjoy an orgasm or even a cup of coffee than it is to enjoy having one's foot sawn off without an anaesthetic; or that it is easier to exercise free choice in the usual sense of the term when we are awake than when we are seriously obnubilated after a head injury – still *pour-soi*, of course, but somewhat confused.

Sartre's twentieth-century updating of an ahistorical, absolute-freedom Cartesianism is a sufficiently compelling bad example to discourage anyone from swinging, when trying to defend the autonomy of the self against postmodernists and others, from system-trance half-truths to neo-Cartesian half-truths. In fact, the postmodern marginalisers of (rational, free) consciousness and the existentialist globalisers of (rational, free) consciousness between them indicate the limits within which any viable theory of the self and of the role of the rational agent in daily life must be found.[15] Interestingly, these opposing visions are vulnerable to the same criticism: they fail to recognise that self-presence, self-possession, freedom, rationality, consciousness have *degrees*. Neither the dissipation of self into an unchosen and hidden system on the one hand nor, on the other, its elevation to an all-powerful legislator over a world created out of its synthetic activity, can accommodate the ordinary facts of life; that, for example, we seem to be more free, more self-possessed and more rational on some occasions than on others – when we are awake than when we are asleep, when we are sober than when we are blind drunk, or when we are walking down the stairs as opposed to falling down them. The Sartre of *Being and Nothingness* could not accept that freedom is contingent and limited by history,[16] and that agency is dependent upon and operates through mechanism, that it is both limited and made possible (as well as being given its content) by 'the given'. The system-trance theorists, conversely, cannot accept that there is freedom and self-possession outside the regulating power of the system, and that individuality contains something real that cannot be dissolved, without remainder, into the system.

Let us examine this freedom and self-possession, and do so through a specific example, one we have used already – that of greeting another person. This is, as already suggested, a particularly useful example, if only because saying 'Hello' seems a classic instance of near-mechanical system-driven behaviour into which nothing personal is inserted. If any speaker is a mere node in the system, a rule-driven non-agent, it is surely the Hello-sayer. If what is going on *here* doesn't yield to post-Saussurean system-trance analysis, such a mode of analysis won't apply *anywhere*. Well, let us see.

Imagine, as not infrequently happens, I catch sight of the potential recipient of my 'Hello' some way off. This gives me time to make a series of decisions. The first decision is whether or not I should respond at all; the second, whether I should respond with something middle-of-the-road such as 'Hello' or something more informal (such as 'Hi!') or more formal (such as 'Good morning'). My decision whether, and how, to respond will be most crucially dependent upon whether or not I recognise the potential recipient. 'Recognise' here has a variety of meanings: there are degrees or levels of recognition. I need to recognise the approaching person as being a human being, not some other physical or biological entity. One could imagine this recognition process being automated and the greeting-response, if appropriate, being secured automatically – rather as a robin will automatically peck at a red patch against a brown background. However, being human is not in itself sufficient to earn a greeting from me. The oncomer will need to belong to certain categories: the next level of recognition, in other words, is classification, allocation to a familiar (or unfamiliar) category of human being, a category towards which I am likely to deport myself in a certain way. This will depend upon things that are specific to myself, though some of the simpler considerations may be cast in general terms. I may be more likely to greet a male of my own age than a child (I don't want, after all, to be accused of being a child-molester) and a middle-aged man rather than a young woman (again, I don't want to be accused of invading the female's personal space, and worse). In other words, my classification of a stranger as an appropriate recipient of my greeting depends upon an enormous number of considerations that could not be captured in even the most complex set of general rules. For their application is dependent upon all sorts of things that are specific to me and/or specific to that moment. What sort of place we and the oncomer are in, what (inner or outer) business I am engaged in, what I feel like today (how grumpy or good-willed, well- or ill-disposed to humanity or particular sub-categories of humanity), etc. will all influence whether and how I greet. The vast majority of these factors is highly personal: the joy I am feeling at having secured an

MRC grant, my awareness from reading about it in the newspaper that this ('lonely', as I now appreciate it) place is where a woman was stabbed a few years before, my toothache, my attitude (as this person draws nearer and I see how smart a suit he is wearing) to something I choose to classify as 'businessmen' at present, etc. The number of considerations, and the way their application is crucially determined by so many things that are specific to me, clearly demonstrate how no finite set of rules could capture my likelihood of greeting the individual, predict the way in which I would greet them, or regulate my greeting behaviour in general. Only if I belonged to an exotic tribe and were being observed by an anthropologist ignorant of what was going on inside me, could these things seem predictable or tightly rule-governed. To a truly informed observer (for example, myself), it is evident that the greeting-rules, and the rules for the application or waiving of those rules, are infinitely complex.[17]

The complexity that attends the greeting of classifiable strangers is, however, only the beginning of the story. Many people I greet fall under unique categories – the single member-class of their unique selves. I recognise exactly who it is that is coming towards me in the proper-name sense: this is not merely 'middle-aged businessman', but Fred whom I met on the train a few years ago, after we hadn't seen each other since we had been schoolboys together. Such specific – token- rather than type- – recognition mobilises a vast additional army of considerations arising out of our actual (not general) shared experiences, but whose potency will depend upon how I am feeling at this moment – cheerful-communicative or grumpy-withdrawn. Again, none of these influences on my decision will belong to 'the system' – of language, of society – or to history in general. Our shared (or unshared) history will be utterly individual: it will belong to our actual episodic, autobiographical memories, whose elements may have certain, general, culturally-specifiable characteristics, but whose overall character and whose combinations will be unique. And it is that which is unique that will be decisive. It will be the interaction between our unique histories (as perceived by us now) and between those histories and our present states that determine whether or not we say 'Hello' and, more specifically, the way we say 'Hello'. Even this is not the whole story. We may be aware of, and resist, the pressures to say 'Hello', or subvert them. The tendency of human beings to parody anything stereotyped in their own behaviour, especially linguistic behaviour, and so to distance themselves from it, or to reclaim the behaviour for the actual moment they are sharing with the other person, has not been sufficiently remarked upon. It is a symptom of something very deep and distinctive about us – the tendency to make things explicit, as I have argued in *The Explicit Animal* – but also an uneasiness about anything that looks mechanical. And so, the encounter with the friend – particularly if that friend is close enough for courtesy, attention, communicative intent, etc. to be taken for granted – may prompt a jokingly assumed voice for the greeting – say a 'posh' voice or a rural dialect – perhaps with reference to a television programme we both of us admit to enjoying.[18] This, in turn, will refer back to shared experience, to a common world or a common set of assumptions about and attitudes to the world, or all three.

The potential complexity, consciously engaged in and profoundly individual – not necessarily in the sense of being original, but in the sense of being rooted in individual knowledge of the relations between the greeter and the greeted, in actual individual experience – can unfold indefinitely. None of this complexity could have been generated by the system; indeed, it represents distances (often consciously underlined) from the system.

Thus even the mechanical 'Hello' is rooted in considerations that are far from mechanical; and its use is influenced by the utterly personal history upon which the recognition and mode of acknowledgement of the other are dependent. It might be objected that while, yes, the determinants of whether or not I do something as seemingly mechanical and stereotyped as saying 'Hello' are autobiographical and specific to me, this is not the end of the story. The autobiographical element simply provides a substrate upon which the general rules can operate. For example, it is a personal, not a system-based, constraint that I shall not say 'Hello' to you again on the very specific grounds that we have already met twice this morning. However, the constraint is still a general cultural constraint: in taking notice of the fact that we have already said 'Hello', I am applying general principles that I did not choose, and to this extent I am caught up in the system, yielding to its constraints. More generally, it could be argued that it is only in virtue of its obeying the general rules that our communicative behaviour is intelligible and actually communicates. If I said 'Hello' at intervals throughout a conversation, my interlocutor would not know how to take it; my greeting would be unintelligible.

This objection is not decisive; indeed, it clarifies and strengthens the point I am making. For in order to apply the rules (or to break them to some specific communicative purpose) I have to be able to relate them to the absolutely specific situation I am in. No rule could determine or automate the application of the general rules to particular situations. Such applications require full consciousness of the particular situation and an understanding of the point or purport of the rule – in short, a sense of what is going on, where I am and what I am trying to do. That sounds very much like a fully developed conscious agent.

Someone might argue that the contents of the 'personal' history that influences the decision to say 'Hello' and the manner in which it is said are themselves impersonal. This, too, is not the case. First, although the elements that make up an encounter with another may be descriptively general ('We first met at a station, when we were both heading for the London train') they are perceptually unique. The elements of the stylised encounter (e.g. Boy meets Girl) have a unique position in the series of experiences that are the lives of the individuals encountering one another and are themselves experientially unique. Secondly, the perceptions are based upon sensations that lie beneath and escape description. More specifically, sensations do not belong to *any* system. This is not merely a restatement of the epistemological point about the incommunicability of the actual content of experience. No, the content of experience goes beyond the epiphenomenal fact of its incommunicability: its very reality, its being, lies in that which is incommunicable. That in virtue of which I am present here, present to this bit of the world and thus present to myself, lies beyond and beneath the mere forms of discourse – language or other discursive systems.[19] This is the core or basis of the self that is not open to dissipation in the system; it is the basis of the personal histories through which our relations with others are mediated, through which we engage with history, society, culture, etc.

That our personal histories – a unique succession of experiences that are not fully communicable – should lie at the core of our social being seems so obvious that it may seem surprising that others have overlooked it. This is because when we reflect on the self, or try to classify ourselves, we factor out what we can neither express nor generalise. In this way, the meetings between us, the history of the meetings between us, my decision to say 'Hello' on this occasion, and the manner in which I say it, are made to seem like positions in a network of general possibilities. But, of course, a meeting between you and me is composed of more than the factors that made this meeting probable or definite. When Goldmann writes:

> We have long since learned from the social history of ideas that *every* mode of human thought and feeling is determined by mental structures which are closely related to the objective life of the particular society in which they develop
>
> (Goldmann, p. 15)

we have to read him carefully: he says *mode* of thought and feeling, not the thought and feelings themselves. This is what the post-Saussurean dissipation of the self overlooks: the fact that my thoughts and feelings (and goals and actions) are not types but actual specific thoughts and feelings (and goals and actions), and these are not determined by 'the objective life of society'. The latter cannot specify the specific; and everything that exists is utterly specific. It is in the utterly specific that our uniqueness and actuality lies; and in this, too, we find the ontological weight of the non-substitutable self.

No system can handle – determine, absorb, dictate – actual individuals: the system of *langue*, for example, cannot legislate over the occurrence of actual *paroles*. And just as *langue* does not determine when and how I actually say

'Hello' (though it may indicate where it is more appropriate for people in my culture to say 'Hello'), so the Unconscious, or the laws of history, do not determine who or what I should like or want to do. There are two related reasons for this: they are not tightly enough drawn to be able to specify what is to take place to the precise degree necessary to secure passage from the possible to the actual; and it is necessary for me to experience them in my own life, in my own body, to be affected by them. Of course, behaviour is rule-governed and culturally constrained; but a knowledge and understanding of the constraints and the ability to apply the rules to particular situations (and, since all situations are particular and have their own quirks, this means to apply rules *tout court*) requires a profound and complex understanding of an individual situation and a tacit but sure sense of the point of the rule. The rule-governed nature of behaviour not only permits individual creativity and the unique input from the rational, conscious, self-present individual – as a kind of 'personal spin between the meshes' – it actually demands such an input. The rules for applying, breaking, playing with the rules cannot, therefore, be mechanically applied or enacted through a helpless node in the system.[20]

To reassert the reality of the self is in essence to reassert the centrality of individual experience and the individual organisation of those personal experiences through which the general influences, common to a group, a nation, an era, are ultimately transmitted. Although we do not choose the cultural and historical context in which we live out our lives and find our own meanings, any more than we choose the rules of the language through which we speak, we are no less present in the lives we enact and the meanings we find in those lives. For at the heart of the *quidditas* – the coarse general framework within which we think of ourselves as living – there lies an unclassified *haecceitas* which is the only true reality. This is always present and it will always fail fully to coincide with, and hence will subvert, the general structures. The incompletely classifiable and communicable first-person sensations that make up our classifiable and incommunicable experiences (and classification gets easier as we ascend the scale of generality, to the level at which we touch the laws that post-Saussureans see as swallowing up the self) continually subvert the generalities of history, culture and the rest – just as Winston Smith's aching varicose ulcer was evidence of his non-solubility in Big Brother's closed universe of general discourse. Actual experience is constant proof of our distance from the collective. The uniformity of a company of soldiers standing to attention on parade – the supreme example of the reduction of the individual to a social atom externally determined in all respects – is deceptive. Even during the moments of the parade, the individual soldiers are possessed by different sensations and by different preoccupations arising from the utterly different personal histories to which they are inescapably attached. They are commutable, equivalent signs only with respect to the particular occasion – the parade to which they each contribute one unit of soldierliness – but beyond that they are profoundly different.

If we exaggerate this inner distance and think of the individual as being composed of incorrigible sensations, we run the risk of espousing, as Sartre did, a neo-Cartesian vision of a transparent self, absolutely self-possessed and self-present. If, on the other hand, we overlook this distance, we run the opposite risk of seeing the self dissolve into objective systems. The first error leads to the fantasy of absolute freedom and delusions of omnipotence; the second error leads to a fantasy of total passivity and impotence (omnimpotence, perhaps), a fantasy in which the individual is seen to be so much part of the system that it is difficult or impossible to partition responsibility for actions between individuals and systems, in which we deny the ontological weight of the individual as an agentive centre, as a place where a difference is made.[21]

I am not self-created – after all, I did not make, nor could I run, the body which is my *sine qua non*, and I did not choose many of the conditions in which I act out my life. Nor am I absolutely transparent, totally revealed to myself; not at least at the level of talk about the self – the level at which I am acknowledged by others and at which I seek acknowledgement – for the process by which I am disclosed to myself at this level is mediated by language and society which structures (though, importantly it does not form the actual content of) even my deepest desire. Nevertheless, ultimately, the content of the self, including even its larger-scale aspirations, is held at a level at which I am both present to myself and distant from, or at least distinct from, the anonymous, external world of *systems*. The actual – actual experiences of the world – is rooted in something that lies beyond the system, beyond the mechanism: the pure system, and the mechanism abstracted from its realisation in a particular event or act, are only schemata of possibilities. The actual is what is suffered, or chosen – in short, experienced. This is the content that fills out the form and it is inseparable from the individual considered as a unique and irreplaceable being with a unique biography. Every actual experience, every real choice, is rooted in that individual and goes beyond the system.[22]

For all these reasons, I believe it is possible to make sense of the notions of self and individuality that do not, on the one hand, elide the differences between mechanisms and agency[23] or, on the other, destroy the notion of responsibility and of the individual as an entity making an independent contribution to the world in which she finds herself. It is necessary only to recall how an individual is both particular and generalisable. At the root of this notion is the tautology of the embodied individual which may be expressed as 'I am this thing'. This notion is suspended between the particularity of presence and generality of absence: I am present and coinciding with myself inasmuch as I am embedded in my experiences and have assimilated their general face; and am absent from myself inasmuch as I am classifiable in accordance with objective criteria that are invisible to me. It would be naive to think of 'the life of a society as a sort of sum, or product, of the thought and action of a large number of individuals', as Goldmann said the leaders of the Enlightenment did – if only because the mass of individuals create, sustain, respond to, are part of, something that the individual cannot know in its entirety. Ignorance, as Hayek repeatedly emphasised, is the most significant fact about human nature in relation to society as a whole and legislators and reformers should take account of this when they are preparing to impose their Utopian dreams on their fellow citizens. There is, however, good reason for seeing those individuals as at least in some sense being 'a free and independent point of departure'. This would suffice to rescue the Enlightenment project – or at least the hope of progress – from the contemporary Counter-Enlightenment's gloating and self-satisfied (not to say self-contradictory) metanarrative of its irretrievable demise.

Notes

1. This phrase derives, I think, from Paul Ricoeur. I am here borrowing it from David Lehman's brilliant *Signs of the Times: Deconstruction and the Fall of Paul de Man* (London: André Deutsch, 1991). I cannot resist quoting his comment about literary criticism in the 'age of suspicion':

   > Acquiescing in the notion that disinterested inquiry is an impossibility and that every value judgement is necessarily a power play before it is anything else, they make their decisions by ideological litmus tests and determining the sexist and racist quotient in any piece of writing, from Plato to the present. This is, at bottom, a conception of the literary critic as an agent of the thought police, single-minded, obsessively concerned to enforce the party line, willing to subject chosen works to a violent form of interrogation, and more than happy to eliminate literature altogether in favor of pure theory.
   >
   > (p. 263)

2. Isaiah Berlin, 'Political Ideas in the Twentieth Century', in *Four Essays on Liberty* (Oxford: Oxford University Press, 1969), p. 18.

   Later in the same essay, he tries to distance Marx and Freud from the bad influence they had on twentieth-century thought:

   > By giving currency to exaggerated versions of the view that the true reasons for men's beliefs were most often very different from what they themselves thought them to be, being frequently caused by events and processes of which they were neither aware nor in the least anxious to be aware, these eminent thinkers helped, however, unwittingly, to discredit the rational foundations from which their own doctrines derived their logical force.
   >
   > (p. 21)

   This is characteristically generous but not, alas, sustained by all the facts.

3. They are not, of course, alone in this. I have already noted how thinking by transferred epithet and misplaced consciousness is not unique to psychologists and philosophers of a cognitive persuasion. How often have we been told that 'It is language that speaks' and it will be recalled that it was Lévi-Strauss who stated that 'myths think themselves out in men and without men's knowledge'. The reader is also referred to my 'A Critical Dictionary of Neuromythology', in *On The Edge of Certainty* (London: Macmillan, 1999), which is devoted almost entirely to examining such dodges.
4. *Times Literary Supplement*, 3 February 1995, p. 6. The contradictions in the postmodern critique of the narratives of emancipation and enlightenment have been uncovered by many critics; see, in particular, note 10 below.
5. Of course, Marx saw the Enlightenment through the eyes of Hegel's critique. So, although he inherited the Enlightenment spirit of criticism and healthy scepticism and was fired by a Voltairean anger at the permanent conditions of oppression sponsored by those in power and the mystifications of their ideologues such as priests and cultural functionaries, he also inherited Hegel's dialectical obfuscations, his belief in historical necessity and his irrationalism – or, rather, his sidelining of ordinary reason in favour of the dialectical unfolding of Great Reason. And all that was necessary for Marx's writings to cause maximum damage was to ensure they had their most enduring effects in countries that had been relatively untouched by the Enlightenment. His writings, therefore, became a means by which feudal autocracies continued their tradition of oppression with a different rationale. The unaccountable czars, bureaucrats and priests were replaced by unaccountable dictators, commissars and ideologues – illustrating not the Hegelo-Marxist laws of history but Pareto's circulation of elites, in which, however, the main motor is not ability but brutality and ruthlessness.
6. Joel Handler, Presidential Address to the Law and Society Association in *Law and Society Review* 26(4) (1992): 697–731, at pp. 697–8.
7. Just in case it might be thought that Barthes was joking, here is an earlier passage from the same lecture:

   > power is the parasite of a trans-social organism, linked to the whole of man's history and not only to his political, historical history. This object in which power is inscribed, for all of human eternity, is language, or, to be more precise, its necessary expression: the language we speak and write.
   >
   > Language is legislation, speech is its code. We do not see the power which is in speech *because we forget that all speech is a classification, and that all classifications are oppressive*. Jakobson has shown that a speech-system is defined less by what it permits us to say than by what it compels us to say ... Thus, by its very structure my language implies an inevitable relation of alienation. To speak, and with even greater reason, to utter a discourse, is not, as is too often repeated, to communicate; it is to subjugate.
   >
   > (Inaugural Lecture, Collège de France, in *Barthes: Selected Writings*, ed. S. Sontag (Oxford: Fontana, 1983), p. 460, emphasis added)

   In common with many of the *maîtres à penser*, Barthes does not pause to differentiate between the legitimate and beneficial use of 'the power which is in speech'. We shall return to this.
8. *After the New Criticism* (Chicago: the University of Chicago Press, 1980, pp. 283–4). For the followers of Paul de Man (blissfully unaware that they were following a real

Fascist), it was not only language but meaning itself that was 'Fascist'. Lehman (ibid.) gives an account of how this was explained to him by one of de Man's disciples:

> We inhabit [Lehman's informant told him] an indeterminate universe. Everything is mediated entirely through language – the only way we can know anything is by using words. And the words of any discourse constantly shift their meaning. Everything depends on interpretation and no interpretation is more correct than any other. The proper attitude is to regard all interpretations as equally 'not true and not false'. To insist that a given piece of discourse means something specific and decided is to elevate one meaning at the expense of others. It is to uphold a hierarchy of values and that renders one guilty of a dictatorial urge. Fascism, in short.

The argument is, of course, self-refuting in two ways. First, it assumes that it has a definite meaning itself and this means that meaning is determinate – at least to some degree. And secondly, it assumes that those who force determinate meaning upon statements must be capable of doing so, even though their words, too, are subject to unlimited indeterminacy. If they are not able to do *that* then there can be no way that meaning can become Fascist.

9. He is reminiscent of many other preachers of disorder who expect their own lives to be cocooned in a high level order. I am reminded of John Weightman's observation about the Marquis de Sade:

> There is something unconvincing, perhaps even comic, in the frantic excess of his Gothic destructiveness, when, in real life, he expected society to function efficiently, at least with regard to his privileges as an aristocrat. In the intervals of preaching chaos in the name of unbridled lust, he wrote indignant letters demanding immediate payment of the feudal dues from his estates.
>
> (*TLS*, 1 May 1992, p. 5)

10. This is a recurrent theme in my *Not Saussure* (London: Macmillan, 2nd edition, 1995). The way in which postmodern thinkers 'saw off the branch upon which they are sitting' (to use Jonathan Culler's metaphor) is also addressed with exemplary clarity in the special issue of *Critical Review* on postmodernism (Volume 5, Issue 1, Spring 1991).

    Carl Rapp's essay on Lyotard ('The Crisis of Reason') deals a fatal blow to the latter's reputation as a thinker. According to Lyotard, it is the achievement of postmodern thought to recognise that the narratives of progress towards the truth are without foundation. Lyotard's *The Postmodern Condition* asserts that there are two different kinds of knowledge – narrative knowledge and scientific knowledge. The 'metanarrative of knowledge' is that the shift from the former to the latter represents true progress. Lyotard asserts that postmodernism now appreciates that this itself is a myth without justification: no form of knowledge gives us access to the truth; and narrative knowledge and scientific knowledge cannot be ranked in the way that intellectual historians usually have done. The problem, which Lyotard overlooks, is that this 'metanarrative of metanarratives' claims itself to be true and to transcend the pre-postmodern narrative, by explaining where the latter stands in the history of thought. It represents exactly that kind of knowledge which Lyotard and other standard bearers of postmodernism consider to be meaningless.

    Jeffrey Friedman, in 'Postmodernism v Postlibertarianism', put his finger on the postmodern 'conceit' that we can have it both ways: that we can gain enough critical perspective on our thought to call it false, at the same time that we deny our ability to transcend our own context. This, of course, merely reproduces the hubris that postmodernists claim was invented by the Enlightenment and that, they contend, they somehow managed to escape.

(p. 152)

Postmodernism, as Friedman phrases it, 'propounds a metanarrative of the end of metanarrative' (p. 151), and claims to have achieved 'a transcendence of transcendence'.

This is particularly notable in those who follow Richard Rorty in deconstructing any hint of universalist pretensions in thought, or context-transcending notions of truth and reality. Rorty's neo-pragmatist attack on philosophy, his assertion that truth is relative to interpretive communities and his rejection of 'the universal, timeless and necessary' is triply self-contradictory: it is itself a philosophical position; it is not itself presented as being relative to a specific interpretive community; and it seems to have the status of a recently discovered universal, timeless and necessary truth. The notion of interpretive communities as the final arbiters of truth is, of course, deeply flawed. It does not, for example, account for the difference between an outbreak of racist 'thought' and a law of physics – both being sustained by 'interpretive communities' in Rorty's sense; between groundless prejudices and useful truths; or between scientific laws that lead to effective technologies and magic that doesn't. Nor does it explain how interpretive communities become established or what determines their boundaries, nor even what we should think of as such a community – 'me on a bad day', 'our household', 'everyone in our street', 'all the people in British medicine', 'Europeans since the pre-Socratics'. Connected with all of these is a failure to explain why the interpretive community which accepts one truth – for example, Newton's laws of motion – should be so much larger than the interpretive community that accepts another, such as the prophecies of the Reverend Jones of Jonestown.

11. When Foucault was admitted to hospital after a road traffic accident, Simone Signoret was the first to be informed of the event. 'All are agreed on her reaction; she was startled and horrified that neither the police nor the hospital staff had recognised Foucault' (David Macey, *The Lives of Michel Foucault* (London: Vintage, 1994), p. 370). This response, which Macey allows to pass without comment, is multiply revealing. It shows, first of all, that the ordinary notion of identity seemed to be applicable to the man who denied it (and who, indeed, had erased the concept of 'man' from the intellectual map). At least his close friends believed so. Secondly, it exposed a deeply anti-egalitarian expectation amongst his friends. Presumably, Foucault would have been treated differently had he been recognised and 'differently' would not, of course, have meant 'worse'. Finally, there is the comical assumption that policemen, doctors and nurses are derelict in not knowing the identity of a certain intellectual who loomed so large in certain intellectual circles. To loom large in those circles is presumably to loom large in the world, and those who cannot identify the large-loomers – doctors, nurses and policemen culpably busy with other preoccupations – quite naturally evoke the 'horrified' reactions of other large-loomers.
12. The reader is referred to my *Enemies of Hope* (Basingstoke: Macmillan, 1997), Chapter 3, 'Magic and Science', and to my *Newton's Sleep* (London: Macmillan, 1995), where the Strong Sociology of Knowledge is criticised. This critique was in

part based upon Lewis Wolpert's excellent *The Unnatural Nature of Science* (London: Faber, 1992).

Of course, Faraday was not working in isolation – he will have been influenced by ideas 'in the air' at the time (though his notions of field-forces were revolutionary); but not every scientist of his time who was equally exposed to such influences made so much of them, rose so far above them, and had such an enduring impact on the way we see and operate in the world. Likewise, his notion of forces and fields was greatly influenced by the world-picture he derived from his Sandemanian background, which had encouraged him to seek a unity of forces. But the proof of his theory was its basis in observation, its ability to be generalised and to predict novel observations and its practical applications. The Clerk Maxwell–Hertz–Einstein revolution in theoretical science, the technological transformation of the world would not have come out of Faraday's work if he had simply been acting out childhood influences. After all, Einstein was no Sandemanian, and one does not have to be a Sandemanian to get a dynamo to work.

13. See especially chapter 6, 'Man, the Explicit Animal', reprinted as reading 3 in this volume.
14. Or at least the pre-Marxist Sartre of *Being and Nothingness*.
15. The post-Saussurean marginalisation of consciousness is, of course, at least in part an over-reaction against Sartre's failure to recognise the bounds of freedom and the historical influences on the self. Foucault's empty cipher, vanishing into the historical transformations of discursive forces, is a response to Sartre's all-powerful, anhistoric, abiological, purely metaphysical *pour-soi*.
16. That 'Men make their own history, but they do not make it just as they please; they do not make it under circumstances chosen by themselves, but under circumstances directly encountered, given and transmitted from the past' (Karl Marx, *The Eighteenth Brumaire of Louis Bonaparte*) is unlikely to be dissented from by many.
17. For a further examination of this problem of specification-by-rules (with an incomplete understanding of its devastating implications for his own theories), see Daniel Dennett, 'Cognitive Wheels: The Frame Problem of AI', in Christopher Hookway, ed., *Minds, Machines, Evolution* (Cambridge University Press, 1984). See also my discussion in *The Explicit Animal*, pp. 223–6. The experience of the imaginary anthropologist, incidentally, should cast doubt on what Louis Althusser ('On Marx and Freud', trans. Warren Montag, *Rethinking MARXISM* 4(1) (Spring 1991), p. 24) describes as 'the golden rule of materialism': 'never judge a being by its consciousness of itself'. I am afraid that a statistical, objective analysis of my greeting behaviour and that of a large group of individuals considered to belong to the same class as myself would yield no insights into why, with what purpose, or what feelings, I greeted, or failed to greet, anyone on a particular occasion. You would have to know a fantastic amount about me really to know why.
18. Man (and woman) is, very importantly, The Piss-taking Animal – and this is a mark of his/her distinctive consciousness – a consciousness of the signs that he/she not only responds to but consciously deploys – a consciousness of signs *as signs*.
19. Ironically, this distance between language and experienced reality has been used as an argument to support the idea that language does not make contact with the world and that discourse is, therefore, a sealed system that refers only to itself. At the same time, discourse theorists overlook actual experience as that which informs, subverts, acts as a critical check upon, the world of discourse. See Raymond Tallis, *In Defence of Realism* (London: Edward Arnold, 1988).

20. The role of understanding – individual understanding – and assent in rule-following has been grossly underestimated. The cloudy notion of 'internalisation' of rules has contributed to this failure. According to internalisation theorists, rules become transformed into something more mechanical and automatic – into unconscious pressures. However, rule-following in many cases is like responding to an appeal to reason. This combines individuality – I have to see and understand and assent to its conclusions – and collectivity – I submit to general, universal rules. (This is also an answer to romantics and those others who see the application of reason in human affairs as being anti-individual and anti-creative.)

    After Grice's detailed and brilliant analyses of the production of meaning in ordinary conversation, there should be no excuse for anyone to forget the extent to which rule-following is explicit and based upon a complex understanding not only of the rules but of your understanding of the rules. This is one of the points implicit in The Frame Problem (see note 17).
21. This is well illustrated by the Critical Legal Studies movement which, for example, suggests that the state should be held responsible in cases of child murder, since 'contemporary modes of social thought ... recognise the pervasive relationship between observer and observed and deny the primitive notion that subjects act upon a background of distinct, fixed objects rather existing in a reciprocal and ever-changing subject–object tension' (cited in Lehman, op. cit., pp. 39–40).
22. And herein lies the deep meaning of the Paul de Man affair which Lehman described and analysed with such brilliance. The question of Paul de Man was not a question about a piece of the endless and undecidable text of society; it was a question about the actual behaviour of an extra-textual individual – as was accepted, without question, by his defenders, such as Derrida, as well as his attackers. De Man had always believed, or pretended to believe, that writing should be approached as examples of the text-system playing with itself. 'Considerations of the actual and historical existence of writers are a waste of time from a critical viewpoint' (op. cit., p. 137). As Lehman says, 'how poetically just it would be if so antibiographical a theory of literature should be vanquished by the discovery of a ruinous biographical fact' (p. 140).
23. Perhaps we should be more intensely and more continuously astonished than we are at the way automaticity and responsibility interact, at how physiological and social reflexes interact with our agency.

From: *Enemies of Hope* (Macmillan, 1997), pp. 303–26, 468–73.

7
The Hope of Progress

In this second reading from *Enemies of Hope*, Tallis defends the values of the Enlightenment and a chastened version of the Enlightenment project, freed of its scientistic and totalitarian aspirations. This means mounting a defence of certain universal values, in opposition to the relativism of much contemporary thought. The minimal principles Tallis wishes to propose are, first, that the individual has the right to choose whether he or she lives or dies, and, second, that we should favour those values that leave individuals who do not share them most free to act in accordance with their own differing values. Out of these minimal or basic principles others – such as accountability and rationality – may be derived. In explaining these ideas, Tallis recognises that there is in what he says a strand of utopianism. However, despite the catastrophic results of utopian ideals during the twentieth century, he is convinced that the two major strands of the hope of progress – first, to alleviate suffering (the world of means), and, second, to extend the capacities of human beings to realise new possibilities (the world of ends) – are essential if mankind is to find any meaning in its struggle to get beyond the brute desire for survival. It is in creativity that the possibilities of human life find their true realisation, and the enemies of creativity, he insists, are such physical and political realities as pain, unreasonable oppression, unchallenged cruelty, unaccountable government, hunger and fear.

Worries about universalism

The most persistent criticism of Enlightenment thought is that it is (arrogantly) universalistic. The charge is that, beneath the differences between individual thinkers, there was a central dogma to which they all subscribed:

> the reality of natural law ... of eternal principles by following which alone men could become wise, happy, virtuous and free. One set of universal and unalterable principles governed the world for theists, deists and atheists, for optimists and pessimists, puritans, primitivists and believers in progress and the richest fruits of science and culture; these laws governed inanimate and animate nature, facts and events, means and ends, private life and

> public, all societies, epochs and civilisations; it was solely by departing from them that men fell into crime, vice, misery.[1]

Although the Enlightenment thinkers were prepared to accept that, since men lived in different circumstances, the same ends might be achieved by different means, their cultural relativity stopped short at relativising those ends themselves:

> they ... retained a common core of conviction that the ultimate ends of all men at all times were, in effect, identical: all men sought the satisfaction of basic physical and biological needs, such as food, shelter, security and also peace, happiness, justice, the harmonious development of their natural faculties, truth, and, somewhat more vaguely, virtue, moral perfection and what the Romans called *humanitas*.
>
> (Berlin, ibid., p. 3)

It is this – and the related assumption that the *philosophes* and their heirs know what is best for all mankind – that is credited with generating the deepest and most enduring resentment. And Berlin, in common with many less temperate contemporary critics of the Enlightenment, seems to think that this resentment is justified: the assumption of universality inevitably leads to oppression; at the worst the often violent imposition of modern European values – or eighteenth-century Parisian values – upon the entire world.

This criticism of the Enlightenment has been, I believe, a serious source of confusion; and that confusion is evident in the list of 'ultimate ends' that Berlin gives. They are actually a mixture of (a) basic or universal *means* (to life) such as food and shelter, (b) arguably universal ends, such as happiness, (c) possibly culturally-specific means, such as justice, and (d) manifestly culture-specific ends, such as moral perfection. We need to keep these separate if we are going to evaluate the Enlightenment justly and separate what is enduring and beneficial in its programmes and dreams from what is either of historical interest only or an insolent and dangerous imposition of Eurocentric or Parisocentric values upon the world. Keeping these things separate, while at the same time noting the interrelationships between them, is essential if our argument about the Enlightenment – and, indeed, the hope of progress – is not going to become enmired in irresolvable disputes about cultural relativism and ideological and axiological colonialism.

Let us begin with groundfloor values, with means–ends pairings that seem to be universals. Can we take it for granted that physiological survival is, other things being equal, a basic desire? It would seem, at first sight, that we can. Of course, there will be circumstances in which death will be preferable to life –

where, for example, an individual is suffering so much pain that life is not worthwhile, or where there has been such loss of face or status that death is preferred to dishonour. We shall assume, however, that there are no cultures or societies where unbearable pain or insupportable dishonour are the norm. If there were such societies (present-day Rwanda may be approaching this condition) we would be inclined to regard them as gravely dysfunctional rather than as a serious challenge to the cultural universal of the desire to live.

We may think of the will to life, then, as a core value, invariant across cultures. If we accept this, then we may derive other cultural invariants; for example, the value of secure, adequate supplies of safe food and water. Ensuring the provision of safe food and water for all creates technological and logistic challenges that, historically, have been most successfully addressed by rational and scientific means rather than, say, by means of magic or prayer. Consider, for instance, the reliable and universal provision of clean water supplies. Historical experience would suggest that this essential requirement is met most effectively not, say, by 'wise men' preaching irrationalist doctrines of 'pollution' but by an approach based upon contemporary scientific understanding of microbiology, the physics and chemistry of pipes, etc., and also upon a clear understanding of the importance of individual accountability amongst those involved in ensuring the supply of water. Not all of this may be explicit – when I select the sort of pipes I am going to buy on behalf of the people on the basis of disinterested advice rather than 'backhanders', or on the basis of sound technical advice rather than the visions of the elders, I do not need to know much about the relevant metallurgy though this knowledge lies in the background of the consumer item in question – but it does need to be implicit. We can thus move very quickly from a small handful of incontestable value-universals to a vast nexus of value-imbued and ethics-imbued technical consequences which, themselves, acquire the status of secondary or consequential universals.

Sharing a universal wish that one should not die prematurely of thirst or diarrhoea already commits one to subscribing to a complex, subtle and boundless nexus of rational, technological and contractual thought and behaviour. Although some of those universals will seem to be purely technological, behind or implicit in them, or their application, will be other things that are not purely technological. It is no use taking on board the principles behind water purification, based upon a knowledge of bacteriology and toxicology, if these principles are not implemented by individuals who feel personally responsible for their own part in a very complex interlocking network of activities involving large numbers of people and agencies. Science-based provision of safe water supplies will not be possible in a world where the individuals employed by the water companies have a fatalistic attitude to life, do not value their work, do not have any conscience with regard to it, or are appointed and promoted on the basis of nepotism and/or bribes rather than on the basis of competence or genuine commitment. Buying into technology means buying into the collective and personal values necessary to make technology work.

We seem now to be well advanced in defending quite a lot of universal values, and thus allaying the fear that even a greatly reduced universalism deriving from, or implicit in, a reassertion of the Enlightenment hope of progress, would involve an oppressive value-colonialism. Before proceeding any further, however, we should go back and question our starting assumption: that there *is* universal consensus at the level of basic biological need originating from agreement about the value of life. Is life, or a life not dominated by pain and privation, an absolute value? Is the desire for such a life a cultural invariant? We noted the fact that there are, in certain cultures, circumstances in which death may be preferred to life, and dealt with this by suggesting that any society in which a preference for death or continuous pain was the norm should not be considered merely as having different values but rather as being pathological. De Maistre, however, has suggested that such cultures may not be all that unusual; on the contrary, they may themselves reveal the deep truth about mankind. As Isaiah Berlin expressed de Maistre's view:

> men's desire to immolate themselves is as fundamental as their desire for self-preservation or happiness.[2]
>
> The rational man seeks to maximise his pleasures, minimise his pain. But society is not an instrument for this at all. It rests on something much more elemental, on perpetual self-sacrifice, on the human tendency to immolate oneself to the family or the city, or the church or the state, with no thought of pleasure or profit, or the craving to offer oneself upon the altar of social solidarity, to suffer and die in order to preserve the continuity of hallowed forms of life.
>
> (ibid., p. 123)

There are several possible responses to this. The first is to repeat the point already made in the Prologue, that de Maistre, by making such general statements about human nature, is committing precisely the essentialist, universalist error for which he so ferociously criticised the Enlightenment thinkers. His pessimistic view of mankind as irrationally committed to evil and self-immolation is no less universalist than the *philosophes'* vision of mankind as essentially rational and beneficent. The second is to note that, although humans do seem sometimes so to order their affairs as to increase rather than decrease the sum total of happiness, the suffering and death consequent upon human actions, even war, is frequently not anticipated even by the chief agents. The English and German Establishments who sponsored the First World War on a wave of patriotic excitement and moral indignation expected a rapid victory, not a protracted blood-and-mud bath in which they lost their own lives or those of their children. (Most of those who participated did not, of course, freely choose to do so.) Immolation, in short, is rarely a primary aim or value, but more frequently an undesired consequence of pursuing other aims or protecting other values. And finally, if it were a primary value, the question arises whether it should be simply accepted as such, as part of the rich pattern of life, a thread in the multicultural variousness of the world, or whether, on behalf of other universal values, it should be opposed. The answer must surely be that it should be opposed.[3]

The reason for this is worth examining in more detail because it opens on to the larger question of the relations between different values and different value-systems – of how, from a non-universalistic standpoint, from a point of view that does not claim transcendent authority, we can adjudicate between fundamentally different, but conflicting, values or value-systems. It may well indeed be the case that for some men, immolation is preferable to life and that the short path of slaughter and glory leading to the grave while crusading on behalf of some higher principle of honour – the glory of God, the glory of the nation, the glory of Glory – may be better than the long littleness of ordinary, comfortable existence. One can even imagine a society in which *all* adults subscribed to this view: Jonestown was a microcosmic example of such a society. Is not this *weltanschauung* entitled to its share of respect? There are two very specific reasons for answering this question firmly in the negative.

The first is the minor practical reason that the self-immolating sword wielded by such societies has to be forged by other societies – or other individuals within that society – who do not subscribe, or have in the past not subscribed to, this value-system. The humane methods of self-destruction, the life leading up to the climactic act of mass suicide, is parasitic upon the work of others who work within a rationalistic, contractual framework. Consider the terrible events at Jonestown when the Reverend Jim Jones persuaded all the several hundred members of his sect to kill themselves and their children. The deaths were brought about by poisoning with cyanide. Cyanide doesn't happen: it has to be made and bought. Expert chemists, transport systems, etc., were therefore necessary to bring about the realisation in Jonestown of this ultimate expression of irrationalism. This tends to be overlooked, just as, in a less dramatically horrible context, principled and articulated rejections of progressive, organised society presuppose a background of progressive, organised societies to be able to achieve the expression they need. Dependency upon a context of reason is true of all irrationalist movements and philosophies, and usually to a much greater degree than is true of that small number of them that, like the Jones cult, are committed to a climactic apocalyptic end.[4]

The second, more important, reason is that the sword that is wielded will not usually be directed exclusively inwards. The Jonestown massacre was untypical in this regard. More commonly, apocalyptic romantics do not confine themselves to their own society or their own circle; they do not bring the temple down exclusively upon the heads of the faithful. The Jungerian Storm of Steel was not an internal affair of the Club of Junkers. The active nihilism of the dispossessed and militaristic right-wing aristocrats, obsessed by the lost honour of their Fatherland, who brought the Apotheosis of the Romantic Will to its realisation in Europe in the 1930s and 1940s, had grievous consequences that were borne by others than themselves, by others who did not share either their preoccupations or their value systems. The freely chosen values of these apocalyptic romantics inspired the most appalling oppression, often unto death, of many millions of others whose freely own chosen values were thus trampled over.

There are two elements in this second argument. First, the values achieving predominance in a particular society may not only not be of material benefit to many members of that society, whatever moralistic or altruistic dress they wear (this is the Marxist point), and secondly, they may be explicitly not shared by all its members. Even if we take a small, closed community like the People's Temple commune in Jonestown, while it is not impossible that the mother gassing her six-month-old child during the collective immolation was doing it as a free agent, it is equally possible that she might have not been acting as a free agent. What is certain is that the six-month-old child was not acting as a free agent.

In larger communities, this disparity of values and wishes is much more evident. So a progressive, liberal commitment to multi-culturalism may well involve not only respecting the different values of a society other than one's own, but incidentally result in colluding with the tyranny of the majority (or, not infrequently, a powerful minority) in that society. My wish not to judge what goes on in your country X by the values predominating in my country Y may mean that I refuse to pass judgement on the way the predominant values in X oppress some individuals in that country. The well-founded fear of being arrogant over values may give rise to a culpable quietism when others' values in other cultures are being trampled on. The judgement as to the point at which laudable tolerance gives way to culpable quietism depends upon two things: one's definition of a society as being other than one's own and therefore outside the scope of one's moral or axiological jurisdiction (Was Jonestown part of America or not? Who is my neighbour?); and, related to this, the sense that one has of the scope of one's responsibility. 'It's none of my business, ducky' may or may not be an admirable response to learning of actions that, although they contravene one's own value-system, are consistent with the values and assumptions of the society in which they take place.

The definition of the society or community to which one belongs is rather more difficult nowadays in a world that has – though to a lesser degree than some of our cultural prophets would claim – moved towards being a global, electronic village. Cultures intermesh through communication and trade. The sale of arms, the conduct of any trade, the provision of Overseas Aid – all of these directly or indirectly support or undermine the value-systems of the countries on both sides of the transactions. In profiting by the sale of arms to an evil regime, one becomes in some degree evil oneself – by sponsoring or supporting their evil. That is obvious. What is less obvious is that, in selling technology to a country that does not have the rationalistic value structure to enable that technology to run effectively (cf. the discussion about unpolluted water supplies above), one is being dishonest, even if the sale is not lubricated by backhanders funded from overseas aid. The non-fraudulent sale of technology presupposes some commonality of values – the values that will create the context in which the technology will work effectively.

In short, one cannot in the modern world avoid some universalism, if one is at all honest. It is implicit in one's dealings with other cultures, even if it is not made explicit as a condition of those dealings. This is not always fully appreciated by those who preach a politically correct value relativism. It may be intellectually pure and morally self-satisfying to jet round the world pointing out that there cannot be universal individual rights because neither the idea of the individual nor that of rights is universal. But it may also be deeply hypocritical because those who are able to do this enjoy freedom of travel, wealth beyond the dreams of most individuals on the planet, and many other things that come from the idea of contractual rights. They would be outraged and inconsolable if they were deprived of them – gaoled, debagged, impoverished at the behest of a theocrat who disapproved on religious grounds of jet travel. And they might be rather anxious if they learned that the quality of maintenance of the engines in the jets were also subject to culturally relative variation and were not subject to a universal agreement on contractual and personal responsibility and the superiority of rational science over magic.

We need some way, therefore, of working out how to separate benign from malign universalism: distinguishing between on the one hand, extending to all human beings the status one automatically grants one's own fellow citizens and, on the other, an arrogant imposition upon other cultures of one's own culture-specific beliefs; separating rational respect and concern from missionary fervour, moral superiority and patronising arrogance. For we can no longer be neutral as to what goes on in other cultures, because we are so deeply implicated in them as to make it difficult to define the boundaries of our own culture and hence the boundaries of our responsibilities. This is not merely a matter of knowledge – modern methods of newsgathering and dissemination prevent us from pleading ignorance about what is going on in the wider world – but also a matter of action and interaction. Whereas we may choose to regard tyranny in remote places as being, unlike tyranny at home, none of our business, we are no longer entitled to do so: it has everything to do with our business in the narrow and the wider sense. Our choices directly or indirectly support or undermine the value-systems in other cultures. And this also has everything to do with our more obvious responsibility for tyranny nearer to hand. Cheap imported goods manufactured under conditions of slave labour in a distant Hell sooner or later contribute to the unemployment that will add to the underclass in our own country and make that Hell a little less distant. We can no longer retreat to cultivating our own garden because the garden belongs to everyone: our spades always dig into global soil. (This globalisation is not an accident, or the product of specific technologies such as those related to communication and travel. It is an inevitable consequence of the mobilisation of indubitably universal scientific knowledge in the service of human needs and wishes.)

Finding a criterion for demarcating benign from malign universalism is, therefore, a matter of some urgency in a world in which diverse cultures are becoming more and more intimately intermeshed – particularly as liberalism has lost self-confidence, in response to the criticism that liberal thought simply cannot take on board the illiberalism that, by its own principles of value-relativism and tolerance, it should tolerate. Many erstwhile liberals purport to believe that a Declaration of the Rights of Man is a Eurocentric (and hypocritical) imposition on cultures in which individual rights are not recognised as absolute indefeasible values.[5] And yet they feel unhappy about an attitude of complete moral and cultural *laissez-faire*, or a mere 'live and let die' *modus vivendi* that does not even aspire to shared moral and political beliefs.

How, then, shall we arrive at the desired criterion? I believe that we can do this by making a very small number of assumptions. Indeed, it may be that we need to assume only two things:

1. That an individual has a right to choose whether he/she lives or dies – except in those circumstances where he/she has committed a crime for which the penalty in his/her culture is death. This does not pre-empt any discussion as to whether there should be a death penalty at all (I personally am deeply opposed to judicial execution); or for what crimes the penalty is appropriate.

This assumption is not vulnerable to the charge that it presupposes that the individual has the right to enjoy rights and values that override those of the culture or society or value-community in which he/she is born and so smuggles in moral or value universals that may be used to judge a culture from the outside. It does not require this further presupposition; for it is difficult to imagine any culture in which all individuals, or even the majority of individuals, would fall foul of the death penalty. Nevertheless this will prove, as we shall see, sufficient to establish an important distance between the individual and the culture of birth without invoking 'individualistic' 'rights' and incurring the charge of imposing an implicit Eurocentric, 'Occidental' liberal individualism upon cultures to which this is alien. My criterion is less vulnerable to this charge than, for example, the Canadian Charter of Rights and Freedoms (quoted in Stephen Sedley's lecture 'Rights, Wrongs and Outcomes', *London Review of Books,* 11 May 1995, pp. 13–15), which asserts that 'Everyone has the right to life ... and the right not to be deprived thereof in accordance with the principles of fundamental justice'. 'The principles of fundamental justice' are, implicitly, cultural invariants that in fact cannot be assumed as a given.

2. That, given a multicultural world and multicultural societies within that world, in which people will have values that are deeply and irreconcilably at odds, we should, if we have to adjudicate between them, favour those values that still leave individuals who do not share them most free to express or act in accordance with their own different values, above those values that do not leave that freedom intact. This is more likely to minimise culture wars – in which no one's values will be respected – but I think, as I shall show presently, it goes deeper than mere pragmatism or political expediency.

With these two assumptions, I believe that we could make considerable progress towards deriving very general criteria permitting a distinction to be made between benign and malign universalism. I also believe that these criteria are sufficient for a reformed Enlightenment programme to proceed without being a Eurocentric imposition. What grounds do I have for believing this?

Once it is accepted as basic that an individual has a right to choose to live, except where he/she has earned judicial execution, then it follows that society has a duty of care towards its citizens; for it has an obligation to ensure as far as possible that its members do not incur avoidable death – at least in the years before they can make a free choice for or against life – in, for example, the years of infancy. (This right, of course, brings with it reciprocal duties: I have a duty to contribute, directly or indirectly, as far as I can, to the process of ensuring that other members of my society do not die an unchosen, non-judicial death.) It might be thought that little could be derived from this criterion for separating benign from malign universalism: motherhood and no arsenic pie and that's about it. It does not tell us, for example, how far the duty of care extends. But it has a very important aspect. It cuts beneath specific, culturally-relative values and mores to something more fundamental: to the individual's existence or non-existence. And it is this that permits one to find a place outside of particular cultures from which some judgements can be made.

Using this criterion, we can accept the cultural relativist's position that, once we are in a culture, we are part of it – it is in a sense constitutive of us – and it is insulting for others to try to impose upon us (or even to save us from) values that are not the values of that culture. And yet, despite being good relativists, we can still retain a universal principle which is derived from the fact that existence is a *necessary* condition for us to enjoy (or not enjoy) the *accident* of being part of one culture rather than another. There is, in other words, the pure fact of one's existence that has logical, ontological, existential priority over one's status as a member of a particular culture. One's belonging to a particular culture is an accidental inflection of one's existing at all. The question of the life and death of its members thus cuts beneath other value questions. I am an Englishman and it would be patronising for someone from Chad to try to rescue me from the nexus of belief-systems that comes with being an Englishman – except inasmuch as my existence itself is threatened by those beliefs – when, in other words, I am in danger of becoming nothing. Being nothing is a greater, a more fundamental danger than being a Chadised Englishman. The right *to be* – or to choose to be, to continue choosing my own existence – is a ground floor right that lies deeper than, in the sense of being a necessary condition of, my right to be in the English manner that I choose or have had chosen for me by the fact of having been born in an English culture. The tautologous right to be this particular entity goes deeper than the semi-tautologous right to be the kind of entity my culture commits me to being. The fact that you exist (or do not exist) is not culture-relative; it is the one indubitably extra-cultural datum; for it is a precondition of being able to participate in a particular culture and accept or reject its values. A person from Chad would thus be in a strong position to disapprove of the English set of values if it resulted in the death of most English people in infancy, before they had the opportunity to choose for or against life and for or against life English-style. The contingent fact that I exist is a necessary condition of the contingent fact that I exist as an Englishman with an English set of values. The fact that my existing at all is a necessary condition of my existing as a certain type of being reveals that there is something deeper than those things that are culturally relativisable.

Several things follow from my right to be able to choose whether I live or die. The most important is that society should be so governed and, as far as possible, so ordered as to minimise, for example, infant mortality (for we are all infants at some time or other). This at the very least will require attention to the provision of basic biological necessities. In the case of something as fundamental as ensuring clean and abundant water supplies, this requires familiarity with the relevant scientific knowledge about sanitation, the flow of fluid in pipes, metallurgy, etc. A preference for science-based technological practices rather than magic thinking will therefore be essential. But beyond this, it requires subscription to certain ethical principles; for example, a sense of personal responsibility in those individuals whose job it is to maintain and protect the water supply. Minimisation of corruption and dishonesty, appointments to senior posts on the basis of skill and experience rather than kinship networks, some minimal level of state investment and regulation, and a degree of commitment to distributive justice, will also be necessary. These take on the status of secondary value universals. Thus, from the simple principle of respecting an individual's right to make a choice about living or dying, about being or not being, we can derive many ethical consequences that are consistent with Enlightenment thought. We may discover that much of the implicit ethos of the Enlightenment is not so narrowly Eurocentric after all.

Let us now look at the second principle: giving preference to those values that still leave individuals who do not subscribe to them free to express their own, quite different values over values that do not leave those options open. I have already noticed that this is more likely to minimise those culture wars that are marked by an intensified loathing of everyone's values by everyone else with other values. But there is more to this principle than its potential to keep the peace. It is intended to address the criticism that the Enlightenment did not appreciate that there are many different ways of understanding the purpose and meaning of human life; that, for example, some human beings may prefer unhappiness to happiness; or prefer the deferred happiness which they are expecting in the next world to happiness in this world. We should, of course, respect these latter individuals; after all, it is possible that they may be right to focus on the After-Life (though I personally doubt it). And because we cannot pre-judge the seekers of unhappiness or early immolation as wrong, we cannot help ourselves to off-the-shelf, 'free' or 'spontaneous' universal values such as 'Nobody wants to live in permanent, unrelieved pain', 'Nobody wants to die young', of the kind that the utilitarians assumed and for which they were execrated by their Romantic critics. We have, instead, to consider how we can reconcile such absolute differences in the valuation of the things of life as between an ascetic who wishes for Hell on Earth and a hedonist who seeks happiness. We would, after all, like to give both of them the respect that is due to their deeply different values.

We could argue that the problem does not have to arise (and can therefore be overlooked) because we are all – hedonists and ascetics – tucked away in the private spaces between the meshes of society, and here we can imagine that we are solitary and practise our own way of life. But this is not an adequate response; for how individuals order their affairs is not entirely separated from how society as a whole orders its affairs; questions of self-government and government *tout court* are not clearly distinct and they have many points of interaction – a truth which would be conceded even by those who do not agree that 'the personal is political' and vice versa. Private ascetics will have their views about how public life should be conducted, what should be permitted to others, what goals society should aim for. And private hedonists will also have views on these matters. And both will expect their views to be reflected in what actually takes place in the public sphere they share. Another-worldly ascetic, for whom flagellation is the proper activity of man, is unlikely to be a good team-player in institutions devoted to limiting human suffering. So how, where there are strongly opposed ascetic and hedonistic views, should society as a whole order its affairs? Where some of its members prefer suffering to happiness (and strongly believe that others should share their conviction), should society be ordered on Hell-on-Earth/ascetic lines; or should it be ordered on the lines of ordinary comfort? We can answer this with the help of the general principle I have just advanced.

Consider scenario 1, in which society gives precedence to the wishes of the ascetic, so that all will have to live in material impoverishment and discomfort. Such a society will live closer to death: inattention to comfort and basic needs will mean that the lives of all – not just ascetics' lives – are in constant danger. Now many in such a society will not have chosen danger and discomfort and early death. Their values will thus be ignored, indeed trampled on. Amongst these dissidents will be immiserated infants and children, a significant number of whom will not, because of the general lack of concern for safety and comfort, survive to adult life to discover, even less to choose and live in accordance with, their own values. They will not even survive to choose *asceticism* or early death.

Now consider scenario 2, in which the values of comfort-seekers have precedence and society is so governed, administered and managed as to maximise happiness in the conventional sense. This option will reflect the wishes of the hedonists, but it will also leave the ascetics free to starve, beat and even kill themselves in their frantic pursuit of the happy unhappiness that is to be found beyond the thick robe of the flesh. If you choose pain on behalf of society, this may deny others the pleasure or comfort they wish; if you choose pleasure or comfort on behalf of society, neither you nor any others are denied the freedom to choose pain for themselves. We should, therefore, support a culture that chooses comfort and still leaves its citizens free to be as uncomfortable as they choose. The Enlightenment thinkers would have found this a perfectly acceptable principle: that society should be so ordered as to free the citizens to make the happiness or unhappiness of their own making.

We therefore admit a hierarchy of values: a more basic value (for example, valuing life) is given priority over a less basic one, since the former is a necessary condition for the choice of the latter; we should give priority to those values which interfere least with the expression of other values. If you say you couldn't give a damn about life and therefore care even less about an adequate water supply, you would, if you were empowered to express your beliefs in the public sphere, increase my chances of premature death from cholera and hence prevent me from fully expressing my values – which wish for and require a long life. If, however, I, who love life, am given power to create a society in which life and longevity and comfort are valued, I still leave you free to choose otherwise – to drink as much infected water as you like in pursuit of your early demise through diarrhoea. Giving my preference for universal health over yours for universal suffering still leaves you at liberty to choose suffering and an early death. I do not need to live in fear of the consequences of your value-system, and you are not obliged to live in fear of the consequences of mine.

In summary, these two minimal criteria, which on close inspection requisition the kind of applied reason and justice that the Enlightenment thinkers worked for, enable us to separate benign from malign universalism; a malign *laissez-faire* cultural relativism – of the kind convenient for the arms salesman who doesn't mind to whom he sells his weapons, classifying his clients only into those who do and those who do not pay their bills – from a benign respect for the variety of human life.[6] After all, to permit or endorse or to look passively upon a culture which does not ensure that many of its members *live* – so that they may freely choose for or against material prosperity, for or against life itself – is to collude in an 'internal cultural colonialism' where some within a society or culture deny others within that society or culture the power even to choose for or against that culture. That seems to me to define a limit to relativism that cannot itself be relativised or dismissed merely as dominant-culture ethnocentricity, as Eurocentric illiberal liberalism.[7] This limit may provide us with the equipment to address John Rawls' challenge (as expressed by Hoffmann, see note 5), 'to reconcile a variety of reasonable conceptions of the good (for instance, different beliefs about the role of religion in society) with a single political conception of justice'. By means of the principle I have advanced, we may accommodate the fact that all values are contingent – even the desire to live: nothing could be more obviously groundless than my desire to continue being this utterly contingent being (me) – with the frequently pressing need to adjudicate between them.

The spectre of Utopia

I could have made the defence of a greatly curtailed Enlightenment universalism easier for myself by taking for granted that certain human wishes are universal. Surely, I could have argued, every culture subscribes to the following:

1. Continuous unremitting pain – or fear of it – is bad.
2. People, in particular children, should not suffer avoidable death.

The reason I did not take even these seemingly basic and universal values for granted is that I am not too sure how universal they are. Yes, there must be very few cultures – even those with their gaze directed to the next world – in which normal people would dissent from those principles. But, to judge from the evidence, there seem to be many more cultures in which the conditions necessary to ensure the general implementation of these principles are not ardently pursued. In some cultures, whilst the death of the young may be regarded as a bad thing in itself, other considerations may override it. A raped daughter may be expected to prefer death to dishonour. Or the collective will may seem to place a higher value upon the esteem that comes from the trappings of wealth over the satisfaction derived from a job discharged conscientiously; and this ordering may mean that life-threatening diseases will continue to be carried by the water supply. There are circumstances in which warring tribesmen or the members of Bomber Command would not shrink from killing children. And so on. That is why, when trying to retain something from Enlightenment universalism, it is important to make as few assumptions as possible.

One of the assumptions made by Enlightenment thinkers – an assumption that, according to Isaiah Berlin, is one of the distinguishing features of Western thought since at least Plato – is that there is a commonality of human ends, howsoever different the means by which they try to achieve them. We have tried to avoid that assumption as far as is possible. Berlin connects this assumption of a unity or harmony of human ends with the notion of Utopia – the idea of a perfect society 'in which there was no misery and no greed, no danger or poverty or fear or brutalising labour or insecurity'. Western Utopias, he says, tend to contain the same elements:

> a society lives in a state of pure harmony, in which all its members live in peace, love one another, are free from physical danger, from want of any kind, from insecurity, from degrading work, from envy, from frustration, experience no injustice or violence, live in perpetual, even light, in a temperate climate, in the midst of infinitely fruitful, generous nature. The main characteristic of most, perhaps all, Utopias is the fact that they are static. Nothing in them alters, for they have reached perfection: there is no need for novelty or change; no one can wish to alter a condition in which all natural human wishes are fulfilled.
>
> (Berlin, *The Crooked Timber of Humanity*, p. 20)

The connection between the idea of a perfect society and universalist assumptions about the ends of life is underlined by Berlin:

> The assumption upon which this is based is that men have as certain fixed, unaltering nature, certain universal, common, immutable goals, identical

> for all, at all times, everywhere. For unless this is so, Utopia cannot be Utopia, for then the most perfect society will not perfectly satisfy everyone.
> (ibid., pp. 20–1)

We may smile at the naivety of those who dream of Utopia, but there is a very real sense in which the hope of progress is implicitly Utopian, inasmuch as it is assumed that progress in specific areas will not be at the expense of progress in others; that, for example, the steps taken to control smallpox do not destroy the liberties which are necessary to ensure a tradition of civil government, or a just society; or, more narrowly, that the measures taken to control smallpox do not create conditions in which a yet more virulent disease may flourish. Even the less ambitious, piecemeal social engineering advocated by democratic socialists carries within it the assumption that all the small advances will point in a certain direction, will converge in the vector of overall progress. Reformers, however modest, are inescapably concerned with the health of society as a whole and even the most cautious, focused or narrow-minded of them – those for whom the branch-lines of social reality are everything – would lose their appetite for specific reforms if they did not feel that the net effect for society as a whole was positive. Speaking personally for a moment, I would not be terribly keen to continue my own work in the neurology of old age if I knew that every gain in this area would be bought at the cost of an equivalent loss in the field of the cardiology of old age, the nutrition of older people or diarrhoeal diseases affecting children in the Third World. Every reformer, every progressively inclined individual, everyone concerned to bring about net improvements, however local, is thus implicitly Utopian: it is only a slight exaggeration to say that every disinterested drive to local improvement contains an implicit drive to global improvement. Anyone who shares the hope of progress, however local or focal, must therefore take account of the fears the very notion of Utopia raises in the minds of contemporary thinkers.

Recent history has made us all too familiar with the way in which Utopian aspirations, in the hands of those who have real power rather than being ineffectual dreamers, have helped to transform backward, unjust and impoverished countries into absolute Hells on Earth. The lessons learnt from the real experience of the twentieth century have been reinforced by numerous fictional dystopias. The former have shown the difficulty of bringing about massive social change without smashing what is worthwhile in the public sphere and replacing the little and inadequate good with universal evil. The catastrophe of communism, in particular, has caused a radical re-think amongst the radicals about what it is that makes a society work for the good of all its citizens, how the individual will to personal and collective advancement is best harnessed to promote the collective good, and how rapid and profound the processes of social change should be. Many fictional treatments of Utopia, however, have gone beyond anxieties about the process and doubts about the achievability of the goal and expressed a deep scepticism and disquiet about the goal itself – beyond questions about the practicability of bringing about Utopia to the very principle of Utopia itself. They have, that is to say, questioned the assumption, identified by Berlin as being central to the ideal of a perfect society, 'that men have a certain fixed, unaltering nature, certain universal, common, immutable goals' and have concluded that, since this assumption is unfounded and oppressive, the decline of Utopian ideals – at least in the West – is to be welcomed. We shall never agree on the ends of life; so a society that appears to express and embody a set of ends for all of its citizens and for all time, must be oppressive:

> Immanuel Kant, a man very remote from irrationalism, once observed that 'Out of the crooked timber of humanity no straight thing was ever made'. And for that reason no perfect solution is, not merely in practice, but in principle, possible in human affairs, and any determined attempt to produce it is likely to lead to suffering, disillusionment and failure.
>
> (Berlin, *The Crooked Timber of Humanity*, p. 48)

This is a deeply disturbing conclusion, not simply because we cannot live without explicitly Utopian ideals. Many men of goodwill have done so. But because, as already indicated, modest melioristic ambitions, dreams of bringing about improvements in a small sphere of one's own expertise and concern, shade imperceptibly into the hope of leaving the world a better place than one had found it – into the hope of bringing about net overall gain. It would be an odd social conscience that was unconcerned if the improvements brought about in one sphere were exactly offset, or worse, by deterioration in other places. The socially concerned, whilst oppressively aware that there is much misery that they must leave to others to sort out, at least assume that the happiness they spread will not bring about deepening immiseration elsewhere. This assumption is not, of course, always well founded: society is not only the sum of intended actions and their intended consequences but also of the unintended consequences of actions. Nevertheless, all melioristic instincts, however narrowly expressed, have the seed of Utopianism in them; bear within them the assumption that many progressive actions will add up to overall net progress for the world; that they have a deeper meaning inasmuch as they may contribute, in howsoever small a fashion, towards the forwards and upwards movement of humanity as a whole out of want, fear, pain, impoverishment of all sorts; that the effects of these actions will converge in similar or compatible goals even if they are not strictly synergistic; and that, while Utopia will not be achieved as the outcome of a single revolutionary convulsion, it will be approximated, even if never achieved, as an asymptote approached by huge numbers of small advances. To abandon Utopian ideas, therefore, is not merely to foreswear the visionary passions of fanatics and lunatics, but to throw into question the very dimension of hope in human affairs. It is difficult to be anti-Utopian without being against progress itself; for there is no clear or sharp distinction between arrogant claims to provide universal – in both senses of 'global' and 'universally applicable' – solutions to the woes of mankind and wanting to contribute, however modestly, to making the world overall a better place.

The two major elements of the hope of progress – to alleviate the sufferings of mankind (the world of means); and to extend the capacity of human beings to realise new possibilities that men and women have invented (the world of ends) – are necessary for mankind to find any kind of meaning in its struggles beyond the brute desire for one's own survival and pleasures and the survival and pleasures of one's children and a circle of dependants and friends. This dimension of hope – making the indefinite future of humanity the secular analogue of the eternity of religious hope – is deep-rooted in our consciousness. Since we cannot, as we have agreed, become 'religious' by decree, we have to ask ourselves what secular society will become without the hope of progress and without fostering the visions of those who dream unselfishly of making the world a progressively better place? The implicitly Utopian hope of progress is an essential regulative idea for collective human morality in precisely the same Kantian sense as the notion of progress towards the truth is the regulative idea of science. Because we cannot forgo the dream of Utopia, however muted and low-key, without denying the hope of progress and hence rendering collective human action headless and amoral, we must take account of the fears that the spectre of Utopia awaken.[8]

There are two fundamental objections to Utopia, however painlessly it may be achieved. The first is that it may be boring and empty; and the second is that it will be rigid, uniformitarian and authoritarian.

Need Utopia be boring and empty?

> The western world is now engaged in constructing a fundamentally secular and deconsecrated technologically-based society. This is a society in which – if it is achieved – all men will live in comfort. Perhaps there will also be a large measure of formal freedom and religious and philosophical toleration. But it is a society that threatens to deprive human life of all spiritual content, a society in which the growth of freedom is likely to be accompanied by the growth of numbers of those whose inner emptiness robs them of the desire to use it, a society in which religious and philosophical toleration will be

> made all the easier to achieve as spiritual impoverishment makes religious and philosophical commitment constantly more rare.[9]

Berlin's deliciously mocking account of Utopia as an essentially static society whose members not only live in perfect harmony but also live in 'perpetual, even light' – making Utopia a rather staider, chillier version of the eternal afternoon of Tennyson's Lotos Eaters – captures the anorexia that many of us feel when imagining any kind of paradise, whether earthly or celestial. Perhaps we all subscribe, if only unconsciously, to the Schopenhauerian notion that humans are doomed to oscillate between suffering – from pain or from a frustrated desire for pleasure – and boredom. If we take away pain and unfulfilled desire, won't we be left only with boredom and a sense of emptiness, a life rendered meaningless by satiety? The answer to this is yes, only if the experience of meaning is exclusively rooted in pain and unfulfilled desires, if it is based upon lack. If this is inadequate as an account of the actual sources of meaning, it is even less adequate as an account of *possible* sources of meaning.

The relationship between pain (or suffering more widely construed) and meaning is that, except in those cases where pain is freely chosen, pain is anti-meaning, privation of meaning. To put this another way, its 'meaning', as I have argued elsewhere,[10] lies almost entirely in the meanings *it takes away*; in the lost meanings of the things it renders meaningless. To be in severe pain is to be rolled in the brazier of anti-meaning. The argument – developed extensively in David Morris's *The Culture of Pain*[11] – that pain is a profound source of meaning, and that life without suffering lacks a dimension of reality, fails to notice this most obvious feature of pain: that any meaning it has is stolen from elsewhere, is lost meaning. If there are new or original meanings created by pain, they are the second-order meanings relating to the ploys we use to alleviate, deal with or endure it. It is part of the Western religious inheritance, the Judaeo-Christian assumption that life is a vale of tears, to accept without question that the deepest meanings are associated with suffering; that a life relatively free of pain – a 'comfortable' life – is inescapably shallow. There is, however, no *a priori* reason for thinking that one sort of sensation, preoccupation or theme touches more closely upon our true nature, or reveals us more completely to ourselves, than another.

It may be historically true that, for humans, pain has had the upper hand over pleasure, sorrow over happiness; but this may be a contingent, not a necessary, feature of the human condition. Admittedly, as things are, it is true that to be in pain, to be acquainted with grief, is to be closer to the reality of most people's lives than is being part of a comfortable minority. But this is how things are *now*; not how they must be, even less should be, for all time. It may be argued that the revelation afforded by pain has a 'deep' permanent truth, for it reminds us of our finitude; that its negative meanings are the profoundest meanings because they underline what a small figure we cut in the universe and how what we are not vastly outsizes that which we are. The demeaning impact of pain, its savaging of our ordinary meanings, tears open the bubble of ordinary sense which encloses us and normally insulates us from the objective reality of our condition. In one sense this is true; but in another sense it is not. We are finite, yes; but we are also the site through which the universe discloses what is not finite. In addition to being existentially finite, finite in our being, we are infinite in our knowledge inasmuch as we are a place of revelation of the infinite, a revelation that pain – along with those other things, such as getting and spending, that dominate the kingdom of means – obscures. In toothache, I am as remote as possible from being a lens on the universe; I am a place of toothache.

It may be argued, finally, that pain not only reminds us of our finitude but also makes us, in a positive sense, more human. This is not noticeable amongst sufferers in ordinary life: chronic pain isolates, degrades and closes off human beings. That is the common testimony of sufferers. However, our experience, though useless in itself may make us more sensitive to the suffering of others. Morris quotes Albert Schweitzer:

> Whoever among us has through personal experience learned what pain and anxiety really are must help to ensure that those who out there are in bodily need obtain the help which came to him. He belongs no more to himself alone; he has become the brother of all who suffer. On the 'Brotherhood of those who bear the mark of pain' lies the duty of medical work.
>
> (quoted in Morris, p. 287)

Levinas, also cited by Morris, goes further. Pain is negative, useless, absurd, yes. But it may be transformed:

> it opens up the ethical dimension of the 'inter-human'. My own useless suffering, that is, takes on a changed meaning if it becomes the occasion for your empathetic, even suffering response.
>
> (ibid.)

There is a terrible sentimentality in this. The reality of the effect of chronic pain – in this case, toothache – is expressed by Dostoevsky's anti-hero writing from under the floorboards:

> Those groans express, firstly, the degrading futility of one's complaint, a legalized tyranny of nature which one despises, but from which one, unlike

> nature, is bound to suffer. They also express a sense of the fact that at that moment one has no other foe than the pain; a sense of the fact that one is utterly at the mercy of one's teeth; a sense of the fact that Providence is in a position either to will that your teeth shall cease on an instant to ache or to will that they shall go on aching another three months; and lastly the sense of the fact that if you do not agree with, but, on the contrary, protest against, the situation, your only comfort, your only resource, will be either to cut your throat or to go on beating the walls ever harder with your fists, since there is nothing else for you to do.[12]

This is life after two days of toothache. The inter-human dimension opened up by this relatively trivial agony is not quite as Levinas envisages it:

> Well [by the third day] his groans will have become malicious and meanly irascible; and though he may continue them whole nights and days at a stretch, he will be aware all the time that he is doing himself no good by his utterances, but merely uselessly angering and annoying himself and others. Better than anyone else he will be aware that his family, as also the public before whom he is cutting such a figure, have for a long time been listening to him with disgust; they think him an utter rascal, and have it in mind that he might just as well have groaned in a simpler manner (that is to say without any turns or roulades), since his present style of groaning is due simply to temper and is leading him to play the fool out of sheer viciousness.
>
> (ibid., p. 603)

There must surely be better ways of promoting mutual assistance, concern, even love, than through the anti-meanings of pain. And I am not aware of any evidence that shared sorrow is superior to shared pleasure and shared joy as a means to opening up and maintaining the 'inter-human'. Unalloyed happiness, the continual pursuit of pleasure, seem hard, empty, shallow, only in a world – such as the world today – in which pain has the upper hand. In Utopia, where pain has been conquered, there may be other means of being profoundly inter-human than through the mediation of pain. 'The great object in life,' Byron said, 'is sensation – to feel we exist, even though in pain.' Yes, but preferably not in pain; or not in involuntary pain.[13]

So much for the anxiety generated by the prospect of a pain-free life in Utopia. What about the consequences of the satisfaction of all desires? Surely, desires are a source of positive, rather than merely privative, meaning and their universal and rapid satisfaction must lead to an emptying of life. Ironically, one of the powerful rebuttals of this assumption comes from the most vicious critic of the Enlightenment dream of progress: Joseph de Maistre.

Man, he said, 'is infinite in his desires and, always discontented with what he has, loves only what he has not'.[14] This was in support of his claim that humans are insatiable for power. But it could equally well be used to demonstrate the inexhaustible possibility for development, elaboration and refinement within desire, reflecting a boundless human capacity for discovering new sources of meaning. Development may occur in one of at least two directions: the folding and unfolding of existing desires – as witnessed by humankind's ability to transform and deepen and enrich the experiences associated with physiological needs;[15] and the discovery of new desires, new modes of rapture, fascination and preoccupation. Let us look at examples of these two possibilities.

First, the elaboration of appetites. Consider human sexuality. It is rooted in physical appetite: this is the *donnée*. But it is also deeply implicated in a specifically human wish to be *recognised* by others, a wish that, as Hegel and many others after him appreciated, reaches into the fundamentally metaphysical nature of the human animal. Sexuality has many dimensions. Here are a few at random: sensual delight; care and mutual support; awe and adoration; responsibility; the many narratives of growing love, of consent and mutual understanding; the sense of privilege; the profound vision of the otherness of the Other. These intersect and interact in an infinite number of ways. And within the sphere of sensual delight, the delightful and not so delightful tensions between orthogonal (and sometimes incompatible) dimensions: maximising sensation; enjoying privileged knowledge; savouring power; asserting companionship; expressing love. There are equally complex tensions between the long narrative – of conquest, of uncovering, of companionship – and the instant of sensation. And between the institutional and the sensational, the discursive and the tactile, the social and the individual, person-as-subject and the person-as-object, the general object of desire and the particular desired person, the physical and the metaphysical. And sexuality has, of course, other less attractive elements: the exertion of power over another; the desire to hurt, to smash, to revenge oneself, to humiliate, to destroy.

Human sexuality is susceptible, therefore, of endless elaboration. This is to be understood not only, or not especially, in terms of exploring the factorial X number of combinations of bodily surfaces and acts involving them, but in terms of an infinitely folded and unfolding consciousness of the other person and through him or her of oneself. This complexity, this foldedness, is, or may be, evident even at the 'purely' physical level. Whereas in animals, the sexual act is an operation performed by one animal upon another, by a subject upon an object – the 'ten second jump and shriek' that Young referred to – in human beings, there is a layered awareness of one's own sensations, of the other's sensations, of the other's awareness of one's awareness of his or her sensations; and so on. A vertigo of mutually reflected consciousnesses can open up at every point. And there are other, richer possibilities at the level of words, symbols, gestures. They are infinite because humans are explicit animals and there is no intrinsic limit to the extent to which explicitness unfolds.

This ever-enhanced mutual awareness was represented in the existentialist literature derived from Hegel's analysis of human relations as a kind of Hell. Sexuality in Sartre's philosophical treatises, books and plays was a battle for domination, and the sexual relationship was an interaction between two roles: that of Master-Sadist and that of the Slave-Masochist. The thirst for recognition – for an affirmation of one's own reality by another's acknowledgement of that reality, through one's consciousness of one's self – underwent malignant change in Sartre's vision into a contest between two beings locked in a life-and-death struggle, each trying to impose their own meaning upon the relationship and to deny the meaning the other would wish to impose. This, in turn, was part of a larger project to enclose the other's existence within one's own world and deny the reciprocal fact that one is part of the other's world.

Sartre's pessimistic view – echoed by many writers in the twentieth century – is at least in part the result of a gross simplification, a reduction of the richness and complexity of sexual relations to a naked battle between categories. Few would accept that the asymmetry in human relationships between Master and Slave is a permanent feature of the metaphysical condition of humanity. It may characterise many relationships – for example, the asymmetrical relationships between most men and women over history. It is not impossible that in Utopia sexual relationships would be between equals and the joyful exploration of bodily and social possibility would not unfold into destructive madness. Sadism would not be necessary, for example, in order to enhance sensation; this would come from mutual awareness of awareness; from increasingly intense acknowledgement of the other's unique reality.[16]

The possibilities inherent in sexuality indicate the wider possibilities for Utopians: a metaphysical journey through an ever-deepening sensuality, a contemplative physical pleasure, towards delight in the mystery of the world, in particular of consciousness and of human consciousness, as revealed in the life of one's companion of choice, to a deeper fascination with the mystery of the perceived world – an enraptured delight in the appearance of light, in the feeling of warmth on one's arm, in the quiet sound of the evening breeze in the trees. Truly understood, all of these are inexhaustible. In Utopia, we may imagine individuals engaging at will in a lucid ecstasy whose object is the ordinary sensations of the body and the sensibilia of the common day. It may be that, at first, the majority of people will need the help of a gifted minority, who will serve a role similar to that of artists in the present, decidedly pre-Utopian, times; ultimately, when the education of the senses – the ability to enjoy experience for its own sake, to experience one's experiences[17] – occupies a central place in the curriculum, all will be artists, not in the sense of producing art, but in the sense of experiencing the world as artists do in their best moments.

If one still wanted to have a use for the term, one could think of the sensibility of the Utopians as being essentially religious. Their religion would not, however, be encrusted with institutions (it would have no institutions, being purely a matter of actual consciousness) or suborned to the service of power; nor would it spawn or be spawned from creeds and dogmas. Its cognitive content would be the indisputed obvious: things no one is going to argue about; meanings beyond differentiated meaning or disputable interpretation. A religion of wonder – about light, about perception, about the fact that we, inexplicably, are – which will be perhaps closer to the true spirit of religion than a thousand child-slaughtering battles over the *filioque* clause, or the persecution of an unmarried mother, or even a twenty-page proof of the existence of God.[18]

Some prophets of such Utopias – most notoriously Aldous Huxley – saw in drugs such as mescaline a rapid route to dissemination of artistic experiences and sensibilities. There are at least two important reasons for doubting the power of drugs to hasten the birth of Utopia. First, drugs are available now and yet Utopia hasn't arrived: they don't fit into the Kingdom of Means in which most of us have to spend our lives. Not only do they fail to help bring about the Utopian future liberated from the exigencies of need: through their induction of dependency, they create new and terrible needs that demand to be met again and again and again. Secondly, drugs would undermine the conditions necessary to maintain Utopia. The lucid trances, the ecstatic enjoyment of the real, that I see as possible for Utopia, would not break up society or damage the bonds of shared delighted and mutual concern. They would be part of, integral with, one's sociality. Drugs, with their isolating and confused delights that are totally unrelated to external reality (including the reality of others' happiness and unhappiness and their needs), threaten to erode everything that makes people supportive of one another.[19] If it is possible, as I have argued, to have a pain-free life, a hunger-free life, which is not lacklustre, boring or empty, if it is possible to delight in satiety, it will not be necessary to import artificial significance into life through drugs to replace the lost meanings that were associated with struggle for survival, with suffering and with unsatisfied desire.

This may not convince those who, like Dostoevsky's Underground Man, believe that if they were transported to Utopia they would want to smash it simply for the sake of asserting their own unique existence and demonstrating that they were not merely insigificant cogs in a vast machine. Such sentiments, echoed by a thousand existentialist and pseudo-existentialist writers and a hundred thousand sympathetic commentators since Dostoevsky, do not take into account the fact that we are already able to cope with the fact that the universe does not perpetually acknowledge our status as its centre and irreplaceable only child. Inside or outside Utopia, in a well-organised Heaven or in an anarchic Hell, we are equally a minute part of a huge crowd. Nor do these anti-Utopian sentiments recognise that the inhabitants of Utopia will have had different formative experiences from themselves; that, unlike Dostoevsky's Underground Man, they will not have known privation, injustice, marginalisation and humiliation, in sum, the damaging experiences that fill them with their impulses to cause damage. Likewise, the Underground Man's impatience with the unremitting rationalism of Utopia would not make sense to those who actually enjoyed the privilege of living in Utopia:

> See here: reason is an excellent thing – I do not deny that for a moment; but reason is reason and no more, and satisfies only the reasoning faculty in man, whereas volition is a manifestation of all life. ... It is true that, in this particular manifestation of it, human life is all too often a sorry failure; yet it nevertheless is life, and not the mere working out of a square root. For my own part, I naturally wish to satisfy *all* my faculties, and not my reasoning faculty alone (that is to say, a mere twentieth portion of my capacity for living).
>
> (p. 613)

This would simply not make sense to a Utopian whose happiness was rooted in a unity of consiousness in which reason and sensation and will were all convergent in experiences of wholeness. There is no *a priori* reason why this should not be possible. Nor why the impulse to evil should remain as powerful in those whose lives have not been damaged as they manifestly are in those like the Underground Man who have been damaged:

> Does reason never err in estimating what is advantageous? May it not be that man occasionally loves something besides prosperity? May it not be that he also loves *adversity*?
>
> (ibid., p. 618)

Not necessarily in Utopia. The assumption that in Utopia we shall be bored, our lives will be empty and sooner or later we shall try to smash something – each other, society – is the result of reading the future of man from one part of his past. And that is a mistake. After all, we are able to live at a great remove from all the things – instincts, impulses, etc. – that are supposed to define us and limit our capacity for change.[20, 21]

Need Utopia be rigid or authoritarian?

Utopian writers tend to assume that their Utopias will be highly ordered. The dystopian consequence of this seems to be that order will be maintained by an intensely authoritarian and obtrusive state, often underwritten by a potentially brutal, quasi-militaristic police force. The social framework which sustains the exquisite sensitivities of the privileged of Utopia will be upheld by rubber truncheons applied to the heads and electrodes applied to the genitals of dissidents.

It is easy to see why this may be considered to be an inevitable feature of Utopias. First, the kind of order Utopias exhibit cannot be relied upon to emerge as a 'spontaneous order' in the Hayekian sense. It is therefore assumed to be intrinsically unstable and vulnerable to the slightest tremors of dissent, unrest or rebellion. Secondly, a society which is well off and comfortable has much to lose collectively. There is a lot invested in not rocking the boat: it is unlikely that unplanned change will bring about further improvements; the results will most likely be deleterious rather than otherwise. Rebellions, or other sources of unplanned change, will have to be dealt with severely. For the same reason, a comfortable society will feel threatened from without and have a high level of anxiety about external enemies and their collaborators from within. 'Fortress Utopia', the result of inevitably uneven development of societies through the world, will be at risk from becoming paranoid – with predictable consequences for civil liberties. This will seem likely even in the best kinds of Utopias; those, for example, which are *not* built on the slave labour of an underclass.

More careful consideration of the kind of Utopia we are envisaging – a Utopia of Ends rather than of Means, of consciousness rather than consumption – may lead us to question the received idea that Utopia will be automatically associated with police batons and a Draconian rule of law parodying Singapore. Are we sure that the citizens will *want* to dissent in a violent and explicit and destabilising way? It is quite likely that they will have better things to do. After all, it is only in the world of tyrannies, want, greed, etc. that dissent seems natural, even noble. Nor will their failure to dissent necessarily be evidence that the citizens have been drugged, bribed ('bread and circuses'), brainwashed or cowed into conformity. For the latter assumes the division of society into a ruling class – of Guardians, Commissars, or whatever – and a ruled class who have to be kept under the thumb of, or in thrall to, the rulers. But it is not impossible that in Utopia we may have moved beyond this. The exercise of power will be diffused into civic duty and the latter will not be considered to be an end in itself; it will simply be what it is – a duty, an interruption to the cultivation of the Kingdom of Ends. Power will not be concentrated and, as such, will be no more likely to lead to corruption than the power of the milk monitor. By such a diffusion of power, Utopia will have stability built into it and the impulse to dissent will be focused on particular technical questions; the adversarial habit will atrophy while individuals pursue their own ends in harmony with others. The standard dystopian image of infantilised citizens free to pursue empty private ecstasies so long as they do not seek power, their lives monitored and patrolled by brutal shock troops ready to pounce if they show any signs of independence or rebellion, assumes that power remains in the hands of a few ruthless Guardians who foreswear the Kingdom of Ends for power; or foreswear delight for power, which has become an end in itself. This is a possible, but not a necessary, scenario.

There remains, however, a further serious question. If the population in Utopia is pacific rather than pacified, then the Utopians are very vulnerable to attack from others outside of Utopia. In order not to be a sitting target, one of two things is necessary: either Utopia should be well armed; or it should be universal, so that it has no outside threat because there is nothing outside of it apart from empty space. There are difficulties with either of these solutions. 'Fortress Utopia' will need a standing army, a tradition of military organisation and discipline, of command and obedience that will be at odds with the ethos that we have envisaged, of diffused power and private citizens living largely in a kingdom of private or privately chosen ends. The spectre of highly disciplined, CS gas-wielding shock troops patrolling outside the dreams of the Lotos-eating citizenry returns. Once the concentration of power and authority necessary to requisition and maintain and run a standing army is granted, then the possibility of corruption and tyranny is raised once more. A citizenry whose power aspirations do not extend beyond that of being a milk monitor seems distinctly vulnerable. If the army is recruited from within the citizens on the Swiss model, so that the soldiers revert to being citizens after a period of duty, there emerges the new problem of transforming successive intakes of Lotos-Eaters into a fighting force. This can be solved only by having a permanent officer class. A much more attractive option is to extend Utopia to the point where it ceases to have an outside. And I suspect that this is the only viable option: in the globally networked world of the twenty-first or twenty-second century, no localised Utopia – even less a localised Fortress Utopia – would be possible. And this must depend upon even development world-wide and upon human beings feeling themselves to be citizens of no particular country, owing an allegiance only to the human race. As we reach the end of the twentieth century, with demagogue-inspired reassertions of ethnic allegiances, this, alas, seems even less likely than at the beginning of the century. However, an economy based upon infinitely renewable bits (of information) rather than exhaustible supplies of available energy required to move atoms (of matter) raises the hope of cooperation rather than brutal and bloody competition between countries. Nicholas Negroponte[22] has sketched an account of some of the possibilities arising out of the 'irrevocable and unstoppable' change from atoms to bits. His optimistic account of the digital future is based upon the fact that digital technology is 'decentralizing, globalizing, harmonizing, and empowering' (p. 229). Nothing could be more remote from the ethnocentric passions of the demagogues.

Utopia, then, may not necessarily be authoritarian, forbidding and prone to dealing brutally with dissent; for, with power diffused and fewer grounds for dissent, the relationship between the individual and authorities will not be an adversarial one; at any rate, the adversarial moments will not be organised into factions and rebellion. The idea that there might be nothing to dissent from may be distressingly unromantic, undramatic to some and may invoke the image of the state (the world-state, one assumes), as a massive herd of shepherdless sheep. It is the uniformity that may be most deeply offensive: the prospect of all the citizens obediently chewing the grass of identical experience is not inspiring. (We have already quoted de Tocqueville on this in note 9.) The assumption of empty, mindless uniformity would, however, be mistaken. There is no reason why what Emerson called 'the infiniteness of the private man' should be eliminated by comfort and contentment. It is pain, rather than lack of it, that rivets us to our finitude. Even rebellion is narrowing: it takes its themes, its agenda from its object. Rebellion 'against the system', if it is anything other than rhetoric and gesture, if it is in any sense constructive, is in danger of converging to single issue narrowness. Utopia, on the other hand, should permit, in the interstices of uniformity, an infinite depth and variety of experience.

The model here is sexual behaviour. From a certain distance its stereotyped nature is almost comic. The picture from within is different. Inside the relationship, inside every act, there is the possibility of an inexhaustible variety of experiences, awarenesses, understandings and misunderstandings. Even between the same two people, no two successive acts of intercourse are the same. In Utopia, where individuals are committed to experiencing and reflecting upon their experiences, such variety would be understood and experienced. The richness and fathomlessness and variety of life in Utopia would come from the content of consciousness, not from its descriptive silhouette or from the remote, third-person viewpoint of comparative ignorance. The actual content of consciousness would provide the essential inner distances within Utopia.

In *Two Concepts of Liberty* Berlin asserted, against an oppressive paternalism that would deny us the right to define ourselves, that 'we must preserve a minimum core of personal freedom, if we are not to degrade or deny our nature'. This is incontrovertible. But it is only from the point of view of material necessity that we may be captured by the generalising gaze, only from the utilitarian point of view that experiences are classified into successive and identical instances of a finite number of types. It is war and hunger that classify weathers into wet and dry, foggy and clear; in peacetime and satiety, the thousand different cloud formations and the thousand modes of shadowiness and sunniness are there to be appreciated. And it is the control exerted by societies dominated by material want that reduces sexual behaviour to recognisable forms that can be allocated to the categories of transgressions or permitted modes.

This last point can be usefully connected with wider doubts that have been expressed about Utopias of all kinds, and about the Enlightenment project in particular: that it is at once too prescriptive and too shallow. The specific target of this criticism is the notion of a society based upon reason. Let us return to Dostoevsky's anti-hero:

> See here: reason is an excellent thing – I do not deny that for a moment; but reason is reason and no more, and satisfies only the reasoning faculty in man, whereas volition is a manifestation of all life. ... It is true that, in this particular manifestation of it, human life is all too often a sorry failure; yet it nevertheless *is* life, and not the mere working out of a square root. For my own part, I naturally wish to satisfy *all* my faculties, and not my reasoning faculty alone (that is to say, a mere twentieth portion of my capacity for living).
>
> (p. 613)

Yes, of course, reason and utility and the Kingdom of Means are not sufficient in themselves; the reasoning faculty is not the whole of what we are. Man doth not live by reason, even less *in* reason, alone. Reason is only a shell. It creates the framework within which we are able to live whole lives. But only the framework. This is not, however, a case for irrationalism. The reason-based technology that liberates us from toothache leaves us free to choose, or to find, our own meanings and values and pleasures and depths and revelations. Reason is the beginning, not the end, of the full life. There is thus no enmity between reason and creativity: reason creates the conditions in which creativity is possible. The true enemies of creativity are toothache, unreasonable oppression, unchallenged cruelty, unaccountable government, hunger, fear, etc.

The two complaints that first, reason does not satisfy the whole man and secondly, political theory based upon Enlightenment thought was too shallow because it did not address the fundamental wishes of mankind are really two aspects of the same complaint and can be answered in the same way. Indeed, they answer one another. Yes, a politics based upon reason is shallow and thank God that it is. The social order should not be, or prescribe, the ends of life: politics should fall short of final ends. A successful political system *should* be 'shallow' in this sense, so that it can free people to discover and make their own depths.[23] May we be protected from political leaders who want to legislate for our depths, who think they can answer to our deepest needs rather than address the things that prevent us from discovering, inventing and meeting our deepest needs. The history of the world has so often been disfigured by religious theocrats and secular dictators (of Right and Left) who busied themselves too much with the people's depths instead of permitting them to be free to find their own depths. Three cheers for the beneficent power of reason. And three more cheers for its shallowness. ...

* * *

Conclusion: the Enlightenment dream and the hope of progress

The deficiencies in the Enlightenment notion of human nature (in so far as a common picture can be extracted from the writings of so many disparate thinkers) and in the programmes of the *philosophes* for improving the conditions of human life are easily stated. The simplistic assumption that there would be a universal solution to human ills – based upon the methods of and guided by the findings of physical science – is foremost among these. Arrogant scientistic universalism has not, of course, been the sole preserve of Enlightenment thinkers, but some of them were perhaps the first to make it programmatic.[24] And like many other thinkers before and since, they failed to recognise the extent to which they were children of their time. It is, however, a historicist exaggeration to see Enlightenment thought, as Goldmann does, as merely a stage in Western bourgeois thought and rooted in a society that is based on exchange value (whence come its ideas of equality, the social contract, toleration, universalism); but it is equally mistaken to see it as Man's first and definitive discovery of his own unchanging essence. We recognise that many of the values that the *philosophes* saw as self-evident, eternal truths are neither self-evident nor eternal; and we also recognise that the assumption that all values can be brought into harmony requires careful interpretation. When Helvetius asserted that moral laws come from the individual's pursuit of his own happiness, and that it is in the individual's interest to promote the general welfare, since his own happiness depends on other people, he not only failed to take account of the people having conflicting interests in the pursuit of the same ends, but also failed to recognise that people might have fundamentally different ultimate ends; that, in other words, it is not only intermediate means but final goals that may be the subject of dispute. The belief that everyone could be paid-up members of the Party of Mankind – patriots for humanity rather than for their country or simply for themselves – that there were values that transcended one's self, one's faction, the interests of one's social group, brings to mind too many memories of doomed ventures into universal brotherhood – malign ones such as International Communism and benign but ineffective ones such as the League of Nations or The Committee for World Government. The scientistic version of universalism carried additional dangers of demeaning those whose only role was to be the substrate of the beneficent, improving intentions of the legislators. We have discovered how important it is to recognise and curtail

> the tendency – difficult to avoid but disastrous – to assimilate all men's primary needs to those that are capable of being met by these methods: the reduction of all aspirations and questions to dislocations which the expert can set right. Some believe in coercion, others in gentler methods; but the conception of human needs in their entirety as those of the inmates of a prison or reformatory or a school or a hospital, however sincerely it may be held, is a gloomy, false, and ultimately degraded view, resting on the denial of the rational and productive nature of all, or even the majority of, men.[25]

This fault is not, of course, peculiar to the *philosophes* and their heirs; indeed, it has been most strikingly practised by anti-Enlightenment (Marxist, Fascist) legislators; but the Enlightenment programme always, on account of its confident universalist scientism, carried the possibility of becoming coercive, patriarchal and physicianly, on the grounds that, as Heracleitus expressed it, 'the beast has to be driven to the pasture with blows'. The Committee of Public Safety was not entirely a travesty of Enlightenment paternalism. The journey to ruthlessness in Utopian dreamers possessed of universal truths is not always a long one, and does not always have to pass first through corruption. Moreover scientism – and the belief or pretence that the pursuit of life, liberty and happiness can be reduced to a matter of utilitarian calculation – harbours other dangers. A morally neutral, purely technical and managerial approach to social problems, runs the risk of creating a moral vacuum which may predispose to political instability. Once this is admitted, it has also to be acknowledged that moral passions infused with a desire to control others, and reinforced by appeal to a transcendental authority and supported by power structures, are no less dangerous.[26]

I hope I have shown that progressive thought does not necessarily entail subscribing to an oppressive universalism. It is possible to identify a core of human values that it is not unreasonable to assume would be invariant across cultures; and from these, much follows that would be consistent with the Enlightenment approach to the woes of the human condition. This would include individual accountability and the deployment of reason. As has already been pointed out, reason does not necessarily strangle creativity and freedom – not only because its intelligent deployment requires a creative imagination, but also because its meshes are not tightly drawn. Likewise, politics based upon certain principles such as reason, accountability of the governors to the governed, a commitment to respecting the lives of all citizens, while it may influence the content of consciousness and the meanings that are available to people, are not themselves those meanings and the whole story of that consciousness. It is important that they are not, that they do not pretend to be. The personal is political only in so far as the political obtrudes beyond its proper sphere – and people are either incompetently or oppressively governed.

Faith in the application of reason to human affairs should be hard to challenge now that we have ample experience of the consequences of irrationalism translated from the private to the public sphere. The 'shipwreck of rationalism' described in John Stuart Mill's *Autobiography*, where he discovers that the fulfilment of utilitarian ends is simply not sufficient an aim to nourish the spirit, has been overshadowed by the greater and more appalling shipwrecks wrought by irrationalism. Likewise, it will be difficult to go back to the charismatic authority of priests with their transcendental warrant to guide human affairs now that we can see what is possible when practice is evidence-based and evidence derived from cooperation in uncertainty rather than fabricated out of autocratic certainty. The occasional outbreak of charismatic leadership – Branch Davidian-style omniscience and other manifestations of the horse-shit of the Apocalypse – does not inspire confidence in the benefits of regression to earlier modes of establishing authority. And while, as Barthes argued,[27] the Enlightenment–universalist notions of the Great Family of Man may be sentimental masks to conceal the reality of exploitation, they are infinitely preferable to the fevered *volkisch* ideology that had its roots in Counter-Enlightenment thought and culminated in the *Volksgemeinschaft* concept in National Socialist ideology, where it provided the rationale for the Nazis' *Judenpolitik* and the concentration camps.[28] And although outrage at inequality and suffering, and a desire *ecraser l'infame*, has sometimes led to outrages of its own and added to human suffering, it is still more likely to improve the lot of mankind than a passionate concern to preserve the privileges of the privileged, concealed beneath some patrician rhetoric about the intrinsic superiority of the upper classes and their God-given right to rule.[29] The fundamental vision of the Enlightenment – that we are all of us, above all, members of the human race – not only elevates the oppressed, but unmasks the oppressors: it strips away the aura behind which they hide from critical evaluation. And the belief in the indefinite perfectibility of man is greatly to be preferred to an inert or paralysed pessimism, 'a drooping despondency that offers no remedy for the abuses it bewails'.[30]

There is much to criticise in dreams and fantasies of the Enlightenment *philosophes*; but it is difficult to quarrel with their wish to make life better and their rage that unnecessary suffering is permitted and that superstition, intolerance and illegitimate authority are allowed to work so effectively to maintain a world in which such suffering continues. Nor can one quarrel with their belief in the essential goodness of man – at least as a 'regulative idea' in the Kantian sense. The fact that Condorcet's dream of the indefinite perfectibility of man received its finishing touches while he was being hunted to his death by his fellow heirs of the Enlightenment is jaw-achingly funny only to the malicious and shallow, to those who, from positions of comfort, may bear the sufferings of the world with considerable ease.

In the Preface, I have described this book as a 'Yes–but' to Berlin's 'Yes–but to the Enlightenment'. In particular, I have focused on those more recent thinkers who believe that there are fundamental reasons why what we call, in shorthand, 'the Enlightenment project' – something between a programme and a dream – of progressive improvement of the lot of mankind is misconceived. These contemporary prophets of the Counter-Enlightenment seemed to be vindicated by the man-made catastrophes of recent history; by the depressing fact that, in Adorno and Horkheimer's words, 'the fully enlightened earth radiates disaster triumphant'. And, indeed, there are some reasons for believing that this age, 200 years on from the *philosophes*, is the worst of ages: wars on an unprecedented scale; monstrous institutions and regimes marked by mass torture, concentration camps and genocide; greed-driven ecological disasters; and so on. However, the scale of wars may reflect technological advance (including better methods of transport and communication permitting mass mobilisation, as well as more destructive weapons) rather than moral decadence. Increased technological capability may also account for the greater expression of evil in evil regimes; after all, mass murder and unremitting persecution is not new and there is no horror in the twentieth century that has not been perpetrated on a huge scale in previous centuries. The treatment of the slaves by the Egyptians, the Mayan sacrifice of the prisoners they captured in wars launched specifically for that purpose, the Athenians' savage destruction of Samos match what has been achieved in the twentieth century, once one allows for the constraints imposed upon earlier barbarism by technological limitations. The history of the world is, as Nietzsche said, the refutation by experiment of the idea of a moral world-order; it has always been a story of injustice, cruelty, chaos, oppression and of privations suffered by ordinary people cheek-by-jowl with over-provision for the privileged few. Indeed, in view of the enormously enhanced power of individual human beings through technological advance, it is a tribute to progress that it has *not* led to universal oppression and universal warfare, along the lines predicted in many dystopic fictions.

For perhaps the first time in history there are sizeable enclaves of comfort and justice in the world and, even more surprisingly, these enclaves include many ordinary people. This is the first century in which, in some countries at least, the rhetoric of the Rights of Man has been taken seriously and translated into the accountability of officials, politicians, the establishment, to the mass of the people. Abuses of power are still present even in these countries, but they are visible and challenged. In the United Kingdom, the experience of work, of illness, of going out into the street, of being a school-child, have all changed for the better – beyond all recognition. To take some aspects at random: work is no longer, or rarely, excruciating labour supervised by a self-indulgent bully against whose reign of terror there is no appeal; the care of ill people is not only technically more competent, but is administered by individuals whose natural tactlessness (we are all born congenitally tactless) is modified by an awareness of how things look from the patient's point of view; a walk down a busy street is not a journey through offal; and school-children are no longer required to tolerate the capricious cruelty of ignorant teachers and malignant peers without redress. This is not to say that cruelty of all sorts does not occur in the United Kingdom: child abuse, wife battering, gang terrorism are daily news. But what has changed is the scale of the cruelty and the disappearance of the assumption that it is normal, acceptable or natural: it is more visible precisely because it is no longer acceptable. In short, in every sphere, individuals treat each other better and with more respect. This may be because, on account of modern technology, they have more spare capacity to do so. If so, this cannot be a case against modern technology – or against this century.[31]

The idea of the twentieth century as a time when people treated each other with greater respect is not one that will receive ready assent: respect for other people was not the notable feature of the 'great' wars, of the concentration camps, of the Gulags, or of the colonial wars any more than it has been particularly in evidence in recent years in Rwanda, the former Yugoslavia, Somalia, South Africa, and so on. The list of times and places where respect has been wiped out by atrocity is dismayingly long. But that is not the point I am making. I am arguing that, perhaps for the first time in history, there are now some societies, where most people, most of the time, not merely the well-off or the powerful, are treated by most other people most of the time, in a manner that is consistent with the assumption that they have equal entitlement to respect. The gross abuse of 'inferiors' is not universal and unchallenged.

This statement may prompt two other questions: Is this improvement more than offset by deterioration elsewhere? Is the deterioration elsewhere actually *caused* by the improvement in those countries such as the United Kingdom where ordinary people are better off? Should we regret the precipitous decline in infant mortality amongst working-class Britons because of its cost to other countries? These are unanswerable questions: answering them would oblige us to carry out a 'global felicific calculus' which is simply impossible; and oblige us to trace causal relations beyond the point at which one can do so with any kind of confidence. Whether, for example, the improved sensitivity of the nurses caring for terminally ill patients in hospices in the United Kingdom has been bought at the cost of more brutal treatment of child workers in sweat-shops in Bombay is not easy to answer. Certainly, it could be argued that the labour- and revenue-intensive care of dying cancer patients is dependent upon the investment of a greater proportion of Gross Domestic Product in health care, and that this depends directly or indirectly upon the importation of cheap goods, and that the cheapness of these goods depends upon a brutalised child labour force. One could equally well say that a country such as India, which has a long and terrible tradition of classifying some of its citizens as 'untouchables', has always condoned the exploitation of the lower orders by the wealthy middle and upper classes and that child labour is eternal business-as-usual.

All that we need to do is to put into question the myth of 'The Myth of Progress'.[32] Yes, it *is* possible that, overall, progress has not been made; that the sum of human suffering is no less now than it was 100 years ago. But this is far from self-evident; so it cannot be taken for granted, as it is by so many humanist intellectuals. There is, in fact, a considerable body of evidence to support the contrary claim that there *has* been overall global improvement in standards of living, and even, possibly, in quality of life. John Tierney[33] has pointed out that:

1. Over the last few decades, infant mortality has decreased and life expectancy has increased, most dramatically in the Third World.
2. Although many people in the Third World have been affected by war, persecution, drought and disastrous agricultural policies, the number of people affected by famine has been declining over the last three decades. The number is lower than it was during the same decades of the last century, even though the world's population is much larger.
3. The average person in the Third World is better nourished now than in the late 1960s. Food production has increased faster than the population.
4. The average worker world-wide can buy more coal, metals and food with an hour's pay than he could a century ago.

But even if life were not overall better for the average human being than it was a century ago, we still have to ask ourselves what message we would draw from this about the way forward. Is there any alternative to that advocated by the Enlightenment thinkers?

Let me put the question more bluntly. If you don't believe in reason – on the grounds that it is an instrument of domination (e.g. of females by males or of non-Europeans by Europeans) – what will you put in its place? Unreason?

As Gellner has said:

> In our human self-image and self-assessment, the claims of unreason appear to be overwhelmingly strong, though it is not very clear just how we should live by the contrary, irrationalist vision. Its oracles speak in nebulous and murky language, and their pronouncements are allergic to clarity.[34]

If you throw away reason (and its despised cousins, logic and common sense), will there be any restraints on choice of actions, on methods, etc. of achieving human ends? And if you relativise all ends and all values, will you be happy to support a global policy that aimed, let us say, for the greatest unhappiness of the greatest number? (In a sense de Maistre takes this path; though he does not make clear whether he regards the eternal bloodbath of life as positively desirable or merely inevitable.)[35] And if you don't believe in science and technology, what alternatives do you have to offer when it comes to meeting human needs – for shelter, warmth, food, drink, etc.? How shall these be provided except by better understanding of how safe, clean food, etc. is produced, and what the body needs, by the kind of understanding exemplified by the discovery of vitamins and the progressively more subtle understanding of their actions? And what do you have to offer when it comes to solving the secondary problems that arise as an unlooked for consequence of scientific solutions to human needs? (As Medawar pointed out, 'the deterioration of the environment produced by technology is a technological problem for which technology has found, is finding, and will continue to find solutions'.)[36] After all, as I have noted on another occasion, it was high science and not The Children of the Celtic Dawn who discovered the hole in the ozone layer (as well as the ozone layer in the first place – and ozone – and its role in filtering out harmful radiant energy – and radiant energy – and the harm it sometimes does). We need as much science in the application of science as in science itself, as much technological tact and subtlety in regulating the application of technology to solving problems as in developing the technology in the first place.[37] And if you don't like modern democracy – which, in principle at least, regards each individual as equal to every other, an equality that is most directly expressed in the principle of one person one vote – what will you put in its place? Is there any other form of government – autocracy, oligarchy, ochlocracy, the varieties of dictatorship of Left and Right – that have proved to be better safeguards of the welfare and aspirations and dignity of ordinary people? Democratic accountability at all levels of public life may be imperfect, but are there other ways in which accountability may be better secured? Or is the unaccountability of a charismatic leader with transcendent authority that comes from either spiritual or temporal power better? History tells us not.

And if, finally, you are disaffected with contemporary 'Western' civilisation, what alternative do you have to offer? If you don't like the comforts it brings, will you seek out discomfort for yourself and your children? If you don't like its emphasis on material progress, will you seek to extend destitution? All the endless talk about 'alienation' and moaning over the modern division of labour that has supposedly reduced individuals to mere functions has not contributed one quantum of light to understanding the precise nature of the discontents humanist intellectuals routinely express with respect to civilisation. The grumblers have never, for example, addressed the question of whether hoeing a turnip field by arthritic hand hour after hour in a biting wind is more or less alienating than typing memoranda on a word processor in a warm office; or whether the rational (and hence, we are to understand, the dehumanising) approach to disease results in more or less alienation – whether a course of antibiotics is more dehumanising than the unremitting savagery of untreated cystitis.

It seems that, if we are really to will progress, we have no alternative but to work within the framework of Enlightenment thought, though our approach will be greatly modified in the light of lessons learnt. These lessons would include:

1. Entertaining more modest ambitions than the *philosophes* did for the scope of interventions and the rate of change. Modest interventions, whose effects are carefully monitored (so that, at the very least, lessons can be learned from the unexpected outcomes) and infinite patience – these are crucial. Humility and admitted uncertainty should be the guiding emotions of social planners.[38]

2. Avoiding scientism – that is to say, using a cargo-cultists parody of what is believed to be '*the* scientific method' in areas where even the approaches of successful science would be inappropriate – and the related assumption that a single method can be used to understand, even less to bring about, desirable social change. This does not, however, mean failing to recognise that there are transferable virtues in science: models of cooperation; a commitment to testable hypotheses; recognising the limits of certainty to which the existing evidence commits us.

3. Thinking through as clearly as possible the nature of universal or species wishes as a guide to identifying culturally invariant values and at the same time learning how to respect differences more actively. This will require all of us being aware of 'repressive tolerance', whereby dissenting world pictures are accommodated by not being taken seriously.

4. Being wary of excessive centralisation of power: men and women of apparently good intention must be as closely regulated and as answerable and accountable as people of less good intentions. Being accountable to invisible

forces, to transcendent auditors – God, the National Interest or the Future of Man – is an insufficient safeguard.

5. Respecting the a-civic heart of man; understanding, as J.S. Mill came to understand in the anguish of his mental breakdown, that reason and duty do not reach to the very bottom of our souls. Thinking how to reconcile this recognition with the need to ensure that all contribute to the process by which the civic order necessary for private depths to be developed is maintained.

6. Recognising that, even in a pre-Utopian world of scarcity, utility cannot be the only criterion of value.[39] This acknowledgement of the validity of non-utilitarian values, recognises that many human activities are expressive – self-exteriorising, self-exhibiting, 'that I am' – rather than usefully directed towards some practical end and cannot be captured by a reforming rationalism that would make them more practical, efficient, etc. Language, for example, would probably not be improved as a means of communication – and certainly not enriched – by being transformed into a *characteristica universalis*. Where non-utilitarian values become anti-utilitarian – even if only by virtue of diverting scarce resources from basic needs to less basic ones – is a difficult and delicate question and will require much careful thought. If a Welshman still insists on having road signs in Wales in Welsh, because of their cultural significance, even if the result is an increase in road accidents; or if he insists on having them in both English and Welsh even though the resource to do this will be indirectly taken from the Special Care Baby Unit budget – how shall we, Welsh and non-Welsh, respond? In setting a legislative course that apportions respect to both the expressive and utilitarian aspects of life, reason in the narrow sense, and reason in the wider sense of a faculty that incorporates an empathetic understanding of human wishes, are both essential.

7. Acknowledging that, ultimately, the Kingdom of Ultimate Ends must be left to itself.

Those lessons would probably be accepted by moderate and reasoned critics of the Enlightenment, such as Berlin. His 'Yes–But', informed by an intense awareness of the horrors unleashed upon the world by intemperate and arrogant social reformers of all kinds, still leaves most of the framework in place:

> Yet what solutions have we found, with all our new technological and psychological knowledge and great new powers, save the ancient prescriptions advocated by the creators of humanism – Erasmus, Spinoza, Locke, Montesquieu, Lessing and Diderot – reason, education, responsibility – above all, self-knowledge? What hope is there for men, or has there ever been?[40]

There may be some who feel that the 'ancient prescriptions' ask too much of mankind; or that Berlin's list of the Great and the Good is suspiciously Eurocentric; or that, even if these 'prescriptions' are acceptable, genuine human universals, they will never bring about net progress because sooner or later they run into contradications – if only because, they argue, the sum of even well-intended actions will inevitably bring about unintended consequences most of which will be unpleasant. To such we can only say that there is no *a priori* reason why progress is not possible. Yes, we still have a long way to go; there is much that is sickening, angering, horrifying about the condition in which a significant part of humanity still lives. But it is nevertheless still possible to admit that there has been progress (in some places) without being complacent or cruelly indifferent to the continuing avoidable suffering of many of our fellow-men and without denying that progress for some has been bought at the cost of further immiseration of others. This, surely, cannot be too difficult to understand – so long as one is not a humanist intellectual with a vested interest in crying universal woe. And acknowledging the serious things that are amiss with the modern world, some of them resulting from misapplied technology, does not justify crying 'failure!'

If we deny or rubbish the progress that mankind has already made, and at the same time are aware of the huge efforts mankind have made to ameliorate the human condition, we shall inevitably conclude that no progress is possible. Such 'principled' despair will be a thousand times worse in terms of quietism than the most arrant care-nothing, do-nothing conservatism. An attitude wavering between fatalism, cynicism and moral superiority may suit the purposes of humanist intellectuals who prefer the comfort of the seminar room to the relative discomfort of the places where the real work of bringing about a better future must take place. It lets them morally off the hook – just as does the idea that there is no truth (only the dominant rhetoric of particular interpretive communities) and no genuine agency (only passivity in the seas of history, discourse, the unconscious, or whatever). 'Drooping despondency' makes very little demands on one's free time.[41] But we must refute those for whom (to parody Keats) 'the miseries are the world are misery and let them rest'. For, as Medawar has pointed out,[42] although humans have been around for 500,000 years, it is only during the past 5,000 years that they have won any kind of reward for their special capabilities and only during the past 500 years have they begun to be, in the biological sense, a success. 'Only during the past 10 to 15 minutes of the human day has life on earth been anything but precarious.' Technology has been really effective – because driven by science and a fundamental understanding of natural laws – only in the last 50 years. Reason is a comparative newcomer in human affairs and a neonate in the history of living things.[43]

Opposition in principle to the idea of progress, based upon assumptions about the nature of mankind – Original Sin, aggressive animal nature (ethology, Social Darwinism), incurable irrationality (anthropology) – or about society (it is too deep to be understood, a collection of opaque forces rather than the summed activity of human agents) – simply fails to see the whole story. None of the theoretical reasons for denying the hope of progress is decisive. Nor, it must be admitted, are there irrefutable reasons for assuming that progress is guaranteed or inevitable. One would have to be a Hegelian or a Marxist to be stupid enough to believe that progress will come about of its own accord. If we believe, as I believe, that it has to be brought about by human effort, human beings mobilising the abstract intelligence and universalising goodwill that they uniquely possess, there is no certainty that the future will be better than the past. So we are left with a secular equivalent of Pascal's wager, which I commend to the reader.

As Pascal pointed out, nobody can be absolutely certain that God exists. We are in the position of best-guessing gamblers, making absolute and irreversible decisions in the context of uncertainty. What, then, should we do? Pascal recommends believing in God, for this will place the believer in a no-lose situation. If he is right, then he will be appropriately rewarded when he meets his Maker face to face. If he is wrong, he will not suffer for his credulity in the after-life of total oblivion. If, on the other hand, he wagers on the non-existence of God, his reward, if there is no God after all, is to enjoy the same oblivion as the believer. But if God really does exist, then he will be condemned to Eternal Damnation as punishment for his error. Pascal's wager is not an entirely full or fair statement of the case, if only because there is quite a range of gods to choose from and the result of choosing the wrong one could be persecution on earth and damnation in the after-life. Nor does it take account of the psychology of religious belief: the true experience of God should be (as Nijinsky proclaimed) 'a fire in the head' rather than the outcome of a prudent calculation of probabilities. We can, however, usefully transpose Pascal's wager to the secular sphere and use it to think about the hope of progress. If we believe in the possibility of progress, we may or may not be successful in bringing it about. But if we deny the possibility of progress, then, since it will not happen of its own accord, we shall ensure that progress shall most definitely not come about. For the sake of the hungry child in the dust, we should not allow those who prophesy doom and gloom to speak unopposed; otherwise their prophecies will help to bring about their own hideous fulfilment. And more hungry children will die in the dust, while the prophets of gloom, of course, continue to enjoy life in the library and the seminar room.

And perhaps for our own sake as well. Once you throw away belief in progress and the desire to make progress – the passion to alleviate human suffering here and now and in the future, on a small scale and on a large scale, locally and globally (and, as we denizens of the global village are aware, the distinction between these categories is not absolute) – then you have thrown away one of the deepest and most noble and fertile sources of goodness in human beings and, effectively, much of the underpinning of civilisation. For a truly human culture is always – though never exclusively – preoccupied with improving the lot of mankind and in modern times this has taken the form of concern about justice for all, about the rights of the many, about enrichment of the poor and empowerment of the powerless. Great, rich cultures have a generosity that is implicitly on the side of progress (even if it is not Utopian or explicitly progressive). The only question for such cultures is whether progress is pursued well or badly, effectively or ineffectively. As Medawar has said, 'The idea of improvement must be pretty well coeval with human speculative thought. In one form or another it embodies almost the whole spiritual history of mankind.'[44]

The enemies of hope have found their own reasons for dismissing the Enlightenment dream, without, perhaps fully realising what they are doing – or what they would be doing if the world took them seriously. Hitherto, those who have rejected earthly happiness have had alternative, next-worldly, futures to look forward to. In the absence of such alternatives, to dispense with the hope of progress, to mock 'the grand narratives of emancipation and enlightenment', is to lead humanity towards a collective despair perhaps unprecedented in articulate cultures. Or, more likely, since even the most articulate pessimists are not notably lacking in personal ambition and concern for self-advancement, to set an example to the well-heeled sections of the race that will encourage them to pursue their own happiness and forget that of humanity as a whole.

For the sake of our humanity, then, as well as for the welfare of those whose lives would otherwise be Hell on earth, we must believe in, and strive for, progress, as did those noble philosophers of the Enlightenment.[45] 'To deride the hope of progress', as Medawar says, 'is the ultimate fatuity, the last word in poverty of spirit and meanness of mind.' This book has been written in the hope that such poverty of spirit and meanness of mind will not have the last word.

Notes

1. Isaiah Berlin, 'The Counter-Enlightenment', in *Against the Current*, ed. Henry Hardy (London: The Hogarth Press, 1979), p. 3.
2. Isaiah Berlin, 'Joseph de Maistre and the Origins of Happiness', in *The Crooked Timber of Humanity*, ed. Henry Hardy (London: Harper Collins, 1991) p. 121.
3. This seems to be Maistre's answer, too. It is because of the intrinsic evil of men that he opposes the Enlightenment. Non-hierarchical societies of equals do not

have the means to constrain that evil: men need to be hemmed in by the terror of authority to be saved from themselves. His remedy, of course, is at odds with his analysis, as we pointed out in the Prologue: if men are evil, it is at least arguable that power should be dispersed rather than concentrated in a few hands.

4. I am reminded by what Gellner (and after him Merquior) pointed out, 'that all the romantic binges proffered by the counter-culture (and soon commercialized) ... depend on the rational basis of the self-same culture they profess to scorn' (J.G. Merquior, 'In Quest of Modern Culture: Hysterical or Historical Humanism', *Critical Review* 5(3) (Summer 1991): 399–420).
5. The supposed Eurocentricity of liberal values, in particular the liberal conception of justice, must, however, not be accepted 'on the nod'. As Stanley Hoffmann points out ('Dreams of a Just World', *New York Review of Books*, 2 November 1995, pp. 52–6), this notion (made in their defence by many repressive regimes) doesn't take into account the fact that one can 'find believers in liberal values, believers who are often repressed, everywhere, and many anti-liberals in the West' (p. 55). And he cites a refutation, by the Asian Yash Ghai, of the so-called 'Asian', anti-liberal point of view. Hoffmann succinctly defines the central philosophical and ethical problems in a non-ideal world:

   > how to produce both order and justice in a world of different 'corporate bodies' and regimes, which reflect different conceptions not only of the social good but of political justice and are based at least as often on coercion and repression as on consent.
   >
   > (ibid., p. 55)

6. I may be thought of as having smuggled in not only rationalism but also western science into those things that are not merely cultural options. My own view (which I have expressed at length elsewhere, e.g. *Newton's Sleep*, London: Macmillan, 1995) is that many human problems *are* technological and that to these a technical solution is required. The background for the most successful technical solutions is so-called 'Western' science. (It is perhaps worth noting that it is *not* 'Western', though it may have begun in the West – if Egypt and Greece may be categorised as parts of the 'West'. It is now part of a universal human heritage and to suggest otherwise is to insult all of those non-Europeans who have made major contributions.) This is recognised even in those countries where much is made of indigenous cultures and crafts and the superiority of native over imported solutions. When the rich fall ill, seek to travel great distances, need to communicate or want to have a good time, they do not hesitate to utilise 'Western' science and technology.
7. It may seem that I am making too much of a meal of defending core Enlightenment values. Surely, no one would oppose – at least in principle – a reign of tolerance, justice, democratic rule by accountable leaders fired by a sense of justice and directed by reason rather than irrationality or expediency. Am I not making a rather dragged out case for Motherhood and Apple Pie? Anyone who asks this question has probably forgotten how these values – which do not seem to be sufficiently valued by humanist intellectuals within the academy, though they are beneficiaries of them – are routinely trampled on in the real world. The Second World War and the collapse of the Berlin Wall did not bring to an end theocratic tyranny, secular despotism and religious intolerance. The enemies of the Enlightenment are at large. In many cases, in common with a significant number of humanist intellectuals,

these enemies believe they have good reasons for rejecting tolerance, accountability, etc. Toleration, for example, is seen in many places of the world to be a lesser value than inculcating the One True Faith that will save the community from Armageddon and its members from eternal damnation. And (to move inwards from the real world to the world of the library) there is a massive literature – the work of a nexus of writers whom we may capture in the portmanteau term 'Boas-deconstructors' – which not only denies that there is such a thing as cultural evolution and progress but that we should do everything possible to protect so-called primitive peoples from development. Their views are echoed by certain romanticising professional travellers such as Wilfred Thesiger who positively regretted that the nomads in the Empty Quarter should share the values of the West. As Michael Asher notes in his biography (*Thesiger*, Viking, London, 1994), Thesiger assumes 'that the primitive only wishes to be left alone and has no desire to see his children grow up healthy, to emerge from poverty and to be able to read and write'.

8. In what follows, I am going to address anxieties about an achieved Utopia, not anxieties about the process by which it is achieved or deeper anxieties about whether the world is in fact moving forward or backwards. I shall deal with the latter question towards the end of this chapter.

   What about the process? Most of the anxieties are relevant to explicit programmes for bringing about Utopia. The latter can provide the immemorial excuse for large-scale iniquities: you cannot make an omelette without breaking eggs. Alas, it is easier to break eggs than to make an omelette – which is why so many revolutions have broken millions of eggs and made no omelettes.

   The alibi of the future has also provided justification for generic injustices directed against entire categories of individuals – those who are identified as being opposed to the coming Utopia, either explicitly in their words and actions or implicitly in virtue of their 'class' or 'historical' situation. Such people – or, as they are often called, 'elements' – may be destroyed, given the overriding importance of realising the Utopian dream. The alibi of the future also justifies the (temporary) further oppression of the oppressed by their liberators: the beast has to be driven to the pasture with blows; things inevitably get worse before they get better; change always hurts even those who benefit from it; etc.

   In short, the Utopian imperative justifies the way in which (to quote Marx, cited in Albert Camus, *The Rebel*, trans. Anthony Bower (London: Penguin Books, 1953), p. 172) 'Progress resembles that horrible pagan god who only wished to drink nectar from the skulls of his fallen enemies.' Explicit Utopianism allows the leaders to subordinate the present experience of the people in the name of the indefinite future, sacrificing several generations to the needs of an infinite series of future generations, giving the commissars and the *nomenklatura* free access to the riches of the earth while they plan the next massacre or prepare the ground for the next unplanned famine. Utopia, in short, makes unacceptable demands, requiring the majority of one generation to abjure the hope of happiness in the only life they will have, to pave the way for the possible happiness of future generations.

   The unquestionable goodness and historical rightness of the explicit Utopian dream and its prophets and guardians license the untrammelled power of those whom the alibi of the future – of being on the side of generations yet unborn – lifts above moral or legal judgement. Since the prophets of the revolution and the midwives of the coming Utopia cannot be contradicted, the failure of Utopia to materialise must be due to saboteurs. The Utopian dream reduces all discourse to brutalising simplifications, as Camus captured in his incomparable analysis in *The Rebel*:

> To the extent to which Marx predicted the inevitable establishment of the classless city and to the extent to which he established the goodwill of history, every check to the advance toward freedom must be imputed to the ill-will of mankind.
> (p. 207)

Or, more precisely, certain 'reactionary elements' within it – capitalist lackeys and other members of the evil classes. These will be singled out for special attention, with the familiar, dispiriting consequences:

> The principles which men give to themselves end by overwhelming their noblest intentions. By dint of argument, incessant struggle, polemics, excommunications, persecutions conducted and suffered, the universal city of free and fraternal man is slowly diverted and gives way to the only universe in which history and expediency can, in fact, be elevated to the position of supreme judges: the universe of the trial.
> (ibid.)

9. Lucien Goldmann, *The Philosophy of the Enlightenment*, trans. Henry Maas (London: Methuen, 1973), p. 95. This is an indirect echo of de Tocqueville's famous critique of democracy:

> I see an innumerable multitude of men, alike and equal, constantly circling around in pursuit of the petty and banal pleasure with which they glut their souls... . Over this kind of men stands an immense, protective power which is alone responsible for procuring their enjoyment and watching over their fate. It provides for their security, foresees and supplies their pleasure, manages their principal concerns, directs their industry, makes rules for their testament, and divides their inheritance.

10. Raymond Tallis, 'Terrors of the Body', *Times Literary Supplement* (1 May 1992): 3–4.
11. David B. Morris, *The Culture of Pain* (Berkeley: The University of California Press, 1991).
12. Fyodor Dostoevsky, *Notes from the Underground*, Part One, chapter 4.
13. Morris looks forward to an era of 'postmodern' pain. This is pain of which the patient takes charge. Taking charge of pain includes 'assuming personal responsibility for its meaning' (ibid., p. 289). This may seem a distinct possibility in the first hour of toothache or vomiting; by the third month, the pain will be calling the shots, especially if it is a symptom of a fatal disease. Assuming personal responsibility for the meaning of a tunnel of barbed wire leading out of the light into endless darkness is not a realistic option and it is an inhuman expectation to suggest that it is. Give me diamorphine and I'll forgo the postmodernism.

    The positive valuation of pain is, of course, intimately tied up with the religious vision of the world as a vale of soul-making. In accordance with this vision, pain is of spiritual benefit both to those who suffer and to those who grow through their self-sacrificing service in tending those who suffer. Even when this vision does not tilt into the overt sado-masochism explored in books as diverse as Nietzsche's *Anti-Christ* and Huysmans' *A Rebours*, it is far from benign. Christopher Hitchens' account of the damage caused by Mother Teresa's mission to the wretched of the earth, the destitute and terminally ill, is an illuminating and terrible example, sufficient by itself to persuade the uncertain of the horrors that may result when a religious agenda hijacks human need (*The Missionary Position*, London: Verso, 1995).

14. Joseph de Maistre, 'Study on Sovereignty', in *The Works of Joseph de Maistre*, selected, translated and introduced by Jack Lively (London: George Allen and Unwin, 1964), p. 118.
15. See Raymond Tallis, *The Explicit Animal* (London: Macmillan, 1991), especially chapter 6.
16. Utopians have often worried over the major barriers to happiness that would come from sexual jealousy. They have suggested two solutions.

    The first is that sexual relations should be free and untrammelled: everyone should screw everyone else. This rather assumes that individuals will no longer want to choose with whom they make love – that no one will find anyone else, or their sexual proclivities, unattractive. This seems rather unlikely and would anyway diminish the 'specialness' of the sexual relationship. Moreover, even amongst small groups, where there has been some pre-selection, free love invariably leads to the exploitation of those with less intense sexual drives by those with more intense drives and, to a lesser extent, vice versa; and of the less powerful by the more powerful.

    The second is to forgo sexual relations altogether (with the continuation of the human race being assured by artificial insemination). The history of abstinence is not encouraging: the imperatives of sexual desire are an inescapable reality.

    There is a third way, where long-term sexual relationships are so highly developed that their metaphysical possibilities are fully realised and the physical specifics of the partners become less important. The more metaphysical sexual relationships become, the less pronounced will become the differences between values of sexual partners. Each will become to the other the means of exploring, understanding, possessing the otherness of the world, a singular who is at once unique and stands for an entire class, a concrete universal, an archetype. This is the path that I am suggesting here; where perfectly developed sexual relationships open on to something wider and even deeper than themselves.

    Incidentally, the lucrative assumption, common to much quasi-literary fiction exploring the 'outer limits' of human behaviour, that the ever more frantic search for enhanced sexual sensation will inevitably modulate into a murderous frenzy reminiscent of Young's hunting pack, is just that – a lucrative assumption. The psychopathic hero of Bret Easton Ellis's *American Psycho*, for example, is utterly empty of emotion and has his murderous sexual experiences with strangers. This is not where most people are starting from. We have no reason to assume that the inhabitants of Utopia will be affectless serial killers.
17. The difficulty of experiencing our experiences and, in the wider sense, of 'arriving' (in the Kingdom of Ends) is explored in Raymond Tallis, *Newton's Sleep* (London: Macmillan, 1995). It is treated biefly in 'The Difficulty of Arrival', reading 15 in this volume.
18. Utilitarianism, and in particular John Stuart Mill's version of it, was dismissed by right-wing romantics such as Carlyle and Nietzsche as 'the philosophy of pigs'. This is utterly unjust. Anyway, my own utilitarianism may escape this charge because (like Mill) I see material comfort as the beginning, not the end, of human development. The pigs fall asleep next to the trough once they have supped their fill. For human beings, satiety is the beginning of wakefulness, of an ever-unfolding consciousness undistracted by the struggle for survival, by the tyranny of hunger, by preoccupation with getting and spending.

19. For an extended discussion of this, see 'The Work of Art in an Age of Electronic Reproduction', in *Theorrhoea and After* (Basingstoke: Macmillan, 1999).
20. The assumption that Utopia is boring may also be based upon the idea that it is static. This is a misunderstanding: it will always be an asymptote towards which humanity will struggle for complete achievement. The future struggle, however, will not be for adequate nutrition or for decent treatment by others or for a cure for toothache but for the perfection of mutual understanding or the realisation of delight inherent in consciousness of the sunlight and for establishing the conditions in which that becomes increasingly possible. Nor will it be the fulfilment of a pre-established blueprint: when it is approached, it will emerge as something unprecedented. And therein lie potential dangers – as well as unforeseen sources of hope.
21. Since the Romantics inaugurated the tradition of rebellion against the social order, it has been natural to sympathise with the rebel. After all, most social orders have been absurd, unjust, obtrusive, etc. – just the kind of thing that should be rebelled against. It would be less easy to sympathise on existentialist grounds with rebels who brought down a genuinely beneficent and harmonious society in order to assert that they were not mere cogs in the machine. Such a collapse would increase suffering. One would not readily forgive a rebel who, for the sake of self-expression, participated in destructive acts that increased infant mortality and, in consequence, denied infants the right to participate in or dissent from the social order. In many ways, Bakunin's psychopathic visions of setting fire to Paris, of the great anarchistic act of destruction, are the purest expression of the 'Apotheosis of the Romantic Will'. The hatred of reason and order, in other words, leads in one direction to the burning of children. In the other direction, it leads to the endearing, impotent, Petrushka-like gestures of the Idiot, or the Clown, or the Pooterish clerk who writes 'I do not like my work' on an official form.
22. Nicholas Negroponte, *Being Digital* (London: Hodder and Stoughton, 1995).

    The major barrier to the switch from atoms to bits, however, is the uncontrolled increase in the population of the world. As Negroponte points out, bits are not edible, they cannot stop hunger. Bodies survive by utilising available energy from the environment in order to maintain the low levels of entropy that characterise physiological life. The more bodies there are, the more energy is required and the more the planet will be polluted. While the shift from an energy-based to an information-based economy will reduce per capita consumption of energy, there is an irreducible minimum for each body. Population over-growth will prevent any kind of Utopia emerging; indeed, it is the recipe for Hell on earth. This is why those who believe in the next world rather than the present one are so adamantly opposed to contraception and are unconcerned about the consequences of this. The earth is *meant* to be a vale of suffering – a doctrine from which the most articulate amongst the believers do not noticeably suffer.
23. It may be questioned whether the private depths individuals cultivate inside the meshes of the public domain are somehow invalidated by lacking public acknowledgement. (In relation to the notion of a private religion see my 'Religion and the Re-Enchantment of the World' in *Enemies of Hope* (Basingstoke: Macmillan, 1997), pp 157ff). If the question is posed in this way, the answer seems fore-ordained. However, the analogy of a 'mesh' may not itself be a valid one. For we are talking about the actual content of consciousness: it is in the very fact that consciousness has content – and not just abstract form, constraints and conditions – that liberation from the public sphere lies. The image of private experience being contained in

small boxes drawn by public (political, social) constraints is misleading. It overlooks the asocial core in all sensation, in all experience.

24. Indeed, those who oppose universalism seem to be unable to do so without themselves being trapped into making universalistic statements. For example, the assertion that all truths are relative to interpretive communities is itself a truth that claims to encompass all interpretive communities, or to transcend particular communities. And the anti-Enlightenment Parisian *maîtres à pensers* were particularly fond of pronouncements laying claim to a breath-taking omniscience.
25. Berlin, *Four Essays on Liberty*, p. 35.
26. Goldmann's observation is apposite here: that capitalist society 'splits ... the individual bourgeois into two fundamentally opposed forms: the "economic man", amoral, unfeeling and irreligious when he is earning a living, and the kind father, affectionate friend and good Christian in the rest of his life.'
27. Roland Barthes, 'The Great Family of Man', in *Mythologies*, selected and trans. Annette Lavers (London: Jonathan Cape, 1972).
28. See Avraham Barkai, '*Volksgemeinschaft*, "Aryanization" and the Holocaust', in *The Final Solution: Origins and Implementation*, ed. David Cesarini (London: Routledge, 1994).
29. Marx cites a prize specimen in *Capital*. He quotes a certain Townsend, a Church of England parson, who glorified the misery of the masses as a necessary condition of the overall wealth of the nation:

    > 'Legal constraint [to labour] is attended with too much trouble, violence and noise ... . whereas hunger is not only a peacable, silent, unremitted pressure, but as the most natural motive to industry and labour, it calls forth the most powerful exertions'. Everything therefore depends upon making hunger permanent among the working class, and for this, according to Townsend, the principle of population, especially active among the poor, provides. 'It seems to be a law of Nature that the poor should be to a certain degree improvident' [i.e. so improvident as to be born *without* a silver spoon in the mouth] 'that there may always be some to fulfil the most servile, the most sordid, and the most ignoble offices in the community. The stock of human happiness is thereby much increased, while the more delicate are not only relieved from drudgery ... but are left at liberty without interruption to pursue those callings that are suited to their various dispositions ... it [the Poor Law] tends to destroy the harmony and beauty, the symmetry and order of that system which God and Nature have established in the world.'
    >
    > (pp. 646–7)

30. Peter Medawar, 'On "The Effecting of All Things Possible"', in *The Hope of Progress* (London: Methuen, 1972), p. 125. This essay is one of the great masterpieces of English prose.
31. Anyone who doubts the reality of progress in some places should read the horrific account of English working-class life in *Capital*. I found it particularly illuminating to read about infant mortality rates in my own town of Stockport; and about life in Doveholes, an ordinary village some 15 miles from where I am writing this. According to the report of the (Poor Law) Relieving Officer of the Chapel-en-le-Frith Union (Chapel-en-le-Frith is another delightful little village), at Doveholes,

    > a number of small excavations have been made into a large hillock of lime ashes [the refuse of lime-kilns], and which are used as dwellings, and occupied by

> labourers and others employed in the construction of a railway ... through that neighbourhood. The excavations are small and damp, and have no drains or privies about them, and not the slightest means of ventilation except up a hole pulled through the top, and used for a chimney. In consequence of this defect, small-pox has been raging for some time and some deaths amongst the troglodytes have been caused by them.
>
> (*Capital*, p. 665)

Some progress has been made since then. (One of the problems of assessing progress, is that one tends to forget where one has come from.)

32. A myth that is bolstered by two other myths: the myth of the organic communities of the past; and the myth of the inorganic non-communities of the present and the future. I have dealt with the former in *Newton's Sleep* (London: Macmillan, 1995) and will not repeat here what I have said there. Let me, however, say a few words about the supposed inorganic non-communities of the present.

    The image that this invokes is of atomised individualistic lives passed in consuming whatever is thrown at them by a television screen or a computer terminal. This image is incomplete. In our household the younger members spend much time interacting with electronic screens of various sorts (though this is punctuated by frequent forays to play football and basketball in the drive and elsewhere). During this time, they are no less in communication with one another than they would be if one were playing football for one team and the other for another. There is much passionate discussion of the game being played on the screen and the supposed inorganic, post-modern, traditionless experience is frequently punctuated by distinctly organic and immemorial traditions such as rolling on the floor, fighting. This is simply an emphatic manifestation of the fact that even the participants in a computer game are not dissolved into an ethernet of elsewhere: they are here and now, rooted in the present tense and the present location. Their experience of events on the screen is clearly situated in their experience of the house, each other, the changing lights and sounds of their immediate environment.

    The myth of the organic unity of the past was that individuals were not separated by their fears and pains; and the myth of the inorganic community of the present is that individuals are not related to their environment through the bodily experiences of warmth, shared physical environments, etc.
33. Data taken from John Tierney's article 'Betting the Planet', published in *The Guardian*, 28 December 1990. Of course, these facts, while undermining the case for pessimism, do not provide grounds for complacency. War, famine, hunger, premature death, oppression, persecution and torture are still all too prevalent on the planet. Even so, it is astonishing how much things have improved, despite the continuation of disasters – natural and man-made – and an explosively rising population. How much better things would be if the population expansion had been curbed and men had behaved better towards men. At any rate, it is a tribute to the power of technology and to human ingenuity that it can still bring about an improvement in the lot of human beings despite the tendency of some of mankind to shoot itself through the foot with an AK–47.
34. Ernest Gellner, *Reason and Culture* (Oxford: Blackwell, 1993), p. 181. Gellner also points out that 'the claims of unreason are not equally persuasive in all spheres. They are not very persuasive in cognition, notwithstanding the fact that the absence of a warranty for rational procedures is undeniable. Cognition continues to function admirably, even given the absence of any such guarantee' (ibid., p. 181).

35. The more intelligent question is not whether we should accept reason or reject it – whether we should on the one hand, see the world in entirely rational terms or, on the other, assume a ferocious irrationality, whether we should be 'dry' or 'wild' – but how much wildness we can allow ourselves without forgetting the thirsty child screaming in the dust. But we are a long way from even beginning to ask this sort of question.
36. Medawar, op. cit., p. 125. The entire passage is worthy of citation:

> Many different elements enter into the movement to depreciate the services to mankind of science and technology. ... We wring our hands over the miscarriages of science and technology and take its benefactions for granted. We are dismayed by air pollution but not proportionately cheered up by, say, the virtual abolition of poliomyelitis. ... There is a tendency, even a perverse willingness to suppose that the despoliation sometimes produced by technology is an inevitable and irremediable process, a trampling down of Nature by the big machine. Of course it is nothing of the kind. The deterioration of the environment by technology is a technological problem for which technology has found, is finding, and will continue to find solutions. ... I am all in favour of a vigorously critical attitude towards technological innovation: we should scrutinize all attempts to improve our condition and make sure that they do not in reality do us harm; but there is all the difference in the world between informed and energetic criticism and a drooping despondency that offers no remedy for the abuses it bewails.

37. This is particularly obvious in medicine, where enormous distances separate the well-validated idea or treatment from its routine good use in everyday practice. One has only to think of the poignant contrast between the care with which drugs are developed and tested and how they are used in the real world; between pre- and post-marketing.
38. Medicine may provide some useful models here. The incremental improvement in the treatment of illnesses, the recognition of uncertainty as an inescapable aspect of interventions and the caution with which changes are introduced (at least by non-charlatans) has much to teach planners and reformers. Recent ISIS studies have led to the recommendation of a series of treatments which, if universally implemented would significantly reduce mortality from heart attacks. Several hundreds of thousands of patients had to be recruited in many hundreds of centres in scores of countries in order to produce robust answers. The next step is to look at ways of implementing this newly established good practice and to investigate how services are organised to ensure this. This brings the challenges of medicine closer to the wider challenges of social reform. The Cochrane collaboration, which is keeping a world-wide database of properly validated double-blind controlled trials for universal use, is another model for social reformers to examine.
39. And this applies to future as much as present utility. Yes, we must work for the future but also live in the present because this is the only life we have; besides, there is a danger that tyrants may use the alibi of the future to justify present suffering, present iniquity. As Camus said, the future is the only estate that the masters freely make over to the slaves.
40. 'John Stuart Mill and the Ends of Life', in *Four Essays on Liberty*, op. cit.

41. I am perhaps being too generous, here, in following Merquior's diagnosis of the diagnosticians of society:

> That a deep cultural crisis is endemic to historical modernity seems to have been much more eagerly assumed than properly demonstrated, no doubt because, more often than not, those who generally do the assuming – humanist intellectuals – have every interest in being perceived as soul doctors to a sick civilisation.

 There may be baser instincts at work. There is a delighted child in all of us that rejoices when things go wrong. And many of those who have loathed the modern world and detested progress have been themselves seriously damaged individuals: Baudelaire, Eliot, Benn – the list speaks for itself.
42. Medawar, 'On "The Effecting of All Things Possible"', op. cit.
43. Just how new it is, and how extraordinary, is captured in Gellner's 'Prometheus Perplexed', the penultimate chapter of his *Reason and Culture*. A few passages will have to suffice:

> Reason is a foundling, not an heir of an old line, and its identity or justification, such as it is, is forged without the benefit of ancient lineage. A bastard of nature cannot be vindicated by ancestry but only, at best, by achievement. ...
> The Cosmic Exile [reason], opting out of culture, is impractical. But it constitutes the noble and wholly appropriate charter of myth of a new kind of culture, a new system of a distinctively *Cartesian* kind of Custom and Example. Custom was not transcended: *but a new kind of custom altogether was initiated.* The separation of referential cognition from other activities, the systematic submission of cognitive claims to a severely extra-social centralized court of appeal (under the slogan of 'clear and distinct ideas', or of 'experience'), and the establishment of a single currency of reference, had burst open the limits of knowledge. It initiated and made possible an age of totally unprecedented, fabulous cognitive and economic growth. Through its associated technology, it brought the Malthusian age to an end. Henceforth resources would, and generally did, grow faster than population. Coercive political systems were no longer imposed on mankind by the need to enforce an inevitably unjust distribution on members of society endowed with inherently limited resources. Oppression, from now on, was to be our option, but no longer our destiny.
> ... in the one great and irreversible transition or *coupure* between the traditional and the rational spirit, pragmatic considerations overwhelmingly and decisively favour one of the two contestants. At one particular crossroads, the verdict of history is categorical, unambiguous, decisive and irreversible.
>
> (pp. 160, 165)

 This should be read in conjunction with the following passage from Hermann Hesse:

> Since the end of the Middle Ages, intellectual life in Europe seems to have evolved along two major lines. The first of these is the liberation of thought and belief from the sway of all authority. In practice this meant the struggle of Reason, which at last felt it had come of age and won its independence, against

the domination of the Roman Church. The second trend, on the other hand, was the covert but passionate search for a means to confer legitimacy on this freedom, for a new and sufficient authority arising out of Reason itself. We can probably generalise and say that Mind has by and large won this often strangely contradictory battle for two aims basically at odds with each other.

(Hermann Hesse, *The Glass Bead Game*, trans. Richard and Clara Winston (London: Picador, 1987), p. 19)

44. 'The Genetic Improvement of Man', in *The Hope of Progress* (London: Methuen, 1972), p. 69.

This essay usefully distinguishes three main kinds of vision of the future of man: the Olympian, the Arcadian and the Utopian. In the Olympian version, 'men can become like gods; can achieve complete virtue, understanding and peace of mind, but through spiritual insight, not by mastery of the physical world'. Arcadian visions of the future are bound up with the ancient legend of a Golden Age, 'it is directed backwards': 'men remain human but in a state of natural innocence. They retreat into a tranquil pastoral world where peace of mind is not threatened, intellectual aspiration is not called for, and virtue is not at risk.' Authority is replaced by fraternity in this 'world without strife, without ambition, and without material accomplishment'. The Utopian vision assumes that man improves the world through his own exertions: 'he begins as a tenant or lodger in the world, but ends up as its landlord; and as his environment improves, so, it is alleged, will he': 'Virtue can be learned and will eventually become second nature, understanding can be aspired to, but complete peace of mind can never be achieved because there will always be something more to do. Men look forwards, never backwards, and seldom upwards.'

My own hope for the future combines elements of all three visions. From the Olympian vision, I would take the emphasis on spirituality. This, however, would be possible only on the basis of universal, or near-universal, liberation from material want. From the Arcadian vision, I would borrow the emphasis upon the light-handedness of authority, itself possible because the emphasis upon the 'metaphysicalisation' of experience (or the discovery of the mystery inherent in experience) would limit the appetite for material gain and the strife that follows from this. The logic of increasing consumption would be challenged by a shift of emphasis towards experiencing more deeply and more thoroughly the things that we have – learning how to possess our possessions. (I have discussed this at greater length in 'The Work of Art in an Age of Electronic Reproduction', in my *Theorrhoea and After*, Macmillan,1999.) And from the Utopian vision, I would take the belief that material progress is a necessary condition of spiritual liberation – to paraphrase Brecht, 'Grub first and then metaphysics' – and the assumption that individuals would behave better towards one another when they were themselves treated better – 'Grub first, then ethics'.

And I would reject elements of each. The Olympian vision seems to suggest that man can live by the spirit alone and that each can survive in a solipsist bubble of ecstatic contemplation. On the contrary, we need the material and spiritual succour of the companionage of others. The Arcadian vision is based upon a sentimental idea about human nature in the remote past, in particular about organic, agrarian communities. We have little evidence that such communities are as fraternal as Rousseau and others would have us believe: spite is not an invention of the drawing room. As Jon Elster has pointed out, pre-industrial societies are riddled with envy:

> A depressing fact about many peasant societies is that people who do better than others are often accused of witchcraft and thus pulled down to, or indeed below, the level of others. Against this background, ruthless selfishness can have a liberating effect.
>
> (quoted in Aaron Wildavsky, 'Can Norms Rescue Self-Interest?', *Critical Review*, (1991) 5(3): 305–25, at p. 315)

And, finally, most Utopian visions focus too exclusively on material advancement.

45. I have expressed the view that lack of belief in progress takes away an important part of the meaning of life. Others have suggested that, on the contrary, belief in progress undermines the meaning of the past and, indeed, of the present in so far as it is regarded as the past of the future. For example, Bryan Appleyard talks of the reduction of 'history to an insignificant landscape of ages that were trying and failing to become our age', adding that 'in time, our age will be reduced to the same condition' (*Understanding the Present*, London: Picador, 1992, p. 237). I think that the hope of progress and respect for the past can be reconciled: we have simply to recognise what those who brought about the better future (which is our present) achieved; to remember, as Newton did, those giants upon whose shoulders we stand.

From: *Enemies of Hope* (Macmillan, 1997), pp. 362–91, 397–469, 476–82, 485–90.

Part IV
The Errors of Post-Saussurean Thought

The domination of the unconscious over consciousness, of the system of signs over the sign-using individual ('language speaks us', 'the signifier dominates over the signified'), and the decentring of the self have been most widely associated with the so-called post-Saussurean thinkers. These thinkers purported to base their ideas on Saussure's linguistics. The argument Tallis has had with them, extending over several books, takes issue, first, with their ideas, second, with their claim that these ideas are founded on Saussure's linguistics, and, beyond that, with their mode of argument.

First, Tallis has argued that the post-Saussureans (and subsequent exponents of what Richard Rorty has called 'Theory') are wrong about the nature of language. In particular, they confuse the signifier and the sign, the signifier with the sign in use, and the language system with speech. The confusion between the system of language and the use of that system on particular occasions results in post-Saussureans overlooking the fundamental characteristic of human discourse – the deliberate formulation and expression of meaning by a situated individual. Post-Saussureans are forced by their errors to absurd conclusions; for example, that texts do not refer to anything outside of themselves and, indeed, that language is non-referential. They are also wrong about the self, the human subject. This includes the developed self (a function of language, according to Benveniste, Barthes and many others); the developing self (the emergence of a fiction, according to Lacan, whose factually baseless and explanatorily inadequate genetic epistemology is an elaboration of an equally baseless Freudian metapsychology); the intending self (a myth, according to Derrida); the reading self and the writing self (more myths, according to the *maîtres à penser*); and so on. They are in addition wrong about literature and, in particular, wrong in the reasons they adduce for despising realism and about the respective functions of literature and literary criticism.

A second part of the argument Tallis has with the post-Saussureans concerns their claim to be grounding their ideas in Saussurean linguistics. Here again, he insists, they are wrong. Furthermore, their misreading of Saussure is only the most spectacular of their misreadings of writers – such as Peirce and Austin – whose work has some bearing on theoretical linguistics. Beyond the particular errors of the post-Saussureans, Tallis takes further issue with their style of argument, which he finds intellectually derelict. He considers their writings to exhibit: (i) an utterly opaque, sometimes near-delirious mode of argument; (ii) a propensity to draw huge conclusions from one or two bits of data, or, worse, a habit of dogmatic, unsupported assertion of massive 'truths'; (iii) inconsistency; (iv) a fondness for argument from authority ('X said this' – as if citation were evidence); (v) as a correlative of this, a dishonest use of sources (strategic misquotation); and, finally, (vi) constant reference to 'results established elsewhere'.

8
Theorrhoea contra Realism

In this reading, from *Theorrhoea and After* (1999), Tallis addresses the various arguments elaborated by theorists against realism. The weakest of these is that it is methodologically *passé*, though a second idea, that reality is no longer realistic, is not much better. A more considerable argument is the ideological position deriving from Althusser, which sees realism as a form that pretends to present reality objectively and by so doing naturalises what is in fact a social and historical construct. The impossibility of realistic fiction has also been argued for on the grounds that stories have a structure different from that of life. However, the most popular arguments against realism derive from post-Saussurean linguistics, and they depend on the false belief that Saussure showed that reference is not possible. One can go further than this, and claim that all structured awareness of reality is mediated by language and therefore reality is only available to consciousness in so far as it is intra-linguistic – a form of linguistic idealism. In opposing these positions, Tallis is led to confront what he describes as the 'topsy-turvy world' of Derrida. Here, language is purely a matter of signifiers that never touch extra-linguistic reality: for Derrida, as for Lacan, discourse is an endless chain of signifiers, attempting vainly to fill the lack corresponding to the absent origin, an absence that is only revealed the more completely the more eagerly one seeks for it in language. Tallis is challenging one of the basic assumptions underpinning a great deal of semiotic and post-modern thought: the idea of the free 'play' of the signifier. It is a confusion based on the entirely erroneous notion that meaning something and existing are alternative states. As Vincent Descombes has noted, the whole set of ideas derives from Hegel's famous dictum, that the word is the murderer of the thing. The result is a muddle, in which it is argued that, since the use of signs is necessary to represent what is absent, the absence of what is signified is necessary for the use of signs. Tallis concludes that the case against the realist novel fails absolutely.

Introduction: the disparaging of realism

Over the last few decades, the realistic novel has been derided by literary theorists associated with the structuralist and post-structuralist schools of thought – the so-called post-Saussurean critics. Their criticisms have not been adequately answered because the underlying theoretical arguments – supposedly derived from Saussure – have not been examined with sufficient care. There has consequently been a tendency to assume that there is a powerful case against realism which must be accepted or ignored with a bad conscience. We are told that realism is dead while the non- or anti-realistic novel is alive and kicking.

Of course, realistic novels continue to be written and read. But this evidence of life is illusory. According to Robert Scholes those who still write in the realist tradition are like 'headless chickens unaware of the decapitating axe'.[1] Michael Boyd asserts that, although 'hacks will no doubt continue to write soporific illusions just as some readers will continue to require such products for their easy consumption ... the modern novel defines itself in terms of its rejection of the conventions of formal realism'.[2] It is not too clear what Boyd means by 'conventions' and by 'formal', but the implication of his views is obvious: we are to look elsewhere for fictional instruments to sharpen our perception of the world, to liberate us from the automaticity that pilots us through our days, and to help us to explore the realities in which we are situated and by which some of us are oppressed. The realistic novel is dead; and such posthumous life as realism enjoys is to be found in the work of middlebrow and blockbusting authors who squat paperbacked ingloriously on railway stations and airports, waiting to be consumed by the mindless looking for an equally sedating but slightly more interesting alternative to sleep.

The acknowledged fathers of the contemporary literary novel – Beckett, Pynchon, Raymond Roussel, John Barth, Borges, Gabriel García Marquéz, Donald Barthelme, to name a few chosen at random – create or created dream-worlds, anti-worlds, word-worlds and non-worlds, as do many lesser figures of equally serious purpose. The house of fiction is overrun by fabulists, by writers with their hands deep in what Philip Larkin once scornfully referred to as the myth-kitty. Science fiction continually looks like becoming mainstream. At least one prominent novelist, Doris Lessing, who was for many years a serious practitioner of realism, took to writing 'space' fiction for a while. This, she claimed at the time, was the only suitable mode for the contemporary novel. Alas for the contemporary novel; for, as Oscar Wilde said, 'It is only the unimaginative who ever invent.'

Even those writers who locate their fictions on earth and still have a use for characters drawn from daily life and for plots remotely related to ordinary experience are pleased to allow anti-realistic elements into their works. Indeed, a modest degree of apparently deliberate implausibility seems to metal the fast lane to academic critical favour. Many 'serious' novelists, in whose work formal experimentation is not especially evident, now include goblins, unfortunates who are twice-born or undergo innumerable incarnations, creatures with magic powers and other such implausibilia in their cast of characters, in an endeavour, perhaps, to look fashionably South American. Pseudo-science, magic, playful erudition, parody and above all whimsy unite practitioners as different as Salman Rushdie and Kurt Vonnegut. It seems to me that whimsy is the temptation of the twentieth-century novel as moralism and sentimentality were that of the nineteenth; the Author-as-Puck has replaced Little Orphan Annie and it is not self-evident that puck-marked modernism is much of an advance over the mushier reaches of Victorian fiction. Having said this, the taxonomy of anti-realism in Cristopher Nash's brilliant, rich and comprehensive *World-Games*[3] reminds us that the house of anti-realistic fiction also has many windows.

Just in case it may be thought that the theoretician's assault on realism – which I have discussed at much greater length in my book *In Defence of Realism*[4] – is now a thing of the past, let me quote from a critical notice by Terry Eagleton of a novel in a recent issue of *The London Review of Books:*[5]

> [In *What a Carve Up!*] High Victorian realism ... has thickened into the paranoid world of the Post-Modernist text, where everything is at once arbitrary and obsessively interconnected, and where – for all the world as in a novel – the contingencies of real life turn out to be densely plotted. The *locus classicus* of this in fiction is the scene where the characters are gathered together in the drawing room of the country house to hear a will revealed or the source of the crime disclosed; and *What a Carve Up!* ends with an adroitly heavyhanded parody of that moment, as the Winshaws – now all potential murder victims – try to figure out which particular movie they are in. The answer ... is *What a Carve Up!*
>
> Yet Coe's novel, so shrewdly conscious of its own busily parodic techniques, that it has the curious effect of parodying Post-Modernism, too, raising it to the second power ...
>
> *What a Carve Up!* shuffles us between signifier and referent ... reminding us that ... life is indeed a product of art.

The symbiotic relationship between a certain sort of critic and certain sort of novelist is self-evident. Their shared needs and preoccupations mean that the former will guarantee the latter extensive and respectful attention. Equally evident from this passage is the extent to which mimesis – successful or otherwise – is no longer even an issue. For a radical critic such as Eagleton (who relishes novels like *What a Carve Up!* where radical critics discourse of Godard and the hegemony of the signifier), plausibility is a literary vice, not the minimal art virtue of fiction. As Nuttall put it in his *A New Mimesis*,[6] 'one of the immemorial ways of praising a writer, that is by saying that he or she is true to life, has become obscurely tabu, as if it involved some misconception of the nature of literature and the world'. To break with plausibility is to refuse to subscribe to the *illusionism* that is the distinctive vice of the realistic novel. Most people reading in the *Sunday Sport* that someone had claimed that Excalibur had suddenly appeared out of a Lake in the Midlands, would probably be rather bored. But their attitude to implausibility in contemporary fiction is to be quite different. So if Donald Barthelme writes a story about a glass mountain inexplicably appearing in Manhattan, then they are obliged to be thrilled – a daring break with the dull conventions of realism. Which is not to say that they believe Barthelme's story; or even that they read it as an allegory. A story that suspends disbelief or is open to interpretation in a quasi-realistic sense has failed to be sufficiently advanced. In order to guard against this, truly modern fiction will signpost its own artefactual – and advanced – state, its status as a piece of *writing*, by referring to itself, contradicting itself, breaking out into a delirium of puns or fading into a blank page where the reader can reflect on the nature of the narrative act.

There is a famous and much-commented-on opening paragraph in Alain Robbe-Grillet's *In the Labyrinth*. The first sentence announces that it is raining and the second that the sun is shining. This has been interpreted by critics to be an attack on the mimetic contract implicit in realistic fiction. The initial assumption that the novel refers to an external reality is ruthlessly brushed aside and we are, according to one critic, 'forced to realise that the only reality in question is that of writing itself which uses the concept of the world in order to display its own laws'.[7] On this basis, it would seem that to tear the mimetic contract to shreds, to subject the referential function of language to a radical critique and, in passing, to undermine the foundations of mindless bourgeois normality, all that is necessary is to enact the Magrittean cliché by writing down:

THIS IS NOT A WRITTEN SENTENCE

As Wilde might have said, one would have to possess a brain of stone not to burst out laughing at the death of Little Reference. But the wild claims made on behalf of many anti-realist writers who – to use Terry Eagleton's characteristically absurd phrase – 'explode our assurance' – are symptomatic of the critic's belief in the perniciousness of realism and its ripeness for destruction. To write, as one of Elizabeth Bowen's characters once said, is always to rave a little. And to write as a critic is not uncommonly to rave a lot.

Antipathy to realism is probably ultimately a matter of taste; but it has mobilised some apparently powerful arguments in its support, and it is these that I wish to examine. I must make clear, however, that my primary aim is not to attack anti-realistic fiction. My defence of realism is not intended as a formal proof of the worthlessness of fantasy or of fiction that consists of word-games. It merely happens that I have a strong personal preference for realistic fiction and I resent the implication of much literary theory that this taste is symptomatic of an infantile disorder. Or, worse, of Podsnappery. Mr Podsnap's world, it will be recalled, was not a very large world, morally or geographically. He resisted whatever was different, whatever failed to conform to his own unthinking expectations, dismissing it as 'Not English!' And he expected art to live up to the high standards of Englishness he set:

> Elsewise, the world got up at eight, shaved close at a quarter past, breakfasted at nine, went to the city at ten, came home at half past five, and dined at seven. Mr. Podsnap's notions of the Arts in their integrity might have been stated thus. Literature: large print, respectively descriptive of getting up at eight, shaving close at a quarter past, breakfasting at nine, going to the City at ten, coming home at half-past five, and dining at seven.

Well that is *not* what a preference for realism is about. Speaking for myself, nothing human is alien to me; only aliens from outer space are, especially aliens who can't make up their minds whether they are crossword puzzles or not. By all means read or even write science fiction or word-game novels yourself; but do not expect *me* to take an interest in people who have seventeen legs rather than two or to enjoy the erudite whimsy of the postmodernist textualisers merely on theoretical grounds.

The most popular and annoying arguments against realistic fiction originate from post-Saussurean theorists. They are not, however, the only ones. For the sake of completeness – and to pre-empt the objection that I have overlooked the best arguments – I shall list and briefly discuss some other popular reasons for claiming that realism is outmoded, though my main concern is with the post-Saussurean assault on referential realism.

Realism is methodologically *passé*

The weakest argument against realism is that it is stylistically conservative and that to write realistically must be to subscribe, implicitly, to an outmoded view of the world. The force of this argument depends entirely upon the mistaken assumption that contemporary realists are obliged to write like certain earlier realists, and to adopt the well-tried methods of Flaubert or Dreiser or even, God help us, Wilbur Smith. This argument can be dealt with very easily: realism, as an *aim* – to represent reality or to situate a novel in a world that operates under the constraints of somebody's world – and these constraints will be different in Manchester and Rwanda – does not entail commitment to the practices of previous realistic novelists. Even less does it entail subscription to their political, moral or metaphysical beliefs. In practice, a realistic novelist is obliged to be a tireless innovator if he or she is to let the world into the printed page. Realists will not be stylistic conservatives or, necessarily, conservatives of any other kind.

Reality is no longer realistic

The case against realism has also been developed from the assumption that there is something rather special about contemporary reality that makes it unsuitable for realistic treatment. This is expressed most directly in Norman Mailer's story 'The Man Who Studied Yoga':

> Marvin asks Sam if he has given up his novel, and Sam says 'Temporarily'. He cannot find a form, he explains. He does not want to write a realistic novel because reality is no longer realistic.

This passage, which has been widely quoted, is ironically from one of Norman Mailer's least incompetent and more realistic presentations of a complex bit of reality.

Different writers give different reasons for asserting that twentieth-century reality is qualitatively different from all that has preceded it, so that its essence, to quote Gerard Graff, is 'unreality'. Certain themes, however, are sounded again and again: first, modern reality is more horrible than anything that has gone before; secondly, it is pre-digested, in a manner that has no historical precedent, by the organs of the mass media; and thirdly, human artefacts intervene between man and nature to an extent not previously seen, so that the individual's environment is a rapidly changing man-made one rather than a stable natural one.

It is a peculiar but not uncommon kind of snobbery to believe that one lives in the worst of all times – the most abominable, the least comprehensible, the most rootless. Such a belief is the diagnostic sign of an underdeveloped historical sense. Anyone with the scantiest knowledge of what happened before today will know that the history of the world is largely a history of pain, injustice and chaos. Local reality has always resisted complete understanding; and the whole of 'reality' has never been within the grasp of an individual mind. Human life has always been torn with extremes that have often outreached the consciousness of the man with a pen in his hand. It is, therefore, no more a sign of moral or intellectual insensitivity to try to write a realistic novel in 1987 than it was in 1857.

It has also been argued that we live in a world that is more fragmented than before. Gerard Graff, for example, speaks of the way in which

> modern technology, war, politics, commerce, social engineering and journalism ... by promoting continuous discontinuity and upheaval have assaulted our assurance of reality.[8]

Everyone will be familiar with such sentiments. They do not stand up to the briefest reflection on the nature of ordinary life. Human consciousness has always been riven by discontinuities. To dwell merely on the physiological facts, the world has always been served up to living creatures through the lens of a body that has fluctuating neurophysiological properties. Ordinary life is marked by intermissions of consciousness: sleep, dreams, delirium, epilepsy and coma are scarcely twentieth-century innovations. The invention of the jet-plane or the micro-processor has not cut deeper into the continuity and uniformity of an agreed-upon reality than do coma or even the ordinary sleep that you the reader may be on the verge of even now.

There is another aspect of the belief that contemporary life is more 'fragmented' than life in the past. We are to believe that not only is the individual more internally discontinuous but that there is more separation between individuals. Modern societies are more atomic. I think there is very little evidence that changes in *Weltanschauung* are a more potent source of separation than the individual (and immemorial) experiences of pain, ecstasy, happy or unhappy love, anxiety or fear for oneself or one's loved ones, and so on. Here is not the place to discuss where the myths of the organically unified societies of the past have come from, but perhaps I may be permitted the suggestion that they are usually based upon the habit of confusing the unwritten history of experience with the history of written ideas. Moreover, as Merquior has suggested, there may be vested interests in sustaining the confusion:

> That a deep cultural crisis is endemic to historical modernity seems to have been much more eagerly assumed than properly demonstrated, no doubt because more often than not those who generally do the assuming – humanist intellectuals – have every interest in being perceived as soul doctors to a sick civilisation.[9]

All of this is really a long aside, but it is enough, I hope, to establish that reality was no more realistic then than it is now. Most of those who try to prove that contemporary reality is so different that it is no longer amenable to realistic treatment do so by giving realistically described accounts of bits of contemporary reality, and so fall victim to pragmatic self-refutation.

Realism is politically naive – or worse

There are political arguments against realistic fiction. The most interesting ones are presented with particular lucidity in Catherine Belsey's impressively articulate and almost persuasive *Critical Practice*,[10] published in the 1980s. At their heart is the claim that reality is an ideological artefact and that realism overlooks or seeks to conceal or deny this. In recent decades, this has been the crux of neo-Marxist hostility to realism; ultimately, it derives from the paranoiac Althusserian vision of literature as being one amongst many of the Ideological State Apparatuses designed to maintain sufficient status quo to ensure the reproduction of the conditions of production. Realism, by pretending to present reality objectively, objectifies or naturalises what is in fact historically and socially derived.

It is not possible, or necessary, to do justice to the rather complex arguments here.[11] Suffice it to say that Pierre Macherey – a Marxist critic and therefore on the side of the ideological angels – has shown very clearly how the most innocent attempt to represent reality is likely to lead to an exposure of the contradictions inherent in it rather than to collusion with the status quo. He makes this point forcefully in *Towards a Theory of Literary Production*:

> A work is established against an ideology as much as it is from an ideology. Implicitly the work contributes to the exposure of ideology, or at least to a definition of it; thus the absurdity of all attempts to 'demystify' literary works, which are defined precisely by their enterprise of demystification.[12]

The works he is is referring to include the novels of L. Tolstoy – scarcely a forerunner of contemporary anti-realism. Macherey mounts a powerful case for realistic fiction as a way of making ideology visible, the realistic epiphany as a means of *exposing* what otherwise would remain silent or invisible and so pass unchallenged. For, he says,

> no ideology is sufficiently consistent to survive the test of figuration.[13]

The ideological argument also falls victim to self-contradiction; for much of its *gauchiste* anger against society is based upon realistic appraisal of what goes on in the world at large. 'Serbs are raping Muslim women while the world stands idly by' is a realistic statement. Moreover, in Althusser's scheme of things, ideology and false consciousness are almost co-terminous with intelligible experience. There is, as Michel Pecheux pointed out, no room outside of ideology for the opposing view to establish itself. So much for the ideological argument.

There are no such things as true stories

The impossibility of realistic fiction has been argued on the grounds that stories are differently structured from life. The basis of this critique of the pretensions of realism is captured in the famous passage from Sartre's (brilliantly realistic) *Nausea*:

> When you are living nothing happens ... There are never any beginnings ... There isn't any end either ... But when you tell about life, everything changes; only it's a change nobody notices; the proof of that is that people talk about true stories. As if there could possibly be such things as true stories; events take place one way and we recount them the opposite way.[14]

The trouble with this as an argument against realistic fiction is that it is also an argument against realistic statements, in particular those large-scale realistic statements that committed intellectuals such as Sartre believed in and acted upon; for example, 'The French are committing atrocities in Algeria'. It is interesting how often epistemological and other modes of scepticism tend to be forgotten when someone is angry or outraged. It would equally be an argument against the truth of any story – such as the story the patient tells the doctor about his/her illness, or a report on a shopping expedition.

The post-Saussurean critique of realism

By far the most popular arguments against the possibility or validity of realistic fiction originate from critics who have been influenced by Saussure's famous lectures on theoretical linguistics. These are the theorists who have contributed most to the avalanche of theorrhoea – a term I owe to the late J.G. Merquior – that engulfs literary studies. And before plunging into post-Saussurean theory it will be appropriate to make one or two general observations about so-called 'theory'.

Richard Rorty has written of 'a kind of writing ... which is neither the evaluation of the relative merits of intellectual productions, nor intellectual history, nor moral philosophy, nor social prophecy, but all of these mingled together in a new genre'.[15] It is this that is called 'theory'. In certain quarters this is seen as the natural successor to literary theory which in turn has displaced literary criticism as the main business of English studies. 'Theory' is not to everyone's taste; for some, it seems to be composed of theories meta-theorised to the point where you cannot remember where they came from and can no longer see or care whether they are true. Theorists mock readers who, after a few pages of 'theory', thirst for first-order discourse, for facts and reports on experiences, for perceptions and ideas. They are amused by the naivety of those who do not wish merely to situate ideas but also to work with them, to try to understand them, to test them, to develop and extend them. For 'theory' is all about knowing all about theories without engaging with them on their own terms; it is about being able to 'place', for example, the

General Theory of Relativity without having to know how to derive its fundamental equations. It is, in short, intellectually derelict, taking to the extreme the vice of substituting allusion for argument in those places where clearly defined premises and conclusions are required.

Critics seem to divide into those who accept post-Saussurean 'theory' and theories with little understanding of the incompetent philosophy and worse linguistics that underpin them; those who dismiss them as merely fashionable but pernicious and try to refute the ideas without engaging with them; and those who ignore the ideas with varying degrees of unease. Now that the post-Saussurean movement is on the wane – though not as fast as may have been expected – the position of the third group may seem to have been proved the wisest. Why bother tilting at windbags? However, the decline of post-Saussurean theory has resulted from extrinsic, not to say extra-textual, causes: the death of some of the major players; the posthumous disgrace of Paul de Man; the accommodation of the academic nervous system to stimuli no longer novel; and so on. For this reason, it is all the more important to see what the theorists were about and why they were wrong; to drive the stake through the corpse's heart to guard against resurrection.

At the heart of the matter are Saussure's revolutionary ideas about language and the use that has been made of them by literary theorists and others. So before going any further, it is necessary to say something about these ideas, which were developed in the lectures published posthumously by his pupils.[16]

The following are the relevant Saussurean principles:

1. The linguistic sign is arbitrary.
2. The linguistic sign is a signifier combined with a signified.
3. Neither the signifier nor the signified enjoys an independent existence outside of the *system* of language.
4. The linguistic system is a set of differences and its component signifiers and signifieds, being purely differential, are essentially negative.

The arbitrariness of the linguistic sign is hardly controversial. Indeed, it is a very old notion that Saussure did not claim to originate. It does not imply (as Saussure was at pains to point out) that the choice of which words to mean what things was left entirely to the discretion of the speaker. No, the linguistic sign was arbitrary in the sense of having no natural connection with the significate. Words do not have meanings in virtue of the fact that their token instances resemble the objects they are used to refer to. 'Cat' does not look, sound, smell, etc. like any cat and it wouldn't do its job better if it did; indeed, non-arbitrariness would be an embarrassment rather than an advantage.

But Saussure's assertion of the arbitrariness of the linguistic sign cuts deeper into the relationship between language and extra-linguistic reality. The linguistic sign, he asserts, is a 'double entity', one formed by the association not of a name and a thing but of a *signifier* or 'sound-image' and a *signified* or 'concept'. Neither the signifier nor the signified enjoys an independent existence outside of the *system* of language; concept and sound-image exist as determinate, identifiable entities only within the system and, in this sense, are intra-linguistic. The units, defined by such differences can be grasped only through the network of other units. This crucial point warrants further elaboration.

Consider first the signifier. According to Saussure, this is a set of contrasting features realised in sound opposed to other contrasting features realised in other sounds: it is a bundle of phonic *differences*. This conception of the signifier led the way to the great advances in phonology that were the main and still largely undisputed achievement of structural linguistics. Jakobson and others were decisively influenced by the Saussurean intuition that the protean sound patterns of natural languages were underpinned by a universal structure, composed of a limited number of elements and a finite range of permissible combinations. The understanding that actual words (spoken or written tokens) served as the physical realisation of abstract, contrasting sound-features opened the way to numerous advances in our understanding of phonological relationships between languages and of the way the brain extracts verbal tokens from the acoustic material served up to its ear.

The signified, too, is not a naturally occurring entity but a 'concept' (a term Saussure uses in a special sense) – and one whose boundaries are determined only within the linguistic system by its opposition to other concepts. It is not, however, intra-psychic – a mental entity like a mental image: like the signifier, it is not a *thing* but a *value*; and it has value only within the system where it co-exists with other opposing or different values. The denial of the pre-linguistic reality of the signified is the most revolutionary aspect of Saussure's theory – and the one that has generated the most lavish and exciting misinterpretations. The signified is not a 'thing' 'out there'; nor is it a pre-linguistic psychological entity. The signified is purely relational:

> The conceptual side of value is made up solely of relations and differences with respect to the other terms of language ... differences carry signification ... a segment of language can never in the final analysis be based on anything except its non-coincidence with the rest. *Arbitrary* and *differential* are two correlative qualities.[17]

So verbal meaning is specified not solely by means of an external relation between a sound and an object but also depends on an internal relation between oppositions at the phonetic level and oppositions at the semantic level.

So far so good. Few people would dispute that language is more a system than a word-heap and that its component signs are arbitrary in Saussure's sense. And it is perfectly obvious that the semantic catchment area of individual terms rarely corresponds either to patches of space–time or to 'natural kinds' (or 'types of patches of space–time'). Most people would be prepared to accept that linguistic value, as Saussure meant it, is negative or differential and that it is the differences between linguistic units rather than their positive contents, that are used to carry verbal meanings. But what has all this got to do with the validity or possibility of realistic fiction?

The post-Saussurean denial of reference

To get from Saussurean linguistics to the post-Saussurean case against realism, we need to believe that Saussure demonstrated that reference, in the sense required for realistic fiction, is not possible. Now many critics think this to be the case. Robert Scholes, way back in the era before structuralism was replaced by poststructuralism, for example, asserted quite baldly that structuralist criticism

> has taken the very idea of 'aboutness' away from us. It has taught us that language is tautological, if it is not nonsense, and to the extent that it is about anything it is about itself.[18]

I think we would all agree that, if this really were the case, then there wouldn't be much of a future for the realistic novel. The question to which we must address ourselves, therefore, is whether Saussure's ideas do in fact undermine the common-sense view that language may be used to refer to an extra-linguistic reality – to a reality outside of language; whether, in short, we have to subscribe to Derrida's notorious claim that there is nothing outside of the text.

Let us examine the nature of reference as it would seem to common sense. It may be illustrated diagrammatically:

This model implies that language and reality are two separate realms but that the one – LANGUAGE – can somehow reach out to the other – REALITY. Post-Saussurean theorists believe either that

1. Written or spoken reality is intra-linguistic:

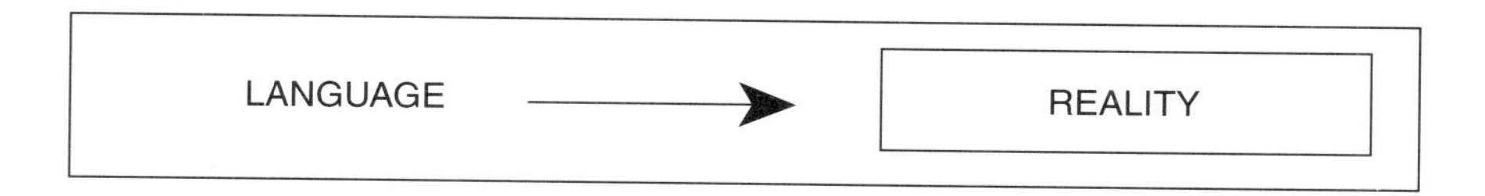

or

2. There is an extra-linguistic reality but language is closed off from it:

If it is further claimed that all structured awareness of the world is mediated through language, then we arrive at the position that reality is available to *us* – to consciousness – only in so far as it is intra-linguistic – a position which may be seen as a linguistic version of idealism.

Weaving in and out of these more explicitly philosophical theses about the relation between language and reality are certain ideas more specifically concerned with the relation between *literature* and reality which have been grouped under the rubric of 'intertextuality'. 'Intertextuality', like 'ideology', is a magic word whose scope can be modified dramatically to meet the polemic needs of the moment. But the central notion is that textual forces are more important than extra-textual ones in determining the form and content of a work of literature; that generic conventions are more influential in this regard than, say, the feelings and experiences or even the biography of an individual writer, or the properties of the reality he or she is seemingly writing about. This is another apparent argument against the claim of realism to be about the external, in this case extra-literary, world.

The more radical accounts of intertextuality see this as an inescapable feature not only of highly stylised literary texts but of all discourse or, indeed, of *any*, however fragmentary, articulation of reality. This opens directly on to the claim that the referent of any text is itself a textual fragment and the further suggestion that society or the world is a boundless text. Edward Said spoke of 'wall-to-wall text' and Julia Kristeva suggested that the notion of intersubjectivity may be replaced by that of intertextuality. Since both reader and writer are texts, the consumption of literature – and indeed living itself – become matters of textual intercourse.

The specific thesis about literature, then, may be expanded to the point where it merges with the more general, and more radical, claims either that reality is intra-linguistic or that language is closed off from extra-linguistic reality. This has been famously advanced by Derrida in the *Grammatology*:

> reading cannot legitimately transcend the text towards something other than it, towards a referent (a reality that is metaphysical, historical, psychobiographical etc.) or towards a signified outside a text whose content ... could have taken place outside of language ... outside of writing-in-general. *There is nothing outside of the text* [there is no outside-text; *il n'y a pas de hors texte*].[19]

Let us now look at these two ideas: that reality is intra-linguistic; and that language is a closed system.

Is reality intra-linguistic?

First, consider the idea *that reality is to a greater or lesser degree intra-linguistic*, that prior to language the world is formless and possibly senseless. This has a long history that antedates post-Saussurean literary theory and, indeed, Saussure himself. But it was Saussure's claim that the signified was intra-linguistic, and that prior to language the mass of thought was shapeless, that led the first generation of structural linguists in the 1930s to search for evidence of this in the apparent relativity of fact to linguistic divisions.

No one, I think, would wish to challenge the obvious truth that language is implicated in the construction of reality. What is at issue, however, is the *extent* to which reality is intra-linguistic and language the agent or medium in virtue of which reality is structured or constituted; more particularly, the radically nominalist assumption, that the traffic is all one way: that language structures reality but reality does not influence the structure, the system of differences, that is the form and content of language.

Now there is a sense in which it is correct to say that reality consists of what gets talked about: to be explicitly there is to be the subject of an assertion. This is certainly true of social reality; and the transformation of an infant into a fully developed human being consists at least in part of a process of induction into an almost infinite set of discourses. Becoming a person, entering language and acquiring a world are intimately connected processes. An historical era transmits itself through time and enters its newest inhabitants largely through words. Much of our world belongs to the realm of knowledge; and this is verbally organised and access to it is verbally mediated. The reality that anyone inhabits is a vast inverted pyramid of discourse poised on a tiny apex of experience.

What of this apex? Is this free of language? Apparently not. Language is not only a means of transmitting general knowledge but also of categorising immediate experience. We make sense of sense-experience by generalising it and at least in part subsuming it under linguistic categories. Though *sensations* may be of particulars, *perception* involves classifying experiences under universal categories, the majority of which will be derived from or enshrined, or stabilised, in language. In so far as it is perceived rather than being merely sensed, an object is at least nascently verbalised. Language, then, not only structures higher order, propositional knowledge of the world but also permeates even our experience of particulars.

So much is incontrovertible. But does this force the conclusion that reality is intra-linguistic to such a degree that 'realistic' novels, novels that seem to be 'about' an extra-linguistic reality, are a kind of fraud? Or that architectural plans are sets of discourse? Or that the law isn't about the rights and wrongs of individuals but about the properties of certain texts? Are we obliged to believe that the manner in which reality is differentiated is an internal affair of language? Does it follow from the intra-linguistic nature of the signified that reality cannot be at once articulated and extra-linguistic? Must we concur with Lacan's claim that 'it is the world of words that creates the world of things'?

The example most often invoked in support of the structuralist contention that factual reality reflects language rather than vice versa is the vocabulary of colour terms. The spectrum of colours is a continuum, but this continuum is invariably spoken of and, it is concluded, often experienced, as if it consisted of distinct and discontinuous segments – the colours. The division of the spectrum into named colours varies from language to language: English, for example, has a range of eleven primary colour terms whereas the Philippine language of Hanunoo makes do with four. This has been taken to imply that the perception and discrimination of even such basic sensory experiences as those of colour are determined by one's native language and it has been invoked in support of the more general hypothesis that reality is experienced in accordance with the manner in which it is linguistically structured.

Over twenty years ago, comparative linguistic studies by Berlin and Kay cast doubt on this relativism by suggesting that there is a universal set of 11 colour categories from which individual languages take different sub-sets. Actually, this evidence, though it may undermine the Sapir–Whorf hypothesis, is an unnecessary weapon in the attack on structuralism since the linguistic relativity argument collapses under its own contradictions. The suspiciously well-worn example of colour terms, far from being a decisive case for structuralism, is a conspicuous own goal.

If it *is* a universal property of the human mind or brain to segment reality in accordance with linguistic categories, how could it be possible that (to use

Jonathan Culler's words in his argument for the structuralist view)[20] 'everyone knows that the spectrum of colours is a continuum'? What do they know it *with*? Not the brain, nor the mind, apparently; for they are supposed to be under the thrall of language. Can it be with ESP? And how, furthermore, are they able to *say* (as Culler does in discussing this example) that it is a *spectrum*? It seems as if the linguistic straitjacket can be taken off at will so that we can inspect it and talk about it and can compare reality as it really is (the continuum of colours) with reality as it is said to be or is conventionally perceived (the segmented spectrum). If we do dissect nature along the lines laid down by our native languages, it would appear that we are not always obliged to do so. Direct experience would seem to be able to circumvent – and so reform – language.

One of the key arguments for extreme linguistic relativism would seem, therefore, to be self-defeating: it depends upon our performing what, *ex hypothesi*, should be impossible, namely seeing the difference between what is said to be the case and what is actually the case. The observation that different races of people dissect the same bit of nature differently according to their different native languages presupposes that that same bit can be repeatedly identified independently of language. As Leech has pointed out,

> even though there is no corresponding concept in one's own language for a concept in another language, one can nevertheless provide a description (if necessary a very detailed description) of its referents.[21]

We often *say* what it is that 'they' or 'we' do not have a word for.

The truth is that the manner in which the world is linguistically differentiated depends upon the needs of the community of language-speakers. The fact that the Esquimaux – to take another suspiciously well-worn example which has anyway recently been disputed[22] – have terms to distinguish ten or more different types of snow whereas Kalahari bushmen do not is a tribute not to the degree to which language shapes our perceptual grids, but to the influence of extra-linguistic experience and need over the development of language – to the fact that snow is a bigger issue inside the Arctic Circle than it is in sub-Saharan Africa. In determining the way in which we speak about reality – and hence describe it – the interaction between linguistic and extra-linguistic factors is two-way. It is not only language that calls the shots.

The earlier post-Saussurean position – held by the structuralists – that articulated reality – or indeed reality itself – is intra-linguistic, is rooted in a confusion between the signified in the precise Saussurean sense on the one hand, and the referent of a sign on the other. Only on the basis of such a confusion could one get from Saussure's observations about the purely relational nature of the signified to the actual business of laying down 'lines along which we dissect reality'. This is a confusion that, as we shall see, has a crucial role in post-Saussurean thought.

Is language a closed system?

One persistent structuralist belief is that, since Saussure demonstrated that language is structured, that it is a system, language must be closed off from anything outside of itself. The more general assumption behind this, that all systems or all structures are in some sense closed, has been expounded with exceptional clarity by Terence Hawkes in his popularising *Structuralism and Semiotics*.[23] Language, he says, is a structure in the Piagetian sense and the transformations of such a structure

> act to maintain and underwrite the intrinsic laws which bring them about, and to 'seal off' the system from reference to other systems. (ibid., pp. 16–17)

In consequence, a language is closed off from reality:

> A language does not construct its formations of words by reference to patterns of 'reality', but on the basis of its own self-sufficient rules. The word 'dog' exists and functions within the structure of the English language without reference to any four-legged barking creature's real existence. The word's behaviour derives from its inherent status as a noun rather than its referent's status as an animal. Structures are characteristically 'closed' in this way. (ibid., p. 17)

Hawkes' use of the word 'behaviour' is revealingly ambiguous. Of course, the word 'dog' does not behave like a real dog. It doesn't for example, make a mess on the pavement. But this merely rules out of court a crude mimetic theory of language; the idea that words stand proxy for objects – and on a one-to-one basis. Such a theory has not been seriously held outside of Swift's Laputa and the Academy of Lagado. Ruling out this theory, however, has a kind of carry-over effect; it seems to suggest that the word's behaviour in another sense – the occurrence of its tokens and the verbal company they keep – is also unrelated to what is happening in the outside world; in particular to the behaviour of dogs.

> A language does not construct its formations of words by reference to patterns of 'reality', but on the basis of its own self-sufficient rules.

Let us consider three formations of words:

The dog   is barking
The dog   is quacking
The dog   is deconstructing mediaeval texts

The first formation is very common, the second very rare, and the third has probably never occurred before. How very like the corresponding situations in life! Is this purely coincidental? Or could it be that formations of words are constructed (*not by language but by language users*) by reference to patterns of reality?

Behind the claim that discourse is closed is a confusion between the system or structure and the specific utterances or writings that utilise that structure – between two things, *langue* and *parole*, that it was part of Saussure's achievement to separate. And this muddle is reflected in the fact that it is unclear whether Hawkes is using the word 'word' to refer to the token or the type. Obviously, no *structure* could determine or influence the use I make of it on a particular occasion and no *type* could legislate over its own occurrences. Of course, the *system* is non-referential, in the same way as the structure of the cerebral cortex is not itself a sensory field.

Consider this claim by Catherine Belsey:

> If discourses articulate concepts through a system of signs which signify by means of their relationship to each other rather than to entities in the world, and if literature is a signifying practice, all it can reflect is the order inscribed in particular discourses, not the nature of the world.[24]

What she says, essentially, is that if language operates in accordance with certain rules and using entities that are intra-linguistic, then all that language can express is those rules and the reality that is referred to is intra-linguistic. The force of this argument depends entirely upon the false assumption that that which is expressed is that in virtue of which expression takes place. Or the meaning of what is meant is that in virtue of which meaning gets specified. This is rather like saying that if I were to point to a dog, that which I point to is not really a dog but a pointee, whose properties reflect the rules governing pointing.

We may accept the validity of the Danish linguist Trier's assertion that the meaning of lexical elements is *specified* by their relatedness to and difference from other elements; but this does not license the conclusion that their meaning in use is constituted by this. As Saussurean linguists – as opposed to post-Saussurean pseudo-linguists – have pointed out, while the words in the lexical field derive their *value* only from their opposition to one another, their *meaning* is fixed only in relation to a particular act of signification. Value and meaning are not the same; the former belongs entirely to the system, whereas the latter does not. The purely notional signifiers and signifieds are such values; they are not meanings. The intra-linguistic nature of the signified does not entail that *meanings* are intra-linguistic.

The confusion between value and meaning leads to the suggestion that meaning is purely differential or structural, or that meanings are sets of differences; that meaning is a matter of binarily opposed forms and not of contents; that the whole of the meaning of 'light' lies in its opposition to 'dark' and vice versa.

In practice, the meaning even of such obviously opposed terms as 'light' and 'dark' is only in part determined by their mutual opposition. They may divide the semantic patch between them through having a common border and give each other semantic shape through their mutual pressure. But this does not imply that their meanings are those borders, are that pressure. It is values, not meanings, that are pure edges or borders, without content. For the opposition between light and dark is based on previously intuited meanings in turn rooted in actual extra-linguistic experience. If they did not already have such meanings, then there would be no grounds for seeing them as being opposed any more than, say, 'light' and 'custard' or 'prime numbers' and 'Terry Eagleton'.

It is a structuralist commonplace that the system allocates meanings to words because 'there is no meaning without structure'. But it is obvious that precisely the opposite is at least as true: that there is no perceptible structure without intuitions of meaning. That this has not been appreciated is due to the fact that the methodological principle of structuralism, the basis of its 'discovery procedures', became thought of as an intrinsic feature of the object under study.

From structuralism to the poststructuralist critique of reference

The post-Saussurean critics, however, go further than suggesting that meaning is the same as value by implying that the referent of a particular utterance or group of utterances is the same as *the signified*. How else would it follow from the intra-linguistic nature of the signified that the referent, too, is intra-linguistic and language is closed off from extra-linguistic reality? To get from Saussure to the poststructuralist attack on referential realism, we have to assent to the following:

Value = Meaning
Meaning = Reference

It would not be appropriate here to dwell on the difference between meaning and reference; this has been the subject of an enormous literature since Frege's famous paper in the 1890s on *Sense and Reference*. Suffice it to say that meaning is general and reference may be particular and that the transition from one to the other often, in daily life, involves the implicit mobilisation of deictic co-ordinates – rooting what we say in the here-and-now defined by one's physical context – which, in ordinary discourse, are indubitably extra-linguistic.[25] There is no way, therefore, other than by extreme carelessness, that one could assimilate reference to meaning, even less reference to (intra-linguistic) value.

In the light of what has been said so far, it might be thought impossible even to imagine how more completely Saussure could be traduced. Nevertheless it is possible. And this is where we come to Jacques Derrida's revision of Saussure and 'the endless chain of signifiers'. Derrida has suggested that language is so enfeebled that not merely is it incapable of reaching a genuine, red-blooded, extra-linguistic referent but that it cannot even reach a signified.

In order to see how he achieves this position, it is necessary to go to his famous essay *Différance* where he tells us that

> as the condition for signification, this principle of difference affects the whole sign, that is both the signified and the signifying aspects.[26]

And he proceeds to conclude from this that the sign as a whole, the sign in use, is also a matter of pure difference.

> the play of differences ... prevents there from being any moment or in any way a simple element that is present in and of itself. (ibid., p. 139)

This helps him to the conclusion that meaning – as it is carried by a particular discourse – is also a matter of difference and that it is an *effect* of language rather than pre-existing, and being expressed in, it. His final position is that the referent is purely negative or differential; from which it follows both that it is intra-linguistic and that it is absent or at least non-present. Since one cannot differentiate between types of nothing – nothing is nothing and that's the end of it – the difference between the signifier and the signified collapses. As Jonathan Culler puts it:

> It follows from the purely differential non-substantial nature of the sign that the difference between the signifier and the signified cannot be one of

> substance and that what we may at one point identify as a signifier is also a signified.[27]

In Derrida's topsy-turvy world, this is taken to mean that language is a matter purely of signifiers that do not touch extra-linguistic reality: discourse is an endless chain of signifiers.

The argument is invalid, as Saussure himself pointed out. What is true of the signifier and the signified is not necessarily true of the sign as used on actual occasions, the verbal token:

> Although both the signifier and the signified are purely differential and negative when considered separately, their combination is a positive fact; it is even the sole type of facts that language has.[28]

This caveat, however, is ignored; or, rather, overridden. Saussure, we are told, simply could not face the implications of his revolutionary insights.

This, at least, is implied in the *Grammatology*. In this abominably written book – bad even by Derrida's standards – he appeals to the writings of the philosopher C.S. Peirce to support his view that discourse consists of an endless chain of signifiers. It is not necessary to go into Peirce's complex and subtle triadic theory of signs or to try to elucidate his concept of an interpretant. For the present purposes, we need only take from Peirce what Derrida has taken. Derrida observes that Peirce has shown that, since signs are interpreted and interpretation generates other signs, one sign leads to another, seemingly *ad infinitum*. Moreover, signs tend to originate out of signs. As Peirce says:

> If a man makes a new symbol, it is by thoughts involving concepts. So it is only out of symbols that a new symbol can grow. Omne symbolum de symbolo.[29]

The chain of signs is thus endless and beginningless.

Should this cause us any concern? Since the chain of signs could be broken only by the emergence of an uninterpretable sign – in short a meaningless object or event – the endlessness of the chain must surely be a reflection of the intelligibility and coherence of the world and the openness of the present to the future and past. It should therefore cause no concern. but Derrida interprets Peirce's sign theory to imply that the chain of *signifiers* – note *linguistic signifiers* not *natural signs* – is endless and thus to constitute evidence for his own quite different view that the signifier never reaches a signified.

To confuse the sign as a whole with the signifier is of course unforgivable – especially in a writer who bases his entire *oeuvre* on the implications of Saussure's ideas. But as we now know this kind of carelessness is routine – nay obligatory – amongst theorrhoeists. Even so, this is clearly too vulnerable to have carried conviction even among those unaccustomed to sustained or consistent thought. In order that the post-Saussurean conflation of sign, signifier and signified should have become a cornerstone of modern literary theory, a further confusing element is needed. This is provided by the introduction of the term 'transcendental signified' in a crucial but very obscure passage in the *Grammatology*.

Since one sign leads to another *ad infinitum*,

> From the moment that there is meaning, there are nothing but signs. *We think only in signs*. Which amounts to ruining the notion of the sign at the very moment when, in Nietzsche, its exigency is recognised in the absoluteness of its right.[30]

One is left only with 'play' – the free play of the signifier –

> the absence of the transcendental signified as the limitlessness of play, that is to say as the destruction of onto-theology and the metaphysics of presence. (ibid., p. 50)

The chain of signs never terminates at anything that is simply present; it always points to the next sign, so that it is reduced to signs of itself – to traces. More generally, we never touch presence unmediated by signs – immediate presence, presence itself. Immediacy is an impossible, elusive dream. Thus Derrida.[31]

It is, of course, untrue that the emergence of 'meaning' in signs results in the evaporation of presence to traces of traces. The paw-marks are a sign to me of a lion. But, over and above their character as signs of a *general* meaning, they have *particular* existence as depressions in the dust. They are that which means 'lion', they carry the meaning 'lion' on this occasion; but that is not all that they are. They continue to exist when they are not meaning and they have features that are quite independent of their meaning, or that are not involved in the specification of the meaning 'lion'. Their location two inches rather than two feet from a particular bush, their being dampened by rain, their being seven in number rather than six, etc. are not features relevant to the discrimination of their general meaning. So, existing and signifying, being present and signifying something that is absent, are not alternative states. On the contrary, being a sign is predicated upon being an existent that is present.

We are no more entitled to infer from the fact that one sign may lead to another *ad infinitum* that the signified is never reached than to conclude from the fact that since every effect is itself a cause and the causal chain is interminable that there are no effects – that the chain of causes never 'arrives at' effects. Of course, there is no 'transcendental effect' which would bring the causal chain to an end; but this does not mean that there are no effects at all. *Omne causa de causis* – all causes themselves arise from causes – does not imply that there are 'no effects/things/events'.

I have taken the example of natural signs, which Derrida's generalisation to all signs justifies. But it is interesting to see how the Derridan argument traduces Saussure in this further way: glossing over the difference between linguistic and natural signs. This is an inevitable consequence of failing to see the force of Saussure's distinction between natural and arbitrary signs or to appreciate the true nature of the signifier and the signified and to see how they differ from signs, meanings and referents. The fact that the signifier does not reach a 'transcendental signified' should be cause for concern only if the signifier were the sign itself and the 'transcendental signified' were a referent. And manifestly they are not.

The 'transcendental signified' is a useful smokescreen. It is used, variously, to mean: the signified; the meaning of a sign; the referent of a chain of signs in use; or the ultimate termination of the chain of signs – in plenitude or closure of meaning, in absolute presence or in God. So those who believe in the reality of the signified and do not believe that language is an endless chain of signifiers apparently also believe in the transcendental signified; and to believe in the transcendental signified is to believe that the chain of signs comes to an end, that a final meaning can be reached and that the place where the latter is reached is identical to that where signs give way to absolute presence – to believe, in other words, in God, Who is both absolute presence and final meaning. Since most contemporary readers are liable to be atheists and since, too, Husserlian 'absolute presence' is so elusive, merging the notion of the signified with that of the *transcendental* signified is certain to discredit it and to give plausibility to the idea that discourse is an endless chain of signified-less signifiers. The concept of the 'transcendental signified' enables Derrida to move almost imperceptibly from the position that no sign opens directly on to a plenitude of meaning/presence, i.e. is under-written by God, to the claim that there is no signified at all, or none, anyway that the linguistic signifier can reach out to.

Conclusion

The conclusion that all signs, not merely linguistic ones, lack signifieds is the inescapable reduction to absurdity – or the self-refutation – of Derrida's 'post-

Saussurean' position rather than its 'daring' conclusion. And the time has come to draw my own, less daring, conclusion – that language *can* refer to an extra-linguistic reality. There is nothing in Saussure's writings to support the post-Saussurean belief that the extra-linguistic referents required by realistic fiction are illusory and that such fiction is therefore a cheap fiddle. Derrida's mishandling of the basic terms in structuralist linguistics underlines the perceptiveness of Saussure's observation in the *Course*:

> No-one disputes the arbitrary nature of the linguistic sign, but it is often easier to discover a truth than to assign to it its proper place.[32]

In short, *post* Saussure does not imply *propter* Saussure. Or don't blame Ferdinand.

More generally, none of the arguments advanced against realism that I have examined withstands close inspection. In particular, the beliefs of the post-Saussureans about the nature of language – based on an elementary misunderstanding of Saussure and a careless misuse of the terms he introduced into linguistic theory – could, if they were true, be neither expressed nor communicated; nor would they have any specific implications for realistic fiction. Once the post-Saussurean critique – and other groundless bases for arguing against realism – are set aside, the many fascinating questions raised by the hopes and achievements of realistic fiction may be fruitfully addressed. Realism is the great unfinished adventure of the novel and one of the most powerful instruments available to us for furthering human consciousness and self-consciousness.

Notes

1. Robert Scholes, *The Fabulators* (New York, 1967), p. 6.
2. Michael Boyd, *The Reflexive Novel: Fiction as Critique* (Toronto: Lewisburg Bucknell University Press, 1983), p. 9.
3. Christopher Nash, *World-Games: The Tradition of Anti-Realist Revolt* (London: Methuen, 1987).
4. Raymond Tallis, *In Defence of Realism* (London: Edward Arnold, 1988; second edition, Lincoln: University of Nebraska Press, 1998).
5. Terry Eagleton, Review of Jonathan Coe's *What a Carve Up!, London Review of Books.*
6. A.D. Nuttall, *A New Mimesis* (London: Methuen, 1983), pp. vii–viii.
7. Jonathan Culler, *Structuralist Poetics* (London: Routledge & Kegan Paul, 1975), p. 193.
8. Gerald Graff, *Literature Against Itself: Literary Ideas in Modern Society* (Chicago: University of Chicago Press, 1979), p. 10.
9. J.G. Merquior, *From Prague to Paris: A Critique of Structuralist and Post-Structuralist Thought* (London: Verso, 1986), p. 260.
10. Catherine Belsey, *Critical Practice* (London: Methuen, 1980).

11. The arguments are set out in detail in *In Defence of Realism*, Part II – 'Althusser and "Ideological" Arguments Against Realism' – pp. 43–90.
12. Pierre Macherey, *A Theory of Literary Production*, translated by Geoffrey Wall (London: Routledge & Kegan Paul, 1978), p. 133.
13. Macherey, ibid., p. 195.
14. Jean-Paul Sartre, *Nausea*, translated by Robert Baldick (London: Penguin, 1965), pp. 61–2. The arguments alluded to here are addressed in greater detail in *In Defence of Realism*, op. cit., Chapter 2, 'As if There Could Possibly be Such Things as True Stories'.
15. Richard Rorty, 'Professionalised Philosophy and Transcendental Culture', *Georgia Review*, 1976, 30: 763–4.
16. Ferdinand de Saussure, *Course in General Linguistics*, translated by Wade Baskin (London: Fontana; Glasgow: Collins, 1974).
17. Saussure, ibid., pp. 117–18.
18. Robert Scholes, 'The Fictional Criticism of the Future', *TriQuarterly*, 34 (Fall, 1975). Paul de Man famously claimed that 'it is not *a priori* certain that literature is a reliable source of information about anything but its own language' ('The Resistance to Theory' in *The Resistance to Theory* (Minneapolis: University of Minnesota Press, 1986), p. 11).
19. Jacques Derrida, *Of Grammatology*, translated by Gayatri Chakravorty Spivak (Baltimore: Johns Hopkins University Press, 1976), p. 158.
20. Culler, op. cit., p. 14.
21. Geoffrey Leech, *Semantics* (Harmondsworth: Penguin Books, 1974), p. 29.
22. See Steven Pinker, *The Language Instinct: The New Science of Language and the Mind* (Harmondsworth: Penguin Books, 1994).
23. Terence Hawkes, *Structuralism and Semiotics* (London: Methuen, 1977), pp. 16–17.
24. Belsey, op. cit., p. 46.
25. I have here skated over what is an absolutely fundamental point. For a more adequate treatment, see my *Enemies of Hope: a Critique of Contemporary Pessimism* (London: Macmillan, 1997), especially Chapter 8, 'The Linguistic Unconscious' and Chapter 10, 'Recovering the Conscious Agent'.
26. Jacques Derrida, 'Différance'. The translation I have used is from *Speech and Phenomena and Other Essays on Husserl's Theory of Signs*, translated by David B. Allison (Evanston, Ill.: Northwestern University Press, 1973), p. 139.
27. Jonathan Culler, *On Deconstruction: Theory and Criticism after Structuralism* (London: Routledge & Kegan Paul, 1983), p. 188.
28. Saussure, op. cit., pp. 120–1.
29. Quoted in Derrida, *Of Grammatology*, op. cit., p. 48.
30. Derrida, ibid., pp. 49–50.
31. Another passage from *Of Grammatology* expresses the key element in Derridean thought, the nub of the Derridean muddle:

    if the signifier is a trace, the signified is a meaning thinkable in principle within the full presence of an intuitive consciousness... . This reference to the meaning of a signified thinkable and possible outside of all signifiers remains dependent upon the onto-theo-teleology that I have just evoked. It is thus the idea of the sign that must be deconstructed through a meditation upon writing which would merge, as it must, with the undoing of onto-theology... . One is necessarily led to this from the moment that the trace affects the totality of the sign in both its faces. That the signified is originarily and essentially (and not only for a finite and created spirit) trace, that it is *always already in the position of*

> *the signifier*, is the apparently innocent proposition within which the metaphysics of the logos, of presence and consciousness, must reflect upon writing as its death and its resource. (ibid., p. 73)

32. Saussure, op. cit., p. 68.

Author's Note

The arguments set out in this chapter have been presented in more detail elsewhere, in particular in two books. *Not Saussure: A Critique of Post-Saussurean Literary Theory* (London: Macmillan, second edition, 1995) examines the defective foundations of structuralism and poststructuralism, in particular their assault on extra-linguistic reference and the notion of truth. *In Defence of Realism* (London: Edward Arnold, 1988; second edition, Lincoln: University of Nebraska Press, 1998) focuses more specifically on the theoretical arguments that have been mobilised against realistic fiction and the inconsistencies in the application of these arguments by critics who purport to subscribe to them.

From: *Theorrhoea and After* (Macmillan, 1999), pp. 3–28, 196–8.

9
The Mirror Stage: A Critical Reflection

The high reputation Lacan's thought still enjoys in Humanities departments, both in Britain and elsewhere, is, so Tallis argues, in this reading from *Not Saussure* (1988, 1995), to be attributed to the fact that those trained in the interpretation of literature (and, one might add, of cinema) have little or no knowledge of scientific method and a less than rudimentary grasp of clinical practice. None the less, it is no good trying to refute Lacan's ideas, since one will seek in vain for the systematic observations on which his conclusions are based. For example, there is little reference to clinical material of his own, which means that his interpretations of his own cases cannot be assessed since insufficient material is given. For Tallis, then, Lacan is a prime example of how not to proceed in diagnostic medicine. He reinforces this view by a detailed account of Lacan's presentation of the so-called mirror stage. This is supposedly the period in infant development between six and eighteen months during which a unified sense of the self, of one's personal identity, is formed and established. Lacan's account of the self has had enormous importance for literary theory; in particular, it has been widely used to justify the notion that referential realism is impossible. The realities of self and world are thought to be composed of fictions that belong solely within the symbolic realm, closed off from any contact with what might lie beyond language. However, as Tallis shows, Lacan's theory assumes that which it sets out to explain. Lacan tries to establish that the child's sense of self is mediated through an identification with his or her own mirror image, and his argument is based on a series of dialectical shifts between self and Other. But, to pull this off, Lacan begins with the assumption he needs to establish, namely, that the child can recognise his or her own image in the mirror. Furthermore, Lacan never explains how, if the self is a fiction, the child is able to refer so many different images of its own body to the same self. These and other objections reveal the fundamental nonsense that Lacan's account succumbs to. It is a nonsense Tallis links to the muddles associated with some versions of genetic epistemology – the process of describing how the child comes to acquire the adult metaphysical world-view. This is to do descriptive psychology and ontology at the same time, and the result is confusion of the sort we find in Lacan.

---

1 Introduction

Over twenty years after the publication of *Écrits*,[1] the volume in which his major papers are collected, Lacan remains highly influential in certain academic circles on this side of the Channel. Catherine Belsey's *Critical Practice*,[2] Terry Eagleton's *Literary Theory*[3] and *The Talking Cure* (a collection of essays edited by Colin MacCabe and written mainly by literary critics)[4] – to name only a few out of many recent articles and books – testify to the high standing Lacan still enjoys as a clinician and a thinker in academic departments of English Literature in the United Kingdom. In contrast, professionals in the fields in which he operated, or touched on, are in the main ignorant of his *oeuvre*. Those few who are aware of his writings for the most part consider them to be unnecessarily obscure, self-indulgent to the point of narcissism and even fraudulent. The consensus seems to be that they can be safely ignored. A similar situation prevails in the United States. In 1984, entire issues of *Poetics* and of *Style*, were devoted to 'psychopoetics', an approach to literary criticism currently almost synonymous with the application of Lacanian psychoanalysis to texts. At the same time, Lacan the clinician and theoretician of the human psyche is neglected by psychologists and psychiatrists.[5] His reputation as a philosopher, developmental psychologist and clinician seems to be highest, therefore, amongst those who are trained in the interpretation of literature but who have little or no knowledge of the scientific method and have only a rudimentary appreciation of the nature of clinical practice.

Any attempt to 'refute' Lacan's idea would be doomed from the outset. One cannot refute fog. Many of the theses most associated with his name are presented with little or no supporting evidence, even though they often look like empirical hypotheses. Such arguments as he offers are often carried along on a stream of what in some circles passes for wit; that 'free play of the signifier' which, to dull sensibilities, seems like a succession of rather academic and feeble puns soliciting a donnish smile. The reader will seek in vain the systematic observations, the measurements, upon which Lacan's conclusions have been based or even indications of the places where such observations are reported or summarised. There is much citation of authorities (Freud, Bühler, Baldwin, and so on) but this is often as imprecisely referenced as name-dropping at an academic cocktail party.

Many of the cases cited in his major papers are taken over from Freud (for example, Wolf Man, Schreber, Rat Man, Anna O.) and the manner in which they are recycled makes it easy to understand why his analyses of them have seemed most convincing to those whose training has been in literary criticism rather than in making and critically evaluating clinical diagnoses. There is little reference to clinical material of his own and, with very few exceptions (such as the report on Aimée, a female psychotic, who was the subject of his doctoral thesis), Lacan's interpretations of his own cases often cannot be assessed because insufficient information is given. If the case histories illustrate anything, it is how not to proceed in diagnostic medicine. The manner in which conclusions are drawn from them is reminiscent of how a first-year medical student, or a hypochondriac, using a few observations to light a gunpowder trail of inference primed with his own preconceptions, might arrive at a wrong diagnosis. The Lacanian *oeuvre* is not unfairly described, therefore, as a huge inverted pyramid of speculation (the word is used deliberately) built upon a tiny apex of fact.

To criticise Lacan on empirical grounds is to play into the hands of his disciples. For Lacan has often indicated his contempt for mere factual truth. Lemaire, in her obsequious and reverential account of the Master's thoughts,[6] refers to the fact that 'some critics have seen fit to use the "factual" insubstantiality' of, say, the mirror stage, as a weapon to 'invalidate it'. She dismisses such pusillanimity as not warranting further attention. 'Factual insubstantiality' does not weigh in assessing the truth of ideas as important as Lacan's; besides, the need to ground hypothesis in observed fact merely symptomatises one's own needs, anxieties and prejudices.

To be fair, Lacan is scarcely unique in exploiting the prestige of the clinic and of scientific diagnostic medicine, while speculating in a manner that patently rejects the rules of clinical inference. This intellectual vice does not distinguish him from other practitioners in a branch of medicine notorious for its therapeutic inefficacy. Jumping to untested and often untestable conclusions, elaborating without independently corroborating the first diagnosis you thought of, submitting to a wild proliferation of unchecked hypotheses (corresponding to the presuppositions with which each patient is approached) – all things an average medical student grows out of after he has made a sufficient number of mistakes – are the stock-in-trade of the psychoanalyst. They cannot therefore be laid at Lacan's door alone and to encounter his writings on the well-trodden battleground between scientists and clinicians on the one hand and those on the other who claim to be scientists and clinicians while at the same time showing little respect for or understanding of the principles of the basic and clinical sciences, would be fruitless.

Instead, I shall examine some of Lacan's central ideas, the arguments he has put forward for them and the use that has been made of these ideas by literary critics and others who think that what Lacan says about human development has profound implications for the philosophy of consciousness, for linguistics, for literary theory and for literature itself. I shall focus particularly on his theory of the mirror stage in infant development as the view has often been expressed that this above all supports his radical nominalism and that it discredits realistic fiction and the realistic view of the self (or subject) and the world.

2 Exposition

(a) Images and the realm of the imaginary

The theory of the mirror stage is regarded as the cornerstone of Lacan's *oeuvre*. It has excited an enormous amount of interest amongst his followers and the essay he devoted to it was written and rewritten over a period of thirteen years. It appears at the head of the English translation of his major papers and its conclusions are alluded to or presupposed in nearly all the papers that follow. The mirror stage, Lacan says, is one of those 'critical moments that mark the history of man's mental genesis' (*Écrits*, p. 17) and it reveals, amongst other things, 'an ontological structure of the human world' (p. 2) and sheds light 'on the formation of the *I*' (p. 1).

From the age of about six months, the child is able to recognise its own image in the mirror. This recognition triggers off a series of gestures

> in which he experiences in play the relation between the movements assumed in the image and the reflected environment, and between this virtual complex and the reality it duplicates – the child's own body, and the persons and, things around him. (p. 1)

According to Lacan, the child takes great pleasure in the correspondence between its own movements and those of its mirror image. The reasons for this pleasure or 'jubilation' go very deep indeed. The mirror phenomenon is to be understood as a moment of *identification* – 'the transformation which takes place in the subject when he assumes an image' (p. 2):

> This jubilant assumption of his specular image by the child at the *infans* stage, still sunk in his motor incapacity and nursling dependence, would seem to exhibit in an exemplary situation the symbolic matrix in which the I is precipitated in a primordial form, before it is objectified in the dialectic of the identification with the other, and before language restores to it, in the universal, its function as a subject.

In other words, the mirror image presents the child with a kind of pre-lingusitic, even pre-social 'I'.

But why should this be an occasion for such rejoicing? Because in perceiving, and subsequently identifying with, his image, the infant 'anticipates on the mental plane the conquest of the functional unity of his own body, which, at that stage, is still incomplete on the plane of voluntary mobility' (p. 18). The mirror stage (which lasts until the child is about eighteen months old)

> manifests the affective dynamism by which the subject originally identifies himself with the visual *Gestalt* of his own body: in relation to the still very profound lack of co-ordination of his own motility, it represents an ideal unity, a salutory *imago*; it is invested with all the original distress resulting from the child's intra-organic and relational discordance during the first six months, when he bears the signs, neurological and humoral, of a physiological natal prematuration. (pp. 18–19)

'Physiological natal prematuration' is an odd phrase but it presumably refers to the infant's immaturity. Being born immature – and hence in a sense prematurely – is uncomfortable; the pleasure afforded the child by its mirror image is due to its anticipating 'in a mirage the maturation of its powers'. As Jacqueline Rose puts it:

> one of the key factors of the mirror stage is that the child is in a state of nursling dependency and relative motor inco-ordination and yet the image returned to the child is fixed and stable, thereby anticipating along the axis of maturation.[7]

Rose illustrates this connection by referring to Lacan's case of a four-year-old whose 'complete motor and linguistic inco-ordination' is attributed to an inability 'to conceptualise its body as total'.

> the rectification of the child's motor inco-ordination during analysis is taken to demonstrate the relation 'between strictly sensorimotor maturation and the subject's functions of imaginary control.'[8]

The logic appears to run as follows: if recovery takes place *during* analysis, then it is *due* to analysis. Analysis is therefore efficacious and the theory behind it must consequently be true. By a similar argument, if I recover from pneumonia after drinking the sacred text of the Koran, the theory that pneumonia is due to possession by evil spirits is upheld. Be that as it may, the claim is that the 'I' or the ego is 'a reflexion of a narcissistic structure grounded on the return of the infant's image to itself in a moment of pseudo-totalisation'.[9] It is this that causes the infant's contemplation of itself in the mirror to be associated with so much pleasure. The infant is jubilant because it *sees* the felt chaos of its existence transformed into the stable image of its physical body.

This image is the basis of the 'Ideal-I' but the latter is 'fictional'. In consequence, while the image 'symbolises the mental permanence of the *I*', at the same time it 'prefigures its alienating destination' (*Écrits*, p. 2). The mirror stage 'establishes a relation between the organism and its reality – or, as they say, between Innewelt and Umwelt' (p. 4). But 'this relation to nature is altered by a certain dehiscence at the heart of the organism, a primordial Discord betrayed by signs of uneasiness and motor inco-ordination of the neonatal months' (p. 4). Since the unified 'I' in the mirror with which the infant identifies is the first of a series of *fictions*, the mirror stage is

> a drama whose internal thrust is precipitated from insufficiency to anticipation – and which manufactures for the subject, caught up in the law of spatial identification, the succession of fantasies that extends from a fragmented body image to a form of its totality ... and lastly the assumption of the armour of an alienating identity which will mark with its rigid structures the subject's entire mental development. (p. 4)

The infant's 'jubilant' identification with the image of his body resolves the uneasiness arising from his premature birth but it does so at a price. The specular 'I' – like all future I's – is founded upon *mis*-recognition. The reified product of a succession of imaginary identifications with the mirror image, it is a fiction even though it is cherished as the stable or would-be stable seat of personal identity. Stability is borrowed and is consequently bought at the cost of self-misrecognition, of identification with something that the infant is not.

> It is in this erotic relationship, in which the human individual fixes upon himself an image that alienates him from himself, that are to be found the energy and the form on which this organisation of the passions that he will call his ego is based. (p. 19)

The subject, as Lemaire says, '*is* his own double more than himself ... consciousness collapses into its double without keeping its distance from it'.[10]

Eventually the price of imaginary identification will be paid. The alienation implicit in the act of referring oneself to something that one is not will become paranoia when the image with which the infant identifies is no longer its own reflection but is another child of the same age; when, at about the age of eighteen months, the mirror stage comes to an end and the specular *I* is deflected into the social *I*. The child will then begin to exhibit 'primordial jealousy' and the phenomenon of 'transitivism'. The jubilant identification of the fragmented and inco-ordinated subject with its totalising mirror image turns sour.

(b) Words

Lacan is a Freudian. Indeed, it is his recurrent boast that he alone has kept faith with the Master's deepest insights. As Malcolm Bowie has said, 'Lacan presents his main task as that of reading Freud well and getting him right.'[11] The mirror stage has therefore to be incorporated into the framework of the orthodox Freudian theory of infant sexuality. The arguments by which this is accomplished are, in those places where they are actually given rather than merely hinted at and the cloud of unintelligible knowingness parts, ingenious in the extreme. The mediator of the processes both by which the infant's specular image gives way to the social 'I' and M. Lacan is united with Herr Freud is, of course, King Oedipus. The Oedipal events mark the transition from a dual, immediate, mirror relationship to a mediate relationship with the other's identification of the self. Successful resolution of the Oedipus complex results in the passage from the imaginary to the symbolic realm, from the world of mirror images to the world of words.

In the mirror stage, the child cannot differentiate himself from the Other with which he identifies himself. Identification with his mirror image will, furthermore, spill over into that of the mother who holds him up to the mirror. This presents no problems until the father appears on the scene. He, of course, disrupts the cosy relationship with the mother and blocks the child's free access to her and certainly prevents his merging with her. The father, in Freudian terms, frustrates the child's wish to become the phallus: the Oedipal conflict begins. Its resolution requires the refashioning of the subject and involves his translocation from the imaginary to the symbolic world; for the Oedipal events are associated with the accession to language. This is explained as follows:

The Father's veto is the child's most fundamental contact with the Law. In order to stand for the Law, the Father must lay it down. Now in human societies, the preferred mode of laying down the Law is speaking it:

> The father is present only through his law, which is speech, and only insofar as his speech is recognised by the mother does it take on the value of the Law. If the position of the father is questioned, the child remains subject to the mother.[12]

In the normal course of events, the Father's speech *is* recognised: padre is padrone. And it is speech – and not, as Freud thought, his role in procreation – which confers his privileged status upon the Father:

> The existence of a symbolic father does not depend upon the recognition of the connexion between coition and childbirth, but upon something corresponding to the function defined by the Name-of-the-Father.[13]

This reinterpretation of the Oedipal moment requires a parallel reinterpretation of the Primal Scene. For Freud, the crucial event was the child's coming upon the parents engaged in coitus, or imagining having done so, and experiencing his access to the mother being literally blocked by the father. For the Lacanian, the child comes upon the parents talking to one another, engaged in verbal rather than carnal intercourse.

The Oedipus complex is resolved in most children. Painful though it is, the child accepts the Law, renouncing its right of exclusive access to the mother and acknowledging the superior and prior claims of the father. The blow is softened by an ingenious strategy in which the child *identifies* with the father and takes him as his model; in other words, he *becomes* his father by introjection of the paternal image. If you can't beat (or displace) them, then you join them; or if you can't join her, become like him who is permitted to do so. The father's phallus is reinstated as the appropriate object of the mother's desire and the child no longer insists on the fantasy that he is the object of his mother's desire. A symbolic castration takes place, the father separating the child from the mother. (In the ill-lit world of the Freudian pre-nursery, being separated from one's mother and being relieved of one's external or internal genitalia are not clearly distinguishable, even if one is a girl.) The reward for submitting to this operation is to receive a name and a place in the family: the child enters into language, society and culture.

The coincidental resolution of the Oedipus complex and accession into language, the trade-off between the primal repression of the desire for the mother and gaining a place in discourse, may still seem a little obscure. In the end, it boils down to a tautology (in so far as it can be understood at all) but this we shall discuss in the next section. For the present, let us note some of the ways in which the connection between Oedipus and language has been interpreted by Lacan's followers. The feeblest argument linking the Father and the Law with the acquisition of language and the transition from the imaginary to the symbolic realm appeals to Freud's observation 'that the admonitions of others are conveyed by speech': when father – or the Father – lays down the law – or the Law – he utters rather than mimes it. One would not expect, however, that a list of regulations, a recitation of the rules of the house, of society, would cut much ice with a child who is presumed to be as yet *infans*, outside of language. A better argument originates from the Lacanian A. de Waelhans, who points out that 'primal repression is the act whereby the subject ... withdraws from the immediacy of the lived experience by giving it a substitute which it is not'. This repression is possible only if the subject has somewhere outside of himself to go to and not be. This place is 'an original signifier of the self which he posits as the negative of his coenaesthesia and which allows him to effect the negation inherent in primal repression'.[14] The child is effaced into language. He has renounced the ambition of being the object of his mother's desire and of having unique access to her; he no longer entertains the fantasy of being the phallus. Instead, he has gained access to the phallus-signifier. Like his father, he *has*, or *has the use of*, the phallus:

> In the quest for the phallus the subject moves from being it to having it. It is here that is inscribed the last *Spaltung* [splitting] by which the subject articulates himself to the Logos. (*Écrits*, p. 289)

The phallus-signifier thus symbolises privation or lack of being:

> The fact that the Phallus is a signifier means that it is in the place of the Other that the subject has access to it. (p. 288)

In entering language, one becomes that which one is not; for language above all provides places where one *can* become what one is not and where, consequently, the primal repression of the desire for the mother can be enacted and the Oedipal conflict resolved. In becoming a speaker, the subject 'crosses himself out'. He suffers the lack of being that necessarily follows from locating one's being where one is not. This is felt more acutely, according to Irigaray, when the child is referred to in the third person. Irigaray's argument has been summarised by MacCabe as follows:

> In the development of the child there is a moment when the infant ... enters language. In the process of entry he/she becomes aware of certain places which he/she can occupy – these are the points of insertion into language. Crucially this involves the learning of pronouns: the realisation that the 'you' with which the child is addressed by the father or mother can be permutated with an 'I' in a situation from which it is excluded – when the parents speak to each other. This realisation is the understanding that the 'you' with which he or she is addressed can be permutated with a 'he' or 'she' and it is through the experience of this empty place that the child enters language. The passage through this empty place is the exclusion necessary to the proper control of language... . It is this which gives language its fearsome quality because the experience of the sign involves a castration at the linguistic level ...
>
> To accede to the world of absence – to the world of the sign where one thing can stand for another – we must wound perpetually, if not destroy, a narcissism which would render the world dependent on our presence... . The name is that which marks the exclusion of the subject from the realm in which he/she is thus constituted.[15]

To enter language is to be decentred; to become a substitutable anyone instead of the centre of the world. The child who has repressed his desire has consented to become a substitutable anyone, a mobile phallus-signifier that will never, except in the symbolic realm, make contact with the object of its desire. A phallus thus cut off from the true or primordial object of its desire is, in the curious linguistics that operate in the pre-nursery darkness, a signifier without a signified. The object of desire has been lost so that it can be conquered only in fantasy by endless expansion along a proliferating chain of signifiers that never touch the ground of the signified. Discourse is, at bottom, the manipulation of the absence of the mother.

Language is the precondition of the process by which the child becomes fully aware of itself as a distinct entity. The linguistic self, the 'I', is a mobile signifier, a fiction even more hollow than the I of the mirror stage. The subject[16] who 'articulates himself in the Logos' (*Écrits*, p. 277) 'undergoes a split in view of being a subject and only insofar as he speaks' (p. 288). This split – which divides the conscious from the unconscious, the latter composed of the material suppressed at the time of the primal repression – allows the subject to become fully constituted. In the mirror stage, the I discovered itself, acquired unity, only by being translocated outside of itself; it *became* through retroactive displacement. In other words, even as far back as the pre-social mirror stage, the Other was involved; its (strictly *her*) presence was at least implicit

> in the gesture with which the child in front of the mirror, turning to the one who is holding it, appeals with its look to the witness who decants, verifying it, the recognition of the image, of the jubilant assumption, where indeed *it already was*.[17]

Nevertheless, the passage from the Imaginary to the Symbolic involves a more profound emptying of the subject and by the very processes through which the social *I* is constituted. The defining image of the mirror stage had a plenitude that is denied to the self constituted through language. For linguistic signs are constituted through differences; they are purely differential, purely relational – in short, negative. So the self as a mobile signifier is even more deficient than the specular *I* of the mirror stage.

Even so, the mediation of the symbolic is essential if the ordering of the world, of things in the world, of the child's life, is to be ensured. Outside of language, there is only the nameless Real – 'the primordial chaos upon which language operates' which is 'radically extrinsic to the procession of signifiers'.[18] Within the realm of the symbolic, on the other hand, there is the unified self and a world of apparently stable objects. Thus

> It is the world of words that creates the world of things – things originally confused in the *hic et nunc* of the all in the process of coming-into-being – by giving its concrete being to their essence, and its ubiquity to what has always been. (*Écrits*, p. 65)

So much for the theory. On the basis of Lacan's ideas, it has been argued that objects and selves are internal to language and that the fundamental presupposition of both literary and philosophical realism – that there is a language-independent reality, is false. Reference outside of language is not possible because everything that one refers to is intra-linguistic; the reality one would wish to describe is composed of fictions that belong inside the symbolic realm. Even the most painstaking *chosisme* does not provide a window upon an extra-linguistic reality, because the *choses* in question have been created by the world of words. Such conclusions would not in fact follow from Lacan's claims about infant development, even if they were true. But before dealing with these conclusions, let us investigate the extent to which the theories themselves stand up to critical examination.

3 Critique

(a) Facts

(1) Infans jubilans

Lacan's theory of the mirror stage is offered as an explanation of an *observation*: the 'jubilation' of an infant confronted with his own mirror image. Anyone who has tried the experiment of holding an infant of the appropriate age up to a mirror, however, will find that its response to confronting its own image is highly variable. It may at first take a great deal of interest in its mirror image as, indeed, it takes an interest in most novel sensibilia. But the novelty soon wears off; and anyone hoping to excite a fourteen-month-old with its mirror image when there is, say, a cat or a moving toy robot in the vicinity, is going to have his work cut out. Even where the child does pay attention, interest is almost as likely to be directed at the frame (especially if it has something, such as a hook that looks as if it could be swallowed, attached to it) as to the image. If the mirror is a small one, the child will often grab it and attempt to bang it up and down in the usual way that tiny children have with delicate objects, as if to torture them into disclosing their name and nature. In any case, attention to the mirror image is usually very transient and is not often associated with elaborate play and the 'series of gestures' that Lacan refers to. If there is elaborate play, it is usually at the instigation of the parent engaging the child in a game of peep-bo. Moreover, the 'startling spectacle of the infant in front of the mirror', in which he 'overcomes, in a flutter of jubilant activity, the obstructions of his support' and fixes an object 'in a slightly leaning forward position' (*Écrits*, pp. 1–2) is by no means specific to the mirror experience: it would as well describe an infant confronted by *any* object of interest – a passing cat, or a rustling sweet paper.

(2) Mothers, fathers and mirrors

The theory assumes that the child is held up to the mirror by its mother. This is essential if the transition from the specular to the social *I* is also to be associated with resolution of the Oedipus complex and accession to the symbolic realm. The complex mechanism outlined above would be hopelessly deranged if the father were the first to hold the child up to the mirror or if, as presumably happens in most households, mother and father were to divide this particular job between them; or if – and again one has no reason to assume this is unusual – siblings, child-minders, aunts and uncles were involved. For the theory requires that mother and child should be glued together at the specular moment when the child identifies with its mirror image – so that the child can suffer subsequent displacement by the father and 'come to realise that he is a third member of the family'.[19] The father has to happen upon a scene where the infant and the mother are united in the infant's fusion or confusion of the mother's image with his own. It is this that triggers the transition from the specular to the social *I*; from the (less hollow) fictional identification with the mirror image to the pure absence of the dispersion of the self into language as an infinitely mobile phallus signifier: 'With the advent of the father, the child is plunged into post-Structuralist anxiety.'[20]

It is extremely awkward both for the child and for the theory, then, if the father is present from the beginning; for the child's imaginary identification with his mirror image would be as likely to spill over into the image of the father as into that of the mother. Indeed, as (according to the theory) the child cannot differentiate himself from the Other with which he identifies himself, nor can he differentiate the components of that other, he would most probably identify with *both* mother and father. Now, except where the father is a sailor, a gaolbird or divorced from the mother, one would expect that both parents, along with anyone who happens to be in the house, would share the task, apparently vital for his metaphysical well-being, of holding the child up to the mirror.

The Oedipal triangle also requires that the child should preferably be male – females can be accommodated only by a scandalous interference with their genitalia – and that he should be an only child, for the second and subsequent children are much more seriously displaced from their mothers by their siblings than by their fathers. But these are difficulties common to all psychoanalytic theories and are not peculiar to Lacan's version of Freud.

(3) The specific immaturity of human infants

Lacan contrasts the 'the triumphant jubilation and playful discovery that characterise, from the sixth month, the child's encounter with his image' with the 'indifference' shown by even the highest animals, such as the chimpanzee (*Écrits*, p. 18).[21] He attributes this difference to the 'specific prematurity of birth in man' and adduces as evidence of this 'the anatomical incompleteness of the pyramidal system and ... the presence of certain humoral residues of the maternal organism' (p. 4). While it is true that a human infant is helpless for longer than, say, a young chimp or a lamb, the helplessness of the child at birth is no greater than that of a kangaroo and its period of total motor incoordination not *proportionally* greater than that of, say, a seal in relation to total lifespan. There is *no* evidence for an *anatomical* incompleteness of the pyramidal tract – all the neurons are present at birth – unless 'anatomical' refers to the *connectivity* of neurons. If that is what is meant, then the argument falls flat on its face, because the immaturity of the perceptual systems is even greater in this respect as the immense amount of research carried out on the visual cortex over the last thirty years has clearly demonstrated.[22] But the interpretation of the significance of the mirror stage depends, as we shall discuss presently, upon the assumption that perception is in some sense ahead of voluntary motor activity. The reference to 'certain humoral residues of the maternal organism' is even less intelligible. Of course the infant carries antibodies which have reached its bloodstream by passive transfer from maternal blood across the placenta. But this adaptive response is hardly a sign of immaturity, is not unique to man and has no relevance to the infant's self-experience, other than protecting it from life-threatening diseases. There is, in short, no evidence to support Lacan's claim (*Écrits*, p. 137) that 'prematuration at birth' is specific to man, as anyone who has observed blind newborn kittens will agree.

(4) The totalising image

The essence of the mirror stage resides in the contrast between the sensed helplessness and incoordination of the infant and the wholeness of the image perceived in the mirror. As Lemaire expresses it 'the Mirror Stage is the advent of coenaesthetic subjectivity preceded by the feeling that one's own body is in pieces. The reflection of the body, then, is salutary in that it is unitary and localised in space and time.'[23] *Is* the reflection of the body that infants receive in the mirror thus unified? Is not the image very often only fragmentary, consisting of part of the body – usually the face plus or minus the neck and shoulders? How often does the child see the whole of its body in the mirror?

When does it see the back of its head as well as its face, its sore bottom and kicking legs at the same time as its arms and chin? Moreover does not the infant frequently catch sight of its image *en passant*, at times other than when it is being held up to the mirror by its mother? Does it not, for example, receive faint impressions of itself in car, shop and home windows? Or glimpses in car mirrors, saucepans and the backs of watches? In short, is not the infant's entire experience of its mirror image both spatially and temporally fragmented and is not the image it is confronted with also highly variable on account of the variability not only of the surfaces upon which his body is reflected but also of the conditions of illumination in which the self-encounter takes place? Nothing could be less likely to ease 'the feeling that one's body is in pieces' than catching casual glimpses of bits of it. Anyone relying on necessarily random encounters with mirrors to provide an infant with 'its totalising image' is going to have a hard time.

The supposed contrast is between the unitary image and the sense of being in a fragmented body arising out of motor incoordination. But surely the sensed helplessness of the child is not constant during the whole period between six and eighteen months. The motor incoordination of a six-month-old is dramatically different from the nimbleness of the eighteen-month-old. Nevertheless, the jubilation is supposed to remain undiminished.

(5) *The impotence of factual evidence*

Psychoanalysts have traditionally been unflustered by facts that seem to contradict their theories. Most facts can be reinterpreted so that they appear to confirm rather than undermine the theory. The lack of evidence for the certain processes described by Freud, for example, provides further evidence for the reality of other processes he described – for the universality and omnipotence of repressive mechanisms, for example – and so apparently increases rather than decreases his credibility. The disagreement his theories provoke is interpreted as active resistance to them and taken to be a sign of the very defence mechanisms postulated by his theories and so further proof of the theories themselves. Lacan himself cites the well-known story of the young lady who reported a very unpleasant dream she had had and asked her analyst whether this didn't cast doubt on the Freudian claim that all dreams enact symbolic wish fulfilment. Her analyst replied that she had had the dream in order to fulfil her wish to disprove Freud's theories.

More generally, the ploy is to point out that the person assessing the validity or otherwise of psychoanalytic ideas is himself their subject and therefore not in a position to be objective. The trouble with this ploy is that it tends to rebound on those who advocate the theories because they, too, are encompassed by them. The argument that we reject Freudian ideas because we are in the grip of precisely the unconscious forces that they describe, invites the counter-argument that Freud himself must have put them forward and his followers now support them for the same reason. A more subtle way of dealing with contrary evidence is to suggest that appealing to factual evidence – or referring disparagingly to the lack of it – is to take the theories too literally: the child does not actually *see* his parents copulating; he only imagines that he has done so. Or, if that does not cut ice, to claim that the primal scene stands for some more fundamental relation to external reality and that stumbling upon the primal scene is not a historic event that took place at a certain moment in the child's life; rather it is a *structure* that represents the unconscious of the society to which he belongs. MacCabe, for example, describes Irigaray's 'linguistic' version of the primal scene (referred to above) as 'a diachronic fable of a synchronic functioning'.[24] Thus reinterpreted, the theory is sealed off from any kind of external assessment.

(b) Arguments

The resistance of Lacan's theories to empirical refutation does not prevent one from evaluating them in accordance with 'internal' criteria, assessing their consistency, explanatory power and plausibility. The theory of the mirror stage falls down on all three counts.

(1) Consistency

According to Lacan, the mirror stage extends from about six to about eighteen months. The moment when the mirror stage comes to an end

> inaugurates, by the identification with the *imago* of the counterpart and the drama of primordial jealousy (so well brought out by the school of Charlotte Buhler in the phenomenon of infantile *transitivism*), the dialectic that will henceforth link the *I* to socially elaborated situations
>
> (*Écrits*, p. 5)

Transitivism is an important concept for Lacan and for his literary and psychoanalytic followers. It is a sign of identification with others and evidence that the Oedipus complex has been, or is being, resolved. It is symptomised by the fact that 'The child who strikes another says that he has been struck; the child who sees another fall, cries' (p. 19). According to Lacan, the period in which transitivism 'dominates the entire dialectic of the child's behaviour in the presence of his similars' comes to an end at about the age of two-and-a-half years. Curiously, however, he says – on the same page – that this period begins *at the age of six months*. Few of us will have been lucky enough to overhear a six-month-old complain of being struck by one of his 'similars'. But that is a mere matter of fact. More serious than its mere factual untruth is that it conflicts with what Lacan himself had said a few pages earlier – which was that transitivism *inaugurated* the *end* of the mirror stage. But six months is the age when, Lacan teaches us, the mirror stage begins. No wonder it is so difficult to observe! In the context of such carelessness, the extreme precision of Lacan's claim that mimicry between children is most 'fruitful' if it takes place between 'children whose age differential is no more than two and a half months' is laughable.

(Incidentally, Lacan is completely at odds with Freud in locating the resolution of the Oedipal phase between eighteen months and two years. For Freud, the *pre*-Oedipal phase did not end until the age of three.)

Another key fact invoked by Lacan in putting forward his theory – linking it with his explanation of why man is unique amongst the animals in having a fully developed language and culture – is that the intensity of the human infant's response to the spectacle of its mirror image is of a different order from that of any other animal. In the paper devoted to the mirror stage, however, Lacan adduces the universal importance *throughout the animal kingdom* of the encounter with the mirror image and its connection with socialisation by giving examples of its influence in other species. A female pigeon will not usually ovulate without seeing another member of the species, nevertheless maturation of the gonads may occur as a result of catching sight of its own image in the mirror. Even more startling, the migratory locust can be changed from a solitary to a gregarious form by being presented with a mirror image 'provided it is animated by movements of a style sufficiently close to that characteristic of the species'. So much for the unique responsiveness of the human infant to its mirror image.

(2) Explanatory power

A theory that is worthy of the name should not assume all that it is intended to explain. Lacan's theory of infant development is enormously ambitious: it encompasses a genetic epistemology. It claims to have something to say about the genesis of the infant's sense of its self, about its perception of Others as in some fundamental sense equal to itself and about its developing the idea of a world of stable objects. Even more ambitiously, it tries to unpick the origin of the adult world picture, claiming that the real world is either primordial chaos or simply unknown to us and that the world of things (and not merely the infant's access to the world of things) is a product of the world of words.

The ontological thesis is readily dealt with. Although it is suggested that the word of differentiated 'reality' is the product of the world of linguistic 'difference', it has already been assumed that, by the time the child accedes to the symbolic realm, certain differentiated things have been interacting. The mirror stage presupposes the existence of at least four separate 'things' – the infant's body, the mother's body, the mirror itself and the mirror image. In addition, a natural standpoint optics is presupposed. How otherwise would the movements of the infant's body be matched by those of the mirror image, and the infant's face be reflected in a consistent fashion in the mirror, so that it could be recognised as being the same on repeated presentation? The pre-linguistic existence of these objects and of the optical relations between them is hardly consistent with Lacan's extreme nominalism or the literary theories that his followers believe his work justifies. If 'the world of words creates the world of things', then we are not entitled to suppose that there are any *things* at all in the pre-linguistic reality of the infant or the extra-linguistic realm of the Real.

Lacan believes he has uncovered the roots of our sense of (unified) self in the infant's identification with his mirror image. To be a self is to enjoy self-recognition mediated through some material or human Other with which one identifies. Since that Other is *not* oneself (by definition), the self or ego thus produced is a fiction. It is a fiction that is cherished, however, because, unlike the unmediated experience of one's bodily being-there, it is stable. The sense of self is consequently founded upon misrecognition. So much for the ontogenesis – and the Lacanian debunking – of the self and the idea of the unified person. How much is this an explanation of the origin of the *I*? How far does it justify the conclusion that the self is a fiction?

It is no kind of explanation at all. In order to construct his theory, Lacan begins with the assumption/observation that the child can recognise his own face in the mirror. This is accepted as a given that requires no further analysis or explanation. He does not wonder what 'own' can mean here where there is no formed conception of the self as being opposed to other human and material objects. Nor does he apparently consider it necessary for his ontology that he should furnish an explanation of the fact that the child can pick out its own image from the background of the person holding it.[25] He also overlooks the extraordinary fact that the child is able to identify its image across a series of transformations and under all sorts of circumstances: he has, in other words, nothing to say about the fundamental puzzle of genetic epistemology, that of object constancy. The self may be a fiction but, if it is, how does the child manage to refer so many different manifestations of its body in the mirror, to the same self? Whence, if the direct, proprioceptive experience of the body is that 'one is in pieces', does the idea arise that 'one is a unity'?

Why should a series of random exposures to quite different images of oneself give rise to a fictitious idea of stability that overrides the more continuous – and, according to Lacan, true – deliverance that one is fragmented? Whence the belief or feeling that the 'salutary' mirror image is 'unitary' and 'localised in space and in time?'

Even less satisfactory is the Lacanian account of the genetic epistemology of objects – an account that is ambiguous as to whether or not it is also an explanation of the nature of those objects or a critique of the concept of an object. According to Rose:

> The identification of an object world is ... grounded in the moment when the child's gaze was alienated from itself as an imaginary object and sent back to it the message of its own subjecthood. Access to the object is possible only through an act of self-identification.[26]

The object seems stable because it is fixated by a stable gaze:

> It is from this fixity, and the images that are thus produced, that the subject is able to postulate objects of permanence and identity in the world.[27]

Primordial chaos is brought to heel by the infant's basilisk stare! Rose notes that

> Janet (quoted by Lacan) compared the formal stagnation of the images just produced to the frozen gestures of actors when a film is halted in mid-projection.[28]

We know, of course, that there is no such thing as a steady gaze: the eye is in constant motion and if the image were held fixed on the same point of the retina, it would fade due to bleaching of visual pigments and accommodation of the nervous system. We have also been told that the infant faced with the image of his own body wriggles around in constant play; so there could be no purely specular basis for the sense of one's own body, or the mother's body, as a stable thing. The theory also assumes a synthesis of visual experiences across time and this presumably could take place only within a self or subject that was united with itself over time. Finally, the suggestion that a stable gaze would freeze the object into a stable thing would be tenable only if the object itself were stable, i.e. already frozen; that the ontogenesis of the object had already been accomplished and the child's gaze was encountering preformed objects. In other words, even if the theory of the mirror stage *were* a contribution towards a genetic epistemology of object perception, it would still have nothing to say about the ontological status of apparently material objects. There is a circularity in Lacan's account of the genesis of the sense of a stable self and of stable objects outside of the self. Objects are endowed with a stable identity through identification of the subject with them. Thinghood, in other words, is displaced selfhood. But selfhood is displaced or introjected thinghood ... all seems to be suspended in the air.

A key assumption of the theory of the mirror stage is that the developing infant is perceptually ahead of its motor capacities: 'The child anticipates on the mental plane the conquest of the functional unity of his own body, which ... is still incomplete on the plane of voluntary motility' (*Écrits*, p. 18). We are expected to believe, in other words, that the child *imagines* a unity he has not *experienced*, to accept that his development is governed by the intuition of a oneness to which there corresponds no experience and for which, according to orthodox Lacanian teaching, there is no basis in reality, in the Real. The sense of self – precisely that which it purports to explain – is therefore *presupposed* in Lacan's account of child development, even though the latter claims to show that the self without external foundation – that it is, in short, a fiction.

And what of Lacan's theory of the accession to the realm of the Symbolic and the acquisition of language? Most of the processes by which this is supposed to take place are predicated upon the prior achievement of a fairly advanced level of linguistic attainment. The child who consents to become a signifier must have suffered the experience of hearing the parents talking about him. He must, that is to say, have understood that the sounds emitted by the parents were *linguistic* and that the conversation referred to *him*. 'There is', the reader will recall MacCabe informing us,

> a moment when the infant (*infans*: unable to speak) enters language: In the process of entry he/she becomes aware of certain places which he/she can occupy – these are the points of insertion into language. Crucially this involves the learning of pronouns: the realization that the 'you' with which the child is addressed by the father or mother can be permutated with an 'I' in a situation from which it is excluded when the parents speak to each other.[29]

An action-packed 'moment'!

There is, of course, no evidence for such a giant intuitive leap on the part of the child. Indeed, all the evidence is to the contrary. Although Humboldt and the earliest linguists thought that personal pronouns constituted the most primitive layer of language, Jakobson has presented convincing arguments (and evidence) that their acquisition represents an advanced stage of linguistic attainment. The personal pronouns are the last elements to be acquired in the child's speech and also the first to be lost in aphasia. Their very nature as 'shifters' – their reference depends upon who is using them – means that they have a double structure, uniting conventional and existential bonds within the same sign; and this makes them extremely complex.[30] Pronouns are an unlikely place for a sensible *infans* to choose to enter language. And if one assumes, as Lacanian theory does assume, that the acquisition of language right up to the appreciation of the shifting reference of pronouns requires no explanation, then one is (yet again) bypassing all that a theory of its apparent scope should take account of and try to explain.

Special pleading may save Lacan's theories from the charge of 'factual insubstantiality' but no amounts of such pleading can save a theory that assumes all the things it pretends to prove or explain.

(3) Inherent plausibility

Enough has been said so far to show that the theory of the mirror stage lacks empirical support and that as Lacan presents it even lacks internal consistency. Moreover, even if it were true and internally coherent, it would explain none of those aspects of infant development that it purports to explain. The final point to be made against the theory is that it is not even inherently plausible.

The basic idea of the mirror stage is that the child's sense of self is decisively influenced – even created – as a result of the accident of its catching sight of itself in a mirror. This immediately raises the question as to what would happen to a child in a household or a country without mirrors?[31] Supposing mirrors were banned on the grounds that they encouraged vanity over one's personal appearance? This is an unlikely state of affairs but the point of this thought experiment is to highlight the absurdity of a theory that proposes an *accidental* basis for a fundamental aspect of human development. One measure of the value, truth or explanatory power of a theory is its ability to predict novel facts or at least to accommodate facts that were not taken into account when the theory was originally formulated. If epistemological maturation and the formation of a world picture were dependent upon catching sight of oneself in the mirror, then the theory would predict that congenitally blind individuals would lack selfhood and be unable to enter language, society or the world at large. There is no evidence whatsoever that this implausible consequence of the theory is borne out in practice.

(c) Style

(1) The dance of the signifier, or Lacan-can

If my exposition of Lacan's theory of the mirror stage has made sense, I may be justly accused of traducing the original which at best consists of tatters of clearness amidst a general fog. Much discussion of Lacan's writing – both by his followers and his opponents – is taken up with his style. This is highly appropriate because without his distinctive manner of writing, it is unlikely that his *oeuvre* – which is divided between original ideas which are either baseless or incoherent and mangled versions of others' ideas – would have made much of a stir. The Lacanian style – now, alas, widely aped by literary theorists (especially those of a psychopoetic persuasion) – has much in common with the verbal chaos of the usual run of psychoanalytic writing. The addiction to jargon, the piling up of abstractions and the citation of authorities without precise reference, the clumsy literary allusions, do not distinguish him from other meta-theoreticians of the human psyche. On top of all these vices, however, he has vices of his own that make him an especially poor writer in a field where competition for the wooden spoon is fierce indeed.

There are many points where, his apologists explain, he tries to mimic the mental operations that he is supposed to be talking about. 'Lacan's own notoriously sybilline style, a language of the unconscious all in itself, is meant to suggest that any attempt to convey a whole, unblemished meaning in speech or script is a pre-Freudian illusion.'[32] Random associations, elliptical allusions, puns, deletion of the steps in arguments, and so on all contribute to the opacity of his publications. Word play is especially prominent and many arguments are carried forward through a series of puns on the grounds that the 'free play of the signifier' will show the reader what the unconscious really is. Malcolm Bowie, a writer sympathetic to Lacan, states that

> A complete account of the characteristic features, syntactic and other, of Lacan's style would include: the ambiguous *que*, disturbances of conventional word order, literal and metaphorical senses interwoven, periphrasis, ellipsis, leading notions alluded to rather than declared, abstractions personified, persons becoming abstractions, widely different words becoming synonyms, synonyms being given widely different meanings... . All this keeps the signified as a palely fluttering presence behind the rampaging signifier.[33]

To attack this style would be to play into the hands of the Lacanians, by betraying one's inability to handle the anxiety aroused by the suspension of definitive meaning, the permanent deferment of closure of sense. Any such attack would anyway be superfluous, since it would be difficult to formulate a more telling criticism than the inadvertent critique assembled by the contradictory claims of the apologists of his style: *qui excuse, accuse*.

> As contradiction is inherent in language, and as all language thereby becomes, in some sense, self-critical, no external tests are necessary. And to fail a test is, in any case, also to pass it.[34]

> Truth which seeks to remove itself from the contradictory processes of language becomes falsehood there and then.[35]

> Lacan is the originator of a coherent and continuing tradition of scientific enquiry.[36]

> With his very first words, Lacan states his trenchant opposition to the fundamental proposition defended by his follower Laplanche ... [who goes] ... directly against the very point on which his own statements leave *absolutely no possible doubt*, namely that, on the contrary, language is the condition of the unconscious.[37] (my italics)

> Thus, if one thinks particularly of the Lacanian theory of the relationship the subject has with spoken discourse ... one is led to recognise in it an astonishingly lucid philosophy of man. Thanks to the efforts of the Lacanian school of psychoanalysis, we can now understand how the unconscious is formed at the beginning of life, what it is composed of, and what its precise modes of arrangement and functioning are... . I would be happy to be recognized as possessing the simple virtue of having proposed reasonable and clear explanations [of Lacan's writings] which will in future allow others to go further.[38]

So much for his apologists who, in defending Lacan's right to be obscure and self-contradictory, end up by contradicting themselves. Charles Larmore offers a more plausible explanation of Lacan's style (in so far as the style is deliberate rather than reflecting an intellect helplessly caught up in an interdisciplinary muddle): 'It is difficult to avoid the impression that his stylistic mannerisms are also aimed at covering over difficult theoretical problems by making it hard to pin down just what it is he is saying.'[39]

(2) Terminology: the slippery phallus

Larmore's criticism of Lacan's slippery style seems far too restrained when we come to consider the manner in which he uses key terms. In Lacan's writings – and that of his followers – it is true to say that anything can be made to mean anything.

Take, for instance, the phallus. In classical Freudian teaching, the phallus is the part of the anatomy that is threatened during the Oedipal stage. The child fears castration as a punishment for being its father's rival for the mother's love. In his almost impenetrable paper 'The signification of the phallus', Lacan 're-reads' Freud:

> the phallus is not a phantasy, if by that we mean an imaginary effect. Nor is it as such an object (part-, internal, good, bad etc.) in the sense that this term tends to accentuate the reality pertaining in a relation. It is even less the organ, penis or clitoris that it symbolizes.
>
> (*Écrits*, p. 285)

What, then, is this phallus, which seems to have taken leave of the infant's body painlessly, and yet without anaesthetic (unless it be the narcotic effect of Lacan's prose style)? The phallus 'is a signifier'. It is not any old signifier – like 'cat' or 'custard'. It is a *privileged* signifier 'intended to designate as a whole the effects of the signified' (p. 285). More specifically, the phallus is 'the privileged signifies of that mark in which the role of the logos is joined with the advent of desire' (p. 287). It is a signifier, in other words, that signifier Lacan's theories about the relationship between primal repression and the accession to language or the Symbolic! We now know that nappy changes may uncover a marvellous little sign that contains, as it were on microfiche, the very essence of the *Écrits*!

The suspicion arises that Lacan's redefinition of the phallus (in the course of which it acquires and loses a capitalised initial letter, doubtless symbolising its alternation between the erect and flaccid state) makes his theories entirely circular. This is amply confirmed by one of his most admiring commentators who has this to say about the Phallus (which is also here The-Name-of-the-Father): 'The exact nature of this "Name-of-the-Father" or of the "Phallus" remains obscure, but can be thought of as corresponding for the child to his confused and varied intimate experiences which go to make up Freudian thought.'[40] Perhaps it is the amount of 'dissemination' ('a linguistic or textual productivity which escapes the domination of or determination by concepts'[41]) taking place that makes the phallus such a slippery customer to get hold of. No wonder, anyway, that 'Lacan speaks with approval of Humpty-Dumpty as "the master of the signifier".'[42] As Bowie says, 'he proves himself a worthy heir of Lewis Carroll's aggressive talking egg'.

A similar serious inconsistency in terminology is to be found in his commentators. As we noted earlier, Lacan seems to use the terms 'subject' and 'ego' or 'I' interchangeably. And yet the distinction between the two is considered to be one of the great achievements of Lacanian thought. Bowie, for example, points out that, for Lacan

> [w]hereas the ego, first glimpsed at the mirror stage, is the reified product of successive imaginary identifications ... the subject is no *thing* at all and can be grasped only as a set of tensions, or mutations, or dialectical upheavals within a continuous, future-directed process.[43]

And, Larmore writes, 'Lacan's important insight has been that theories of the constitutive subject fail through not having distinguished between subject and ego.'[44] Lacan himself, however, speaks of the subject 'being a subject only insofar as he speaks' (*Écrits*, p. 269). The subject then would appear to exist on the far side of the entry into language rather than being merely that which is *behind* the successive identifications that give rise to the ego. The Lacanian subject, in other words, seems to be unable to decide whether it is the shaping spirit – or, rather the shaping emptiness, like Sartre's *pour-soi* – behind the imaginary or symbolic identifications; or whether, like the *I*, it is a product of those identifications. Whether, in short, it is *constituting* or, like the ego, merely *constituted*. Althusser, of course, assimilated both conceptions of the subject to the political subject and has been criticised by Lacanians for that reason.

4 Further reflections

The discussion in the preceding section may go some way towards explaining why in the United Kingdom and elsewhere, Lacan's standing as a genetic epistemologist and clinician is higher in departments of English and French Literature than amongst philosophers, whose tastes are for more coherent argument, psychologists acquainted with the scientific method and medical practitioners aware of the pitfalls of clinical diagnosis. Some of his ideas – such as, for example, that the infant is comforted by the spectacle of his wholeness in the mirror – have a temporary intuitive appeal and the training of literary critics consists for the most part of learning how to articulate intuitions. That training is less directed towards acquiring proficiency in weighing the competing claims of rival theories, collecting empirical evidence or assessing the extent to which available or offered data support one theory rather than another. Lacan's major metaphysical conclusions seem often to be taken over on trust as *results* by critics who may be unable to follow the steps by which they were derived or to appreciate the absence of such steps. It is of course a good deal easier to take exciting ideas 'on board', as part of one's 'intellectual equipment', than it is to make a responsible evaluation of them.

As a contribution to the theory of child development, Lacan's *oeuvre* has one outstanding virtue: it is in tune with the helplessness and pathos of infancy, with its *difference* from the adult world, with the imperatives of need and desire that drive the little *hommelette* to seek a shape for itself and the urgency with which it tries to find order in its world and the catastrophe of madness that ensues if this fails. The very implausibility of Lacan's theories sharpens one's sense of the inexplicable miracle of infant development. But this single virtue is cancelled out by the many vices I have outlined in this chapter. I should like to end with some general observations: (a) on the character of Lacan's theorising; (b) on the relevance or otherwise his theories may have to realism in fiction; and (c) on what they teach us, by their bad example, about the requirements for any account of child development that has pretensions to being a genetic epistemology.

(a) The character of Lacan's theorising

It is frequently unclear whether Lacan is describing, explaining or hypothesising. Consider his account of the stages of self-recognition in the mirror.[45] In the first stage, the infant confuses his reflection and reality: he tries to seize hold of the reflection or find it behind the mirror. At the same time he confuses it with the image of the adult holding him. In the second stage 'he acquires the notion of the image and understands that the reflection is not a real being'. In the third, and final, stage, he realises that the image is his *own* and manifests intense joy.

At first this seems like an intelligible narrative of events based upon observation or the laying bare of a mechanism. It soon becomes apparent that many of the 'observations' are not observations at all but hypotheses; or at least fairly shaky interpretations of what may or may not have been observations in the first place. We are offered something that looks like a 'descriptive explanation'. It is in fact no such thing: it is neither a description nor an explanation but a chain of conjectures presented as pseudo-description. We are told that the child learns: (i) to distinguish between reflection and reality; (ii) to dissociate its own image from that of the adult; and (iii) to identify the appropriate image as being its own. The reader will consult Lacan's writings in vain for an empirical description and even less for an explanation of these fundamental processes. But without an account of *how* the child is able to distinguish between the real and the non-real or between itself and others, the sequence of events outlined above does not amount to an *explanation* of anything. It bypasses the very mysteries it purports to confront. But if it is not an explanation what is it? It is certainly not a set of empirical observations – we are not told of the frequency with which the events referred to have been observed to take place or the conditions under which the observations were made. Lacan's version of the evolution of the mirror stage, in other words, is a patchy rational (or quasi-rational, or semi-rational) reconstruction, supported by a dubious periodisation, that survives precisely by being ambiguous as to whether or not it is a description, an explanation or a series of hypotheses.

(b) Linguistic and literary implications

It has often been thought that Lacan's 'discoveries' about the genesis of the self and the acquisition of language have profound implications for our interpretation of the relationship between language and reality and of the nature of the self and that they undermine, on both counts, the pretension of realistic fiction to give an account of how things 'extra-linguistically' are.

According to Lacan, the sense of self is based upon identification with something that is not the self: in the mirror stage there is an imaginary identification with the mirror image; after accession to language a symbolic identification with the father results in a self that is a 'mobile signifier'. In either case, the self is a 'fiction'. Access to objects, moreover, requires identification with them; so, by the same token, things, too, are fictions: they belong to the realm of the Symbolic. The Symbolic realm is composed of signifiers without signifieds since the true signified, the mother as object of desire, has been foresworn, under the threat of castration, in the resolution of the Oedipus complex. Since signifiers cannot exist outside of the linguistic system, everything relating to the Symbolic realm must be internal to language. The self and its world is intra-linguistic: 'It is the world of words that creates the world of things. ... It is in the world of meaning of a particular language in which the world of things will come to be arranged.'

There is, as we have already noted, not a shred of evidence that the acquisition of language (significantly referred to as 'accession' to the symbolic, as if language were something the child could pick up all at once, or 'entry' into language, as if it were something he could just walk into) is linked in this way to the resolution of the Oedipus complex. Indeed, Freudian theory is against any such link, in so far as the resolution of the Oedipal conflict is supposed to take place between the ages of three and six years, whereas the entry into the symbolic realm apparently occurs at the end of the mirror stage which, we have been told, is at about eighteen months. Let us suppose, however, that Lacan's account of things were true. Would it support the linguistic and literary conclusions that have been drawn from it – that language cannot refer outside of itself and that realism in fiction is a sham? Not at all. For if object perception and the sense of self are based in the first instance upon imaginary identifications of the subject with that which is not itself, then the entirety of human consciousness and experience must be founded upon such fictions. The pre-linguistic world of the infant confronting its mirror image must be as fictitious as the post-linguistic one. If realism is impossible because *all* discourses are founded upon misrecognition, then, by the same token, so is all consciousness. Realistic fiction is no more imprisoned inside an illusion than any other discourse or indeed consciousness; if it is thus imprisoned, the illusion is one to which there is no alternative and the prison one which has no outside. A specifically Lacanian theory of language and, more particularly, a specifically Lacanian case against realism is not upheld. In short, if Lacan's theories were true and they did have the implications his literary followers seem to believe they have, the implications would only be those of any idealistic philosophy which casts doubt on our ability to have access to a 'real' world outside of consciousness.

(c) Genetic epistemology and ontology

A further problem relates to *levels* of argument and the validity of drawing ontological conclusions from developmental observations. Lacan's theory of the mirror stage and beyond is immensely ambitious. It purports to explain how the developing infant comes to construct a world of things and a thing-like self as the moving centre of that world. With his emphasis on desire (desire for the Other, desire to be unified, and so on) and on the role of arbitrary signs (in the Symbolic realm), he is presenting an alternative genetic epistemology to those advanced by the cognitivists (who emphasise the interaction between perception, motor activity and innate mental structures in the acquisition of the adult world-picture) and those of associationist or learning theorists (who emphasise non-arbitrary signs and a world picture whose coherence simply reflects the spatio-temporal coherence of the world outside the organism accessed through direct experience and extended through 'stimulus generalisation'). (Although desire in Lacan, rather as in Sartre, is perhaps too self-transparently and continuously metaphysical, lacking in specific, even erotic, detail.) As a contribution to genetic epistemology, Lacan's theories are unsatisfactory for a variety of reasons of which their lack of empirical basis, their internal inconsistency and their incompleteness are foremost. But there are additional grounds for concern.

These further problems cannot be laid solely at Lacan's door but are inherent in the project of genetic epistemology, of describing how the child acquires the adult *metaphysical* world picture. We have to consider our own attitude towards the *end-point* of intellectual development; to examine whether, when we describe how the child comes to see the world as we see it, we imagine we are explaining how he came to have access to the 'truth' about the world or whether we think we are discovering the aetiology of an *illusion* he shares with us. Our view about the mind-independent reality of material objects, say, may determine our whole strategy in investigating or thinking about the acquisition of object constancy. The very nature of our question will be influenced by whether or not we think of objects as genuinely out there for perception to gain access to or whether they are artefacts of the perceiving subject, constructs out of sense data. It is important that we make the kind of question we are asking quite clear; otherwise we are in danger of conflating two tasks – that of seeing how the child acquires our world picture and that of *evaluating* that world picture – and hence of wobbling between descriptive genetic epistemology and critical epistemology, between ontogenetic psychology and ontology. If we are unhappy with the received world-picture, we may find ourselves writing a premature 'teratology' of adult consciousness, a critique of the adult world picture based upon a few conjectures about its genesis in developing individuals. At any rate, we may not be aware of the extent to which our account of the 'metaphysical development' of infants is *tendentious* until we clarify our attitude towards the destination of this process. Only when we have done so will we be able to separate ontogenetic psychology from ontology. For we cannot do developmental psychology *and* ontology at the same time: to try to do so would be rather like using a certain method of measurement to test a particular hypothesis while at the same time using the measurements to assess the validity of the test. The fundamental problems of Lacanian theory are symptomatised in his claim that the mirror stage is both 'one of those critical moments in man's mental genesis' (*Écrits*, p. 17) *and* that it reveals 'an ontological structure of the human world' (p. 2).

Separating psychological ontogenesis from an evaluative or even revisionary ontology may not be easy. To fail to do so, however, is to succumb to 'the genetic fallacy' that Margaret Boden has defined succinctly as 'thinking that one can justify some belief (or impugn its validity) simply by detailing its history'.[46] Hamlyn has argued that 'philosophical questions about the nature of a certain form of understanding and about its conditions and criteria are utterly divorced and distinct from psychological questions about the conditions under which such understanding develops in individuals'.[47] This is, of course, too extreme, but Hamlyn's further assertion that 'a theory that rests upon both empirical and philosophical considerations must have a degree of incoherence', though directed against Piaget's genetic epistemology, puts a finger upon what is most awry with Lacan's speculations.[48]

Whether or not the genetic fallacy is a fallacy, one should be cautious – as Lacan and the Lacanians have, conspicuously, *not* been cautious – in using conjectural genetic epistemology as a critique of ontology. Once one judges the adult view of 'what kinds of things there are' in the light of psychological ontogenesis, then scepticism is a foregone conclusion. The very process of proposing *mechanisms* by which the developing infant comes, say, to form an idea of a self or acquires the belief that there are mind-independent objects must inevitably cast the validity of those entities into question. For the mechanisms by which the child acquires adult concepts and gains access to the objects and structures of the adult world can never seem less questionable than the grounds for adult belief in them are shaky. There is as yet no philosophical proof of the existence of mind-independent objects; so the infant's grounds for inferring their existence will fall short of absolute proof. If, as Bradley said, metaphysics is 'the finding of bad reasons for what we believe upon instinct', then genetic epistemology must seem like the art of unmasking the child's even shakier reasons for believing what we believe; or reinterpreting those reasons as mere mechanisms or structures within a developing organism, validated only by some unexplained survival value.

By so signally failing to confront the problems implicit in genetic epistemology, Lacan does us the unwitting service – perhaps the only one performed by his *oeuvre* – of emphasising the importance of doing so. Only after these problems have been faced are we in a position to approach infant development with the rigour appropriate to the great intellectual challenge it represents. The challenge – almost as great as that of epistemology itself – is that of uncovering the mechanisms whereby the human infant becomes free of mechanism – or is able at least to rise above it, in part to control it and in part to know it. Of establishing, in short, how it is that an organism comes to live a life that it seems in part to choose rather than merely live. Despite the claims usually originating from academic departments of English and French literature that the Master has 'suggested ways in which intellectual rigour might be possible in branches of psychology where vagueness and guesswork have reigned until now',[49] the Lacanian muddle contributes nothing, apart from its singularly intense vision of the *difference* of infancy, to meeting that great challenge.

Notes

1. Jacques Lacan, *Écrits*, selected and trans. Alan Sheridan (London: Tavistock, 1977). The translations are Sheridan's.
2. Catherine Belsey, *Critical Practice* (London: Methuen, 1980).
3. Terry Eagleton, *Literary Theory* (Oxford: Basil Blackwell, 1983).
4. Colin MacCabe (ed.), *The Talking Cure* (London: Macmillan, 1981).
5. Ellie Ragland-Sullivan, 'The Magnetism between Reader and Text: Prolegomena to a Lacanian Poetics', *Poetics* (December 1984) pp. 381–406.
6. Anika Lemaire, *Jacques Lacan*, trans. David Macey (London: Routledge & Kegan Paul, 1977).
7. Jacqueline Rose, in MacCabe, *The Talking Cure*, p. 137.
8. Ibid., p. 136.
9. Ibid.
10. Lemaire, *Jacques Lacan*, p. 81.
11. Malcolm Bowie 'Jacques Lacan', in J. Sturrock (ed.), *Structuralism and Since* (Oxford University Press, 1979).
12. Lacan, 'Les formations de l'inconscient', *Bulletin de Psychologie* (1956–7); quoted in Lemaire, *Jacques Lacan*, p. 83.
13. Ibid.
14. Lemaire, *Jacques Lacan*, p. 86.
15. MacCabe, *The Talking Cure*, pp. 194–6.
16. This is discussed in more detail in Section 3(b).
17. Lacan, quoted in MacCabe, *The Talking Cure*, p. 149.
18. Sturrock, *Structuralism and Since*, p. 133.
19. Lemaire, *Jacques Lacan*, p. 180.
20. Eagleton, *Literary Theory*, p. 108.
21. Lacan is, of course, wrong about chimpanzees. They are also fascinated by their mirror images. A recent book on Lacan (Bice Benvenuto and Roger Kennedy, *The Works of Jacques Lacan* (London: Free Association Books, 1986)) quotes Köhler's account of the behaviour of chimpanzees presented with a mirror.

    They concentrated all their interest on the image; this interest did not decrease ... but remained so strong that playing with the reflecting surfaces became one of the most popular and permanent of their 'fashions'.

(W. Köhler *The Mentality of Apes*, trans. E. Winter (Harmondsworth: Penguin, 1957); quoted in Benvenuto and Kennedy, p. 53)

Curiously, Benvenuto and Kennedy find this passage from Köhler *illustrative* of Lacan's point about the mirror stage, rather than contradicting it. They do add this, however:

> It might be that the chimpanzee does not recognise what he sees as his own image, unlike the child, and this is what distinguishes the human as subject from the animal who merely remains fascinated by reflections. (p. 53)

But this is, of course, mere conjecture.

22. Including, of course, the Nobel Prize winning work of Hubel and Wiesel and the elegant studies of Colin Blakemore.
23. Lemaire, *Jacques Lacan*, p. 81.
24. MacCabe, *The Talking Cure*, p. 193.
25. For a full philosophical discussion of the mysterious process by which one identifies oneself – in a mirror and elsewhere – see P.F. Strawson, *Individuals* (London: Methuen, 1959). The world picture he deduces from self-identification is precisely the opposite of Lacan's – 'the world of words creates the world of things' – as are the rigour and honesty with which he conducts his argument. See especially chs 1.6 and 3.
26. Rose, in MacCabe, *The Talking Cure*, p. 138.
27. Ibid., p. 137.
28. Ibid., p. 160.
29. MacCabe, ibid., p. 193.
30. R. Jakobson, *Shifters, Verbal Categories and the Russian Verb* (Cambridge, Mass.: Harvard University Press, 1957).
31. This possibility is considered by Benvenuto and Kennedy in *The Works of Jacques Lacan*:

> Of course, an infant may never actually see a real mirror image reflecting himself. In this case he may not have an image of himself which is distinct from the mother's gaze. (p. 54)

Curiously, this is not regarded as a stumbling block for the theory. They merely go on to say that:

> Lacan's mirror stage refers to a particular moment of recognition and jubilation, when the infant is moving away from the simple reflection of the mother's gaze.

Whether this is meant to imply that the mirror stage is in truth a metaphor, or that one can have a mirror stage without mirrors, is unclear.

32. Eagleton, *Literary Theory*, p. 108.
33. Sturrock, *Structuralism and Since*, p. 145.
34. Ibid., p. 149.
35. Ibid., p. 146.
36. Ibid., p. 150.
37. Lemaire, *Jacques Lacan*, p. 249.
38. Ibid., pp. 247–8.
39. Charles Larmore, in MacCabe, *The Talking Cure*, p. 120.

40. Lemaire, *Jacques Lacan*, p. 88.
41. Sturrock, *Structuralism and Since*, p. 160.
42. Ibid., p. 144.
43. Ibid., p. 131.
44. Larmore, in MacCabe, *The Talking Cure*, p. 126.
45. Summarised in Lemaire, *Jacques Lacan*, p. 177.
46. Margaret Boden, *Piaget* (London: Fontana, 1977) p. 96.
47. Ibid., p. 97.
48. It is interesting to compare the genetic epistemology of Piaget and Lacan. Scientifically and stylistically, they are, of course, worlds apart. But their approaches differ in other significant respects. The Lacanian infant seems insufficiently cognitive: the world is the internal accusative of its desires; it encounters not objects but 'the Other'. The Piagetian infant on the other hand seems excessively 'cognitive', operating with no motivation other than a rather abstract curiosity that is divorced from immediate need.
49. Sturrock, *Structuralism and Since*, p. 150.

From: *Not Saussure* (Macmillan, 1988, 1995), pp. 131–63, 260–2.

10
The Shrink from Hell

This is a review of Elizabeth Roudinesco's *Jacques Lacan & Co.: A History of Psychoanalysis in France*, 1925–1985, translated by Jeffrey Mehlman and published in London by Free Associations Books in 1990. The translation is that of the second and final volume of Roudinesco's history of French psychoanalysis, which was published by Editions du Seuil in 1986, under the title *La Bataille de cent ans: histoire de la psychanalyse en France*, 2. Tallis's review appeared as 'The Shrink from Hell' in *The Times Higher Education Supplement*, 31 October 1997, p. 20.

Future historians trying to account for the institutionalised fraud that goes under the name of 'Theory' will surely accord a central place to the influence of the French psychoanalyst Jacques Lacan. He is one of the fattest spiders at the heart of the web of muddled not-quite-thinkable-thoughts and evidence-free assertions of limitless scope which practitioners of theorrhoea have woven into their version of the humanities. Much of the dogma central to contemporary Theory came from him: that the signifier dominates over the signified; that the world of words creates the world of things; that the 'I' is a fiction based upon an Oedipalised negotiation of the transition from mirror to symbolic stages; and so on. The English translation of this biography by one of his disciples is therefore an event of the first importance. It is a harrowing read, but no one who inflicts on students Lacanian readings of literature, of feminism, of the self, of child development, of society, or of life, should be spared the experience.

Lacan was born in 1901 into a wealthy middle-class family and trained as a doctor. He was attracted first to neurology but soon abandoned this because the patients' troubles were too 'routine', as his biographer (who clearly sympathises with his inhumanity) explains. If Elizabeth Roudinesco's account is accurate, he must have made a hash of his first case presentation to the Société Neurologique: his patient, she says, supposedly had 'pseudobulbar disorders of the spinal cord' – a neurological impossibility. (The innocence with which Roudinesco reports all kinds of clinical cock-ups makes this book a particularly disturbing read for a medic.) Abandoning neurology was obviously a wise career move. Unfortunately, though he lacked all the qualities necessary to make a half-way decent doctor (e.g. kindness, common sense, humility, clinical acumen and solid knowledge), Lacan did not abandon medicine altogether, only its scientific basis. He chose to be a psychoanalyst where, instead of elucidating diagnoses, he could impose them.

He fastened on Marguerite Pantaine, a tragically deluded woman who had attempted to kill a well-known actress. For a year, he and Marguerite were, according to Roudinesco, 'inseparable'. (She had no choice, being in detention.) The elaborate story he concocted about her became the basis of an entire theory of the sick soul and formed his doctoral thesis. In the great tradition of psychoanalysis, 'he listened', Roudinesco says, 'to no truths other than those which confirmed his own hypotheses'. More precisely, the truth was that which confirmed his hypothesis: into her case, 'he projected not only his own theories on madness in women but also his own fantasies and family obsessions'. For this soul-rape Lacan was awarded his doctorate and his reputation was made. To the end of her days, Marguerite remained bitterly resentful of the use he had made of her. With good reason: Lacan's crackpot theories, partly expropriated from Salvador Dali, probably prolonged her incarceration. To add insult to injury, he 'borrowed' all her writings and photographs and refused to give any of them back.

Lacan published few further cases of his own. Instead, he recycled some of Freud's well-known cases, in pursuit of his avowed aim of restoring the truth of Freud's ideas which he believed had been traduced by Freudians. Unfettered by data, he was free to soar and to promulgate those large, untestable and obscure ideas – they were too difficult even for Melanie Klein to understand – that made him into an international superstar and which were cherished by his followers and are foundational for theorrhoeists. His doctrines – a magpie muddle of often unacknowledged expropriations from writers whose disciplines were alien to him, cast in borrowed jargon and opaque neologisms – were Rorschach ink-blots into which anything could be read. Lacan's ideas were insulated against critical evaluation by his writing style, in which, according to Roudinesco, 'a dialectic between presence and absence alternated with a logic of space and motion'.

The most powerful support for his doctrines, however, was the aura which surrounded him. Lacan was a handsome dandy and, like many physically attractive psychopaths, he was able to command unconditional love. He exploited this to the limit in support of his boundless appetite for wealth, fame and sex. He kept his disciples, who 'worshipped him like a god and treated his teachings like a holy writ', in constant fear of excommunication: the absence of Lacan was an ontological catastrophe equal to the absence of

God. Anyone who fell under the spell of the Master laid aside their critical sense.

He justified his intellectual terrorism on the grounds that he was surrounded by enemies whom he had to fight. One lot of enemies he conspicuously did not fight were the occupying German forces during the second world war. Although he remained in France, he so ordered his affairs as to be entirely safe and entirely comfortable. He felt, according to an admirer, Jean Bernier, that 'the events that history forced him to confront should have no effect on his way of life, as befits a superior mind'. As a doctor he had many privileges and he made full use of them. The major battles of his life were therefore in peace-time, most notably with the International Psychoanalytical Association (IPA) from which he was eventually expelled in 1963.

Lacan portrayed this break as the result of an ideological conflict between the old school and the progressive, true Freudians represented by himself. Actually it was about his greed. He needed to maximise his throughput of patients in order to finance his lavish lifestyle. (He died a multi-millionaire.) He started to shorten his sessions, without a pro rata reduction of fee, to as little as ten minutes. Unfortunately, Freudian theory fixes the minimum length of a session at 50 minutes. Lacan was therefore repeatedly cautioned by the IPA. According to Roudinesco, he gave several lectures to the Société Psychanalytique de Paris arguing that shorter sessions produced a beneficial sense of frustration and separation in the patient, 'turning the transference relationship into a dialectic' and 'reactivating unconscious desire'. Additionally, he lied to the IPA about the duration of his sessions. Despite this belt-and-braces approach, he was rumbled and out he went.

Faced with loss of income, he established his own French School of Psychoanalysis, over which he had absolute power. Its work, Roudinesco says, 'concentrated on desire, transference and love, and all of these came to be focused on the person of Lacan himself'. Now he could make his sessions as short, and as expensive, as he liked. Even when they had contracted to a minute or two, he would often see his tailor, his pedicurist and his barber while conducting his analyses. In the final years, the process of shortening reached its natural conclusion in the 'non-session', in which 'the patient was not allowed either to speak or not to speak' as Lacan 'had no time to waste on silence'. With the help of non-sessions he averaged 80 patients a day in the penultimate year of his life. Non-sessions were perhaps an improvement on sessions, in which, disinhibited through dementia, he would indulge his bad temper, raging at patients and occasionally punching them or pulling their hair.

The calamitous consequences of his style of doctoring were entirely predictable: his clients committed suicide at a rate that would have alarmed a man armed with less robust self-confidence. He claimed that it was due to the severity of the cases he took on but it may also have had something to do with the way he would start and stop analysis at whim and would sometimes cast aside, at very short notice, people who had been under his 'care' for years. The brilliant ethnologist Lucien Sebag killed himself at 32 after having been discharged abruptly from treatment – because Lacan wanted to sleep with Sebag's teenage daughter. Not that Dr Lacan was always so constrained by such exquisite moral scruples. He frequently chose his mistresses from his training analysts (who were additionally vulnerable because they relied on him for the pass necessary for them to practise as Lacanian analysts) and also from his ordinary analysands. In his defence, Roudinesco points out that Lacan never pursued the physical side of things in his consulting rooms. One suspects that, given the design of the analysts's couch, this was dictated by mechanical rather than ethical constraints.

On the principle of *credo ut intelligam* his disciples still believed him even when, in his last few years, he was manifestly suffering from multi-infarct dementia. He became obsessed by a particular mathematical figure called a Borromean knot, in which he saw the key to the unconscious, to sexuality and to the ontological situation of mankind. His quasi-mathematical, pseudo-logical fantasies – the culmination of the cargo cult science of his school – propounded in interminable seminars, were agonised over by his congregation who suffered appallingly from their inability to make sense of them. They felt unworthy of the Master. Even his episodes of aphasia, due to mini-strokes, were taken to be 'interpretations', in the technical sense of conveying 'the latent meaning of what the analysand has said and done'. When, towards the end, he became deaf and his responses were even more disconnected from what was said to him, this occasioned protracted arguments among his followers over the meaning of his words and deeds. Even when, in his last year, Lacan's mind was entirely vacant, he was still brought to meetings 'to legitimise what was being done in his name' and 'suggestible people heard him speak through his silence'.

When he died in 1981, total war broke out among his disciples. Within a decade, there were 34 associations claiming to be the sole representative of the true spirit of Jacques Lacan and the sole heirs to his intellectual estate. Even now, 15 years after his death, this extraordinary charlatan can still command the adoration of the vulnerable and the gullible. Roudinesco, for all that she dishes enough dirt to hang Lacan ten times over, seems to forgive him everything for his 'genius' as a clinician and thinker. Nor does she question any of his fundamental ideas, though in the course of a 500-page book she disdains either to expound them in any coherent way or to offer any evidence for them: she is too busy with splits, schisms and influences. It is apparently enough proof of their truth that Lacan asserted the doctrines associated with his name.

His lunatic legacy also lives on in places remote from those in which he damaged his patients, colleagues, mistresses, wives, children, publishers, editors, and opponents – in departments of literature whose inmates are even now trying to, or pretending to, make sense of his utterly unfounded, gnomic teachings and inflicting them on baffled students. Aleister Crowley, the 20th-century thinker whom Lacan most resembles, has not been so fortunate in his afterlife.

Lacanians may argue that the great edifice of the *Écrits* is not undermined by revelations about his life. The Master's thoughts should be judged on their own merits. However, in the absence of any logical basis or empirical evidence, the authority of the thought has derived almost completely from the authority of the man. The discovery that Lacan was the shrink from hell is not, therefore, irrelevant. Roudinesco's biography is consequently an act of liberation on behalf of those students, forced by uncritical teachers who do not know Stork from butter, to try to understand and make sense of his nonsense. This act of liberation is all the more compelling for being the work of a disciple and thus in part involuntary.

From: *The Times Higher Education Supplement*, 31 October 1997, p. 20.

11
Walking and *Différance*

In the reading given here, also from *Not Saussure*, Tallis considers the significance of Derrida, who, like Lacan sought to undermine the possibility of determinate meaning by emphasising the play of the signifier, arguing that meaning was based not only on differences (as in Saussure's account of the language system) but also on deferral. Every signified may turn into a signifier, so that no closure of meaning is possible – there is no transcendental or final signified. Signification, founded on differences and constantly undermined by deferral, is an effect of *différance*, the inescapable lack conditioning the self-differing of language from itself. As Tallis notes, what all this comes to is the idea that verbal meaning – and hence speech-acts and speaking subjects as much as written texts – is shot through with non-presence. I cannot be present in what I say since meaning is inseparable from absence. If what I am is somehow dependent on the signifier 'I' – and, according to the theory of the mirror stage, it must be – then my very being is like a maggot wriggling on the hook of *différance*. The word that names me, and gives me my place in the social and symbolic order, also murders me: it annihilates me in the uniqueness of my presence and alienates me from myself in the self-division and otherness that make language what it is. For Derrida, it would seem, the only kind of self-presence that would overcome so catastrophic a fall from the origin, an origin where the self was fully coincident with itself, would require the shedding of localised bodily being. Only through the replacement of the particular by the general could one achieve such a coincidence of one's being with consciousness and meaning. And yet, of course, this project is an impossible one. On this showing, Derrida has constructed a metaphysics of disappointment and tragic loss. The elusiveness of the self and the unattainability of the present moment at once oppress him and provide the mainspring for his thought.

The Street

Here is a long and silent street.
I walk in blackness and I stumble and fall
And rise, and I walk blind, my feet
Trampling the silent stones and the dry leaves.
Someone behind me also tramples stones, leaves:
If I slow down, he slows;

> If I run, he runs. I turn: nobody.
> Everything dark and doorless,
> Only my steps aware of me,
> I turning and turning among these corners
> Which lead forever to the street
> Where nobody waits for me, nobody follows me,
> Where I pursue a man who stumbles
> And rises and says when he sees me: nobody.
>
> Octavio Paz

If we are not present in our speech acts then, surely, we cannot be present in any other acts; indeed we must be non-present in our entire lives. For deliberate speech acts are the very paradigm of self-conscious behaviour, of self-expression, or embodied self-presence. They seem to be intentional to a degree exceeding all else that we do; for the primary purpose of such an act is the production of meaning whereas other acts serve non-signifying intentions and only secondarily or incidentally convey meaning. If we cannot mean what we talk we certainly cannot mean other things that we do. If we deny intentions to speech then we must banish them from our lives.

Consider a non-linguistic act such as walking. If I believe that I am present in my act of walking, it is because that act is informed by an intention that it may also incidentally signify. I know what I am doing, in so far as I have some notion of a goal towards which I am progressing and it is this notion of a goal that directs and coordinates the many separate movements of my limbs. Of course, my knowledge of the purpose and nature of my own actions will inevitably be generalised or abstract: the intelligible is necessarily general; and the more explicit that intelligibility, the more abstract my knowledge will be. My recognition of what I am doing – 'that I am doing *this*' – will be mediated by universals. An action will be recognised for what it is in so far as its profile is congruent with the silhouette of its general kind. Walking, analysed as a set of physical events, may not have discernible formal properties. The individual movements comprising my journey to the pub cannot easily be related to 'movement-types' whose successive realisations amount to a 'sentence' whose resultant meaning is 'arrival at a pub'. I may dawdle on the way, deviate to avoid a particularly unpredictable dog, pause to look at some flowers, and so on. There will be, in other words, continuous, non-systematic variation in the physical elements that go to make even such a stereotyped act as my nightly visit to the same local. Nevertheless, inasmuch as my journey makes sense to me, my walking can be analysed as the realisation of a series of elements, though it is not sufficiently segmented to make a formal '-emic' analysis anything other than strained and implausible. Recognition of such elements as they are realised, however, is the middle step in the organisation of the afferent feedback from my walking into a sign of what it is, of the process that it was intended to be. Nothing could be more conventional or more ready-made than the signs that give me online reassurance that I am doing what I think I am doing and what I intended to do. Walking, then, if it is recognised by the walker for what it is, is composed of iterable signs.

My sense of the meaning of my action, my confidence in the coincidence between intention and action, the process by which the action is informed by its intention, will be mediated by more indirect, more abstract, more complex signs. Such signs derive their meaning from the boundless context of my current location; ultimately from the limitless horizon of my consciousness and its history. For the meaning of my action will be context-dependent and in a way that I will certainly not be able to specify. The meaning of a walk to the pub may plausibly be related to everything that I have been up to that moment. In so far as any action is meaningful, its meaning is differentiated. An action implies choice and implicit in any given course of action are the many alternative actions that have been rejected. The meaning of my action therefore also depends upon the opposition of at least some of its elements to other actions that have different meanings. Choice implies differentiation and exclusion.

Differing and *difference* are therefore intrinsic to non-verbal meaning as well as to verbal meaning. (This is in addition to the verbalised meaning that many actions have and to the fact that perception itself is language- and theory-ridden.) Furthermore, the meaning of an action such as walking always points to a future – the future in which the action is completed and the goals attained. That future, however, points to another future and so on. The meaning of walking escapes the present in so far as it refers to this elusive future. Non-verbal meaning, too, is therefore characterised by *deferral*. Walk-acts as much as talk-acts exhibit the features of iterability, context dependency, difference and deferral. It is not only speech that is riddled with *différance*.

Must we conclude that we are really or typically absent in our walking? Is a man who is deliberately walking to the pub self-deceived when he believes that his action is expressing his intention to walk to the pub? It is certainly true that when we are walking we may forget what we are doing; our intentions may occultate and our intending selves may temporarily absent themselves from what we are doing. We do not continuously intend even our most deliberate actions throughout their duration. On the way to the pub I may become totally absorbed in the conversation I am having with the person who is walking with me. There is often a time-sharing of attention, whereby we switch from one on-going action to another. For part of my journey to the pub, I may walk deliberately; at other times I may delegate my walking to the automatic pilot while I turn my attention (and so my intentions) to other things. It does not, however, follow from the fact that my intention sets my action in motion, rather than being necessarily present throughout, that I am not-present in my action. Even less does it follow that my walking is entirely without authorship. Fluctuating attention and braided intentions do not imply non-intention. A man who is walking and talking at the same time is not, from the point of view of his walking, a headless automaton.

It is perfectly obvious that we are present in our walking. Nevertheless, the reasons for Derrida's denying presence in our speech acts seem to be equally applicable to other flesh acts such as walking. Indeed, they seem to be more applicable to the latter. And this already fits with ordinary intuitions: speech acts, in addition to having the features shared with other voluntary acts of being purposeful and deliberate, also have as their primary intention that of conveying meaning. We would therefore expect speech to include those acts in which we are most present and self-present; within which it is most easy to discriminate grades of automaticity, or stereotyping – and hence of conviction, sincerity and so on. Speech acts are the flesh acts in which we are most present. If we are absent from our speech then we must be absent from our lives and we must abandon the notion that we are present in any of our purposive acts.

Can I intend what I walk? Well, what would count as intending my walking? If we require that 'the intention animating (the walking) should be through and through present to itself and to its contents', could we ever intend walking? All bodily actions have physiological, psychological and social causes or frameworks wholly or mainly inapparent to the actor. Must we then conclude that we are not the authors of our actions, that we are non-present in them? I could not run my body for ten seconds if it did not run itself. My most deliberate acts are predicated on the unwilled health of my body and operate through mechanisms of which I am unaware. Can I therefore in any sense be entitled to believe that I intend any of my life? So much of what I *am* is *given*. And what could be more general – and more particular – than the body and its functions?

Since every argument Derrida uses to 'prove' that we are non-present in our speech acts could be equally well applied to other flesh acts, must I conclude that walking is a kind of writing; indeed, that writing is the condition of possibility of walking? And if I do not, indeed cannot, will not, accept this, am I the hopeless victim of a 'legocentric' fallacy? Is my belief that I am present in my walking an illusion generated by the circuit of 'se regarder marcher' or 's'entendre marcher'? (Cf. the 'I' of Octavio Paz's poem.) Since every act is a sign of itself – and it is by virtue of this sign that the actor recognises what he is doing so that he is able to continue doing it – walking is haunted by *différance*. Should I not believe that walking has differences but no positive terms? Should I not therefore deny that there is a walking subject? Would it not be reasonable for me to maintain that a falling corpse reveals the true nature of walking more than ordinary ambulation, that a headless hen shows us what ambulation really is?

These questions are not frivolous or unfair. The extension of Saussurean analysis to the whole of experience was at one stage the goal of structuralism and, more specifically, of the '-emic' analysis of behaviour that was so fashionable in the 1950s. Moreover, Gayatri Spivak, Derrida's translator, tells us that 'according to Derrida, Husserl's text is tortured by a suppressed insight that the Living Present is always already inhabited by difference' (*Of Grammatology*, Baltimore & London: Johns Hopkins University Press, 1976, Introduction). So it is not just speech but consciousness itself that is hollowed by non-presence. As we walk, our feet may touch the ground, but the play of signs that is our walking will never touch the ground of meaning, the transcendental pavement.

A *reductio ad absurdum*. Non-verbal acts and even the world of natural signs such as grey clouds are as difference-ridden as speech and writing. Difference, therefore, doesn't seem to make much difference. And for this reason, where Derrida's dazzling gnomic darkness has caused others to defer, I beg to differ.

Mr Pickwick to the rescue

> Pickwickian sense. In a technical constructive or conveniently idiosyncratic or esoteric sense; usually in reference to language 'unparliamentary' or compromising in its natural sense.
>
> (*Oxford English Dictionary*)

> The chairman felt it his imperative duty to demand ... whether he had used the expression ... in a common sense. Mr Blotton had no hesitation in saying that he had not – he had used the word in its Pickwickian sense.
>
> (*Pickwick Papers*)

There are signs that Derrida himself has never been entirely comfortable with some of the ideas most associated with his name. Though he usually manages to avoid drawing conclusions that can be readily tested against experience, he does feel the need to use more than obscurity to elude or baffle his readers and to deflect the sceptical astonishment of those who might be inclined to dismiss his views as nonsensical.

In a characteristically caustic passage, Austin writes as follows:

> One might well want to ask how seriously this doctrine is intended, just how strictly and literally the philosophers who propounded it mean their words to be taken ... It is, as a matter of fact, not at all easy to answer, for,

> strange though the doctrine looks, we are sometimes told to take it easy – really it's just what we've believed all along. (There's the bit where you say it and the bit where you take it back.)[1]

Austin is here referring to the doctrine that we never *directly* perceive or sense material objects; but he could well have been speaking of many of Derrida's claims; for Derrida spends a good deal of time retreating from things we might think he may have said. (Though it has to be admitted that many of the positions most notoriously associated with his name are vulgarisations of his views by his less gifted but more publicity-conscious followers.) The process by which he executes his U-turns and wriggles out of positions that seem, on the surface, to be an affront to common sense and ordinary experience involves a continuous redefinition of words that would seem not to require definition in the first place. This is the Pickwickian method and we shall examine how it is applied to 'writing', 'presence' (and 'absence'), 'intention' and 'auto-affection', though many other key words are handled with equal unscrupulousness and cunning.

(1) Writing

According to Derrida, 'To affirm ... that the concept of writing exceeds and comprehends that of language presupposes of course a certain definition of language and of writing' (*OG*, pp. 8–9). So, for Derrida, writing is not merely

> the penning or forming of letters or words; the using of written characters for purposes of record, transmission of ideas etc.; the action of composing and committing to manuscript; the expression of thoughts or ideas in written words.
>
> (*Oxford English Dictionary*)

That is the narrow 'graphic' acceptation of the word. Derrida interprets writing in a more generous sense:

> and thus we say 'writing' for all that gives rise to inscription in general, whether it is literal or not and even if what it distributes in space is alien to the order of the voice: cinematography, choreography, of course, but also pictorial, musical, sculptural 'writing'. One might also speak of athletic writing, and with even greater certainty of military or political writing in view of the techniques that govern these domains today. All this to describe not only the system of notation secondarily connected with these activities but the essence and content of these activities themselves.
>
> (*OG*, p. 9)

If writing *were* all of these things, then it would be scarcely surprising if it were to exceed, indeed encompass, speech.

This greatly expanded definition of writing has not been arrived at as the result of a careful examination of the object in question. It is to be found at the very *beginning* of *Of Grammatology*. As Derrida himself admits, the belief that 'oral language already belongs to this language presupposes a modification of the concept of writing that we for the moment merely anticipate' (*OG*, p. 24). It proves, in fact, difficult to anticipate what directions this modification will take. 'Writing' acquires a larger and larger catchment area and Derrida cites Plato and Hegel in support of an extraordinary extension of the concept of writing. (The citations are, to put it mildly, imprecisely referenced so that the reader is not in a position to evaluate the Platonic or Hegelian uses of the term. But the names invoked are so big that the ordinary reader is disinclined to do anything other than take what is said on trust.) For Plato, Derrida tells us, writing is at once mnemotechnique and the power of forgetting; whereas for Hegel, writing is 'that forgetting of the self, that exteriorisation, the contrary of the interiorising memory, of the *Erinnerung* that opens the history of the spirit' (*OG*, p. 24).

The most powerful redefinition of writing, and the one from which most of Derrida's most striking positions have been derived, is insinuated and developed intermittently in the early pages of *Of Grammatology*:

> If 'writing' signifies inscription and especially the durable institution of a sign (and that is the only irreducible kernel of the concept of writing), writing in general covers the entire field of linguistic signs. In that field a certain sort of instituted signifiers may then appear, 'graphic' in a narrow and derivative sense of the word, ordered by a certain relationship with other instituted – hence 'written', even if they are 'phonic' – signifiers. The very idea of institution – and hence of the arbitrariness of the signs – is unthinkable before the possibility of writing and outside of its horizon.
>
> (*OG*, p. 44)

> Even before it is linked to incision, engraving, drawing, or the letter, to a signifier referring in general to a signifier signified by it, the concept of the *graphie* (unit of a possible graphic system) implies the framework of the *instituted trace*, as the possibility common to all systems of signification.
>
> (*OG*, p. 46)

The 'if' at the beginning of the first quotation is characteristic, indeed pathognomomic, of the post-Saussurean style of argument. It is not clear why, if writing *does* signify the durable institution of a sign, it should cover the entire field of linguistic signs. The force of the argument, such as it is, seems to depend upon confusion between the 'durability' of the institution – presumably '*langue*' as opposed to '*parole*' – and the durability of the particular signs that are used. Naturally, a written word is durable in the way that a spoken one is not. In either case, however, the institution – the system of differences in the Saussurean sense – is durable. So much is clear, if of dubious validity.

Once, however, linguistic signs are related to 'the framework of the instituted trace', the gates of obscurity are flung wide open:

> The instituted trace cannot be thought without thinking the retention of difference within a structure of reference where difference appears *as such* and thus permits a certain liberty of variations among the full terms. The absence of *another* here-and-now, of another transcendental present, of *another* origin of the world appearing as such, presenting itself as irreducible absence in the presence of the trace, is not a metaphysical formula substituted for the scientific concept of writing.
>
> (*OG*, pp. 46–7)

Perhaps not, but absence has insinuated itself into the concept of writing which, as we have been told, encompasses the whole of the linguistic institution. The space of writing 'constitutes the absence of the signatory, to say nothing of the absence of the referent. Writing is the name of these two absences' (*OG*, pp. 40–1). Writing as the name of the absence of the subject and the absence of the referent of writing strikes one as curious; but the 'modification of the concept of writing' is still not complete. In the essay on '*Différance*', writing (or proto-writing) conquers yet more territory:

> and it is this constitution of the present as a 'primordial' and irreducibly nonsimple, and, therefore, in the strict sense non primordial, synthesis of traces, retentions and protentions ... that I propose to call protowriting, prototrace, or différance.
>
> (*SP*, p. 143)

Jonathan Culler accepts this quite without protest and asserts baldly that 'writing in general is an *archi-écriture*, an archi-writing or protowriting which is the condition of both speech and writing in the narrow sense'.[2]

Long live the narrow sense! If we read 'proto-writing' as 'Pickwick-writing', then we should be in a position to see some of Derrida's more extraordinary positions for what they are.[3]

(2) Presence/absence

If we are not present in what we say, it might be reasonable to suppose that we are absent from it. But things are not so straightforward in Derrida's writings (or proto-writings): 'nothing, either in the elements or the system (of language) is anywhere simply present or absent. There are only, everywhere, differences and traces of traces.'[4] Derrida frequently uses the term 'non-presence' to signify the middle position between presence and absence. 'There is the bit where you say it and the bit where you take it back.' (Or: one can write – or speak – '*sous rature*'.) Derrida says it by asserting that we are not present in our speech but takes it back by saying that we are not absent either – rather non-present. Supposing we were to say that that which is non-present is also non-absent, would we not deprive Derrida's conclusions of much of their power to astonish? Few people would object to being told that they were 'non-absent' from their speech. Or does 'non-absent' mean something different from 'not-absent'? In the dazzling chaos of Derrida's gnomic texts it would appear to be possible to deny the presence of something, to deny also its absence, and also to give slight preference to the denial of presence over the denial of absence.

(3) Intention

One not unreasonable reading of Derrida is that we cannot, indeed we do not, mean what we say. But, as pointed out earlier, if we cannot mean what we say, we certainly cannot mean what we walk. By abolishing intention from speech – or treating the idea that what we say is informed by our intentions as an aspect of the logocentric fallacy – then we must abolish intention from our entire lives. This conclusion must be unpalatable to Derrida himself. After all, he must have, in some sense, intended to write *Of Grammatology* rather than to earn his living as a harpooner or a tattooist. And he must take a far greater share of the blame for that book than either Queen Elizabeth I or myself can be expected to do. His recognising this may be why he smuggles intentions back into ordinary life:

> the category of intention will not disappear: it will have its place, but from that place it will no longer be able to govern the entire scene and system of utterance ... the intention animating the utterance will never be through and through present to itself and to its content.[5]

But whoever thought that 'the intention animating the utterance' *would* be 'through and through present to itself and to its content'? As the ever-helpful Culler says, 'it is not a matter of denying that signatories have intentions, but of situating those intentions'.[6] So that's what it is all about! On closer inspection, Derrida's conception of intention is no more subversive of ordinary understanding than those of a Marxist or a psychoanalyst; and they are considerably less radical than those of a physiologist[7] – or a social psychologist such as Mead.[8]

(4) Auto-affection

In the essay on Husserl, auto-affection almost evaporates before the demonstration of its own impossibility. As a condition or criterion of 'full' presence, it proves a major stumbling block to the phenomenological enterprise. Elsewhere, however, it seems to be flourishing to an extraordinary degree:

> Auto-affection is a universal structure of experience. All living things are capable of auto-affection. And only a being capable of symbolizing, that is to say of auto-affecting, may let itself be affected by the other in general. Auto-affection is the condition of an experience in general. This possibility – another name for 'life' – is a general structure articulated by the history of life, and leading to complex, hierarchical operations.
>
> (*OG*, pp. 165–6)

By an inexplicable miracle, Husserl's impossible dream becomes life's inescapable structure.

(5) Conclusion

The continuous process of on-line redefinition of crucial terms is the key to Derrida's ability to arrive at astonishing conclusions. It is blatant enough to cause Mr Pickwick himself to cry out in protest. Those of us who still think of 'writing' as typically something that is committed to paper and who insist that absence is different from – indeed the opposite of – presence and vice versa, may remain unimpressed. Even less impressive is Derrida's habit of blurring elementary distinctions – such as between type and token in order to sustain the idea that all communication is 'the durable instituting of signs'.

It might be appropriate to end this section by introducing a new term of my own. It is intended to encompass the misreading and miswriting necessary to pull off the Derridan conjuring trick. I shall christen this process (in memory of one of Derrida's most fervent disciples who made much of the 'fruitfulness of misreading') *léger de Man*.

The tragic meta-philosopher

> [*Différance*] must be conceived without *nostalgia*; that is, it must be conceived outside the myth of the purely paternal or maternal longing belonging to the lost fatherland of thought. On the contrary, we must *affirm* it – in the sense that Nietzsche brings affirmation into play – with a certain laughter and with a certain dance.
>
> (*Speech and Phenomena*, p. 159)

It is tempting to dismiss Derrida's attacks on phonocentrism, logocentricity and the metaphysics of presence as merely misconceived, muddled and fraudulent. But we must look beyond his tendentious accounts of 'Western Culture' and 'Western philosophy', his misrepresentations of individual philosophers, his cavalier use of certain key terms, his tendency to confuse and conflate issues and arguments that are most fruitfully kept apart and his many stylistic vices, to the intuitions that may lie behind his *oeuvre*. These are considerably more interesting than the texts to which they have given birth. His is in some ways a tragic case: a man of immense talent and massive erudition, gifted with profound insights, who could not say the things he most wanted to say but who, nevertheless, has built a huge *oeuvre* out of his circlings round them. The publicity his ideas have attracted has only deepened the tragedy: the bad influence of those he has himself influenced has added frivolity to the obscurity; the ridiculous, indeed despicable, response to John Searle's criticism of his views is a characteristic production of recent years.[9]

Derrida would be quite comfortable with the charge that he is no philosopher. He anyway undermines the claims of philosophy to be more than mere writing, to be free of the influence of the textual forces that govern other, more explicitly literary, modes of writing. Nevertheless, he is, whether he likes it or not, a metaphilosopher – of a certain tragic strain in post-Kantian philosophy. Derrida's refusal to accept the reality of ordinary presence stems from his refusal to settle for less. This is a hunger he shares with Hegel, Husserl, Heidegger and Sartre. Behind the more technical arguments of these philosophers' writings is a disappointed longing for the union of absolute lucidity and undeniable substantiality, of thing-like thereness with thought-like transparency, for an absolute coincidence of knowing and being. The latter is impossible: as being or presence moves towards transparency, it attenuates to insubstantiality; as it gains substance, it thickens to opacity. The actual cannot be both absolutely general and utterly particular.

He has very stringent criteria for what may be accounted 'real' presence and these explain why he denies presence to the speaker; why presence for him, as for Husserl, according to Derrida, must be absolute or nothing; why he overlooks or dismisses the graded presence of everyday reality and diagnoses non-presence. Since, according to his analysis, absolute presence is impossible, the idea of it being riven by contradiction, ordinary presence as it is given to daily experience must be a mirage. It is not 'the absolute matrix form of being but rather ... a "particularisation" and "effect". A determination and effect within a system that is no longer that of presence but of difference' (*SP*, p. 147). Presence is not an autonomous given, a primordial, primitive fact that both faces consciousness and is the givenness of consciousness to itself. The concept of the temporal present, too, is riddled with absence and contradiction. The idea of a current event seems to presuppose a synthesis across two absences – the no longer of the past and the not yet of the future. The present as the seat of change, of activity, of events, the temporal seat of presence of what is actually there, incorporates self-differing, *différance*. The very notion of the present is an effect of differences or (since the notion of change involves the future and hence deferral) of *différance*.

Derrida denies that the speaker is present in his speech act – or, indeed, in any signifying or even significant act – because, like some philosophers before him, he will accept nothing less than an absolute coincidence within voluntary acts of consciousness and meaning. Self-presence *chez* Derrida requires total self-possession. If the signs I use do not originate with me and if I do not explicitly intend all the conventions and, indeed, all the utterance-conditions, that make meaning possible, then I am not present in my act. Since what I say to some degree escapes my control, exceeding or falling short of any formulated or formulable signifying intention, since it is not inwardly lit through and through by such an intention, I cannot be said to have intended the meaning of my utterance.

The disappointed vision behind these impossible criteria for presence is of a self entirely given over to its intelligible acts, without any residue of opacity – either of disengaged self or of unintended meaning. Derridan presence implies total self-knowledge, a consciousness utterly turned over to explicit meaning, fully signifying itself to itself, rendered without remainder into transparent signs. A sign, however, must be iterable to be intelligible, that is to say general. To be present or self-present on Derrida's terms we should have to be given over entirely to generality. Our acts would have to become the universal profiles of themselves, to be entirely silhouette. It would not be sufficient that they should become, like structuralist signs, all form and no content; they must also be independent of any system that is not fully on display. At the very least, the actor should shed his particularity, including his specific locations in space and time and all the deictic co-ordinates that constitute 'being here'. Presence in the Derridan sense would demand replacement of localised bodily being by pure generality; the shedding of particularity, because particular being always exceeds the saturation of a finite number of variables and so falls short of full articulation.

Even if this were possible, we still could not possess ourselves through the signs we use in speech acts. No actor could ever achieve total coincidence within his act of being, consciousness and meaning. He could not dissolve, without residue, into a kind of pure semantic light; for some of him would have to remain undissolved in order to receive that light and be lit by it. The project of absolute self-knowledge is frustrated by the need for that knowledge to have a knower, itself not contained within that knowledge. In the case of a speech act, the speaker could not be present in the Derridan sense in the meaning of the utterance because the meaning would have to mean to someone: the speaker would have to be, at least in part, the consumer of the meaning of his utterance as well as the meaning itself. If total coincidence between being and meaning is the criterion for being present in a speech act, it is scarcely surprising that such presence proves impossible.

Much of Sartre's philosophical megalith *Being and Nothingness*[10] is devoted to agonising over this: 'The being of consciousness does not coincide with itself in a full equivalence' (p. 74). Worse still, 'consciousness – the for-itself – is a being which is not what it is and which is what it is not' (p. 79). But of course 'the *phenomenon* of the in-itself is an abstraction without consciousness' (p. 658). Because consciousness is consciousness 'of' – of something other than itself – it has to be distanced from itself in order to be, in order to have content. If Husserlian immediate presence is impossible it is not because speech is riddled with *différance* but because consciousness is necessarily an intermediary; because self-presence is necessarily indirect. One cannot, to use Sartre's example, be oneself as an oak tree is an oak tree. Put another way, one cannot become a word – confined to its borders, filling its semantic catchment area uniformly with one's self-presence. Even less can one achieve this state by filling out the contours of an act to which a word can be attached in absolute definition or rigid designation.

The presence that Derrida denies is a special type of metaphysical self-presence that goes even beyond Husserlian absolute presence. His assertion that meaning and presence are effects of language rather than existing prior to them are really reformulations of ancient worries about agency – the feeling that even in our apparently voluntary actions we are not fully the agents of what our actions mean. We are not, and cannot be, transparent to ourselves and the significance even of our speech acts cannot be 'rounded up' in our intentions or our consciousness of them. There is nowhere where we can coincide with ourselves – certainly not in our perceptions where we are given up to that which is not ourselves – and equally certainly not in our actions, where we engage an outside world through the mediation of a body that is other than the moments of our consciousness. The world we experience and act on always exceeds in weight, and falls short in purity, of the world of our articulate imagination or our explicit recollection.

The double 'failure' of language – as a vessel in which we can deposit, and so repossess, ourselves and as a means of expressing extra-linguistic reality – the lack of coincidence between word and self, and between word and world – is a dominant theme in Proust. Recollection and anticipation are closer to names; the present moment, unconfined by words, laden with a particularity that exceeds language, is, by comparison, flawed. Unexpressed even in our speech acts, we are 'never quite there': in the present, we elude ourselves and the world eludes the grasp of a fully self-possessed experience. For Proust, as for many continental philosophers, 'the systematic elusiveness of the I' is a consequence of the nature of time itself which denies us total self-possession, rather than being merely a consequence of the grammar of the word. The flawed present is like music; it inheres in hastening away from itself and towards itself.

The elusiveness of the present and the unattainability of undivided self-presence have been fundamental preoccupations of thinkers over the centuries. An impatience at 'never quite being there', at not being identical with oneself, marks a point where the artist and the mystic meet. Hunger for sharper, more continuous self-presence, for a shadeless internal lucidity, for a more acute realisation of the world and the fact that one is in it, lies at the root of many spiritual quests. Ouspensky has expressed this very clearly, in his reporting of Gurdjieff's teaching:

> 'Not one of you has noticed the most important thing that I have pointed out to you' he said. 'That is to say, not one of you has noticed that *you do not remember yourselves* ... You do not feel yourselves; you are not conscious of *yourselves*. With you 'it observes', just as 'it speaks', 'it thinks', 'it laughs'. You do not feel: *I* observe, *I* notice, *I* see. Everything still 'is noticed', 'is seen'... . Only those results will have any value that are accompanied by self-remembering. Otherwise you yourselves do not exist in your observations ...'
>
> I said that we have overlooked a fact of tremendous importance, namely that *we do not remember ourselves*; that we live and act and reason in deep sleep, not metaphorically but in reality ... we *can* remember ourselves if we make sufficient efforts, we *can* awaken.[11]

A less tragically inclined thinker than Derrida might accept that presence and self-presence could never be established through acts because they are presupposed in the very concept of an act. The generality and the iterability of the signs we use do not undermine that ordinary presence – just as the stereotyped or even ritualistic nature of much human behaviour does not absent us from that behaviour. Generality is essential for self-recognition; for it is under the aspect of generality that we recognise ourselves and so 'come to' ourselves. Even – or especially – the objects of our desires are socially coded – that may be how we recognise that we desire them, recognise them as desirable[12] – but the desires are no less fiercely felt for that. That desires are differentiated as values belonging to a system is not the end of the matter.

The question of the context of acts can be approached in a non-Derridan spirit. The boundless text of society which no one can fully specify but which is requisite for acts to have their specific meanings is not necessarily alien to the actors. It is arguable that the sum of our contexts, of circumstances, is what we are; or rather we are that in virtue of which all of these loci are specified or designated *as* contexts. There is no absolute difference between the self that has a context and the context that surrounds it. The ultimate context from which my speech acts derive their felicity is myself; only that self can change a material or social reality from the status of virtual contexts to that of being the actual conditions of a particular utterance. My presence, in short, is that in virtue of which my utterances have deictic co-ordinates to anchor them – is that in virtue of which their transformation from general values to specific assertions, from non-specific possibility to determinate meaning; is possible. My presence, my being here-and-now, furnishes the necessary deictic input required to give my words specificity. Without the opaque residue of unexpressed self or context behind my signs, the latter would drift in a void of generality; my particular existence is what gives determinacy to the truth conditions of my utterances.

Of course, we are never 'there' in the absolute Hegelian or Husserlian sense. Complete coincidence of being and knowledge, of explicit self-presence and facticity, is not possible. The for-itself is fatally divided and Derridan presence is therefore unachievable. We cannot be totally rendered up to ourselves without remainder; we cannot unite within ourselves the solidity of thing-like existence with absolute transparency of consciousness, perfect lucidity with complete changelessness. These demands are conflicting. We are not made in the image of Rilke's angel 'a perfect consciousness ... a being in whom thought and action, insight and achievement, will and capability, the actual and the ideal are one'.[13] For we 'when we feel evaporate; oh we breathe ourselves out and away; from ember to ember yielding a fainter scent'.[14] The angels, on the other hand, 'only catch up what is theirs, what has streamed for themselves'. Accordingly, we are doomed from the start if we wish to be what we know and do and to know what we do. In Sartre's vision, we are given over to a lifelong futile passion to be God, to become a self-founded self, the for-itself-in-itself:

> Every human reality is a passion in that it projects losing itself so as to found being and by the same stroke to constitute the in-itself which escapes contingency by being its own foundation, the *ens causa sua*, which religions call God.[15]

Octavio Paz's poem is aware of this futile passion, this doomed attempt to found oneself. The walker through the deserted street discovers the non-coincidence of the self with the self through the vertigo of solitary, uninterrupted self-awareness, the vortex of auto-affection.

This is perhaps Derrida's inaugural, and unacknowledged, insight. He shares the Hegelian/Husserlian dream of absolute self-presence, of the self-world 'coming to' itself without ever going outside of itself. Why otherwise would he move from the impossibility of absolute self-presence to denying the reality of ordinary presence? His position is reminiscent of those who will not settle for less than total wakefulness and, when they fail to find any state of consciousness answering to this notion, denounce all of life as a dream.

No one would dispute that absolute presence in the Derridean sense is impossible. It does *not* however, follow from this that:

(i) We are no more present in one activity than in any other. Or, more specifically, that speech is a type of writing so that we are no more present in what we say now than Homer is now in the epic poems he wrote millennia ago.
(ii) We cannot intend or mean what we say and that meaning is an effect of language (bits of extra-linguistic reality having no intrinsic difference in meaning) so that what we say is no more true of one bit of external reality than of another and what we say does not refer to one bit of external reality rather than another.
(iii) There is no difference between use and mention, assertion and quotation, being a reader and being a writer.

Likewise, it does not follow from the fact that we are not Rilkean angels or Sartrean gods that we do not or cannot mean what we say; that we cannot mean to say one thing rather than another; or that dead authors are as present in their texts as living speakers are in their utterances.

It would be rather extraordinary if such highly *specific* conclusions as that writing has priority over speech should follow from such profoundly metaphysical premisses – as surprising as if a decision for or against the mind-independent reality of space–time could enable one to decide whether or not cricket had priority over football. Since *différance* is supposed to be primordial, since it haunts not only language but also 'The Living Present', its discovery should hardly influence our decisions about the relative status of speech and writing.

So rational phonocentricity may still be regarded as rational after the 'discovery' of *différance*. And so, too, does logocentricity (not to speak of legocentricity). And this is not entirely unexpected: if meaning of things were *not* differentiated prior to language, there would be little point in a system of differences established to signify different meanings. In direct contradiction of Derrida – and pending more convincing arguments than the ones whose feebleness he has concealed beneath his intellectually irresponsible prose – we roundly assert:

Il y'a de hors-texte

as the hands with which I wrote and those with which the reader holds this book amply confirm.

We conclude that the not inconsiderable interest of Derrida's works lies in the insights that gave rise to them, his reiteration of the metaphysical hungers that motivated the early Sartre, and before him Husserl and Hegel. But a sympathy for those starting intuitions is quickly extinguished by the antipathy roused by his dubious methods of conducting philosophical discussion and the baseless paradoxes to which he owes his doubtless temporary fame.

Appendix: a note on intention

The whole question of the 'through and throughness' of an intention, of the completeness with which our intentions animate our acts, of the extent to which an action realises an intention, is of the greatest interest.

We tend to think of agency and chance as opposites; but there is always an element of chance in agency, even in an act that goes precisely according to plan. I am walking on the beach and I pick up a stone. There can be no doubt that I intend to pick up *a* stone; but the *choice* of this particular stone out of the many thousands that lie to hand is left to chance.

This illustrates the general point that our intentions cannot be utterly specific, with absolute values assigned to all possible variables. The actual moves constituting the action do not uniquely realise the intention; or, to look at it the other way round, the intention cannot legislate over all the features of the action, even if one is not knocked off course in the passage from intention to realisation.

This is a consequence of the fact that, in order to make sense to us, our intentions must be of a general character; from which it follows that there must be unsaturated variables in the original intention. When one intends an action, the intended action is *any* action that corresponds to a certain form. The objects of intentions are, in other words, to a certain degree abstract.

These points become clearer when we consider the ideal of an absolutely lucid intention – and an action that knows itself through and through. How do we elucidate our intentions; how do we make our intentions clearer to ourselves, know them at a higher level of self-awareness? Most typically by articulating them to ourselves. But when we verbalise our intentions we are really describing them and evaluating or interpreting them at the same time; indeed we may be altering or even forming them for the first time. Moreover, even if we accept the notion of a pre-formed, pre-verbal intention, there is still the problem that nothing can be totally elucidated linguistically. There is the element of chance in the choice of words and the unexamined forces at work in the selection of descriptors of one's planned actions. A *description* of an intention, in other words, is a plant that, like the intention itself, grows out of a humus of unexamined self. And even if we pretend that the idea of the formulation of a pre-existing intention is unproblematic, there remains the fact that the mesh of descriptors cannot be drawn so tightly as to determine the character of the action uniquely – so that nothing is left to chance.

Actions, then, can never be totally transparent, even (or especially) to the actor. An intention can never absolutely specify a unique action corresponding to it and the intention itself can never be fully elucidated. Chance penetrates to the core of agency not merely because intentions are externally prompted, formed on the spur of the moment, in response to something that is external to oneself, but also because there can be no 'uniquely referring' intentions (cf. there are no 'uniquely referring' expressions). There is a darkness at the heart of intention and there is an inescapable indeterminacy in their relation even to the actions that seem most precisely to realise them.

None of this, however, supports any of the specific post-Saussurean conclusions about the relation between speech and writing, or about the nature of reference, meaning and truth.

Notes

1. J.L. Austin, *Sense and Sensibilia* (Oxford University Press, 1962) p. 2.
2. Jonathan Culler, *On Deconstruction: Theory and Criticism after Structuralism* (London: Routledge & Kegan Paul, 1983), p. 104.
3. Not content with rendering the concept of writing totally opaque, Derrida does the same for the that of 'the book'. In *OG*, he speaks of 'the death of the civilisation of the book which manifests itself particularly through a convulsive proliferation of libraries' (p. 8). A strategic redefinition of the term 'book' – as that upon which any durable sign has been inscribed – would permit one to conclude that books antedate writing 'in the graphic sense'. For, as everyone knows, stones, sand and the bark of trees (all forms of arche-paper) were around long before the invention of writing.
4. 'Positions', quoted in Culler, *On Deconstruction*, p. 99.
5. Marges, quoted in Culler, ibid., p. 127.
6. Ibid.
7. Benjamin Libet, 'Unconscious Cerebral Initiative and the Role of Conscious Will in Voluntary Action', *The Behavioural and Brain Sciences*, in press.
8. George Herbert Mead, *Mind, Self and Society* (University of Chicago Press, 1934).
9. The exchange between Searle and Derrida is examined in detail in section 2.2 of Culler, *On Deconstruction*, pp. 110–34.
10. Jean-Paul Sartre, *Being and Nothingness*, trans. Hazel Barnes (London: methuen, 1957).
11. P.D. Ouspensky, *In Search of the Miraculous* (London: Routledge & Kegan Paul, 1950) pp. 117–18, 121.
12. We desire that which we see others desire as Spinoza argued in his *Ethics*.
13. J.B. Leishmann in his introduction to his translation of *The Duino Elegies* (London: The Hogarth Press, 1967).
14. Rainer Maria Rilke, 'The Second Elegy', *The Duino Elegies* ibid., p. 228.
15. Sartre, *Being and Nothingness*, p. 615.

From: *Not Saussure* (Macmillan, 1988, 1995), pp. 215–34, 264.

Part V
The Two Cultures

Humanist intellectuals are frequently hostile to science. This hostility encompasses not only the misuses (atom bombs) and miscarriages (global warming) of technology but also its supposedly inhuman, mechanistic approach to the natural and human world. Tallis considers such hostility, coming from individuals who are beneficiaries of science-based technology, enjoying comfort and security unprecedented in history, deeply hypocritical. Moreover, it offers no positive suggestions as to how the undoubted benefits of science-based technology may be more widely disseminated nor its adverse effects controlled. Most important of all, for Tallis, is the fact that such hostility fails to recognise the true mystery of scientific knowledge, which he regards as the most miraculous phenomenon in the universe and the most extraordinary manifestation of the capacity of human beings to transcend the here and now and make that which is around them explicit.

Tallis would contend that of almost equal concern is the failure of many humanist intellectuals to understand anything about the methods of science. They have failed to learn from disciplines in which, unlike their own, there are robust methods of acquiring reliable, universalisable knowledge, and strong institutional controls on fraud and powerful strategies for identifying and correcting error. Not only have these lessons of science been lost on some humanist intellectuals, but, he would argue, there has also been a concerted effort to suggest that scientific knowledge is subordinate to the power formations of discursive communities, or that it is equivalent to magic. In other words, scientific enquiry is presented as being as unreliable a source of knowledge as the disciplines dominated by charismatic leaders whose *obiter dicta* – often summing up the entire human universe in an aside – are accepted without being questioned (and sometimes without being understood). The fact that science has enormously enhanced our power to control nature remains unexplained by those who would sociologise its discoveries about the natural world.

Tallis believes that ignorance of science – mainly spontaneous, but sometimes wilful and cultivated – amongst humanist intellectuals has had many adverse effects. The quality of the debate about many social issues – where a certain degree of numeracy and an understanding of how causal relations may be determined are essential – dominated as it is by individuals unschooled in the methods of acquiring robust knowledge is correspondingly low. For Tallis, many humanist intellectuals not only deprive themselves of acquaintance with what he would certainly describe as humanity's greatest imaginative adventure, but also, through their disparagement of science, discourage others from exploring what he sees as undoubtedly the central cultural fact of our age. His writings are an attempt to see to it that art and science are given their due place in the discourse of intellectuals, in the hope that a new understanding, arising out of the convergence of the two, might come into being.

12
Evidence-based and Evidence-free Generalisations: A Tale of Two Cultures

In this selection, from *The Arts and Sciences of Criticism*, ed. David Fuller and Patricia Waugh (1999), Tallis contrasts the scholarly procedures of science, and in particular medicine, with those prevalent in those Humanities departments where Theory holds sway. He gives an extremely clear account of the way drugs are tested, eliminating bias and the undue influence of preconception. He then contrasts this degree of rigour with what passes for evidence amongst the masters of Theory, Lacan and Derrida. In his theory of the mirror stage, Lacan simply ignored empirical evidence that challenged his claims, while Derrida's misrepresentations of figures as various as Plato, Saussure, Peirce, Husserl and E.R. Curtius have of recent years been carefully documented. The practices of these men, and their epigones, amount, in Tallis's view, to nothing less than a scandal. So why is it that no one seems scandalised? In fact, of course, some writers *are* scandalised, but their responses to what is going on have been pushed to one side or simply ignored. There is in place what Tallis is not afraid to call 'institutionalised fraud'. The hard work of exact scholarship and the close critical response to a given text cannot possibly compete with the lure of the 'big ideas' and the glamour associated with them. This tendency – always a temptation in literary study – has been reinforced by the need of universities, here and in the USA, to maximise income. Those who will expound 'big ideas' are those who get hired, on the expectation that they will prove a bigger draw than those who base their work on scholarship and exact criticism. The consequences of this for genuine thought can be seen in the Sokal Hoax, to which Tallis devotes the last part of the reading.

---

1 Introduction

To an outsider, it seems that, since the study of literature was first established as an academic discipline, there has been almost continuous disagreement over the best or most appropriate approach to criticism. Recently, the very legitimacy of appreciation, evaluation and interpretation of individual works and individual authors has been questioned. Dissent within literary studies has acquired a bitter edge and there are deep divisions amongst academic critics.

The major catalyst has been the emergence of a family of approaches in literature arising out of post-Saussurean schools of thought: structuralist and poststructuralist literary criticism and theory; and the various brands of criticism that have been directly or indirectly inspired by them. The striking feature of these new schools is a shift from the endeavour to understand individual works of literature on what is perceived to be their own terms towards an aspiration to an 'overstanding' of literature as a whole. Literary criticism and traditional scholarship have been displaced by literary theory which has in turn given place to something called 'Theory'.

The emergence of Theory was announced by Richard Rorty over twenty years ago in a widely cited article. Theory, according to Rorty, is a general method of approaching texts or discourses, 'a kind of writing ... which is neither the evaluation of the relative merits of intellectual productions, nor intellectual history, nor moral philosophy, nor social prophecy, but all of these mingled together in a new genre'.[1] The ascent of Theory has been reflected in an increasing tendency to look *through* individual works of literature to the structures of the system(s) of discourse which are said to underlie them, or *past* them to the wider cultural – intellectual, social, political – formations which they are thought involuntarily to mirror or express.

This shift was decisively signalled a couple of decades ago by Barthes' enormously influential *S/Z*,[2] which atomised a novella by Balzac, breaking up the text into lexias or 'units of reading' and allocating those lexias to five classes – the semes, and the hermeneutic, the proairetic, the symbolic and the cultural codes. Barthes' approach was implicitly and explicitly an expression of his belief that the significance of an individual work of art is best sought through seeing it as part of a larger discursive formation or social text rather than as a stand-alone artefact produced by an individual consciousness. 'The author' is merely a site where boluses of the collective consciousness, packets of the *n*th hand – shot through with various kinds of unconsciousness – are sequestrated, brand-marked and emitted. A poem or novel is but a faint precipitate out of the super-saturated solution of the already-written, the already-read. In the absence of an individual author intending, making, shaping the work, there is only the operation of impersonal systems acting through the work. The work, consciousness, the self, the reader, are structured by language, or, more generally, by the sign systems of the collective consciousness and unconsciousness.

Barthes' methods and their underlying rationale, once revolutionary, are now the almost universal convention. The massive and overwhelming influence of Lacan and Derrida and their innumerable epigones has made the emphasis in literary studies on various forms of collective unconscious – linguistic, psychoanalytical, historical, and so on – the norm. The poststructuralist challenge to the distinction between structure and content, and even between the signifier and the signified, has prompted critic to parrot critic in asserting that literary art is about signifiers without signifieds and has little or nothing to do with any reality outside of the text, except in so far as reality is more text. Because, moreover, the conditions that have given rise to the systems that underlie literary texts are self-contradictory – for a variety of Marxist, Freudian, and other reasons – texts are doomed to be at odds with themselves (unless they are written by practitioners of Theory). A crucial function of the critic is therefore 'deconstruction': this is (to use Barbara Johnson's neat encapsulation) to 'tease out the warring forces of signification within the text'. The critic will use deconstruction and other techniques to read the work 'against the grain', so as to challenge the already-written, the already-read. This is a good – 'radical', 'subversive', 'revolutionary' – thing to do because the already-written and the already-read incorporate the 'taken for granted' and the taken for granted is bad since, in an unjust world, taking things for granted, like confusing history and nature, is to collude with injustice.

The result of much of this work has been predictably dull: *S/Z* is more like *S/ZZZZZ* ... But the idea of unpacking from within the text the (textual) world around it and the conventions that structure it has remained attractive to advanced critics, as has the related assumption that works of literature are, above all, texts, and their interpretation should be guided by the fact that texts do not refer to an outside world, except inasmuch as the latter is composed of more text, and that any and every text is to be understood in relation to the systems of signification that regulate discursive practice.

Not everyone, however, is happy with this approach to literature and a few critics have been brave enough to express their unhappiness robustly in print. They feel that Theory is, above all, mechanistic and reductionist – which is hardly surprising since every text is approached with the aim of drawing the same pre-formed conclusions. And although 'overstanding' now has numerous brands – feminist, postcolonial, Lacanian, Marxist, New Historicist, etc. – this modest variety has done little to alleviate the monotony. Under the homogenising gaze of the overstanding critic, the differences between Jane Austen and Wilbur Smith, or between Henry James, Barbara Cartland and the Venerable Bede, are less important than their deep similarities: all five failed to challenge the colonial enterprise; none of them understood the first thing about the Oedipalised negotiation of the transition from the mirror to the symbolic stages, though their work shows they were up to their eyes in its consequences – to the point of believing the fictitious self to be real; all five were blissfully innocent of the ways in which their texts undid themselves; none of them challenged the confusion between nature and culture that enabled the historically derived to be passed off as the eternally true; and they all took for granted the taken for granted, thereby colluding with those power/knowledge structures that keep the oppressed in their state of oppression.

Approaching works of literature with preconceived ideas, and preventing the interpreted works from speaking for themselves, not only guaranteed a monotonous similarity of interpretation; it also encouraged the imposition of interpretations on the basis of very scanty independent evidence. Critics who are not progressive enough to reject close and careful readings of individual texts have bitterly resented the anti-scholarly habit of using tendentious readings of classic or canonical works to support vast presuppositions about the nature of society, the relationship between language and the world, the origin of the self, the interaction between knowledge and power, and so forth. Advanced critics have in their turn accused traditional scholars of timidity and of a failure to recognise the implicit theory within their own practice and to reflect upon it.

My own position is highly sympathetic to the concerns of traditional scholars, a position that has firmed up since I have observed how Theory has managed to survive, indeed to flourish, even when many of its fundamental assumptions have been examined and shown to be groundless and/or self-contradictory;[3] how its practitioners have carried on regardless,[4] with the flow of publications undiminished; and how, to an outside eye, professional advancement seems to be assisted rather than hindered by commitment to criticism that works within, rather than contests, the assumptions of Theory.

This remarkable indifference to counter-argument may in part be because, as I have argued elsewhere, Theory is consonant with wider trends within the humanities: the pathologisation of culture and the marginalisation of the role of the conscious agent in all activities, including such distinctively and seemingly highly conscious ones as writing literature.[5] There are, however, other possible explanations, and, in the present chapter, I shall advance a less ambitious 'internalist' thesis: that Theory, far from being an aberration from, is a culmination of, certain tendencies that have always been present within literary and cultural studies. In particular, I shall suggest that the widespread and uncritical acceptance of the evidence-free assertions of the founders of Theory is an extension of a much longer tradition of accepting evidence-poor assertions; that, because of their methodological weakness, literary studies have always been at risk of being expropriated by fashions led by charismatics and charlatans. More specifically, I shall argue that the discrepancy between the scope of the general statements made within literary and cultural studies and the minute size of the database upon which such statements are founded is not new. What is novel about Theory is only that its 'truths' are of a wider, indeed, global scope: that it looks beyond literature and, on the basis of few or no facts, makes assertions about, for example, the nature of discourse, or of the metaphysical mindset of Western Culture. That, in other words, the difference between Theory and what preceded it is in many cases only a matter of degree rather than of kind.

My general point will be that it has always been possible 'to get away with murder' in a discipline that has no tradition of adequately testing general statements. I shall conclude that one of the most pressing projects within the humanities as a whole (for the problem, of course, extends far beyond literary studies) in the wake of Theory, is, perhaps, to learn how to determine the legitimate scope of general statements – which are often implicitly causal and quantitative – when there is rarely access to adequate empirical evidence.

2 Evidence-based medicine

As medicines become more powerful, the opportunities for doing good with the right treatment and doing harm with the wrong one increase and the burden of responsibility carried by clinicians grows proportionately. The rise of consumerism, in which patients are in more equal partnership with their doctors, means that the latter are more explicitly accountable to patients for the decisions they make. For these and many other reasons, doctors have become more concerned about the quality of the evidence upon which therapeutic choices are made.

The only truly robust method for obtaining good evidence is the double-blind randomised controlled trial which entered clinical science in the 1940s. Prior to being made widely available, new drugs, for example, are required to be evaluated by assigning carefully matched patients randomly either to the drug under study, or to a placebo, or to the best existing treatment. During the period of the trial, neither the patient nor the assessing doctor knows which treatment the patient is receiving. This 'double-blind' arrangement is essential to ensure that enthusiasm for the new treatment does not bias the observers: it embodies the medical profession's own suspicion of itself and its awareness of the potential of both patient and doctor for self-deception and for consciously and unconsciously shaping observations to conform with their wishes. The double-blind arrangement, in short, reflects an acute awareness of the occupational hazard of all empirical enquiry, that of confirmatory bias. In the last few decades, the design of such trials has become considerably more sophisticated, with a better understanding of the ways in which to balance treatment and placebo groups to eliminate bias; with more precise power calculations to determine the numbers of patients that need to be studied to avoid false negatives or false positives; with the use of quality of life and other qualitative outcome measures to complement the more traditional quantitative parameters; and so on. The culmination of this trend has been a series of 'mega-trials' involving tens of thousands of patients in many different centres and often in many different countries.

Mega-trials were pioneered in Italy and they have dramatically influenced our management of common and life-threatening conditions such as heart attacks.

One such mega-trial was the International Stroke Trial (IST). For some time, doctors had wondered whether it might be useful to give aspirin acutely in patients with strokes due to clots in the cerebral arteries. There were good reasons for thinking that this might be a desirable thing to do: aspirin has anti-clotting properties, and animal experiments had shown that early restoration of blood flow may prevent or reverse some of the damage caused by stroke. There were, however, anxieties about the potential of aspirin for causing cerebral haemorrhage even in patients with thrombotic strokes. Similar arguments related to the anti-coagulant heparin. In order to determine the appropriateness of using either aspirin or heparin or both in acute stroke, Charles Warlow and colleagues in Edinburgh established a trial which included 467 centres in 36 countries. Patients were randomised to receive aspirin or no aspirin plus or minus heparin. A prior power calculation indicated that roughly 20,000 patients would be needed and these were recruited over several years. Nearly a decade after the trial was first proposed, the results from IST were reported in *Lancet* in 1997.[6] They were clear-cut: heparin was not beneficial and was possibly dangerous, and aspirin produced a small but definite benefit and should be used in acute stroke. The following week the Chinese Acute Stroke Study (CAST), designed on very similar lines, likewise involving about 20,000 patients, was published.[7] It, too, showed the benefit of aspirin, thus confirming the robustness of both trials and also how international good science is.

Of course not all good trials have to be so large. Where much greater benefits are expected in individual patients, or more complex outcome measures, employing interval rather than categorical scales, are used, smaller numbers may suffice to produce robust results which avoid both false positives and false negatives. It all depends what the power calculation, and the prior hypothesis, require. Sometimes the results of several small trials may be pooled to generate a 'virtual trial' of sufficient power. This approach, however, has potential pitfalls, particularly if the individual trials use different criteria for patient selection or different outcome measures. The science of so-called meta-analysis is therefore now very sophisticated. One of its most important contributions has been to correct the bias that comes from favouring the publication of positive results over negative ones, thereby giving a drug or some other therapy a better press than it may deserve.[8] In meta-analysis, the search for unpublished studies and for raw data from published trials is highly systematic, involving not only massive electronic medical databases, registers of clinical trials, 'grey literature' (theses, non-peer reviewed journals), and literature in all languages but also unpublished sources known to experts in the field whose knowledge is tapped as systematically as possible. Once all the data have been gathered, pooled and analysed, it is possible to indicate whether or not the treatment has a beneficial effect to a measured degree of certainty ('confidence intervals') and the scale of the average benefit patients might expect.

This is scrupulous scholarship of the highest order, and so it should be: patients' lives and happiness are at stake. Even so, doctors are conscious that the evidence from clinical trials is still imperfect, and there has been much criticism, not only of the inadequacies of techniques such as meta-analysis,[9] but also of the wider assumption that all decisions made with individual patients can be entirely based on evidence from clinical trials. No amount of general evidence can predetermine the outcome of the discussion between patient and doctor or take into account all of the factors that are relevant for an individual person.[10] This is, of course, true, but the aim of evidence-based medicine must be to narrow the meshes within which decisions are made rather than to reduce clinical decision-making to the enactment of an algorithm. A doctor who is any good should be able to work within a framework of probability rather than apodeictic certainty.

3 Evidence-free theory: two case reports

The contrast, when one moves from clinical science to Theory, is such that it is difficult to believe the two pursuits belong to the same stage of evolution of the human species. I do not for a moment wish to suggest that the evidence-free theories of post-Saussurean thought – parroted by generations of teachers to generations of students – are typical of literary scholarship. What they illustrate is the vulnerability of the humanities to colonisation by charlatans and how far charlatans can travel unchallenged – because of the lack of a tradition within the literary studies of requiring evidence proportionate to the scale and scope of assertions. Ironically, the demand for evidence seems to fall off as the scope of assertions expands. Rigorous scholars may argue forcefully over the interpretation of a particular word in *Hamlet*, while statements with a global reference will be allowed to pass on the nod – perhaps because the demand for evidence seems almost comical – at any rate misplaced.

Let me illustrate the contrast between Theory and the kind of rigorous scholarship that is regarded as industry standard in the comparatively soft science of clinical medicine with two case reports on well-known practitioners.

Prelude: The omniscient Roland Barthes

Barthes was one of the major figures in literary studies over the last forty years. These are some of the assertions he made publicly and yet escaped mockery:

1. About all language: 'But language – the performance of a language system – is neither reactionary nor progressive; it is quite simply fascist; for fascism does not prevent speech, it compels speech.'[11]

2. Of all signs since medieval times: 'Replacing the feudal index, the bourgeous sign is a metonymic confusion' (*S/Z*, 40).
3. Of all writing: 'Writing is in no way an instrument for communication.'[12]
4. Of all art in the West: 'In the West at least, there is no art that does not point to its own mask' (*Writing Degree Zero*, 41).
5. Of all writers after 1850: '[After the 1850s] the writer falls a prey to ambiguity, since his consciousness no longer accounts for the whole of his condition' (ibid., 66).
6. Of the relationship between all writing and all power: 'Power, or the shadow cast by power, always ends in creating an axiological writing, in which the distance that usually separates fact from value disappears within the very space of the word' (ibid., 26).

Barthes is not alone in his claims to omniscience. Derrida and Lacan are, if anything, more sweeping in their pronouncements. They have taken care, however, to avoid the lucidity that makes Barthes perhaps an easier target, and for this reason have become more potent role models, more widely imitated, and are worthy of more detailed study.

Case 1: Lacan and the insufficiency of facts[13]

Lacan's presence in literary studies is particularly instructive. He wins the prize for obscurity, and the few conclusions that seem half-way comprehensible are glades of seeming lucidity in a thicket of argument composed of allusions and enthymemes – a prose style that was described by a disciple as follows:

> A complete account of the characteristic features, syntactic and other, of Lacan's style would include: the ambiguous *que*, disturbances of conventional word order, literal and metaphorical senses interwoven, periphrasis, ellipsis, leading notions alluded to rather than declared, abstractions personified, persons becoming abstractions, synonyms being given widely different meanings ... All this keeps the signified as a palely fluttering presence behind the rampaging signifier.[14]

In such circumstances, the illusion of meaning created by a bald assertion, however daft, must be gratefully received. What is interesting about Lacan is that his assertions seem unchallengeable because they are apparently rooted in science. Lacanian critics, who are humanist scholars, take them as read; they do not, perhaps, feel qualified to challenge the white-coated boffin. Supporting evidence is never sought. Which is as well – as there is no such evidence.

Consider the claims – central to Lacanian literary criticism – that the self is a signifier without a signified, that it is a fiction, that its unconscious is structured like a language, that the world of words creates the world of things. So far as these widely quoted and much-invoked positions have any evidential base, it should be available in Lacan's *Écrits*.

Lacan claimed to base his beliefs mainly in his theories of child development in which he brought together structural linguistics and Freudian psychoanalysis. He argued that there were two crucial stages in child development: the mirror phase when the child first acquired the notion of a unified self; and the symbolic phase when that self was preserved, in the teeth of its ontological groundlessness, by being inscribed in language and was consequently rewarded by receiving a name and a place in the family, and by an entry ticket into society and culture. The mirror phase is supposed to begin at about six months and end at eighteen months. The child, seeing itself in a mirror, identifies with the image and internalises an image of wholeness that is in advance of its undeveloped physical self, its unmediated sense of being a helpless mess. It embraces this image with jubilation and identifies (or misidentifies) with it. The wholeness of the specular image, Lacan says, is the first version of the fiction of the ego, of the unified or coherent self. In fact, Lacan says, contrary to what the mirror tells the child, we are not whole, we are profoundly split; worse, this thing that is split is not something positive – it is a negative, a lack. We are a nothing cut into many pieces; so our lives, which presuppose enduring identities, are founded upon lies which are compounded when we move from the Mirror to the Symbolic phase: then we are best understood as signifiers without signifieds.

The evidence that Lacan gives for this theory is shaky to say the least. He contrasts the behaviour of infants with that of other animals and claims that there is a distinctive jubilation exhibited by human infants faced with their own mirror image. Actually, there are no data to support this claim: a child looking at itself in the mirror is very easily distracted to more interesting things, for example, a passing cat or a rustling sweet paper or (according to the classic experiments of Lewis et al.[15]) the reflection of a toy in the mirror. Moreover, Lacan himself notes the specific delight – the '*Aha erlebnis*' – experienced by chimpanzees in this situation, although he claims that the chimp does not pursue this any further, unlike the human baby. This, again, is at odds with experimental observations by Gallup et al.[16]

Lacanians, faced with the threat of empirical refutation, argue that the theory is not an empirical theory at all but a metaphor or even 'a diachronic fable of a synchronic functioning' (see my *Not Saussure*, p. 146; and this volume, p. 267). One wonders then why specific empirical claims, including assertions about the duration of the mirror and other phases, are made and why 'facts' are invoked to support it.

If Lacan's hypothesis were genuinely scientific – as opposed merely to clothing itself in the rhetoric of science – one would have expected a vast number of observations to support the pivotal assertion that the child has a special relationship to its mirror image. These would have to be obtained in such a way as to ensure that confirmatory bias was guarded against, and the findings would have to be subjected to statistical analysis to be sure that any association between the encounter with the mirror and certain patterns of behaviour was more than might be noted by chance. None of this is offered by Lacan. Nor have Lacanians even attempted to obtain such data in the sixty years or so since Lacan first put forward his theory.

Arguments about the factual basis for the mirror phase would be of greater moment if the theory itself were not fatally flawed by explanatory inadequacy. What Lacan does not explain is how the infant connects all the different images of itself – corresponding to the various occasions of its being exposed to reflecting surfaces – with the same self if there is no real basis for that self. Such images will take many different forms depending upon the position in which the child is held up, the background lighting, and the nature of the reflecting surface: a mirror, a teapot, a puddle, etc. Without the prior and persisting intuition of a self, to which all the different images refer, the child could not derive a sense of wholeness from a series of quite different images of parts of its own body. Where, if the self is a fiction – dreamed up by a nothing that only imagines it is a something – does the very idea of identity come from? Why am I on the lookout for candidate entities to identify (or misidentify) with? What is it that is doing the identifying, or misidentifying? Nor does Lacan explain how or why the child connects that image with other concurrent experiences – that of its full stomach, its sore bottom, its wriggling legs. Nor – and most damningly – does he account for the connectivity over time, the link between the successive moments of its being. In other words, the specular explanation of the so-called fiction of the self requires the prior existence of precisely that which it has to explain – the synchronic and diachronic unity of apperception, of consciousness. That is an unassailable fact, not a fiction, of our ordinary life in which we take responsibility for our actions. (Lacanians are, of course, entirely insincere in pretending to hold that the self is a fragmented nothing that has no unity: they still believe that there is a difference between their ordinary selves and those of sufferers from end-stage dementia; like the rest of us, they claim ownership for their actions, their works, and their possessions; and they have a sense of rights that would not be coherent if there were no continuous self to assert entitlement. Some of them even have a sense of responsibility that, likewise, presupposes the notion of a real self extended over time.)

As if the lack of evidence for the theory of the mirror phase were not bad enough, Lacan's theory of the symbolic phase has an additional vulnerability: it is based on Freud's notion of the Oedipus complex, for which, it is now known, Freud obtained no independent evidence.[17] What little 'evidence' he adduced was extracted from patients (sometimes under duress) in whom he had implanted the idea of the Oedipus conflict in the first place. Lacan's notion of child development, central for the doctrines which he propounded and which are echoed by his non-medical disciples, is therefore a card castle built on quicksand. It is, however, enclosed in a bell jar, being entirely protected from exposure to empirical testing, though its form is that of an empirical theory.

Case 2: Jacques Derrida and non-facts

Jacques Derrida has made his reputation as a theorist of the human universe. His scope is enormous. His assertions regularly encompass 'Western philosophy', 'Western thought', etc., and he has much to say about (all of) 'writing', (all of) 'text'. In short, he feels able to speak with authority about the entire history of human discourse and declare that (for example) writing (in a very special sense) has primacy over speech; that Western metaphysics has certain distinctive characteristics, including a penchant for immediate presence, unmediated Being; that there is nothing outside of the text; etc. These positions – asserted in the teeth of Derrida's own professed and profound scepticism about our knowledge of the real world and his belief in the total indeterminacy of the meaning of texts – have been accepted without challenge by his numerous disciples. Much of what he says is unsupported by evidence: he is the supreme contemporary master of the evidence-free assertion. Where he provides evidence, it is usually laughably insufficient to the position being argued.

His favoured technique is to discuss a handful of writers, or a single writer, often approached from an egregious angle, and to use them as mighty synecdoches for the entirety of Western thought and Western consciousness, etc. In this regard, he is no worse than Lacan, Barthes, or, indeed, Alf Garnett – for whom a brief encounter in a Curry House will generate sufficient data to support a five-word summary of the Indian sub-continent. In another respect, however, he is less innocent. There is prima facie evidence that his misrepresentation of thinkers key to propping up his cartoon account of 'Western thought' is not entirely accidental. Some of those who have chosen not to be his disciples have taken the trouble to check his sources and have found that they have been misquoted or misinterpreted in strategic ways.

Derrida's misrepresentation of thinkers and scholars initially escaped detection in the 'soft touch' world of interdisciplinary studies. Now it seems that the game is up. The misrepresentations of Plato,[18] Saussure,[19] Peirce,[20] Husserl,[21] and E.R. Curtius[22] have been carefully documented. There is evidence that these errors are systematic rather than accidental, not only because they serve the ideas that Derrida wishes to foist upon the world – most notably that the meaning of discourse is indeterminate, that signs never reach a signified, and that human consciousness is absent from language – but also because some quotations with which Derrida supports his interpretations of the thinkers he suborns to his cause have been mis-edited with great care.

Take, for example, his misuse of E.R. Curtius's *European Literature and the Latin Middle Ages*, discussed by James Drake (see n. 22). Here, in order to make Curtius confirm Derrida's view that 'writing' means more than inscription and that this has been obscured by privileging speech over writing, he stitches together phrases from different parts of Curtius's book (so that their referent is displaced by 1,000 years!) and thereby forces the latter to say the opposite of what he manifestly intended. It is interesting to note that this distortion had to be pointed out by a non-academic and was published, not in a scholarly journal but in a literary weekly – *The Times Literary Supplement*.

Peirce is a crucial witness in support of Derrida's absolutely central notion of 'the deconstruction of the transcendental signified'.[23] Earlier criticism of Derrida's mishandling of Peirce (e.g. in *Not Saussure*) was based upon the assumption that the errors were accidental. It is clear from Vickers' and others' investigations that the accidents have been too central to Derrida's purposes to be entirely accidental. In particular, Derrida's deliberate removal of reference to intelligent consciousness in Peirce's discussion of the chain of signs (*Of Grammatology*, 48–50) is obviously intended to make Peirce sound like Derrida, for whom intelligent consciousness must be left out of account.

4. Lack of scandal: the institutionalisation of fraud

The examples given above of evidence-bent theorising could be multiplied many times over, especially if one were to include the vast following attracted by the *maîtres à penser*. After all, Derrideans number many thousands. What I have described is a scandal of the greatest magnitude. So why is no one scandalised? Had a scientist misrepresented data in the way that Derrida seems to have done, he would have been the subject of a serious enquiry. Is it because, in the world of postmodern 'scholarship', where there is no such thing as truth (or even reference), anything goes?[24] This may be part of the story, combined with the fact that, as Drake has pointed out, people rarely check primary sources, and, as Vickers has noted, they frequently simply quote the passages others have quoted without reading the originating text. A second-order argument-from-authority – whereby truth is asserted by quoting authority (e.g. Derrida) who quotes an authority (e.g. Peirce) – seems to be sufficient to secure assent.

In fact many academics *are* scandalised by what is happening. Serious and scrupulous scholars, such as Brian Vickers (see n. 3), have protested against the distortions and errors of the glamorous critics working in their fields. But matched against the promises irradiating from charismatic figures, the dissent of those who are wedded to factual truth may seem mere carping. To an outsider such as myself, it seems that a mighty work of scholarship such as Vickers' recent edition of Bacon, with its 300 pages of carefully argued footnotes drawing upon a huge knowledge of Renaissance political, social and cultural history, of its literature, and a profound understanding of philology,[25] cannot possibly compete with an immediate understanding of the big picture based upon a few anecdotes and contrived readings which promises to be 'subversive' – both in overthrowing received ideas and supporting a fashionable Foucauldian paranoia about political power in the contemporary world. The competition is as unfair as that which George Steiner noted between science 'which amasses one grain after another in its storehouse only by hard, fatiguing, individual work' and knowledge acquisition by 'a spontaneous spiritual knowing, which would deliver truths about the outer as well as the inner world, without the trouble of recourse to mathematics or experiments'.[26] And yet, despite the unfairness of the competition, in medicine at least, the cautious clinical scientist has won against the omniscient witch doctor. Why has this not happened in literary studies? Why are the quacks – with their instant diagnoses and instant cures – in the ascendant? Why does being a rotten scholar peddling exciting ideas attract tenure rather than scandal?

There are many reasons for this. One possibility is that in the United States of America, and latterly in the United Kingdom, the pressure to maximise income from student fees encourages institutions to appoint 'big draw' teachers, and Big Ideas – even wrong or muddled or daft ones – are a bigger draw than rigorous scholarship, which is inescapably narrowly focused. (This is a hypothesis which would need to be tested by properly controlled case studies.) An alternative – or contributory – explanation is the intrinsic methodological weakness of much literary studies. This weakness is evident not so much at the end of the spectrum where we find detailed scholarship relating to a small number of works – editing, glossing, footnoting – but at the other end, where literary history shades into wider cultural history. There is an aphorism among medical scientists (designed to puncture the pomposity of those who appeal to their clinical impressions or 'experience' to settle issues regarding the course or treatment of disease): *the plural of anecdote is not data.* Cultural history, in particular, is more often than not anecdote driven.[27]

5. The Sokal hoax

The methodological weakness of the higher reaches of cultural criticism and theory was exposed dramatically when the peer review system of one of the leading Theory journals, *Social Text*, was tested. A spoof paper – 'Transgressing the Boundaries: Toward a Transformative Hermeneutics of Quantum Gravity'

– was submitted to this journal: it purported to relativise the claims of quantum mechanics to be in any objective sense true. The paper, written by a professional physicist, was deliberately planted with elementary errors in physics and was logically inconsistent in a very unsubtle way. Finally, it was peppered with totally incomprehensible phrases and assertions. The paper was accepted and published.

The success of the hoax gave powerful support to those who believed that there was now a complete breakdown of quality control in the field of cultural criticism and theory. A paper could be accepted, it seemed, if it appeared to be supporting the prejudices of the editorial board. As Paul Boghossian[28] has written, the journal was prepared 'to let agreement with its ideological orientation trump every other criterion for publication, including something as basic as sheer intelligibility'.

There was a further element to this tale: the paper was written by a scientist who had been provoked to write it by the attacks upon science emanating from the postmodernist critics: the relativisers who pretended to believe that science had nothing to say about Nature, having only social power rather than objective truth to support its claims to be taken seriously; who pretended with equal hypocrisy to equate the scientists who have made modern technologically based society possible with the magicians whose technologies are singularly useless; in short, who regard science as being merely one among many competing discursive formations.

This hostility to science[29] has a particular relevance to the issue of the disabling methodological weaknesses of some aspects of the humanities. It amounts to a pre-emptive strike on a superior rival. Moreover, as José Merquior suggested:

> In the age of cognitive growth and universal literacy, the humanist clerisy is a kind of antique. It no longer holds the monopoly on writing, and knows that its expertise, verbal knowledge, is no match for the authority of science. One possible strategy, therefore, is to disparage this unfavourable setting by decrying modernity.[30]

Ernest Gellner has underlined this connection between 'the crisis-mongering of humanist intellectuals' and 'the archaism of their intellectual equipment'.[31]

At any rate, the Sokal affair exposed the weakness of the peer review process in certain sectors of the humanities. Where there are no objective checks on the claims made in a piece of scholarship, the personal views of peers become all-important. Peers may be as bad as, as well as as good as, oneself. And this is the step by which fraud may move from the personal and individual to the institutional and collective. Moreover, where (as appears to be the case at present) post-Saussureans are in powerful positions in many humanities departments, the chances of publishing work hostile to post-Saussurean thought must be diminished.[32] In science, by contrast, there are numerous checks to prevent the domination of one school of thought over another simply on the basis of the powerful placement of its proponents: the most obvious of these is that the most junior researcher can test whether the results obtained by the Nobel prize winner are repeatable and whether the theory matches the data. No adoring herd of disciples can protect the eminent from scrutiny, from exposure to empirical checks.

In the absence of empirical tests, theoretical writings are liable to be selected for publication by their conformity to the received ideas which are favoured by the editorial boards of the journals to which they are submitted. Barthes' declaration in 1963 was an unconscious warning of the solipsist scholasticism to come:

> the human sciences are losing some of their positivist obsession: structuralism, psychoanalysis, even Marxism prevail by the coherence of their system rather than by the 'proof' of their details: we are endeavouring to construct a science which includes itself within its object, and it is this infinite reflexiveness which constitutes, facing us, art itself: science and art both acknowledge an original relativity of object and enquiry.[33]

What the Sokal hoax has underlined is that, when an academic discipline loses its 'positivist obsession', fraud has an easier time; or something close to it: the editorial policy of journals 'prepared to let agreement with [their] ideological orientation trump every other criterion for publication, including something as basic as sheer intelligibility'.

6. Beyond the anecdote

> Let every student of nature take this as his rule: that whatever the mind seizes upon with particular satisfaction is to be held with suspicion.
>
> (Francis Bacon, *Novum Organum*)

In his discussion of New Historicism, Vickers cites Jean Howard's objection to Stephen Greenblatt's 'anecdotal method'; namely, that it offers no way of determining whether the 'illustrative example' is 'representative, and if so, on what grounds, statistically, say, or just by one's own authority'.[34] This, in a nutshell, is why 'the plural of anecdote is not data' and why medical therapeutics remained pre-scientific and unreliable so long as it was based upon anecdotes – uncontrolled and isolated observations gathered at random. Reliance on anecdote, on impressions whose selection has been influenced by the hypothesis to be tested, becomes the royal road to untruth or at best half-truth as soon as literary studies raises its sights above scholarly attention to individual works or to a small corpus of work and attempts to become cultural criticism, cultural history or Theory. The stage is set for confirmatory bias to regulate scholarship and the critic becomes more like a lawyer making a case – focusing on supporting evidence, ignoring contrary facts – than a scientist trying to uncover robust general truths; or (to be a little kinder) more like a hypochondriac making a diagnosis ('Everything fits!') than to a clinician. If you then add in a little cross-disciplinary travel, so that one's audience is for the most part playing an away match, then the constraints are finally broken. The scene is set for global assertions, for glamorous opacity – in short for Theory.

I am uncomfortably aware that I am not above this process as I write the present chapter. Indeed, Trisha Greenhalgh's description of how one put together an overview in the bad old days before meta-analysis (see n. 8) fits my present procedure, which has been anecdote-driven and dependent upon a selection of quotations from primary and secondary sources. However, so long as my comments are understood as the first word and not the last, this may be acceptable. Scientific medicine, after all, necessarily began with anecdotal clinical observations setting the agenda for systematic clinical enquiry.

The lack of appropriate quantitative methods to acquire the data necessary to underpin descriptive general statements and to ensure the validity of causal explanations – such as those that purport to demonstrate the political, social, cultural, economic and internal 'literary' influences on the structure and content of works of literature – lies at the heart of the present crisis in the humanities. In an age in which it is increasingly expected that general statements should be supported by robust evidence if they are to command credence, the humanities are in danger of being simply anachronistic, acceptable only to arts graduates who have known no better and are unacquainted with adequate methodological discipline. More specifically, by drifting further and further away from careful, evidence-based readings of individual texts and abandoning the traditional virtues of scholarship in favour of a *kulturkritik* of enormous scope, exponents of Theory are increasingly exposing 'the archaism of their intellectual equipment'. Theory shows the extent to which literary studies are still at the stage of clinical impression and personal charisma: the equivalent of the quackery of pre-scientific medicine.

Given that 'the plural of anecdote is not data', what new approach will protect the humanities from the kind of charlatanry that, much to the disgust of many honest scholars, threatens to overwhelm it? Huge collaborative effort would be necessary to acquire data adequate to support the kinds of claims that are routinely made in cultural history and criticism. In certain areas – for example, the work that is being carried out in mining archives – something that resembles this is taking place. Otherwise, however, the tradition of the independent, isolated scholar predominates. This is in sharp contrast to the collaborative model of contemporary science – where collaboration is not merely explicit, as in the IST and other mega-trials, but also implicit and all-pervasive in the sense of building on others' methods, techniques, and findings.

Of course, mere data acquisition is not enough. In science, data are acquired in the context of a hypothesis being tested. The priority of hypotheses raises the danger, already alluded to, of confirmatory bias, particularly where one is dealing with the massive singularities of historical epochs; as Crews expressed it so eloquently, 'any thematic stencil will make its own pattern stand out'.[35] This is particularly likely in a discipline relatively new to the methods of empirical enquiry and where, as in the history of literature or cultural criticism, there are no checks available from independent tests and predictions on the basis of repeated run-throughs.

Avoiding confirmatory bias is central to the morality, as well as the methodology, of science. This is expressed with wonderful persuasiveness by the great physicist Richard Feynman in his moving commencement address to Caltech students in 1974:

> But there is one feature I notice that is generally missing in cargo cult science ... It's a kind of scientific integrity, a principle of scientific thought that corresponds to a kind of utter honesty – a kind of leaning over backwards. For example, if you're doing an experiment, you should report everything that you think might make it invalid – not only what you think is right about it: other causes that could possibly explain your results; and things you thought of that you've eliminated by some other experiment, and how they worked – to make sure the other fellow can tell they have been eliminated.
>
> Details that could throw doubt on your interpretations must be given, if you know them. You must do the best you can – if you know anything at all wrong, or possibly wrong – to explain it. If you make a theory, for example, and advertise it, or put it out, then you must also put down all the facts that disagree with it, as well as those that agree with it ... When you have put a lot of ideas together to make an elaborate theory, you want to make sure, when explaining what it fits, that those things it fits are not just the things that gave you the idea for the theory; but that the finished theory makes something else come out right in addition.[36]

Nothing could be further from this than the evidence-poor, evidence-free or evidence-faked theorising of certain cultural critics and theorists, who, where they are not confabulating their data, are simply redrawing with highly selected facts the outlines of their thematic stencils or hobby horses.

In science, of course, Feynman's morality is not an optional extra: anyone transgressing will soon fall victim to public refutation. It is not that scientists are morally superior to humanist intellectuals but that there is no mileage in propounding untruths: you will very soon get found out, and whereas mistakes are allowed, faking is punished ruthlessly, and a scientist who sticks to his pet ideas in the teeth of refutation soon loses his reputation. In short, the institutional forces favour honesty; science fraud, while real and ever-present, is a minority pursuit. In the humanities, as James Drake has suggested to me (personal communication), the institutional forces work in precisely the opposite direction, and so it is very much down to personal morality. Rampant, unchecked theorising not only adds to the quantity of falsehood in the world but is also counter-educational inasmuch as it teaches the opposite of the kind of scrupulousness that Feynman regarded as essential to science.

To establish large (or even large-ish) truths about cultural and literary history would require an enormous effort of data gathering which would in turn presuppose extensive co-operation and organisation. While this effort is unquestionably worthwhile when one is evaluating a new treatment for a serious condition such as stroke, it may not be thought to be justified merely in order to establish some general truths of cultural history. Indeed, it may be deemed absurd to try to establish assertions about (say) 'the cult of sensibility in the eighteenth century' with the same level of certainty as that which should underlie clinical practice. Humanist academics often defend their data-poor assertions by suggesting that this would not only be difficult; it would also be inappropriate. And they cite Aristotle to the effect that one should apply to any given area of enquiry only the level of precision that is appropriate to it. Against this self-serving defence, I would argue that large-scale empirical statements – such as are made by many cultural theorists and historians – have to be underpinned by properly designed large-scale empirical enquiries. Without such an approach, one can have no guarantee that the body of higher-level 'knowledge' about cultural history is anything other than a reflection of the unsubstantiated opinions and prejudices of the most forceful and charismatic practitioners of the art – providing one of the few examples where intellectual activity actually does conform to the Foucauldian paradigm of the subordination of knowledge to power. If one does not have the means to acquire the data to support higher-level generalisations, one should avoid them. In short, if you can't substantiate statements, don't make them.

The bad examples of the *maîtres à penser* who have dominated literary theory and critical thought in recent years should be enough to encourage submission to such a self-denying ordinance. It cannot, surely, be a worthwhile use of one's life to add to the quantity of untruth in the world and thereby increase the contempt in which literary studies are sometimes held by those engaged in more exact disciplines. For this might lead to throwing out the baby of good literary scholarship with the bathwater of theorrhoea.

Notes

1. 'Professionalised Philosophy and Transcendental Culture', *Georgia Review*, 30 (1976), 757–69 (pp. 763–4), repr. in R. Rorty, *Consequences of Pragmatism (Essays, 1972–80)* (Brighton: Harvester, 1982).
2. *S/Z: An Essay*, trans. Richard Miller (New York: Hill & Wang, 1974).
3. See, for example: Brian Vickers, *Appropriating Shakespeare: Contemporary Critical Quarrels* (New Haven: Yale University Press, 1993); J.G. Merquior, *From Prague to Paris: A Critique of Structuralist and Post-structuralist Thought* (London: Verso, 1986); Raymond Tallis, *Not Saussure: A Critique of Post-Saussurean Literary Theory* (London: Macmillan, 1988; 2nd edn. 1995); Raymond Tallis, *In Defence of Realism* (London: Edward Arnold, 1988, 2nd edn. Lincoln: University of Nebraska Press, 1998); John Ellis, *Against Deconstruction* (Princeton: Princeton University Press, 1989).
4. See Raymond Tallis, 'The Survival of Theory', in *Theorrhoea and After* (London: Macmillan, 1999).
5. Raymond Tallis, *Enemies of Hope: A Critique of Contemporary Pessimism* (London: Macmillan, 1997).
6. International Stroke Trial Collaborative Group, 'The International Stroke Trial (IST): A Randomised Trial of Aspirin, Subcutaneous Heparin, Both, or Neither among 19,435 Patients with Acute Ischaemic Stroke', *Lancet* (1997), 349: 1569–81.
7. CAST (Chinese Acute Stroke Trial), 'CAST: Randomised, Placebo-Controlled Trial of Early Aspirin Use in 20,000 Patients with Acute Ischaemic Stroke', *Lancet* (1997), 349: 1641–9.
8. Trisha Greenhalgh, 'How to Read a Paper: Papers that Summarise Other Papers (Systematic Reviews and Meta-analyses)', *British Medical Journal* (1997), 315: 672–4.
9. Editorial, 'Meta-analysis under Scrutiny', *Lancet* (1997), 350: 675.
10. J.A. Knotterus and G.J. Dinant, 'Medicine Based Evidence: A Prerequisite for Evidence Based Medicine', *British Medical Journal* (1997), 315: 1109–10.
11. Inaugural Lecture, College de France, in *Barthes: Selected Writings*, ed. and introd. Susan Sontag (Oxford: Fontana, 1983), 461.
12. *Writing Degree Zero*, trans. Annette Lavers and Colin Smith (London: Jonathan Cape, 1967), 25.
13. For a detailed critique of Lacan's mirror phase, see Tallis, *Not Saussure*, ch. 5, 'The Mirror Stage: A Critical Reflection'; and reproduced as reading 9 in this volume. See also the damaging evidence for Lacan's fraudulent approach to 'science' in Elizabeth Roudinesco's *Jacques Lacan*, trans. Barbara Bray (London: Polity, 1997), reviewed by Raymond Tallis, *Times Higher Education Supplement*, 31 October 1997.
14. Malcolm Bowie, in John Sturrock (ed. and introd.), *Structuralism and Since: From Lévi-Strauss to Derrida* (Oxford: Oxford University Press, 1979), 145.
15. The experiments are summarised in M. Lewis and J. Brookes, 'Self-Knowledge and Emotional Development', in M. Lewis and L.A. Rosenblum (eds.), *The Development of Affect* (New York: Plenum, 1978), 205–26. (Mirror recognition and self-naming in fact develop at almost the same time, which hardly supports Lacan's notion of a sequence in which a mirror stage is followed by a symbolic stage.)
16. Gordon G. Gallup, 'Self-Recognition in Primates: A Comparative Approach to the Bidirectional Properties of Consciousness', *American Psychologist*, 32 (1977), 329–38.

17. The illusion that Freud amassed a huge body of evidence for the theory that he described as the cornerstone of psychoanalysis theory is just that. For full details see Allen Esterson, *Seductive Mirage: An Exploration of the Work of Sigmund Freud* (Chicago: Open Court Books, 1993); Richard Webster, *Why Freud was Wrong: Sex, Sin and Psycho-analysis* (London: HarperCollins, 1995); Robert Wilcocks, *Maelzel's Chess Player: Sigmund Freud and the Rhetoric of Deceit* (Lanham, Md.: Rowman & Littlefield, 1994). The fact that Lacan feels at liberty to displace the Oedipal stage by two years (taking it back from the age of 3 to 5 that Freud claimed for it to his own 18 months to 3 years) without provoking any challenge from his Freudian followers testifies eloquently to the lack of empirical evidence for either version of this idea of psycho-sexual development.
18. See Mary J. Devaney, *'Since at Least Plato ...' and Other Postmodernist Myths* (London: Macmillan, 1997).
19. See Tallis, *Not Saussure*, 169–71, 211–13.
20. See Brian Vickers, 'Derrida's Reading of C.S. Peirce', *Times Literary Supplement* (9 May 1997), 15; Tallis, *Not Saussure*, 213–14; Ann E. Berthoff, 'Why Peirce is Hard to Read', in *The Mysterious Barricades: Language and its Limits* (Toronto: Toronto University Press forthcoming).
21. Tallis, *Not Saussure*, 189–202; Kevin Mulligan, 'How Not to Read: Derrida on Husserl', *Topoi*, 10 (1991), 199–208.
22. James Drake, 'Derrida's Reading of E.R. Curtius', *Times Literary Supplement* (2 May 1997), 17.
23. Jacques Derrida, *Of Grammatology*, trans. Gayatri Chakravorty Spivak (Baltimore: Johns Hopkins University Press, 1974), 49.
24. Just how far contempt for referential truth has trickled down from the commanding heights of Yale and the Collège de France is illustrated by a recent Open University collection on Representation. The introduction advises students that: 'We should perhaps learn to think of meaning less in terms of "accuracy" and "truth" and more in terms of effective exchange – a process of translation, which facilitates cultural communication while always recognising the persistence of difference and power between different "speakers" within the same cultural circuit.' Stuart Hall (ed.), *Representations: Cultural Representation and Signifying Practices* (London: Sage, in association with the Open University, 1997), 11.
25. *Francis Bacon: A Critical Edition of the Major Works*, ed. Brian Vickers (Oxford: Oxford University Press, 1996).
26. George Steiner, *Real Presences: Is There Anything in What We Say?* (London: Faber, 1989).
27. I owe this explanation to James Drake (in a personal communication).
28. For a lucid account of the Sokal hoax and of the lessons to be drawn from it, see Paul Boghossian, 'What the Sokal Hoax ought to teach us', *Times Literary Supplement*, 13 December 1996. The pernicious impact of postmodernist Theory on academic standards and academic life is explored in Barbara Epstein's brief 'The Postmodernism Debate: More on the Sokal Parody' (*Z Magazine* (October 1996), 57–9). See also Raymond Tallis, 'Sokal and Bricmont: Is the Beginning of the End of the Dark Ages in the Humanities?', *PN Review*, 128 (1998), 35–42.
29. Discussed at length in Raymond Tallis, *Newton's Sleep: the Two Cultures and the Two Kingdoms* (London: Macmillan, 1995), and Tallis, *Enemies of Hope*.
30. J.G. Merquior, 'In Quest of Modern Culture: Hysterical or Historical Humanism', *Critical Review*, 5 (1991), 399–420.
31. Quoted ibid., 409.

32. Where criticism is published, it is ignored. As Bruce Charlton points out (*Journal of Evaluation in Clinical Practice*, 3 (1997), 169–71), one can minimise the impact of valid dissent by denying it the publicity involved in rebuttal.
33. Quoted in Vickers, *Appropriating Shakespeare*, 422.
34. Ibid., 229.
35. Quoted in Vickers, *Appropriating Shakespeare*, 430.
36. 'Cargo Cult Science', in Richard P. Feynman, *'Surely You're Joking, Mr. Feynman!' Adventures of a Curious Character*, ed. Edward Hutchings (London: Unwin Paperbacks, 1986), 341.

From: *The Arts and Sciences of Criticism*, ed. David Fuller and Patricia Waugh (Oxford University Press, 1999), Chapter 4.

13
Anti-Science and Organic Daydreams

In this reading, taken from *Newton's Sleep* (1995), Tallis takes up the theme of the response of intellectuals to science. He begins from the fact of pain. There is a connection that he detects between the attitude of certain intellectuals to suffering and the attitude cultivated by the Church. There is, however, little spiritual content in unrelieved toothache. Death from neonatal tetany – in which the baby spends its first and only week of life convulsing to death – is even less compelling as an example of the spiritual benefits to be obtained from physical suffering. He cites a remark of C.P. Snow's, one of those who, as Tallis sees it, understood the issues at stake here, to the effect that the 'tragic' sense of life opens a moral trap. It is all too easy to believe that, because human life is tragic, it does not matter if two-thirds of the world are starving to death. Pursuing his theme in relation to AIDS, Tallis notes that Susan Sontag, a 'leading intellectual' if ever there was one, has questioned the whole idea of a disease characterised by immune failure and has tried to suggest that AIDS is 'really' a 'product of definition and construction'. Scientists, on the other hand, have worked out the mechanism of the virus and developed treatments and strategies which may in time lead to a vaccine. The problem that certain humanists have with science is that, while it has dramatically diminished human helplessness before the non-human universe, it seems to have done so at the cost of diminishing our communion with the vital forces of nature. Tallis challenges this assumption, which emerged with the Romantics and continues to enjoy a wide following today.

For many of those who find science distasteful, the question of whether or not it is of net material benefit to mankind is irrelevant. Science is condemned precisely in so far as it is preoccupied with meeting material needs and wants, and (to use Bacon's terms) its 'experiments of use' outnumber its 'experiments of light'. Worse, the successes of science have encouraged scientists – and many others in the centuries dominated by science-based technology – to believe in progress. Progress, however, is an illusion: technology has not commuted the common sentence of mortality nor has it brought a definitive understanding of the universe, even less of our place in it. So the scientists' optimism – even their commitment to improving the world – is condemned as 'shallow'. Technological advances, however impressive, do not solve the tragedy of the human condition, they merely blunt our perception of it. It is this, perhaps, rather than the disenchanted world pictures of mechanistic science, that accounts for its despiritualising influence. Science, with its many solutions to specific problems, induces a collective amnesia of our condition, of the terrible mystery of a life in which death is inevitable. The ordeal of privation is to be welcomed: by waking one out of a cocoon of material satisfaction, it may expose one to a sense of the possible that goes beyond the ordinary, closed sense of everyday life.

The defender of science would be justified in pointing out that no human activity has solved the problem of our finitude and that very little contemporary art even pretends to transilluminate the mystery of living. And if science has not cancelled mortality, it is surely better to die at eighty than at eight months. He might also draw attention to the significant fact that second-order humanist intellectuals tend to be more at ease expressing unqualified contempt for the endeavour to solve material need than first-order creative artists. The latter, in an age when technical intervention can make a huge difference, and when it is therefore possible to be of practical use to the world, are commonly weighed down by what Martin Seymour-Smith has christened *Kunstlerschuld*.[1] For many of the greatest writers – Vallejo, Broch, Rilke – the fact that 'poetry does not change anything' is a source of deep anguish: if art is not concerned with the remediable miseries of the world, it is condemned by its inutility. They concord with the judgement, expressed in Keats' *Hyperion*, that the highest art is infused with an urgent sense of the miseries of the world:

> 'None can usurp this height' returned that shade,
> 'But those to whom the miseries of the world
> Are misery, and will not let them rest.
> All else who find a haven in the world,
> Where they may thoughtless sleep away their days,
> If by a chance into this fane they come,
> Rot on the pavement where thou rottd'st half'.
>
> (*Hyperion* ll. 147–53)

The twentieth-century preoccupation with 'commitment' in art is a direct expression of artists' wish to be of practical benefit, and of the conviction that the obligation to serve in the Kingdom of Earthly Means cannot be offset by service in the Kingdom of Transcendental Ends.

The defender of science may also be tempted to cite Hegel: Seek for food and clothing first, then the Kingdom of God shall be added unto you (quoted by Walter Benjamin, *Thesis on the Philosophy of History*, ed. H. Arendt (London:

Cape, 1970)). He might also point out that the spiritual content of unrelieved toothache, of constant shortness of breath from anaemia due to tapeworms, of unrelieved vomiting is limited and hardly justifies the suffering involved. The case of death from neonatal tetany – in which a baby spends most of its first and only week of life convulsing to death – is an even less compelling example of the spiritual benefits of physical suffering.

C.P. Snow pointed out (in *The Two Cultures and the Scientific Revolution* and the later *Recent Thoughts on the Two Cultures*) the 'moral trap' which comes from a tragic sense of life. Scientists, he added, 'are not prepared to believe that because the individual life is tragic ... you need not worry if two-thirds of the world die before their time and while they are alive have not enough to eat'. An awareness of the irremediable in the human condition does not lessen responsibility for the needs of others, or justify condemning as shallow the melioristic instincts of the scientist. Notwithstanding that every finite life, howsoever protracted by technology, falls infinitely short of immortality, it is presumably better to give birth to living rather than dead children and not to die in the process, to be well-fed rather than hungry, to be out of pain rather than in it. For the sake of those who are in want, we must therefore work for progress; we must hope for the sake of those who have no hope. As Medawar said, 'To deride the hope of progress is the ultimate fatuity, the last word in poverty of spirit and meanness of mind.'[2] T.H. Huxley's sentiments expressed in his essay 'On the Physical Basis of Life' will be echoed by many scientists:

> We live in a world which is full of misery and ignorance and the plain duty of each and all of us is to try to make the little corner he can influence somewhat less miserable and somewhat less ignorant than it was before he entered it. To do this effectually it is necessary to be fully possessed of only two beliefs: the first, that the order of Nature is ascertainable by our faculties to an extent which is practically unlimited; the second, that our volition counts for something as a condition of the course of events.[3]

Of course, it is very easy to sneer at progressive dreams when you are not yourself hungry, cold or facing death from disease; but very few of those who despise science are careless of whether they themselves live or die, or whether they are hungry or well-fed.

If it is agreed that it is honourable to seek to improve the lot of mankind, we must ask ourselves how this is to be achieved. Those who despise the scientific approach and the technology based upon it never make clear what they would put in its place. Magic, wishful thinking, priestly authority do not seem to offer much to alleviate Adam's curse and to make the planet more amenable to human need.

Of course, science cannot solve all the problems of living or even of meeting physical need. While, for many of us, technology has been extraordinarily successful in pacifying nature, it has been less successful in dealing with the suffering that human beings, rather than nature, visit on human beings. The world would be a better place if individuals behaved better and if the institutions which in part determine and often legitimate their behaviour were replaced by better institutions. The dream of achieving this scientifically is a scientistic, rather than a scientific, ideal; real life and fiction have provided sufficient dystopian exemplars to put us off centralised quasi-scientific management of society. The equation

BUMPER HARVEST
+
CORRUPT AND INEFFICIENT INSTITUTIONS = MASS STARVATION
+
SCIENTISTIC AND MORALISTIC RHETORIC

which summarises the politico-economic programmes of many centralised dictatorships, is a shorthand reminder both of the limitations of science and of the difficulty of implementing ingenious and honest technology in a stupid and dishonest world. Genetic engineering that makes two blades of grass grow where one grew before may only swell a grain mountain into a Mont Blanc and bankrupt third-world farmers. However, even in the sphere of cooperation and organisation, science has much to teach the world.

Consider the effortless internationalism of science. The edition of the *Lancet* on my desk has contributors from 22 nations. If one publishes a paper in a prominent journal, it is not unusual to get reprint requests from countries as far apart as Czechoslovakia and Brazil. A scientific journal is a permanent international conference in which the participants are agreed on terminology, on methodology and on the kinds of facts that are needed to back up assertions. All of these limit international misunderstanding to a degree unique in human affairs. There is no human activity less provincial than science. Although debate is sometimes heated and genuine discoveries or novel paradigms may take time to get accepted, the rules of engagement are such as to facilitate, as far as is possible in human life, the uncovering of truth. With the exception of certain notorious horrors – the attempt to refute relativity theory on the grounds that it was 'Jewish physics', Lysenko's ideological advocacy of Larmackism – scientists do not invoke the provenance of ideas or of observations as grounds for discounting them. *Argumentum ad hominem, argumentum ad locum,* argument from authority (except in so far as writers may refer to others' findings in published papers which have been peer-reviewed for rigour of method and statistical analysis) is unacceptable. Those who doubt reported findings can attempt to repeat them in their own laboratories and either succeed or – as in the case of Benveniste's claims for the immunological potency of homoeopathic solutions, or Fleischman's seeming demonstration of fusion at room temperature – report their failures to replicate them. Or they can check through the page of equations, searching for inconsistency. Such constraints impose a collective honesty, whatever the individual temptation to fraud. They make it impossible for a charismatic and dogmatic figure – a Leavis or a Lacan – to dominate a field simply by virtue of force of personality, or an aura of moral or intellectual superiority. Criticism and self-criticism are constant features of scientific discourse which shows how disagreement can be handled, without merely destructive conflict, on the way to the truth.

The scientific community provides models, that the non-scientific world would do well to study and perhaps imitate, of large-scale cooperation between individuals from widely differing backgrounds working towards a common goal. Multinational clinical trials are now commonplace: a stroke trial to which I am a minor contributor has participants from 30 countries, ranging from Italy to the People's Republic of China. The European Centre for Nuclear Research brings together hundreds of scientists from dozens of countries. Science is thus not only the most successful of all human enterprises but also the most co-operative.

Science is, consequently, comparatively guru-free, and free of the self-legitimating authority that characterises much of human activity inside and outside of academe. There are geniuses in science but they do not thereby gain an authority that extends beyond their actual achievements, and their theories are up for testing like anyone else's, their experimental results for checking like anyone else's. Quantum theory was not discredited in the 1930s and 1940s simply because of Einstein's hostility to it, or at least to the dominant Copenhagen interpretation, even though he had successfully developed one of the most beautiful and admired and far-reaching theories in the history of the human mind. It would be naive to believe that the authority of great men or of the established consensus carries no weight in science; but the argument from authority – 'This is true because I say so/X says so' – is less potent here than in any other collective human activity.

Scientific co-operation and organisation seems to work in places where virtually nothing else does. Whatever one thinks of the use of human resources to explore space, the space programme in the former USSR was one of the few major enterprises in that country that had been driven and directed by scientific experts, and was, despite its enormous intrinsic difficulty, one of the few that had been exempt from the failure that has dogged most of the great projects in that country. The smallpox eradication programme, shaped by scientists and executed in accordance with a plan rigorously based upon a scientific understanding of the mode of spread of the disease, was a complete success. Investigation of how scientists work together, as well as how they think in private, might help mankind to overcome some of the barriers it erects in implementing the solutions scientists make available.

However, humanity is faced by more than man-made problems: fundamentally, our manacles are not mind-forg'd or even society-forg'd but body-forg'd. Ultimately, they derive from the fact that nature has no particular care for one species, or one individual. It does not favour the anaemic child over the hookworm leeching it of blood. Indeed, nature does not particularly favour living matter over non-living, the head upon which a stone falls over the falling stone. So I return to the question that should – but sometimes does not – seriously exercise those to whom the scientific approach is intrinsically repugnant: what, if science and technology were rejected, they would put in its place to assist mankind in its battle to survive in an essentially indifferent, overwhelmingly non-human, universe. To give this question the necessary edge, let us relate it to a specific problem that nature has recently served up to humankind: the catastrophe of HIV infection, the scale of which is only just being appreciated.

It is estimated that, if no cure is found, the HIV/AIDS pandemic will kill, in addition to many millions of males, 3,000,000 or more women and children in the 1990s; that in the major cities in the Americas, Western Europe and sub-Saharan Africa infant and child mortality will rise by 30 per cent; and that more than a million uninfected children will be orphaned because their HIV-infected mothers and fathers will have died from AIDS.[4] The world is in need of help. To whom should it turn? Politicians? Except in one or two countries such as the UK, their role in the crisis has been less than admirable. United States politicians, needing to be in tune with a homophobic electorate, for ten years ignored the problem or made suggestions that would have been at home in Nazi Germany. African politicians have, with a few honourable exceptions, lied to protect the tourist trade and a misplaced sense of nationalist *amour propre*, with the result that in, for example, the Central African Republic, between 20 per cent and 30 per cent of the adult male population will die of AIDS in the next decade.[5] Should we look to journalists? After a disgraceful period in which this ghastly disease was treated in the UK at least as a delicious scandal, the tabloids and the broadsheets have settled down to dishing out information and misinformation in equal proportions: fifteen years into the epidemic prominent newspapers (amongst them *The Sunday Times*) are trying to reassure their readers that AIDS is not a heterosexual disease. Can *Kulturkritiks* help us? Susan Sontag's well-meaning but deeply muddled *AIDS and its Metaphors* is not encouraging. Apart from her irrelevant critique of metaphors of battle in the struggle to control the disease, she questions the idea of a disease characterised by immune failure and consequent opportunistic infection (of which there are many examples other than AIDS) and tries to deny that AIDS is 'really' a disease at all.[6]

What, in the meantime, have the scientists been up to? They have established diagnostic criteria for the disease, have accumulated a gigantic body of knowledge about its manifestations at every stage in every system of the body in every type of sufferer, have determined its cause and its method of transmission, have developed precise and sensitive tests for establishing HIV status, have identified some of the co-factors which determine whether and when HIV carriers actually develop AIDS, have found ways of dealing with many of its manifestations, and of palliating its later stages, and, by brilliant experimentation, have worked out the mechanism of action of the virus and a strategy which may lead to a vaccine in the near future and a cure in the not-too-remote future.[7] All of this has been achieved as a result not only of the highest level of scientific rigour but also of a freedom from the primitive attitudes and prejudices of most of the non-scientific community. Apart from the courage of certain individual sufferers and their supporters, the majority of the wholly admirable players in the AIDS crisis have been clinical and non-clinical scientists and those who have taken a scientific view of the problem. A comparison between the attitudes and approaches of doctors and scientists to AIDS and that of politicians with their talk of quarantine for HIV carriers, and opinion-formers such as journalists, who talked for so long of the 'Gay Plague', reinforces the belief that science is not merely the most successful but also one of the least contemptible activities man engages in.

And yet the public view of the role of scientists has often been hostile. The priority dispute between Robert Gallo and Luc Montagnier over the identification of the causative virus has been given huge publicity, as it provides pleasing evidence that – surprise, surprise – scientists too have personal ambitions. Scientists have been accused of using the AIDS crisis as a platform to self-advancement. And so on. Even if one granted to these fringe matters the importance they are given in the press, to whom should one trust one's hope for the future? The cultural diagnosticians who delight in putting science in its place with the total authority that comes from complete ignorance? Or the patient researchers working out the docking mechanisms of CD_4 in order to thwart the plans of HIV to write, by reverse transcription, its sentence of death into DNA, the book of life itself? Indignant journalists who write under banner headlines like 'Western Technology Spreads AIDS' (the *Observer*) – a reference to the spread of AIDS by illicitly used dirty needles in Africa (as if all unhygienic practices, such as are routinely observed in certain non-western technologies did not spread infections) – or individuals who make precise and clear statements on the basis of observations obsessionally checked and re-checked even before they are submitted to the rigours of peer review?

The crucial role of the despised – and supposedly inhuman – science and technology in dealing with the greatest health threat of the century will grieve those who would like to adopt other, ideologically more pleasing, approaches. And yet the alternatives to science are unsatisfactory. Blaming the victims and seeing the problem as a manifestation of divine justice have ceased to be fashionable now that the general population feels itself threatened. For a similar reason, the views of the 'deep' ecologists and the 'anthropofugal philosophers'[8] that AIDS is to be welcomed as nature's way of dealing with the population problem and correcting man's total domination of the planet, are now whispered *sotto voce*. Doing rain dances, advocating alternative medicine, hoping the whole problem will simply go away, have also lost their appeal as the epidemic has closed in on people who earlier thought they and their lovers and their children were safe. Of course, scientific medicine is not the whole answer. Education in public health is crucial – though how you educate people out of their desires is as yet an unsolved problem. And science will be less effective than it might be so long as nations and individuals continue lying. Individual, corporate and national greed will also prevent the AIDS vaccines and cures, when they are developed, from being made available precisely where they are most needed. As was pointed out in a *Lancet* editorial ('AIDS Vaccine: Hope and Despair'[9]) the current story is of scientific hope and political despair.

It is revealing that disparagement of conventional science goes side by side with the expectation – often wildly optimistic as regards time-scale – that scientists will 'find the answer'. The assumption that there will be a solution forthcoming from this quarter is deeply ingrained in contemporary consciousness. This raises a connected point: when there is a real problem, the world turns to conventional science and technology to solve it. Just as when you have a real, serious disease – cardiac failure, appendicitis or a broken leg – flower remedies, reflexology, aromatherapy, etc. are quietly laid to one side and orthodox treatments are sought. This suggests that those who claim to believe in anti- or non-scientific approaches to solving human problems do not, ultimately, believe in them. So why do they profess them? What is it that people dislike so much about science that they will devote so much wishful thinking to advocating quackery of various sorts? That, except when the chips are down, so many (daft) answers to the question 'If you reject science what would you put in its place?' are forthcoming.

Quackery, medical and non-medical, is appealing for many reasons: first, it often offers instant answers; and second, its answers and procedures have intuitive appeal. These characteristics are, of course, closely connected, as is brought out in George Steiner's contrast between science 'which amasses one grain after another in its storehouse only by hard, fatiguing, individual work' ... and knowledge acquisition by 'a spontaneous spiritual knowing, which would deliver truths about the outer as well as the inner world, without the trouble of recourse to mathematics or experiments'.[10] Magic thinking has the virtue of coinciding with prejudices of unreformed common sense – the sun goes round earth – and offering immediate results, like the witch doctor who can diagnose you without taking a careful history, examining you or seeking help from investigations carried out by colleagues.[11] But there is more to it than this.

Anti-scientific thought often personalises problems and, indeed, the natural world which gives rise to them. This is, for example, a feature of alternative medicine where general treatments for diseases recognised to be instances of universal types are eschewed in favour of individualised treatment that relates the remedy to the personality of the individual. Conventional medicine regards the disease as a universal – for which there is a standard treatment; individuality resides in the patient's experience of the disease and the relationship to the doctor. Personalising pathological processes is both comforting – as it seems to offer new areas of control and to make additional sense of senseless suffering – and oppressive, as it turns the sufferer from a blameless victim into someone whose personality carries part of the responsibility for the illness. The importance Rilke attached to the rarity of the manifestations of the leukaemia from which he suffered[12] is a poignant testimony to the desire to believe that our suffering is not an impersonal process but a personal destiny, a message addressed to oneself. Diseases in which the causes are unknown and treatment unsatisfactory – tuberculosis in the nineteenth century, some cancers in the twentieth – are more likely to be personalised than those in which the cause is known – fractured femur or tuberculosis in the twentieth century. And they are for the same reason more attractive to quacks. When orthodox medicine can offer a successful treatment for a disease, the quacks find it prudent to move on.

The personalisation of the disease process itself (as opposed to the experience of disease) is an extreme example of the magic thinking – 'mind among things' – that characterises anti-scientific thought and its nostrums for the world's ills. Understanding its background returns us to themes sounded earlier in this work, for it is rooted in hunger for a vision of the world that anthropomorphises the universe, or at least organicises it.[13] Although science has dramatically diminished human helplessness before the non-human universe, its successes derive from a determinedly objective view that outrages our sense of our own centrality and importance in the larger scheme of things. 'The view from nowhere' cultivated by science is remote from the egocentric particulars of everyday life and the gossipy self-absorption that is our natural and comforting standpoint. To the developed intellect, this view diminishes us to a brief nano-nothing in the endless history of the mega-something. It also empties the natural world not only of mankind but also of spirits. The displacement of the theistic and animistic philosophy of nature by a mechanical one has reduced humankind to a very small event on a minute planet. The Copernican revolution that made the earth 'one of the heavenly bodies' (Galileo) demoted rather than promoted that planet. That process of demotion has continued as expanding knowledge has expanded the universe in both space and time. Coleridge's assertion in *Biographia Literaria* that 'We have purchased a few brilliant inventions at the loss of all communion with life and the spirit of nature' both overstates the adverse impact of science and understates its achievements; but it does capture what lies behind those who would seek alternatives, however ineffective, to the science and technology of our age.

As Wolpert has pointed out (see note 11), it is debatable to what extent we are living in a secular age and the role of science in any secularisation there has been. Let us for the present assume that this is an age without transcendence; how much was this prefigured in the Newtonian heritage? Newton himself was not entirely at ease with the mechanistic world picture to which his discoveries made such a decisive contribution. His case is for this reason especially interesting – and instructive.

As well as being perhaps the greatest scientist Europe has known, Newton was also one of the most revered and productive alchemists of his time.[14] In his science, the non-mechanistic idea of Absolute Space – introduced to explain inertia – as God's sensorium stimulated his greatest achievements. However, his great laws were formulated within a mechanistic framework; and they were tested against empirical observations consistent with a mechanistic nature that boiled down to qualitatively neutral matter differentiated only by the size, shape and motion of its atomic or corpuscular constituents. The sharply different world picture he espoused as an alchemist was informed by the notion that mind or spirit plays the role of an activating principle in physical nature, and he regarded the elements he experimented with as humours rather than inorganic chemicals. Many would today find the world picture of his alchemy more attractive than that of his science. But twentieth-century alchemy is no further on than seventeenth-century alchemy, while mechanistic chemistry has long achieved things – including the transmutation of elements – that alchemists only dreamed of. Newton's own *oeuvre* therefore permits a comparison: futile gropings in an attractive, animistic, organic, anthropomorphic world picture (in which the properties and unions of chemicals were understood in sexual, not to say sexist, terms);

and gigantic enduring achievements in an unattractive mechanistic world picture.

The question as to what, if we reject science and technology, we should put in their place remains unanswered by the critics of science. And so long as it is unanswered (and not infrequently unasked), we are left with random activity, inoperant gestures, magic and witchcraft to arm us in the struggle against natural and humanly caused disaster. Hostility to science is rather like hostility to government: there are bad governments and good governments and even bad things in good government; but without government, there is only lawless anarchy. If there has ever been a time when the planet could be a pleasant place to live on without the comforts of science-based technology, the present is not such a time. With the current level of world population, science, technology and rational, science-based social policies of public health, have ceased to be a mere option. We need the huge unit productivity that technology has permitted in order to ensure that, for example, the present quality of life in developed countries should be maintained. The displacement of the combine harvester by the sickle would soon lead to starvation in the United Kingdom. A barrier to realising this is, as I have indicated, that science has so entered into our thinking that we don't notice how much of ordinary common sense is rooted in science, or reflects the transformation of human thought, consciousness, and our world picture, by science. Many of our views about hygiene, for example, are based in bacteriology as it was developed, argued and tested in the nineteenth century, and a mechanical, rather than a spiritual, view of illness.

Of course, it would be nice if the objective reality of the natural world corresponded to one's most immediate intuitions; if the animistic philosophy of nature turned out to be the true one and the mechanical philosophy had turned out to be false; if alchemy and not chemistry had delivered the goods. But this is not how things are. The unattractive philosophy of nature – which began with the assumption that it boiled down to 'qualitatively neutral matter differentiated only by the size, shape and motion of its atomic or corpuscular constituents', though it has moved on a long way since then[15] – has produced results that the rival, more attractive view – that mind or spirit plays the role of an activating principle in physical nature – has not. I repeat: twentieth-century alchemy is much the same as – and as ineffectual as – seventeenth-century alchemy.

The case of Newton points to an obvious moral to be drawn about the relative value of thinking and of wishful thinking, and about their respective places in science – expressed so well in Claude Bernard's aphorism: 'outside of my laboratory, I let my imagination take wing; but once I go into my laboratory, I put my imagination away.' Mechanistic science, in its appropriate field of operation may not yield so much immediate joy as, for example, Blake promises to those who succumb to his anti-mechanistic system. But it delivers. The promise of instant cleansing of the doors of perception may be more attractive, but if they are cleansed in order to see more clearly that one is starving and that one's children are dying of disease, the vision of eternity might not be all that different from that available to the dead of all species.

Notes

1. Martin Seymour-Smith, *Guide to Modern World Literature* (London: Hodder & Stoughton, 1974), p. xviii.
2. Peter Medawar, *The Hope of Progress* (London: Methuen, 1972).
3. T.H. Huxley, 'On the Physical Basis of Life'; this widely available essay was delivered as a lecture in 1868 and reprinted in successive editions in Huxley's Collected Works.
4. J. Chin, in 'Current and future dimensions of the HIV/AIDS pandemic in women and children', *Lancet*, 336, 1990, pp. 221–4.
5. G.C. Schild and E.J. Stott, 'Where are we now with vaccines against AIDS?', *British Medical Journal*, 306, 1993, pp. 947–8.
6. 'That AIDS is not a single illness but a syndrome consisting of a seemingly open-ended list of contributing or "presenting" illnesses which constitute ... the disease, makes it more a product of definition or construction than even a very complex, multiform illness like cancer' – Susan Sontag, *AIDS and its Metaphors* (Penguin: Harmondsworth, 1990) p. 28. This is, of course, nonsense. There are many other immune deficiency diseases which may have an enormous variety of presentations depending on the opportunistic infections the individual may catch due to the failure of his/her immune system. No one, surely, is going to say that agammaglobulinaemia is socially constructed.
7. Since this was written, we have made more progress in treatment than could have been hoped and less progress in developing a vaccine than the optimists had forecast.
8. This movement is discussed in Rainer Friedrich's critique of the postmodernists: 'The Deconstructed Self in Artaud and Brecht', *Forum for Modern Language Studies*, xxvi, 1990, pp. 282–95.
9. Editorial, 'AIDS Vaccine: Hope and Despair', *Lancet* 336, 1990, pp. 1545–6.
10. George Steiner, *Real Presences* (London: Faber & Faber, 1989).
11. Lewis Wolpert, in *The Unnatural Nature of Science* (London: Faber & Faber, 1992, p. 43) interestingly relates the enduring appeal of Aristotle's ideas to their conformity to unreformed common sense and uncontested intuition:

    > The authority of Aristotle's ideas derive in large part from his ability to express in an abstract and consistent manner a perception of the universe that embodied a spontaneous conception of the universe which had existed for centuries. They embody the ideas of many primitive tribes and children.

12. See J.R. von Salis, *Rainer Maria Rilke: The Years in Switzerland*, translated by N.K. Cruickshank (London: The Hogarth Press, 1964).

13. See, for example, Rupert Sheldrake, *The Rebirth of Nature: New Science and the Revival of Animism* (London: Rider, 1993).
14. There is a detailed and fascinating discussion of Newton as alchemist in Richard Westfall's *Never at Rest: A Biography of Isaac Newton* (Cambridge: Cambridge University Press, 1980).
15. John Gribbins and Paul Davies, *The Matter Myth* (London: Macmillan, 1991), is a very readable account of the revolutions in contemporary science that have distanced us from the relatively uncomplicated mechanistic natural philosophy of the seventeenth century.

From: *Newton's Sleep* (Macmillan, 1995), pp. 55–67, 222–3.

Part VI
The Nature of Art

For Tallis, the scientific investigation of the physical, biological and human worlds and the creation of art are the two great, and distinctive, accomplishments of The Explicit Animal. Progress in science has been driven by the twin aims of advancing human understanding and of increasing human control over the natural world and the human body: to make the world on the one hand safer and more comfortable and on the other better understood. At times, art, too, has been thought to aim at improving the world – for example, through improving the behaviour of people in the world by refining sensibility – and to advance our understanding, even if that understanding is informed by a tragic sense that things cannot be ameliorated. For Tallis, however, the central function of art is not so much to make the world a better place or to advance our knowledge of it, as to round off our sense of the world, to perfect consciousness.

Tallis would argue that our explicit awareness of the world and of ourselves in the world is haunted by the feeling that the response we have to the world is incomplete. This is experienced most poignantly in our inability fully to experience our experiences: no experience is precisely congruent with the idea of itself and no complex experience encompasses at any one moment the whole of itself. There is an ineradicable flaw in the present tense of experience. Tallis believes this to be why we never quite arrive in the present: there is no moment at which we have an experience corresponding to our idea of how experiences should be.

Art offers us experiences that do correspond to the ideas we have of them. The key to this, for Tallis, is form, the 'moving unmoved' which links the passage from one moment to the next with a static structure, so that the whole is signalled, shines through, the part. This is most completely realised in music, where each note exists as an explicit part of an unfolding and yet already prefigured whole. Tallis argues that through art the most fundamental division within us – between our general ideas and our particular experiences – is temporarily healed and that for a time we are made whole.

14

The Freezing Coachman: Some Reflections on Art and Morality[1]

In this fairly short reading, from *Theorrhoea and After* (1999), which condenses views already set out at greater length in *Newton's Sleep*, Tallis begins by drawing on a story of Tolstoy's: an aristocratic lady is at the opera weeping at the imagined tragedy on the stage, while outside her faithful old coachman is freezing to death. Tallis's purpose here is to open a consideration of the moral value of art, and in particular of the novel. One might argue, as many critics have done, that by showing how people are corrupted by others, how they influence one another, and so on, the novels of Henry James, say, increase our sensitivity to the reality of the lives of other people, and by deepening our imaginative grasp of their lives open us up to more profoundly human relationships. Tallis rejects this view. There is no empirical evidence for it – indeed, what would constitute such evidence? – and all claims to that effect must be based on an *a priori* assumption, and, as Tallis argues, there are many reasons for thinking this assumption unacceptable. He wants, in short, to argue that claims for the value of art based on claims for its ability to influence behaviour for the better are without foundation. The value of art lies elsewhere, in the kingdom of ends: while it may not improve life, a great novel will introduce those who are its readers to a greater awareness of the complexity of the meanings that the world may bear, and so widen and deepen their experience of life. The appreciation of literature – and appreciation is inseparable from evaluation – is a matter of responding to the way disparate themes vital to human concerns are drawn together and unified.

Tolstoy tells the story of an aristocratic woman at the theatre weeping at the imaginary tragedy enacted on the stage. At the same time, outside in the cold, a real tragedy is taking place: her old and faithful coachman, awaiting her in the bitter winter night, is freezing to death. The point of the story is obvious: art does not necessarily make people better behaved, or more considerate.

The dissociation between the consumption of art and the promotion of good behaviour angered Tolstoy and in *What is Art?*,[2] he savagely attacked what he perceived as the contemporary reduction of art to a mere amusement, recreation or opiate for the leisured classes. Against this, he asserted that 'art should be an organ co-equal with science for the life and progress of mankind'. He regarded art as, most essentially, an activity by which a man 'infected' his fellow men with feelings that he had himself experienced. The purpose of aesthetic form was simply to ensure that those feelings were transmitted effectively. Art should be judged not only according to how well the feelings were invoked but also according to the quality of the feelings themselves. Great art, which must be accessible to and significant to all men, to peasants as well as to the idle classes, transmits feelings that draw men together in brotherly union.

Using these criteria, he rejected most of the art approved by his contemporaries: not only the works of Baudelaire, Wagner and Ibsen but much of Beethoven, Bach and Pushkin belonged to the category of bad art. And by the criterion of simplicity and accessibility, his own incomparable novels, whose greatness lay at least in part in their delineation of the complexity, ambiguity and vagaries of character, were worthless.

Tolstoy's late views – sharply at odds with earlier beliefs he had expressed with equal passion – are the more disturbing for emanating from the supreme practitioner of the art of fiction. In *What Is Art?* we recognise the ancestor of those doctrines that have fostered a thousand mediocre, state-sponsored novels in totalitarian regimes; the aesthetic that elevated 'tractor realism' – in which cardboard cut-out revolutionary heroes struggle bravely and politically correctly against cardboard cut-out counter-revolutionary forces – above Pasternak and Mandelstam. Tolstoy's criterion of greatness in literature would certainly lead to some major re-evaluations: after all, Barbara Cartland's *oeuvre* is more accessible to the masses and contains more unequivocal examples of goodness and badness than, say, *War and Peace*.

Tolstoy's beliefs about the nature and purpose of art are too readily dismissed as part of the gathering madness of his old age, his descent from Tolstoy the artist of genius to Tolstoy the Tolstoyan. Even so, the belief that literature may be – indeed should be – a positive moral influence is tenacious. The opposite view – epitomised in Wilde's assertion[3] that 'there is no such thing as a moral or an immoral book. Books are well written or badly written. That is all' – can still shock even those who are not cultural commissars in totalitarian states.

Some critics claim or hope or imagine that literature may promote *public* morality; that the representations of the artist can deflect human society from a course dictated by greed, tyranny, cruelty, selfishness, vested interests, fear, servitude and the rest; that, by awakening the conscience of the oppressor and helping the oppressed to realise their power, art may hasten the reforms or the revolution that will bring oppression to an end. Others have emphasised the role of literature in promoting *private* morality, through refining our consciousness of others, our sensitivity to them, our ability to imagine into them.

It is not only critics but also artists themselves who believe in, or dream of, a morally useful art. For Keats, true poets are 'those to whom the miseries of the world/Are misery, and will not let them rest'. And this is a sentiment shared by many contemporary artists. Indeed, Martin Seymour-Smith has identified *Kunstlerschuld* or artist-guilt as the occupational hazard of modern poets and writers who fear that 'literature fulfils no useful, only a selfish function'.

The claims made on behalf of politically engaged art are easily disposed of. History demonstrates that literature is as impotent as music in the face of tyranny and terror. Auden's assertion that 'poetry changes nothing' has been empirically proved again and again in the twentieth century. The eloquent outrage of great, humane writers has been and is unavailing – quite apart from the fact that a good many major artists have not been on the side of the angels anyway.

One should not be surprised at the political impotence of art. Rigour, scrupulosity, precision, concern for the exact curve of the thing, render the artist unfit for the kind of blunt, direct, usually one-sided, invariably simplifying and often dishonest communication that is most effective in political life. Great art does not simplify but makes more complex. The artist's deepest wish to *see things whole* undermines his polemic power: seeing all sides is the true glory of art and its utilitarian weakness. The sphere of public discourse is too shallow for artists to swim in with their most powerful strokes. In the world of marches, public meetings and newspaper editorials, his or hers is no longer a special, just another, voice. And a rather feeble one at that. You cannot chop down a tree with a scalpel. The political history of the United Kingdom since 1979 has demonstrated that one editorial in the *Sun* newspaper has the opinion-forming clout of a thousand politically committed plays by, say, David Hare. Moreover, the artist has no particular authority or expertise outside of the aesthetic sphere – as is illustrated by the terrible misjudgements of passionately committed artists. Pound, Céline, Brecht, Gorky and others of equal stature lent their support, directly or indirectly, to the Great Terrors. Finally, works of art take time to create and to make their way in the public domain; so art is too late and too slow to intervene decisively in particular, evolving situations.

In short, good art – complex, ironic, self-questioning – is feeble propaganda, just as good propaganda, which tannoys the convenient wisdom, is bad art. Which is not to say that art should not have its political angers: they may flow from the generosity of its vision. But the angers, the generosity, while they add to the work's intrinsic merits, do not give it extrinsic force; they may be accounted part of its internal moral texture, but do not strengthen its external moral force. And the morality of art may lie as much in form as in content, in the distribution of light and shade, as in what it shows forth in the light.

There may have been a time when art, and in particular literature, was less impotent; a period when mass literacy was novel, and relative political liberalism and the awakening of artists from the hierarchy where they had occupied a subservient place created a favourable context in which protest literature would not only be widely read but would also influence the thinking of those who could change things. If there was such a time – a golden age of Dickens and *Uncle Tom's Cabin* – this has now passed. This may be in part because the mass media have taken over much of the investigative and protest function of arts. The arts have lost those offices, just as they have shed responsibility for conveying practical information – the *Georgics* dimension. What poem could usefully add to our knowledge of, and our ability to alleviate, the atrocities in Bosnia, Iraq or Rwanda?

Many of those who would concede, however regretfully, the impotence of art to influence the course of public events may still cling to the idea that it has a beneficent moral influence in the *private* sphere. Surely it will inspire better behaviour in ordinary individuals even if it is unable to reform power-mad tyrants, and corrupt institutions and those whose vested interests lie in supporting them. This effect will not be through direct exhortation. The influence of art in heightening moral consciousness may be more subtle than that of the sermons, parables and plain tales Tolstoy saw as exemplars in *What is Art?* By showing us how people are destroyed by others, how they are corrupted, how they influence one another, do not, say, Henry James's novels increase our sensitivity to others' needs and vulnerabilities and, by enlarging our imaginative grasp of their lives – how they are made and unmade – open us up to deeper, richer, more truly human relationships?

I am unaware of any empirical data to support this claim. The impact on individuals or populations of particular books, or of their cumulative reading experience, would be impossible to study and has not, so far as I know, been studied. All claims as to the morally beneficent effects of art must therefore be based on an *a priori* assumption and there are many reasons for regarding this assumption as intrinsically improbable.

The first, as is brilliantly illustrated by Tolstoy's story, is that the conditions under which one consumes art and the very business of being committed to art either as a consumer or a producer are more likely to subvert than to reinforce moral resolve. In order to pay art the attention it demands and perhaps deserves, we need to be insulated from the distractions of everyday life, including those that come from our suffering fellow humans – such as freezing coachmen. The consumer of art wants above all to be undisturbed and therefore creates the conditions, either explicitly or structurally (library, theatre, gallery, book-lined study), to ensure this. As George Steiner said, in reply to an interviewer's question as to why a nation of *dichter und denker* allowed the horrors of Nazi Germany: 'We love our texts and we do not hear the cry in the street over the cry in fiction.'[4]

Secondly, art fosters values that are orthogonal to those of everyday morality (and to describe those values as the basis of a 'deeper' morality is to beg the question); for example, aesthetic values relating to form, and values that transcend the 'merely' utilitarian – the 'merely', assumes that you're not hungry, oppressed or in pain – such as the preservation and celebration of past experience *for its own sake*. Art also generates secondary values of its own – those of the connoisseur, of the art-snob and of the scholar. The corruption implicit in such secondary values is illustrated by individuals whose reading prompts them to exhibit their erudition; for example, the present writer who recalls Tolstoy's famous story of the freezing coachman not to learn from it but only in order to use it to support an argument about the relationship between art and morality.

Thirdly, the manner in which situations and dilemmas are packaged and presented in art is utterly different from the way in which they are presented to us in everyday life. Life recounted is inescapably different from life as it is lived. Even the soberest and least sentimental story has an operatic element and is a poor preparation for the pitiless actualities of ordinary life, for a world in which signals are inextricably caught up with noise (at least in part because twenty stories are going on at the same time). It is therefore even arguable that extensive reading of great novels may corrupt one's judgement of, and response to, other people. After the brilliantly delineated characters on the page, the companions of one's own life may seem drab, inferior and, above all, *ill-defined*. It is unlikely that the sentiments we feel for literary characters whose lives we can see as a whole, and from within as well as from without, helpfully educate our emotions for, or train our responses to, real people. Anyway, as Whitehead pointed out, the emotions sought through art are largely 'cultivated for their own sake'. If the essence of sentimentality is expressed emotion separated from the commitment to action, imagined responses divorced from most of the reality in which one would have to act, then art, the 'contemplation of the object independently of the will to act upon it', must be quintessentially sentimental. The truth is that art is primarily a spectacle or a reduction of the world to a spectacle. Certainly, representations on the scale and ambition and complexity of novels must develop the detached, spectatorial element in us. Even those novels that are not intended as jewels to be contemplated in abstraction from the world, but lenses through which we see the world more clearly and brightly, are weak moral motors. Tolstoy's expectation that 'the feelings awoken by art would lay in the souls of men the rails along which our actions will naturally pass' seems a pious hope – however great, sincere, moral or earnest the art.

I have so far assumed that the emotions stimulated by literature would be intrinsically good. This may not always be the case. Even identification with characters who have endured injustice or undergone some ordeal may be in some degree masochistic. Fantasies of being subjected to injustice and subsequent vindication (the latter with a completeness possible only in represented worlds) are all-pervasive in literature – in *The Winter's Tale* as much as in rescue operas or Westerns. Such emotions are infantile and arguably corrupting, firing dreams of satisfaction and moral revenge. And there are, of course, other, darker emotional pleasures to be derived from literature.

It may be that the moral influence of good art is more indirect than has been considered here. In reply to an interviewer's assertion that 'Art can be considered good only as it prompts to action', Robert Frost famously said 'How soon?' However, the assumption that art may not have an immediate beneficial effect but may result indirectly in such effects (the poets are 'the unacknowledged legislators of the world' fantasy) must be at best speculative. As soon as we start thinking about indirect and remote effects, we are into the realm of total uncertainty. Chaos theory has taught us that causation in complex dynamical systems – and what system could be more complex than the interaction between books, readers and their worlds? – is unpredictable and untraceable once one goes beyond a couple of steps in the chain.

The claim for the power of art as a moral influence – to improve public or private, individual or collective behaviour – seems baseless. Is art therefore without value? Should the government cease to sponsor art since it will not make the people better citizens? Should parents discourage their children from reading great literature, since it will not make them kinder in their private lives? Of course not. While art may not make individuals morally better, it will introduce them to a greater selection of the meanings that the world may have, and so widen and deepen their experience of life. Though art is impotent to change the course of history for the better, its image of the terrible and wonderful things that happen in history may in some small sense redeem them, if only for a privileged few: helpless to intervene, it will bear witness, and be true to, the world. Indeed, without taking account of the terrible, art will be empty, trivial; and there may be an element of ordeal in the experience of a great work of art. A masterpiece is a place where many disparate, partial meanings meet and are synthesised into a whole; a Utopia of consciousness where much that is scattered or fragmented in life is drawn together.

When he said that a pair of old boots was of more use than the entire works of Shakespeare, Nekrasov – who was the first to discover and proclaim Tolstoy's genius – was not condemning art, but clarifying its function. Art is only weakly effective in the utilitarian world of practical need and practical morality. Its true sphere is the kingdom of ends: it addresses the final purposes of life rather than the means by which life (and comfort and safety and freedom from want or terror) may be secured. And although it has only a slight external moral force, it does have an intrinsic morality. This is evident in Tolstoy's own incomparable novels. They illuminate the world with an even and just light, and reach with a generosity of imagination into all sorts and conditions of men and women, linking the great facts that enclose us – that we are unoccasioned, that we are transient, that we nonetheless make the world our own thing – with the small facts that detain us. The temptation to believe that this will translate into an influence on practical morality – on behaviour in the public or the private sphere – so that with a finer awareness, will come a richer, deeper sense of practical responsibility, may be overcome by remembering the weeping princess in the theatre and the coachman freezing to death outside.

An after-thought on theatre

Tolstoy's story relates to the theatre and, since in modern times, drama is the art that above all has lent itself – or been lent – to moral causes, it has a special poignancy today. Although theatre is potentially the most persuasive of the arts because it may represent the human world most directly and comprehensively, it is also most self-evidently a *spectacle*. (Indeed, the spectatorial element is present in the etymology of the word.) Our participation in the events is at best that of witnesses and our witnessing is constantly undermined by the artificiality of the occasion – an occasion that is always, above all, whatever else happens on the stage, or to us, a *theatrical* occasion. There is the trip out, the dressing up, the tickets to be purchased, the conventional rising of the curtain at the beginning, the applause at the end. The latter reminds us, if reminder were necessary, that what we have witnessed is at bottom a *performance*: it turns us all into pocket critics, who *judge* the performance, thinking back not only upon what was enacted but also upon how well it was done, and comparing this performance with other performances. The applause and the curtain-calls draw a double line beneath the performed art and make sure we do not confuse it with anything in our life. And though we may praise the 'authenticity' of the performance, and the extent to which it commanded our belief, this only further distances ourselves from the performed events – and draws attention to our own expert judgement and knowledge. The laudatory review we read the following day completes the process whereby the play is tidied away from our lives and is reduced to a treat ('taking in a show').

Dramatists and directors who want the theatre really to change people's lives and, in particular, their private and political behaviour, tackle this problem of artificiality in one of two ways. The first is to increase the participation of the audience, to engage them with spectacles that are ever more realistic, sickening, horrifying, etc. This is the way, for example, of the Theatre of Cruelty, where the audience is threatened by a breaking-down of the boundaries between stage and auditorium. The opposite approach is to underline the artificiality of the theatre and to bring it yet more to the foreground. This is the way of Brecht and the 'alienation effect'.

Brechtian distancing has a further rationale. Brecht recognised that the Tolstoyan notion of the artist 'infecting' his audience with the feelings he had put into his work was, to say the least, dubious. The version of Tolstoy's conception of the function and mechanism of art implicit in realistic revolutionary or committed or protest theatre – that the audience should go to (or 'take in') a show, be moved to anger and pity (and perhaps delight) by what it sees and then act out that anger and pity in the real world – is manifestly simplistic. It is the easiest thing in the world to invoke empathy for characters on a stage and to arouse emotions. Any writing can operate on the emotions: not only trash novels but the most trivial conversation may prompt tears of pity or arouse great anger. What is at issue is the quality of the emotions and the extent to which they connect with the extra-theatrical prose of everyday life; the degree to which they are illuminated by thought and animate thought; how far they connect with, reach out to, the world. According to Brecht, conventional 'realist' theatre merely plays on the unthinking sentimentality of the audience; there are too many people who lack the stone-like heart necessary to laugh at the death of Little Nell. The point is to awaken *thought* as well as emotions: to awaken emotions that are connected with thought; to link the death of Little Nell with the economic circumstances, the political system, the social presuppositions that make it likely that Little Nell and others like her will die prematurely. Without these connections, the theatrical catharsis is merely self-indulgent, emotional masturbation. In order to ensure that the connections are made, the theatrical spectacle should retain its status as a *spectacle* so as to avoid being reduced to a device for inducing physiological tempests in sentimental middle-class theatre-goers who do not wish to look at the circumstances that underlie the tragedies they enjoy weeping at or to consider the extent to which their own privileged situation as comfortable theatre-goers may be connected with those circumstances.

Brechtian dramaturgy is fine but the resultant drama less so. Just as the strategy of the Theatre of Cruelty adds to the discomfort of theatre without prolonging its impact (the very term of classification itself speaks volumes: here is another experience that can be talked about), so Alienation theory may add the tedious sense of depthless spectacle without moving one to wish to change society outside the theatre.

The weak moral situation of the theatre is not unique. Television is not surrounded by so much razzmatazz – it has less of a plinth, we do not dress up, or consciously dress down, to watch it – but it can, for that reason, be more casually switched off and there are fewer apologies for interruption. Changing channels is easier than making one's way out of the auditorium mid-act. The novel (which one may treasure as a possession and admire for its cover) can, without much ceremony, be laid aside. A redirected glance can obliterate a picture. And music may be extinguished when the lift reaches the floor we want.

Notes

1. A much longer version of this essay has already appeared in *Newton's Sleep* (London: Macmillan, 1995). The present text is based upon a talk broadcast on Radio 3 in 1994.
2. Leo Tolstoy, *What is Art?*, translated by Aylmer Maude (Oxford University Press, World Classics, 1930).
3. Oscar Wilde, *The Picture of Dorian Gray*.
4. Perhaps this explains how artists of considerable merit, even genius, managed to accommodate to the Nazi regime. How, for example, some of the greatest conductors of Beethoven flourished under Nazism, accepting the patronage of mass murderers. It was not so much that they conducted the Prisoners' Chorus without listening to it but that they listened to it so carefully that they did not listen past it to any extra-musical world to which its message might be applied.

From: *Theorrhoea and After* (Macmillan, 1999), pp. 99–107, 205.

15
The Difficulty of Arrival: Reflections on the Function of Art[1]

In this reading, a chapter from *Theorrhoea and After*, which like the preceding selection is a condensed version of themes worked through in *Newton's Sleep*, Tallis again takes up the question of the uselessness of art. To argue that art is useless, that it fulfils no function in the kingdom of means, is not to diminish its value, but to show where its value truly lies. It has to do with the final purpose of living and not with the means to survival or comfort. Tallis puts this dramatically by saying that the idea that art is useless would cause less upset if it were also appreciated that consciousness itself is useless. It too has nothing to do with ensuring our survival, and there is no evidence that conscious beings survive better than unconscious creatures like the amoeba. As self-conscious, explicit animals, we find ourselves burdened with the task of making sense of our lives, and completing our sense of things. To exemplify his point, Tallis gives a description of the way he finds it impossible to feel that he has ever actually arrived when he goes on holiday. The sense he has of how the holiday should be never seems to coincide with the experiences that make it into the actuality that it is. He argues that we are condemned to journey towards *ideas* of experience that no experience could ever realise. And yet in art, and especially in music, for Tallis the paradigm case of art, this gap is overcome. The experience of great music and the idea of music expressed in that experience are one.

Paul Valéry captured the essential uselessness of art when he compared prose and poetry in a brilliant analogy. Poetry, he said, is to prose as dancing is to walking. You walk in order to get somewhere, whereas you dance to enjoy movement.

People find it very difficult to accept the uselessness of art. But attempts to confer an external use upon it are signally unconvincing. It has already been pointed out that no one's survival would be threatened by cutting off the Bach supply, that Matisse does not cure chest infections and that Hölderlin's verse has not made the roads safer for children. And we have observed how exposure to art doesn't seem to do much for the morality of nations or of private citizens. After millennia of great art, people behave collectively and individually just as badly as they ever did. If anything has softened the brutish egocentricity of the human animal, it has been technological advance in meeting material want, rather than art. Well-fed individuals in a warm room may be more sensitive to one another's feelings than hungry bodies in the cold air. To quote Brecht: grub first, then ethics.

My intention in emphasising the practical and moral uselessness of art is not to diminish its value but to show where its true value lies. Art, of course, gives pleasure. But then so do drinking alcohol and stroking the cat and, it is rumoured, playing football; and yet some (though not all) people assume an entirely different attitude to these other pleasure-giving, time-killing activities. We are convinced that there is something more serious, more important, about art than playing tiddley-winks or even tennis. Did not Nietzsche say that the creation of art is the only metaphysical activity to which life still obliges us? This is my own position and it connects with my belief that the uselessness of art is an essential, deep uselessness; for, like religion, it is concerned with the Kingdom of Ultimate Ends and not that of means to an end; with the final purpose of living and not with the means to survival or even comfort.

The notion of the uselessness of art would cause less upset if it were appreciated that consciousness itself is useless.[2] If you ask people what consciousness is for, they will usually say that it assists survival. This common-sense answer is flawed because it looks at the matter from the viewpoint of an organism that already possesses consciousness, one in whom mechanism has in part been superseded by deliberate action. We all know that a usually conscious animal is vulnerable in coma: once you're conscious, it's a good idea to stay that way. But that doesn't explain why there are conscious organisms. For this, we look to evolutionary arguments: an animal with a teeny-weeny bit of consciousness could plan ahead and so have an edge over the competition. It, and its genes, therefore enjoyed preferential survival, so that there was a trend towards increasingly conscious organisms. The implicit assumption is that survival is better served by increasing consciousness than by developing better unconscious mechanisms; that deliberate action is always or usually a better bet than automatic behaviour. But this is not so. Much life-preserving activity takes place better in the absence of consciousness and the most complex life-supporting actions – for example, the development of a brain in an embryo – can be accomplished only by unconscious and automatic processes. Trying to bring a brain about by deliberate thought would be an unsuccessful enterprise. There is no evidence that conscious individuals or species survive better than organic automata: as Mary Midgely said, 'if the aim were just surviving, amoebas would be just the thing to be'.[3] The notion that there are evolutionary pressures towards progressively increasing consciousness is due to looking backwards along a process that led up to us.

So consciousness is unexplained. More to the point, it is useless. Perhaps worse than useless; for just as there would have been no pleasure without consciousness, there would equally have been no pain, either; and history suggests that pain has probably got the upper hand. And if the unique capacity of man to murder his conspecifics and to enjoy the infliction of suffering is taken into account, the moral sense that comes with heightened consciousness does not improve the balance sheet, either.

Consciousness is no more useless, though, than life seen as a whole or matter seen as a whole. Anyway, we are stuck with it. We are explicit, self-conscious animals burdened with the mysterious gift of making sense of things – including ourselves. An equally mysterious side-effect of this burdensome gift is a hunger to complete, or bring to some culmination, this sense of things: hence man the metaphysical animal. Historically, this hunger has its most universal expression in religion, but in a secular age is expressed in non-religious art. Art is about rounding off the sense of being consciously alive and finding the ultimate purpose, if there is such a purpose, of that to which so many of our conscious purposes are directed.

The function of art, then, is not to be found in the world of Use, of Means, but in the Kingdom of Ends. It is not, of course, the only feature in the landscape of that Kingdom. There are many other things we do for their own sake. So what's special about art? To answer this, I want to examine the problems that bedevil the Kingdom of Ends; in particular to subject to sympathetic but critical examination the most sustained attempt to dwell in that Kingdom that most of us undertake: the annual summer holiday when we are liberated for a uniquely long period of time from the productive process in order to seek experience for its own sake. The difficulties that attend this secular *haj* tell us a lot about human consciousness and why it needs art. I shall argue that our need for art is rooted in the difficulty, perhaps the impossibility, of arrival in the Kingdom of Ends and there experiencing our experiences.

Let me descend from the universal to the particular and talk about my own annual family holiday. We have holidayed in the same place in Cornwall for over a decade.[4] So the outward journey is a relay of landmarks and each year, we look forward to that climactic moment when we *arrive* in Cornwall, *arrive* in our holiday. And therein lies the difficulty. As the years go by, increasingly we note the lack of an absolute sense of arrival; in particular, our inability to determine the precise moment at which we have definitely arrived – after which we can confidently say 'We are here. The holiday has begun.' Is it when we cross the Tamar and know that, geographically, we are in Cornwall? When we read TIREDNESS KILLS TAKE A BREAK and Mrs Baggit tells us to look after Cornwall and take our litter home? No, we are still fifty miles from the cottage. Is it when we first see the sea? Well you can't do anything with the mere sight of the sea. Surely, then, it is when we reach the cottage. But there is so much unloading to do and pressure to do it quickly before our illegitimately parked car becomes a road-block and our arrival is celebrated with official fines and/or unofficial abuse. After the unloading, there is the unpacking. Putting a particular pair of socks in a particular drawer, or discovering that a treasured toy or an essential gadget has been forgotten, is hardly arrival. Besides, the children have unnegotiable ideas about what shall count as arrival: the holiday hasn't begun until bare feet have touched sand.

And so in an endeavour to arrive as quickly as possible ('weather or not' – the annually re-dusted joke), we prepare for the beach. We pack food, drink and toys, and clothes for all contingencies. At last, oppressed by the weight of our possessions, we hit the beach. We find a suitable place: out of the wind, not so close to the sea that the tide will soak our sandwiches, nor too near to the youths with the ghetto-blaster. The windbreak is erected, our mallet adding to the chorus that simulates the forging-room in Nibelheim. We spread out our possessions. We sit down on the blanket, already covered with sand and spilt coffee, exchange smiles and prepare to subside into stillness. But not for long. Someone's spade has been forgotten and a packet of football stickers has mysteriously disappeared. Several additional journeys are indicated. And numerous further adjustments – of the position of our camp, of the direction of the windbreak, of the distribution of our bits and pieces. Eventually, everything is in place.

Have we now at last arrived? Not at all. Even leaving aside the cloud homing in on the sun like a heat-seeking missile, we know that it is not enough merely to be touching sand. A *game* must be underway. Cricket, for example. So up we get to define a pitch, to put in whatever stumps have survived the journey, assign individuals to teams and try to resolve without recourse to the European Court of Human Justice the dispute over who is to bat first.

This, surely, is the moment of arrival: standing with bat in hand, ready to hit the ball so hard that it will land in the sea. Or is it? Even those few minutes, when you are the privileged one with the bat, are riddled with waiting. You have to wait for the bowler to get the ball, and to complete his run up. There is more waiting when you miss the ball – extended by discussion as to whether it is you or the inattentive wicket-keeper who should chase after it. And when you have hit the ball, and almost score what looks to you like a six, you are rewarded with more waiting – more motionless journeying towards the point of the holiday.

Perhaps this is the wrong model of arrival. Isn't *doing* things on the beach – even archetypal, much-looked-forward-to things – a way of losing the beach, and of losing sight of, and so failing to be arrived in, Cornwall? Is there not an alternative (adult) model in which arrival is the achievement of a certain passivity, rather than engagement in a specific activity? A rather more genteel version that requires a bit more negative capability than an often contentious game of cricket? Isn't arrival really a matter of sensation: the first time you feel the breeze on your bare legs (bared more in response to a sense of occasion than to meteorological realities) or the wet sand under your shoeless, sockless feet? Or when you first look properly at the sea? Well, two days into the holiday, when you at last enjoy an uninterrupted moment, it doesn't seem enough merely to dandle the sea at the distal end of telereception. To be fully arrived, you must be *engulfed*. Immersed.

Journeying is therefore resumed: a change of clothes; a long walk across the beach; and an inch-by-inch, sensitive-part-by-sensitive-part, entry into the water, negotiating past the shocks of cold that still, after all these years, retain their power to shock. The inaugural dip seems less arrival than a tribute paid to tradition and expectation. Hardly are you in than you are thinking about another journey: getting out and a version of arrival that includes dry towels and the sun in a sheltered spot behind the windbreak. Quick in and quick out and, all duties and arrangements suspended, giving yourself up to the absolute comfort of solar energy.

You lie back and close your eyes. Your lids and the world turn to dazzled orange. The warmth on your arms penetrates beneath the skin. The contingent sounds that fill the 360 degrees solid angle around your repose mingle with the multi-dimensional dance of your thoughts. Is this the moment of arrival? Consider what happens next. Is it not typically the case that at such a moment all the year's fatigue gathers up in you and demands satisfaction, that you willingly accede to these demands, and that you dissolve into *sleep*? And that when, an hour or so later, you wake, the world has a greenish tinge, it doesn't look like Cornwall at all, you have a slight malaise and if you have arrived it could be to anywhere.

We keep on trying to arrive – right up to when we have to shake the sand out of our towels for the last time, fold up the windbreak, pack up our belly-boards and our wet suits, draw stumps, return to the cottage, clean it up (an activity dominated by the lamentations of the vacuum symbolically bellowing emptiness) for the next arrivees (or would-be-arrivees), load the car and drive home.

That moment of arrival, after which we would have *remained* arrived, in journeyless continuation, seems to elude us – and systematically. Every candidate point of arrival exhibits a tendency to turn into a piece of *en route*, to be porous with further journeying. Journeys end only in more journeys, macro and micro journeys constituting the activity one had arrived at or for, taking one past the point of arrival. And so it goes – until it is time for departure and the journeys that lead all the way home.

What is true of holidays is true wherever experience is sought for its own sake; where we are concerned not with means to ends, but with ends in themselves; not with journeying but with arrival. This is true even (or especially) of human relationships. The difficulty of arrival seems built into the very structure of human experience. When we dismount from function, when we leave the Kingdom of Means and enter the Kingdom of Ends, we are haunted by a sense of not being quite there; of not being able fully to experience our experiences.

There are various ways of getting round this, or of preventing the feeling from coming on. Consider Camcorder Man who devotes most of his holiday to recording what he cannot experience, in the deluded belief that when he plays back his video tape the experience will happen.[5] Or those for whom holidays are a chance to catch up on something – gardening, reading, cataloguing the butterfly collection. Or those who turn holidays into a series of tasks that mimic the seriousness of work: those hiking holidays with miles to be got through before the pub; the ten-country tour with great distances on the clock and towns ticked off; the terrible ordeal of the orienteering holiday at the end of which there is something called 'satisfaction' or something else called 'achievement'. But these ploys seem to solve the problem only by avoiding it. And what is this problem?

Very baldly, it is that we journey towards *ideas* of experience that no experience can realise. These ideas are derived either from anticipation shaped by words and pictures or, when it is a case of revisiting, from those postcards of the mind that have developed in our memory. Ideas differ from any possible experience in two rather fundamental ways: firstly, sense experience is baggy, obese with contingencies (my conception of the game of cricket on the beach did not include any of the very particular items of which it is composed – that particular shot, that seagull flying overhead, that thin man shouting to his wife); and, secondly, the idea is given all at once in an instant of anticipation or recall, while the experience unfolds over time. The idea has a clear *form* which the experience lacks. Experience is thus riven by a sense of insufficiency: we feel that we are not quite experiencing it. Hence the difficulty of arrival which, we discovered, is not accidental but quite systematic.

To put this more starkly: experience is undermined by the general ideas it fails fully to instantiate. There is consequently an incurable wound in the present tense (the only tense that human consciousness really has) which cannot be solved by camcorders and can only be concealed but not healed by turning our holiday into a series of tasks to be completed. The purpose of art – its true purpose – is to address this wound, and to dress it, and perhaps for a while to heal it.

How? To understand the function of art and how art functions, we need to see how this tension in the Kingdom of Ends between the idea and the experience is essentially a battle between form and content. The content is the actual experience, with all the sense data served up by the accidents of the moment; and the form is the idea of experience. In a truly realised work of art, form and content are in harmony. This is most easily illustrated by music which, for the present discussion, we may think of as the paradigm art. (It was not for nothing that Pater famously said that 'all art aspires to the condition of music'.)

Think of the relationship between idea – or form – and sensation in the experience of a melody. Each note is fully present as an actual physical event and yet is manifestly part of a larger whole, of an idea. There is no conflict between the form or idea of the music and its actual instants. Our moments of listening are imbued with a sense of what is to come and what has passed. The form to which the music conforms – that ties what has gone and what is to come with each other and with what is present – shines through its individual moments. There is both movement and stasis; in Aristotelian terms, the unfolding sound realises form as 'the unmoving moved'.

Of course, the music has its journeys – it manifestly *is* a journey from a beginning to an end – and in great music we feel as if we have travelled great distances to and through a remote *paysage* of sound. But the journeying is never merely a piece of *en route*: the unfolding of the form fills and fulfils the sensation of the present moment with the past and the future, rather than undermining it with the past and the future. The *leitmotif*, recurring throughout the music like an involuntary memory, ties together the beginning, the middle and the end, making it all one. The retrospective light it casts on all that has gone before creates the feeling that we have been arriving all the time and that, indeed, we are arrived. Which is why there are moments when, listening to music, we have the sense of enjoying our own consciousness – its present and its past – in italics.

Art, then, offers us intermittent relief from the otherwise permanent condition of never having been quite there, of not quite arriving. This is at least as important as education or preaching or politics or all the other things that art does so badly and other things do so much better. Useless and necessary, art – like holidays – is about experience for its own sake – but – unlike holidays – such experience perfected. So let there be art, rounding off the sense of the world, celebrating the wonderful and beautiful uselessness of human consciousness.

Let walking know and perfect itself in dancing.

Notes

1. A considerably longer version of this essay has already appeared in *Newton's Sleep* (London: Macmillan, 1995). The present text is based upon a talk broadcast on Radio 3 in 1994.
2. Does consciousness have a value that transcends use? No; for consciousness is that in virtue of which there is value. It cannot therefore be something that of itself has value. Unfortunately, it is rather easy to be seduced into imagining that the value

that human consciousness imports into the world is already there in the non-human world, even in the absence of consciousness, especially if one is confused by teleological talk which inescapably projects values into unconscious processes taking place in unconscious entities. While it is obviously 'good' for an unconscious amoeba to avoid certain concentrations of pH, the repository of this judgement, and hence of the value carried by it, is the consciousness of the biologist who can see what is necessary for the survival of an amoeba. The question of the value of consciousness *per se* beyond use cannot, therefore, arise. (I discuss this at greater length in *The Explicit Animal*.)

3. Mary Midgely, *Beast and Man: the Roots of Human Nature* (London: Methuen, 1980), p. 150.
4. I have presented a best, rather than a worst, case scenario. After all, I have ignored the stream of trivial accidents to which family life is prone and which themselves may frustrate arrival. I have also overlooked inner obstacles. For example, a worry one has failed to leave behind at work. (The frequency with which serious work preoccupations cloud the early days of holidays may reflect a law of psychology, analogous to Dalton's Law of Partial Pressures in the physical world, to the effect that a worry will occupy the space made available to it. In the absence of competing worries, it will fill consciousness. Other preoccupations may prosper through lack of competition. For some, holidays are a breeding-ground of hypochondriacal concerns about their own health or that of others. Minor ailments assume a higher profile.) Finally, I have assumed that holidaymaking is the only business of the holiday. But there may be other agenda items. Holidays are, after all, a time to look at and address one's family head-on instead of in passing – to grasp, that they are here and what they are like. It also offers the one chance in the year for sustained reading and thought.
5. Some of these thoughts were triggered by the spectacle of a man at the table next to mine in a café overlooking a perfect Cornish sea camcording his wife drinking a cup of coffee. I could see that, as the event changed from a spontaneous occurrence into something being set up, he was irritating her: a small act of pleasure was turned into a pleasureless enactment. In trying to capture the perfect image of the moment – and so perfect the moment in an image – he was ruining it. She in her turn was irritating him by seeming to be unable to do 'drinking a cup of coffee' in the way that she had been doing it all her life until he wanted to film her doing this doing. He was not, I hasten to add, an *avant-garde* film producer but a simple chap – in the sense that only chaps, and wealthy ones, can be simple.

From: *Theorrhoea and After* (Macmillan, 1999), pp. 125–32, 212–13.

16
Metaphysics and Gossip: Notes Towards a Manifesto for a Novel of the Future

The subtitle of this chapter from *Theorrhoea and After* is 'Notes Towards a Manifesto for a Novel of the Future', and it consists of a further reworking of the theme of the relation between the particularities of experience and the general ideas that organise that experience. Tallis contrasts metaphysics and gossip: these are the two poles around which fiction moves. It is the achievement of the major novel to bring together what Tallis calls the small facts that detain us with the large facts that enclose us, so that, even if we are not unified by this integration of elements, it may perhaps be that we are, in some sense, *composed* by it. The pun here captures both the idea of how our experience of ourselves may achieve a certain order at the same time as we reach to a certain degree of rest. We are moved by that 'moving unmoved' which is the form of art. Unlike Henry James, of whom Eliot remarked: 'He had a mind so fine no idea could violate it', the novelist of the future will have a mind so fine it can be violated by many ideas, without thereby losing its refinement. For Tallis, being conscious of ourselves is to be conscious of how utterly particular, how utterly unique, we are; at the same time, we are open to generalities of the highest order. The achievement that brings these two distinctive aspects of our lives together is the achievement that makes us whole.

> The poet's function is to describe, not the thing that has happened, but a kind of thing that might happen, i.e., what is possible as being probable or necessary. The distinction between historian and poet ... consists really in this, that the one describes the thing that has been, and the other a kind of thing that might be. Hence poetry is something more philosophic and of a graver import than history, since its statements are of the nature rather of universals, whereas those of history are singulars.
>
> Aristotle (*Poetics* 1451)

(1)

In my more honest moments, I am inclined to admit that I find only two things in the world truly fascinating: metaphysics and gossip. Everything between these two limits, between the general structure and meaning of the universe on the one hand and, on the other, who went to bed with whom and what they did there, is of less compelling interest. Most of the things that are important to the material well-being of the human race lie in this in-between zone – how to cure pneumonia, how to overthrow tyrants, the structure of polymers, etc. are equidistant from metaphysics and gossip. And I take these important things as seriously as anyone. But I am not concerned here with the serious and the important. I am concerned with the truly interesting; I am concerned with art; in particular with the art of fiction.

(2)

Somewhere in his massive and wonderful unfinished masterpiece *The Man without Qualities*, Robert Musil's hero and *alter ego* Ulrich remarks rather snobbishly that there are two sorts of mind: the superior mind that is interested in the (general) *what* and the common mind that is interested in the (particular) *who*. Musil is not being entirely true to himself here. For if he were concerned exclusively with the most general *what* he should never have been a novelist.

Novelists, I believe, are inescapably interested in the *quis* as well as the *quid*, the who as well as the what, the particular as well as the general; otherwise they would have concerned themselves with purer intellectual pursuits such as cosmology, ontology, theology and the like – or not been writers at all.

(3)

There has been interesting and intriguing resistance to acknowledging and valuing the hybrid nature of the novel, its dual attraction towards the two poles of metaphysics and gossip. There are those who reject the metaphysics and those who reject the gossip.

(a) The rejection of metaphysics

Nabokov famously despised the novel of ideas, not to speak of the philosophical novel, singling out Thomas Mann as a crashing bore, the archetype of the novelist who wanted to subordinate his fiction to the ideas he wished to purvey. This is, of course, a caricature. Mann's greatness lay in his ability to dissolve large ideas in the situations, characters and events of his narratives. Yes, his characters utter ideas – almost endlessly, at times, as in *The Magic Mountain* – but they are also uttered *in* those ideas. Think of Settembrini, of Naphta, even of that *tabula rasa* himself, Hans Castorp. And Nabokov's own novels and novellas are charged with implicit philosophy. Nabokov was right to detest novelists who had rather obvious designs on readers; authors of *romans à thèse* for whom the *thèses* could spare the novelist his essential craftsmanly obligation to 'caress the details', to describe the real world or, as Nabokov so often insisted, *a* real world.

The thesis-novel offended Nabokov because he didn't believe in *the* world – corresponding to the monolithic vision of the ontologist or political theorist – and partly because he saw invocation, not analysis, as the novelist's essential business. To forgo the observation that a character's chin might triple as she glanced down to brush off the crumbs from her large bejumpered bosom is to renege on the novelist's essential responsibility to make the reader *see*. And he would have concurred with Proust's observation that art subordinated to the conveying of ideas is like a gift with a price ticket on it. (Proust was, of course, among the greatest of all philosophical novelists.)

(b) The rejection of gossip

> '... the fatal futility of fact'
>
> Henry James

Paul Valéry despised the particularity and contingency of the novel. Why should I care, he famously asked, whether the Marquise went out at five o'clock? Not a bad question. For fictional facts risk a double nullity: like non-fictional facts, they are trivial, or have only a narrowly local interest; and, in addition, they are not even true. To this there corresponds a double arbitrariness: to the arbitrariness of real worlds (a real marquise might just as well have gone out at six o'clock or not at all) is added the arbitrariness of confabulation – there is no limit to one's ability to make up any number of marquises and their comings and goings. (And it is true that most novelists are too busy inventing (or cribbing) to discover anything – though, admittedly, in fiction as in science, one does need to do some inventing to kick-start the process of discovery.) For Valéry, fiction failed to be of interest because it did not address either of the aims he thought non-trivial writing should have: investigating the fundamental nature of consciousness; and uncovering the system of language.

It is difficult to know how sincere Valéry was. His own great works are by no means free of the particular, even his most abstract poems. The *récit* of *La Jeune Parque* gains resonance from the contingent fact that the voice is attributed to a female. As for *Le Cimitière Marin*, the local details and their personal reference give this most philosophical of poems a poignancy crucial to its power to engage our ravished attention. Moreover, for the reasons he himself set out in his early prose masterpieces such as *M. Teste* and *Introduction to the Method of Leonardo da Vinci*, he did not write metaphysical treatises on language or on consciousness, but poems, dialogues, essays ... in short, gossip.

And gossip has been robustly defended by some authors who are serious to the point of austerity. Listen to Joseph Conrad, responding here, through his *alter ego* Marlowe, to the charge of 'seeking amusement through mere gossip':

> From gossip there springs in us compassion, charity, indignation, the sense of solidarity; and in minds of any largeness an inclination to that indulgence which is next to affection (*Chance*).

(4)

The future of the novel, I would like to propose, lies in more explicit recognition of the two poles, metaphysics and gossip, to which serious fiction tends and in more ingenious and convincing and effective ways of mediating between the two. For the novel has the potential – by connecting the small facts that detain us with the large facts that enclose us – to be a means by which we are, if not unified, at least *composed* in a larger sense. Its future lies in exploiting to the maximum the power of the storyteller – who is able to invest a withheld fact with our curiosity, who can awaken in us a ravenous appetite for knowing a particular thing, a specific future – on behalf of the larger wonder of the metaphysician. By reconciling the vector of the journey towards revelation with the stasis of certain knowledge, such fiction would seem to fulfil one idea of the purpose of art: that of putting our minds and hearts into their least local mode without loss of intensity or interest.

If we think of fiction and philosophy as they are conventionally understood, each by itself is insufficient: fiction is concrete but too regional in its reference; philosophy, on the other hand, is universal in its range but abstract to the point of near-emptiness, and, except in the case of a gifted few readers, themselves usually philosophers, gives nothing for much of the imagination to get a purchase on. Appetite is necessary to italicise our sense of being there and this depends upon links to locality, to particulars. By uniting strong appetite to wide wonder, the fiction of the future might fulfil the dimly intuited dream of a utopian consciousness in which, in the same moment, we know ourselves as subjects experienced from within and as objects seen from afar.

(5)

Perhaps the fiction I am talking about will look increasingly essay-like. In his discussion of Diderot, author of one of the earliest fictional essays, *Le Neveu de Rameau*, Lucien Goldmann noted that

> The essay is both abstract and concrete. Its nature, like that of philosophy, is chiefly to raise certain conceptual questions fundamental to human life; but, unlike most philosophy, it has neither the desire nor the ability to answer them. Like literature, it puts these questions not in a conceptual form but attaches them to the 'occasion' of a concrete person or situation taken both from literature and (as the greatest essayists do) from real life. The true essay thus necessarily inhabits two worlds, and is necessarily ironic: it seems to be talking about real people and situations, but these are mere 'occasions' for the essayist to raise crucial abstract questions.

The fictional essay of the future, however, will be animated with a longing to answer the questions fundamental to human life. It may not have the ability to answer them but the writer will be one of those, like Wittgenstein, of whom Russell said it *hurt* him not to know the answers. And that hurt will not be separated from the other hurts – and delights – that come with our peculiar condition of being transcendent minds embodied in warm flesh.

(6)

Such fiction will, of course, have precursors. I have already mentioned Musil with admiration. Proust, Borges, Mann, Benn – even, at a lower level, Kundera – also figure large in my own *Antologia Personal*. Each of these writers has struck his own balance between gossip and metaphysics, found his own way of ensuring that the spider of abstract thought does not break the web of enchantment, his own way of dealing with the anxiety, so eloquently expressed by Amiel, that abstract reflection should not 'dissolve reverie and burn her delicate wings'. (An excessive concern with negative capability should not override the supposedly 'philistine' rage for deeper understanding.)

Perhaps in Borges' case the ideas sometimes precipitate out too decisively from the solvent of the story; but even a piece such as 'A New Refutation of Time' has sufficient human presence to dramatise the ideas. In the hands of such a master, the mere use of a woman's name – who this 'Helen' is to whom he refers in the midst of his elegiac meditation on time, I do not know – is sufficient to infuse a sense of personal loss into the universal and abstract mystery of transience, to create a luminous anguish which does something like justice to the condition of some lives. If we are to be whole, our sadness and happiness should animate our most profound reflections on the great questions; and the novelist should, to take a phrase of Babel's far out of context, ensure that her meditations on the enigmas of the future and the past convey the autumn in the heart as well as the spectacles on the nose.

Such fiction might earn the respect of the shades of Paul Valéry and even of William James. The latter's letter to Gertrude Stein, explaining why he has not yet read the copy of *Three Lives* she had sent him, is worth reflecting on:

> I promise you that it shall be read *some* time! You see what a swine I am to have such pearls cast before him! As a rule reading fiction is as hard to me as trying to hit a target by hurling feathers at it. I need *resistance* to cerebrate!

Of equal relevance here is T.S. Eliot's characterisation of William's brother Henry:

> James's critical genius comes out most tellingly in his mastery over, his baffling escape from, Ideas; a mastery and an escape which are perhaps the last test of a superior intelligence. He had a mind so fine that no idea could violate it.

The novelists of the future will not be afraid of ideas, nor even of taking them seriously. They will have minds so fine that they can be violated by many ideas without losing their refinement. In this way, they will avoid the emptiness that sometimes haunts the perfections of idea-resistant geniuses such as William's brother, of whose method William said:

> To avoid describing it [the object] straight, but by dint of sighing and breathing all around it, to arouse in the reader, who may have had a similar perception already (Heaven help him if he hasn't!) the illusion of a solid object, made ... wholly out of impalpable materials, and the prismatic interferences of light, ingeniously focussed by mirrors upon empty space...

(7)

Of course there will be problems:

(a) A gossip-yeasted novel will often find it difficult to transcend the gossip which animates it, just as contemporary a-philosophical novels, by intermittently appealing to the reader's appetites, sometimes lose the latter's attention for long stretches. The aroused reader hurries impatiently from one undressing to another, resenting the intervening descriptions of the grass and trees and the scrupulous dissections of feelings. The novelist of the future will have to find new ways of mediating between the warring claims of the reader's cerebral cortex and limbic circuit.

(b) The standard implausibilities of serious fiction will remain a perpetual temptation; for example, the contrived attribution of polished thoughts to ordinary, ragged consciousness and the turning of busy consciousness into articulate, or diagnostically inarticulate, voices to help the plot (metaphysical or gossippy) along. This attribution may also be a form of authorial cowardice: half-baked thoughts can be off-loaded on to characters (forced to think to themselves with improbable coherence) whose creation permits the author to be at once didactic and ironically distant from didacticism.

(c) Whimsy, magic, etc. will still tempt the idle writer shrinking from the 'the ordeal of mimesis'. The penalty of requiring of the reader that she suspend her disbelief is that she will at the same time let go of the greater part of her critical intelligence, her native sensibility and, into the bargain, her propensity for a wider wonder. The mystery of goblins distracts from the mystery of children; horses that speak deafen us to the miracle of human speech; a concern with the doubtful magic of ESP blinds us to the indubitable magic of P. Enough said.

(d) The natural state of the reader is boredom seasoned with impatience. The novel of the future will require new kinds of readers, trained in new sorts of expectations. They will need a special sort of forebearance to persist with fictions that demand two kinds of patience at once: the sort of patience necessary to follow arguments; and the sort necessary to engage with the contingent quiddities and the punctations of a protracted narrative.

(e) A philistinism of seriousness will remain a constant danger. The philosophical fiction of the future must not fall into the trap of merely illustrating pre-formed ideas; it must transfigure the great ideas by marrying them to the gossip of everyday life. Metaphysics and gossip should be equal partners. This means taking gossip as seriously as we take it in real life: it should not be subordinated to the ideas. It also, however, means that authors should not be inhibited by pusillanimous fear of being philistine according to the old understanding and consequently being afraid of breaking spells with thoughts. A thought, properly realised, is a spell. (To vary what has been said before: the novelist of the future will not be afraid of ideas, having a mind so fine that many ideas can violate it without detriment to her refined sense of the actual.)

(f) Etc.

Let me end, where I began, with metaphysics and gossip. We may relate these to the two great projects or aspirations of human consciousness: the achievement of what Thomas Nagel poignantly titled 'The View from Nowhere' that endeavours to see the whole of things in the light of eternity; and the equally difficult achievement of 'The View from Here', of utter immersion in the particulars of experience. The future of the novel lies in mediating these two impulses of a creature that is conscious of being both utterly particular, even singular, and at the same time open to generality of the highest order. By this means, fiction may contribute to bringing together those two halves of ourselves and making us whole.

From: *Theorrhoea and After* (Macmillan, 1999), pp. 152–9.

Index